BOOKS FOR B

# BOOKS FOR BURNING

## Between Civil War and Democracy in 1970s Italy

◆

ANTONIO NEGRI

Translations edited by Timothy S. Murphy

Translated by Arianna Bove, Ed Emery,
Timothy S. Murphy & Francesca Novello

VERSO

London • New York

First published by Verso 2005
© Verso 2005
Translations © Arianna Bove, Ed Emery, Francesca Novello, Timothy Murphy 2005
First published as *I libri del rogo* © Castelvecchi, Rome, 1997

1 3 5 7 9 10 8 6 4 2

**Verso**
UK: 6 Meard Street, London W1F 0EG
USA: 180 Varick Street, New York, NY 10014-4606
www.versobooks.com

Verso is the imprint of New Left Books

ISBN 1-84467-034-1

**British Library Cataloguing in Publication Data**
A catalogue record for this book is available from the British Library

**Library of Congress Cataloging-in-Publication Data**
A catalog record for this book is available from the Library of Congress

Typeset by Andrea Stimpson
Printed in the USA

# Contents

# Editor's Introduction:
# Books for Burning

The original Italian title of the volume you are now reading is *I libri del rogo*, which we have translated as *Books for Burning*. The Italian publisher, Castelvecchi, chose that title to highlight the fact that the pamphlets included in this volume played a key role in Antonio Negri's arrest, imprisonment, and trial (in that order) on charges of kidnapping, murder, subversive association, and armed insurrection against the powers of the state; the subtitle has been added to this edition, with Negri's approval, in order to indicate the focus, scope, and historical context of the arguments contained herein. The title as a whole serves to emphasize the importance of these pamphlets, first in the development of the Italian radical social movements of the 1970s, and later in the Italian state's attempt to criminalize those movements and their members.

As Negri notes at the beginning of his preface to the 1997 Italian edition, these texts were written between 1971 and 1977, and despite his claim that they should be viewed as sequential chapters of a single book, they are neither entirely consistent in argument nor fully coherent in form.[1] This is the result of the discontinuous way in which they were written, as programmatic documents or position statements for the organizations in which Negri was involved, as well as the evolving social and political situation to which they attempted to respond. Perhaps the best way to view them is as a series of provisional attempts to sum up the then-current state of the movements, a kind of theoretical tacking into the wind or surfing on the riptides of the seething Italian counterculture. To take one particularly crucial example, the issue of the *party* as an organizational form within the movements is a recurrent focal point throughout these pamphlets, yet the specific form or structure of the party that is proposed, as well as its logical and practical relationship to the proletarian subjects whose will it expresses, is constantly mutating. Very schematically, one could say that, in the course of these texts, Negri moves from a fundamentally Bolshevik notion of the party as an elite, factory-centered, vanguard controlling working-class subversion from above (the "new Leninism" of *Crisis of the Planner-State*) to a paradoxical—and ultimately untenable—conception of the party as the effective and non-separable totalization of mass initiatives and workers' leadership (the "party of Mirafiori" or "party of mass vanguards" of *Workers' Party Against Work*), and finally in *Domination and Sabotage* to a model of the party as an external and subordinate tactical appendage of the class that functions only in situations of direct conflict with the capitalist adversary but has no control over the internal production and organization of proletarian needs and desires that Negri calls *self-valorization*.[2] Conversely, the general definition of self-valorization remains relatively consistent throughout the book, but its subjective referent changes significantly, from an exclusive focus on the needs and desires of male factory workers to a more inclusive consideration of the needs and desires of students, women, the unemployed, prisoners, and other subordinated groups. In other words, the *composition* of the class engaged in self-valorization changes in the course of Negri's analysis, and his categories change accordingly. What ultimately links these three fluctuating concepts—class composition, self-valorization, and the party—is Negri's gradual recognition of the self-sufficiency of the proletarian masses themselves: their ability to conceptualize, produce, and organize their own forms of struggle without the need for external command of any kind. This results in their fundamental *autonomy* from command, both that of capital and that of Leninist "professional revolutionaries," and hence in the blanket name of the movement.

Thus if we are to read these pamphlets as sequential chapters in a single argument, we must do so not in terms of some systematic logical coherence or unity they do not actually possess, but rather in terms of the historical narrative of development they embody. In sailing or surfing rough seas, one rarely travels in a straight line, even if one does manage to reach one's destination. Negri's theoretical trajectory in these pamphlets is likewise anything but a straight line, as was the historical trajectory of the movements whose innovations and goals he struggles to articulate here. The first pamphlet, *Crisis of the Planner-State*, was originally written in 1971 for a national convention of Workers' Power [*Potere Operaio*], the factory-centered organization Negri had helped to found in 1969. The second, *Workers' Party Against Work*, was completed a few short months before Workers' Power, faced with the changing class composition, formally dissolved at its June 1973 conference in Rosolina. The third, *Proletarians and the State*, dates from the period of fragmentation and flux following the dissolution of Workers' Power and prior to the stabilization of the decentered framework of worker, student, feminist, and other struggles that came to be called Workers' Autonomy [*Autonomia Operaia*]. The last two texts, *Toward a Critique of the Material Constitution* and *Domination and Sabotage*, were written six months apart during 1977, just as Organized Workers' Autonomy was taking coherent shape amidst the apparent chaos of the "area of autonomy." These chapters, then, are addressed to structurally divergent organizations, composed of vastly different social subjects, at different points in their evolution within the context of the overall development of Italian working–class militancy in the seventies.

I do not have the space to continue this explication of the historical narrative underlying and informing this book (which others have already accomplished with exemplary thoroughness and sophistication[3]), but this much at least needs to be clear in order to understand exactly how the Italian state and mass media forcibly reshaped this narrative into the straightest of lines in order to criminalize the radical movements in general and the thought of Antonio Negri in particular. In that process the pamphlets in this book played a major part.

The process of criminalization did not actually begin on the infamous date 7 April 1979, when Negri and many of his colleagues in the Institute of Political Science at the University of Padua were arrested, but much earlier. This becomes clear when we examine the initial arrest warrants. There were two addressed to Negri, one from Padua prosecutor Pietro Calogero and one from Rome judge Achille Gallucci. The Calogero warrant ordered the arrest of Negri and his colleagues on charges of having

> organized and led an association called the Red Brigades, constituted as an armed band … aimed at promoting armed insurrection against the Powers of the State and violently changing the constitution and form of government by means of the propaganda of armed actions against persons and things and by means of the planning and execution of robberies and kidnappings, murders and woundings, arson and property damage, and attempts against public and private institutions.

These charges may sound odd to the US or UK reader because they do not correspond directly to any criminal activities defined in the Anglo-American legal tradition. The crimes of "membership in an armed band" and "armed insurrection against the powers of the state" were initially defined during the Fascist period in order to outlaw the nascent Italian Communist Party; Mussolini's government charged Antonio Gramsci with these crimes, among others.[4] After the liberation of Italy in 1945, these offenses were kept on the books but modified in order to outlaw Fascist organizations. Perhaps the closest analog to these charges in the Anglo-American tradition is the charge of sedition, used especially during wartime in the US and the UK from the eighteenth to the early twentieth century, often against radical workers' movements.

In a second paragraph of the same warrant, Negri and his colleagues were further charged with having led

> an association called "Workers' Power," as well as other analogous associations with various names that are all linked together and tied to so-called "Organized Workers' Autonomy," which aims to subvert by violence the constituted order of the State by means of propaganda and incitement to practice so-called mass illegality and various forms of violence and armed struggle (proletarian expropriation and perquisition; arson and damage to public and private goods; robberies and kidnappings; beatings and woundings; attempts on prisons, barracks, party and association headquarters, and sites of off-the-books labor), by means of training in the use of arms, munitions, explosives, and incendiary devices and by means of recourse to acts of illegality, violence, and armed attack against some of the objectives mentioned.[5]

These apparently unconnected charges claimed to establish two things. First, they argued that Negri and company, while appearing to be merely the public spokespeople and theorists of mass political organizations like Worker's Autonomy, were actually the clandestine leaders of the most infamous and effective leftwing terrorist organization in Italy, the Red Brigades, a group whose elitist, ahistorical Leninism Negri and friends had thoroughly criticized from the standpoint of the mass organizations' new class composition. Second, the charges insisted that, despite the apparent opposition between the mass organizations and the clandestine terrorist group, both were distinct wings of the same underlying command structure, a structure that had remained coherent and in control of its members and activities despite the outward appearance of radical disagreement, criticism and even extensive reorganization.[6] If the first charge appeared patently absurd in light of the defendants' long record of public disagreement with the Red Brigades' structure and methods, the second appeared equally ridiculous in light of the discontinuous organizational history I mentioned above. The warrant treated the self-dissolution of Workers' Power, the regular criticisms of terrorist violence, and the gradual formation of Workers' Autonomy as shams, illusions that served to conceal a linear continuity of command and an underlying unity of subversive method among all those organizations.

In a defense memorandum written after six months in prison, Negri attempted to rebut this assertion of continuity between Workers' Power, Workers' Autonomy, and the Red Brigades by patiently narrating the development and dissolution of Workers' Power from 1971 to 1973, the lengthy gestation period of Workers' Autonomy from 1973 to 1977, and finally the formal emergence and immediate crisis of Workers' Autonomy in 1977–78.[7] He made similar attempts during his interrogations and press interviews, and in collaboration with his co-defendants he circulated several other texts reiterating the validity and indeed the necessity of this narrative in any attempt to understand their theoretical and organizational work.[8] He and his co-defendants also denied that they had been in uninterrupted contact from the dissolution of Workers' Power in 1973 to the time of their arrest, emphasizing the very different paths they had each taken through the counterculture.[9] But these efforts were only a small part of the work of explication and interpretation Negri would have to do as a result of the strategy the prosecution adopted in order to substantiate its claims of continuity.

Let us return to the original warrants. In a lengthier and more specific warrant than Calogero's, Gallucci charged Negri, along with twenty-three active members of the Red Brigades, with seven murders, including those of former prime minister Aldo Moro and his five bodyguards on 16 March 1978, as well as involvement in several robberies, kidnappings, and falsifications of automobile registrations used in the crimes.[10] Although Calogero is rightly considered to be Negri's nemesis, in that he is the original source of the "theorem" of continuity sketched above that attributed to Negri and his colleagues virtually every act of leftwing terrorism in Italy from 1971 to 1979, it is in fact Gallucci's warrant that first reveals the strategy the state would use against him, and against the radical movements more generally. It accuses Negri of "promoting armed insurrection against the powers of the State, inciting civil war in the State's territory, subverting by violence the current order of society, and destroying the democratic State and its institutions with the aim of violently changing the State's constitution and form of government" by all the means already listed in Calogero's warrant: assassination, destruction of property, kidnapping, robbery to support acts of subversive violence, sabotage, and so on. But Gallucci adds one more means: "the publication and distribution of pamphlets and communiqués that incite armed insurrection and faithfully follow the ideological lines that Negri presents at meetings and in his publications, including *Domination and Sabotage, Proletarians and the State*, and *Crisis of the Planner-State*."[11] This inversion of chronological order of Negri's texts is important, and we will return to it. Gallucci's warrant goes on to cite brief passages from these and other writings by Negri, which constitute the only evidence offered by either warrant in support of its charges.[12] This warrant makes it clear that Negri would go on trial not just or even primarily for the criminal acts his organizations had supposedly performed, but for subversive words he had spoken and written.

In his 7 July 1979 ruling rejecting a defense motion demanding the release of Negri and his co-defendants from pre-trial detention, Gallucci offers more precise citations from Negri's published works in support of his decision. He cites a number of lengthy passages from four of the five pamphlets in this volume: eight from *Domination and Sabotage* (1977), two from *Crisis of the Planner-State* (second edition, 1974), one from *Proletarians and the State* (1975), and six from *Workers' Party Against Work* (1973), in that order.[13] Let me cite just one from the list for each pamphlet, in order to suggest what the prosecutors sought in Negri's writings and how they intended to use it.

- This violence [of the working class] is *contrary* to capitalist violence; it aims at the destruction of capital's system and regime; it is founded on class self-valorization; it is *not equal* in intensity to capitalist violence—it is *stronger*, more efficacious than capitalist violence … we are speaking of opposing terror with an operation of sabotage and the reappropriation of knowledge [*conoscenza*] and power over the whole circuit of social reproduction, in such a way as to make the capitalist's recourse to terror into a suicidal prospect. (Section 10 of *Domination and Sabotage*, 1977, p. 283 below)
- The problem of organization unfolds between two tasks that are equally fundamental: to ensure the effectiveness of instances of reappropriation of social wealth by the masses and—at the same time—to strike with vanguard violence, in equal and opposing measure, at the bosses' mechanisms of command. ("Postscript" to *Crisis of the Planner-State*, 1974, p. 48 below)
- *If the class adversary seeks in the short term to readjust its power by force,* as well it might—and it is necessary for the first time to insist strongly upon this—*we must develop … a force capable of responding effectively on the militant plane* … (Thesis 14 of *Proletarians and the State*, 1975, p. 174 below)
- Within these [terrorist] positions we certainly do not need to combat the use of violence … In terrorism, what we need to combat is the programmatic will that refuses to incarnate the moments of class power and is unable to grasp *an organic relation* between the subjectivity of workers' power and the subjectivism of the use of violence. (Section 4 of *Workers' Party Against Work*, 1973, p. 91 below)

These four passages, like the others Gallucci cites, are not arbitrarily chosen. Taken in the correct order and in full (without the ellipses he inserts), they are in fact representative of Negri's general argument throughout these pamphlets that working-class resistance must be prepared to meet the legal, institutional violence of the capitalist state and factory with its own organic forms of illegal mass violence. They also suggest how Negri criticized the elitist forms of violence associated with the Red Brigades as being isolated from the mass level of struggle (and thus at best uncoordinated with that level and at worst in opposition to it), an ongoing critique that justified his claim to have been consistently and adamantly opposed to their strategy and tactics.

But in the ruling as in the warrant, Negri's texts are cited in an order that is almost exactly the reverse of their order of composition and publication. What effect does this produce? As Negri himself notes in his defense memorandum, in which he attempts to re-establish the original order and context of these writings against the prosecution's distortions, the prosecution's sequence reverses not just the order but the very meaning of the texts.[14] Specifically, it appears to show Negri's thought evolving from a notion of defensive party organization as unambiguously subordinate to the mass movement, and hence a perspective categorically opposed to clandestine organization and terror, toward a classically Leninist conception of hierarchical party command over the mass movement that could be seen as broadly compatible with the elitist rationale of the Red Brigades. This damning inversion of chronology and meaning led Negri to propose criteria for the correct interpretation of his writings: (a) consider only complete texts, in terms of both form and content, and not just isolated passages torn from context; (b) situate the texts in the context of the author's career, by comparing them with other texts contemporary with them; and (c) situate the texts also in relation to the broader historical context that they attempt to confront.[15] Throughout the memorandum, and indeed throughout his interrogations, he gives examples of how to carry out such an interpretation. With the publication of this volume it is finally possible for English-language readers to undertake such an informed interpretation of Negri's most directly political writings. His reading lessons would have little impact on the prosecution's interpretive strategy, however, and one passage that Gallucci cites suggests why.

In addition to the example passage I listed above, Gallucci also cites the section from *Domination and Sabotage* that is perhaps the most infamous in Negri's vast body of work, one that has widely been read as an open confession of his involvement in terrorism. It is worth citing at length:

Nothing reveals the immense historical positivity of workers' self-valorization more completely than sabotage, this continual activity of the sniper, the saboteur, the absentee, the deviant, the criminal that I find myself living. I immediately feel the warmth of the workers' and proletarian community again every time I don the ski mask ... Nor does the happiness of the result escape me: every act of destruction and sabotage redounds upon me as a sign of class fellowship. Nor does the probable risk disturb me: on the contrary, it fills me with feverish emotion, like waiting for a lover. Nor does the suffering of the adversary affect me: proletarian justice has the very same productive force of self-valorization and the very same faculty of logical conviction. (Section 6 of *Domination and Sabotage*, 1977, p. 259 below)

Here Negri adopts the language and persona of an agent of working–class violence, to the point of metaphorically donning the infamous ski mask often associated with the Palestinian terrorists of the 1972 Munich Olympics but widely adopted by others to conceal their identities from the police. He goes so far as to describe the affective charge that the experience of violence produces for the subversive subject. There is nothing else quite like this in the rest of the pamphlets (though Negri's other works, especially his later writings on Spinoza, contain analogous expressions of profound affective intensity that are not linked to the issue of violence), and the press as well as the prosecution would make much of it, to the point of labeling him the "*cattivo maestro*" of terrorism, meaning both "bad teacher" and "evil genius."[16] Even before his arrest, Negri had been compelled by his comrades in the movements to explain this rhetorical excess, and in his defense memorandum he admitted once again that this passage was a regrettable example of "stylistic forcing" that produced "at times singularly bad writing." Yet he went on to insist, against the prosecution's literal reading and the hysterical denunciations of the press, that "to assume that stylistic variations or risky metaphors are proof of guilt, or even signs of it, seems patently ridiculous to me."[17] Even though no objective evidence linking Negri to the commission of any act of violence had (or has ever) been found, public opinion largely turned against him, his publisher Feltrinelli (whose chief executive was found dead next to a power station he apparently intended to dynamite) dropped him, and all of his books, including these pamphlets, went out of print for some twenty years.

Since the charges against him depended upon substantial citations from his writings (and not only from these pamphlets), however, it comes as no surprise that Negri's interrogations by the prosecutors and judges included detailed attempts to explicate those writings.[18] The transcripts of his interrogations read like lost drafts of Kafka's *Trial*: a distinguished philosopher and teacher desperately trying to teach a menacing and incorrigible classroom full of hostile judges, lawyers, police, and journalists how to understand abstruse tracts of radical political philosophy. The almost legendary difficulty of the pamphlets themselves—which are widely conceded to be among the most conceptually and rhetorically challenging texts Negri ever wrote—as well as the arrogant self-certainty of the prosecution in its presumption of linear continuity between Workers' Power, Workers' Autonomy, and the Red Brigades doomed most of these attempts to failure. But not all of them: during 1980–81 an outside magistrate was appointed to examine and assess the validity of the prosecution's case against Negri and his co-defendants. After completing a thoroughly documented reconstruction of the history of Workers' Power, Workers' Autonomy and their shifting factions, investigating judge Giovanni Palombarini refuted Calogero's theorem of continuity on the basis that it was in contradiction with the known historical facts, largely tautological in form, and thus effectively untenable, and as a result the little evidence that remained unaffected by these problems did not support most of the serious charges against the defendants.[19] Following Calogero's appeal, Palombarini's refutation was overturned almost immediately by a higher court, thus preventing the defendants from being released from pre-trial detention and shielding the prosecution's strategy from further judicial oversight, but it does demonstrate that this travesty of justice should not be blamed on the Italian legal system as a whole.[20]

Not unlike Kafka's trial, Negri's would be characterized by an almost unlimited series of postponements. Arrested on 7 April 1979, he would not actually go on trial until 24 February 1983. In the almost four years between those dates, all of which he spent in prison (and during which time he wrote five books, including his famous study of Spinoza, *The Savage Anomaly*[21]), the charges against him would be modified many times. First, the words "Red Brigades" were deleted from the warrants accusing Negri and his Paduan colleagues of membership in an armed band. Next, the charges relating to the kidnapping and assassination of Aldo Moro were dropped, but new, more abstract charges were immediately brought to keep them in preventive detention.[22] This became a regular cycle during the wait for trial: whenever the time limit on pre-trial detention for a particular charge was reached, new charges were filed to keep the defendants in prison, often in reference to the same events and using the same evidence as the earlier charges. To make matters worse, in December 1979, while Negri was still hoping for a relatively speedy trial, the Italian Parliament passed the so-called "Cossiga law"; this piece of "emergency legislation" extended the maximum length of preventive detention authorized in cases of terrorism from six to almost eleven years. At the same time, laws encouraging "repentant" terrorists (called *pentiti*) to cooperate with the prosecution by implicating others were instituted. This led to a further avalanche of charges against Negri and his colleagues (as well as many other militants) when the convicted kidnapper and murderer Carlo Fioroni implicated them directly in his own crimes (and others) in order to reduce his own sentence.[23] After providing this "evidence," Fioroni was given a false passport and flown out of the country by the Italian secret service. Despite his refusal to return for cross-examination during the trial, and his own lawyer's repudiation of his claims, his "evidence" was not stricken from the record and it was used extensively in the written judgment against the defendants.[24]

Despite the systematic collusion between the Italian judiciary, the established political parties (primarily the Christian Democrats and the Communist Party, who were then attempting to form a coalition under the ambiguous title of the "Historic Compromise") and the press in portraying Negri and his co-defendants as guilty until proven innocent, the irregularity of their judicial situation did not go unnoticed in Italy and around the world. Defense committees were set up immediately in Italy, France, the UK, and the USA, and one of their first acts was the mobilization of intellectual opinion to support the defendants. Discussions and protests began to appear in the Italian media almost immediately, from many political perspectives, and continued unabated until the trial began; well-known figures like Umberto Eco and Noam Chomsky intervened in the early weeks to criticize the orchestrated press hysteria that sprang up around the case.[25] Just one month after the arrests, French philosopher Gilles Deleuze published a letter in the centrist newspaper *La Repubblica* analyzing the contradictory logic underlying the charges, and a few weeks later the US defense committee published a newsletter on the case that contained statements of support from Deleuze's intellectual partner Félix Guattari, respected Italian legal philosophers and jurists Norberto Bobbio and Luigi Ferrajoli, and Italian Socialist Party Senator Mancini, as well as a protest petition signed by Paul Sweezy, Howard Zinn, Immanuel Wallerstein, Perry Anderson, Stanley Aronowitz, and many others.[26] On the first anniversary of Negri's arrest, 7 April 1980, the Parisian newspaper *Le Monde* published an interview with Michel Foucault in which he ironically noted that "We don't, it's true, live under a regime in which intellectuals are sent to the ricefields. But have you heard of a certain Toni Negri? Isn't he in prison simply for being an intellectual?"[27] Over the ensuing years leading up to the trial, Ferrajoli, a leading figure in the Union of Democratic Magistrates, would publish a series of incisive critical articles in both popular and legal journals which revealed the violations of due process and basic civil rights that characterized the 7 April case.[28]

Among many other problems, Ferrajoli singled out as most disturbing what he called the "inquisitorial model" that governed the arrests, interrogations,

and general preparations leading up to the 7 April trial.[29] His argument, based
on an analysis of the phase of secret assembly of evidence prior to the issuing
of warrants (similar in some ways to the grand jury phase of US trials, which
results in an indictment) and the interrogation phase, demonstrates that
evidence and testimony that contradicted or falsified prosecution claims was
regularly discarded or discredited, not because it was shown to be false, but
because it did not fit the pre-established "theorem" of organizational continuity and theoretical agreement between the mass movements and the
clandestine groups. In using the term "inquisitorial" in this context, Ferrajoli
is speaking metaphorically and not making any detailed attempt to liken the
prosecution's methods to those of the historical Inquisition. Cultural historian Carlo Ginzburg, on the other hand, does attempt to demonstrate in some
detail how the prosecution of his friend, the former academic and leader of
Lotta Continua Adriano Sofri, did in fact take a form that was directly analogous to the model of an Inquisition trial such as the ones Ginzburg famously
reconstructed in his books *The Cheese and the Worms* and *Ecstasies*.[30] In *The
Judge and the Historian: Marginal Notes on a Late Twentieth-Century Miscarriage
of Justice*, Ginzburg demonstrates that Sofri's prosecutors and judges manipulated and misrepresented evidence, most importantly the testimony of *pentito*
Leonardo Marino, in order to assure the conviction of Sofri and his friends
for the murder of a police official in 1972. The end result of this process of
manipulation was what Ginzburg calls a "witch trial."[31] With regard to due
process, the handling of physical evidence and the treatment of testimony and
cross-examination, it is clear that Negri and his colleagues too underwent a
witch trial that was intended to guarantee their conviction for something,
though the prosecution never seemed certain of what.[32]

The cumulative force of all these postponements, alterations of charges,
lapses of due process, distortions of evidence, and examples of tautological
reasoning led Amnesty International to decry the 7 April trial in every one
of its comprehensive annual reports on prisoner mistreatment from 1980 to
1988, as well as in a separate paper on the trial's long history published in
1987.[33] An appeal hearing in June 1987 ultimately resulted in the total acquit-
tal of many of the defendants; all of them were acquitted of the charges of
armed insurrection against the powers of the state, on the grounds that no
such insurrection ever took place.[34] The verdicts of most contemporary historians on the case have fully vindicated the concerns of Negri's supporters,
legal critics like Ferrajoli, and Amnesty International. For example, terrorism expert Alison Jamieson remarks that

> The aim of the "7th April" arrests was to prove continuity between the
> public pronouncements of revolutionary ideologues such as Negri and the

clandestine terrorism of the Red Brigades. If there was some truth in the allegations of incitement to violence, the blanket accusations which enveloped Autonomia were the result of near-paranoia, ignorance and misplaced revenge.[35]

In his standard history of contemporary Italy, Paul Ginsborg argues that

> The [Italian] authorities were all too willing to organize witch-hunts and hand out sentences which neither aided the fight against terrorism nor guaranteed impartial justice. The most notorious incident was the case of those arrested on 7 April 1979 ... The "7 April" group languished in prison for a period of years before being brought to trial. One by one the most serious charges against the great majority of them were revealed as false, either at their original trial or on appeal. The politics of the group, which were those of Autonomia, could hardly be called attractive, but too little distinction was ever made by their prosecutors between what had been said and what had been done.[36]

Historians have taken particular note of the grotesque disproportion between the lengthy prison sentences served by defendants convicted of abstract, victimless crimes like subversive association on the basis of their writings (such as Negri's close friend Luciano Ferrari Bravo) and the much shorter sentences served by self-confessed murderers like Fioroni and Antonio Savasta, who had become *pentiti*.[37]

By the time these more rational verdicts were reached, however, Negri was no longer in prison, or even in Italy. Shortly after the start of his trial in early 1983, he was drafted to run for a seat in the lower house of the Italian Parliament, the Chamber of Deputies, by the small, media-savvy, libertarian Radical Party (which would later offer porn star Cicciolina as a candidate for the same legislative body).[38] In the general elections of 25–26 June 1983, Negri was elected to the Chamber of Deputies as a representative of districts in Milan, Rome, and Naples. In the midst of the general uproar caused by this result, the trial was suspended and on 8 July 1983 Negri was released from prison under the protection of the immunity from prosecution traditionally granted to elected representatives in Italy.[39] Upon the opening of the legislative session on 12 July, opposition deputies launched a campaign to strip Negri of his immunity. Formal debate on the motion opened on 14 September with Negri's own speech criticizing the emergency legislation that had kept him imprisoned for so long before trial and that still threatened to send him back on the basis of little more than the testimony of known killers.[40] Despite his efforts, the

Chamber voted 300 to 293 to strip him of his immunity and send him back to prison on 20 September. The ten other Radical Party deputies elected along with Negri abstained from voting, allegedly as a result of intimidation. The day before, in anticipation of the vote, Negri made his escape to France by boat with the aid of sympathizers. The 7 April trial resumed at the end of September, and Negri was subsequently convicted *in absentia* and sentenced to thirty years in prison; appeals and reversals would ultimately reduce his sentence to thirteen years, none of which was for crimes of violence.

Negri was not the only Italian defendant to flee to France; by the mid-eighties several hundred political refugees sought asylum there—a small fraction of the thousands of militants who were eventually caught up in the Italian state's crude dragnets. As Vincenzo Ruggiero has shown, the refugees' status was particularly precarious. The French authorities regularly rebuffed extradition requests from the Italian authorities because they perceived the prosecutions of these people as fundamentally political, and thus ruled out by both the French and Italian constitutions. However, in order to avoid antagonizing and embarrassing their Italian counterparts, French officials refused to grant the Italian refugees formal political asylum, which would lead to citizenship. This left the Italians in political limbo, without the right to work or to participate in the political life of their host nation.[41] As an intellectual celebrity, Negri was spared the worst aspects of this limbo, though he did face the relative indignity of being compelled to teach introductory political science in the University of Paris system as a temporary or adjunct lecturer only a few short years after he had been Louis Althusser's invited guest at the prestigious École Normale Supérieure on the Rue d'Ulm—a visit that resulted in his famous book *Marx Beyond Marx*.[42] Although he was soon appointed a council member of the Collège International de Philosophie, founded by Jacques Derrida and Jean-François Lyotard, he made a living teaching introductory courses and doing sociological research for French government agencies.[43] During his period of exile he founded several critical journals (including *Futur antérieur*), wrote at least ten books, and began his now-influential collaboration with American Michael Hardt.

In 1997, the year that the pamphlets he wrote for Workers' Power and Workers' Autonomy were finally assembled by Castelvecchi into the book you are now reading, Negri decided to return to Italy and to prison in order to help catalyze some kind of solution to the problem of political prisoners in Italy and political refugees abroad. These people remain as unwanted reminders of a historical period whose memory the Italian state and media (now unified more completely than ever before in the figure of Silvio

Berlusconi) have largely succeeded in criminalizing through the indiscriminate use of the techniques developed to frame the 7 April defendants. At the end of June, the very month this book was published, Negri boarded a plane for Rome, which was met at the airport by the police; on 1 July he re-entered Rebibbia Prison to serve what remained of his thirteen-year sentence (minus the four-plus years he had already spent in preventive detention, often in Rebibbia, between 1979 and 1983). Two years later, upon reaching the midpoint of his overall sentence, he was admitted into a program of "semi-liberty" that allowed him to leave prison during the day so long as he returned each night. Two years after that, he was granted something closer to parole, and was allowed to leave prison permanently on condition that he return to his Rome apartment every night; in addition, his passport was withheld, so he could not leave Italy. Finally, in 2003, he was granted full parole, a situation which permitted him to regain his passport and travel freely throughout Europe, the UK, and most of the rest of the world. As of this writing he still cannot travel to the US because of longstanding visa restrictions on ex-convicts and the new security precautions set up following the 9/11 events.

The paranoia and hysteria that sent Negri to prison because of the writings in this book may have passed—in large part because their methods triumphed and were integrated into the status quo—but expanded and intensified versions of them have emerged in the aftermath of 9/11.[44] The detention of suspected terrorists and "enemy combatants" in extraterritorial sites such as Guantanamo Bay, without recourse to legal counsel or courts, is preventive detention all over again—but on a global scale. Anti-Muslim sentiment inspired by unfamiliar languages and rituals and fanned by the fear of "sleeper cells" is the theorem of continuity all over again—but on a global scale. Offers of streamlined, expedited access to citizenship made to immigrants who are willing to implicate others in terrorism is *pentitismo* all over again—but on a global scale. These theoretical analyses of the seventies that you are about to read may have laid the groundwork for Negri's influential investigations into biopolitics, postmodernity, and Empire, as he says, but his practical experiences in the Italian judicial system during a state of emergency may well offer an even clearer glimpse of what resistance movements during the open-ended "War on Terror" will have to face in the future. Thus it is vitally important, for reasons beyond mere historical accuracy, to contest the way that the social movements and cultural memory of seventies Italy have been criminalized and suppressed. May this book help revive that memory.

**Notes**

1. Contrast the formal dissimilarities between these texts with, for example, the elaborate formal parallelism among the parts of Hardt and Negri's *Empire*, Cambridge, MA: Harvard University Press, 2000.

2. On the issue of the party in Negri's writings of this period, and in the area of Autonomy generally, see Steve Wright, "A Party of Autonomy?" in Timothy S. Murphy and Abdul-Karim Mustapha, editors, *The Philosophy of Antonio Negri: Resistance in Practice*, London: Pluto Press, 2005. On the issue of class composition, see Steve Wright, *Storming Heaven: Class Composition and Struggle in Italian Autonomist Marxism*, London: Pluto Press, 2002, especially chapters 6 and 7.

3. In Italian, see Nanni Balestrini and Primo Moroni, editors, *L'orda d'oro: 1968–1977—La grande ondata rivoluzionaria e creativa, politica ed esistenziale*, new edition Milan: Feltrinelli, 1997, and Guido Borio, Francesca Pozzi, and Gigi Roggero, *Futuro anteriore: Dai "Quaderni Rossi" ai movimenti globali—Ricchezze e limiti dell'operaismo italiano*, Rome: DeriveApprodi, 2002; in English, see Robert Lumley, *States of Emergency: Cultures of Revolt in Italy from 1968 to 1978*, New York: Verso, 1990, and Wright, *Storming Heaven*.

4. See *1923: Il processo ai comunisti italiani / 1979: Il "processo" all'autonomia operaia*, Milan: Collettivo editoriale 10/16, 1979, pp. 5–6. The overall intention of this small volume, evident in its unwieldy title, is to demonstrate a strict parallelism between the Fascist case against Gramsci and the fledgling Italian Communist Party in the twenties and the case against Negri and his colleagues in 1979, which was pressed most forcefully by members of the Italian Communist Party itself, such as Calogero. On PCI collusion in the criminalization of the extraparliamentary left, see David Moss, *The Politics of Left-Wing Violence in Italy 1969–1985*, London: Macmillan, 1989, pp. 132–36.

5. Arrest warrant reproduced in *Processo all'Autonomia*, edited by Comitato 7 aprile and the team of defense lawyers, Cosenza: Lerici, 1979, pp. 3–4. This volume, published in late 1979, documents only the earliest stages of the case against Negri and his co-defendants; by the time they actually came to trial, in early 1983, documentation of the case had swelled to more than 50,000 pages of court orders, motions, and transcripts as well as hundreds of newspaper articles and dozens of books (to say nothing of radio and television reports). The cited translation and all subsequent translations from this volume are mine.

6. For Calogero's own comprehensive exposition of this "theorem," see pp. 29–35, 49–88 and 107–10 of Giuseppe De Lutiis, editor, *Attacco allo stato: Dossier 7 Aprile*, Rome: Napoleone, 1982. See also David Moss's summary of the theorem in his *Politics of Left-Wing Violence in Italy 1969–1985*, pp. 204–07.

7. Negri, "Il memoriale difensivo di Toni Negri," part one, sections I and II, and part two, section III, written in late 1979 and published in *Lotta continua* issues for 19 and 20–21 January 1980. All translations from this text are mine.

8. See Negri's interrogations in *Processo all'Autonomia*, pp. 133–203, as well as the collective document produced by the 7 April prisoners on 24 May 1979, published in *1923: Il processo ai comunisti italiani / 1979: Il "processo" all'autonomia operaia*, pp. 142–84. A partial translation of the latter may be found in *Working Class Autonomy and the Crisis*, London: Red Notes, 1979, pp. 155–59. Just before the start of their trial, Negri co-wrote with some of the same comrades another "proposal for the interpretation of the Italian movements of the seventies" entitled "Do You Remember Revolution?", which was originally published in *Il Manifesto*, 20–22 February 1983, and translated into English in Negri, *Revolution Retrieved*, London: Red Notes, 1988, pp. 229–43.

9. Negri, "Il memoriale difensivo di Toni Negri," part two, section IV, *Lotta continua* 20–21 January 1980.

10. *Processo all'Autonomia*, pp. 5–8. Negri would ultimately be charged with eighteen murders, and convicted of none. He would also be charged with terrorist activity in a dozen or more different cities and regions, all of which could hold separate trials. As a result of the insurrection and Moro assassination charges, his case was transferred to Rome, the capital, and all the regional trials were postponed until the conclusion of that trial.

11. *Processo all'Autonomia*, p. 8.

12. *Processo all'Autonomia*, p. 9. Calogero also discusses the pamphlets in his exposition of the theorem; see De Lutiis, editor, *Attacco allo stato*, pp. 53–55 as well as scattered brief references throughout his discussion.

13. *Processo all'Autonomia*, pp. 262–64.

14. Negri, "Il memoriale difensivo di Toni Negri," preamble, *Lotta continua*, 19 January 1980.

15. Negri, "Il memoriale difensivo di Toni Negri," part two, section V, *Lotta continua*, 20–21 January 1980.

16. For a relatively restrained example, see Sergio Zavoli's 1988 interview with Negri in the context of a comprehensive television documentary on seventies terrorism, published in Zavoli's *La notte della repubblica*, Milan: Mondadori, 1992, pp. 257–68; Zavoli questions Negri about the ski-mask passage on pp. 263–64.

17. Negri, "Il memoriale difensivo di Toni Negri," part two, section V, *Lotta continua*, 20–21 January 1980.

18. Negri's interrogations between late April and July 1979, many of which focus on his writings, occupy seventy pages of *Processo all'Autonomia* (pp. 133–203); discussions of the pamphlets translated in this volume may be found on pp. 168–69, 172, and 187–89. Selections from these interrogations have been translated into English and published in Negri, *Revolution Retrieved*, pp. 261–68, corresponding to pages 137, 140–50, 155–59, and 162–63 of *Processo all'Autonomia*.

19. Palombarini, *7 Aprile: Il processo e la storia*, Venice: Arsenale, 1982, especially pp. 157–67. The bulk of Palombarini's book consists of the historical reconstruction,

which is remarkably detailed, accurate and perceptive, that formed the basis of his ruling. For a more extensive summary of both the reconstruction and the ruling, see Moss, *The Politics of Left-Wing Violence in Italy 1969–1985*, pp. 207–09.

20. See excerpts from Calogero's appeal in De Lutiis, editor, *Attacco allo stato*, pp. 139–44.

21. *The Savage Anomaly: The Power of Spinoza's Metaphysics and Politics*, 1981; Minneapolis: University of Minnesota Press, 1990, translated by Michael Hardt.

22. The first revised warrants are included in *Processo all'autonomia*, pp. 281–82. See also Luigi Ferrajoli, "The Prosecution's Case Collapses," in *Italy 1980–81: After Marx, Jail!*, London: Red Notes, 1981, pp. 52–53, as well as Moss, *The Politics of Left-Wing Violence in Italy 1969–1985*, pp. 200–02, *Amnesty International Report 1981*, London: Amnesty International Publications, 1981, p. 304, and *Amnesty International Report 1984*, London: Amnesty International Publications, 1984, pp. 291–92.

23. On the new preventive detention laws, see *Amnesty International Report 1980*, London: Amnesty International Publications, 1980, pp. 279–81. For a much more detailed chronology of Negri's period of imprisonment and trial, see "Éléments de chronologie politique" compiled by Yann Moulier, in Negri, *Italie rouge et noire: Journal février 1983–novembre 1983*, Paris: Hachette, 1985, pp. 318–21, as well as my extension of this chronology on the "Amnesty for Antonio Negri" website, http://lists.village.virginia.edu/~forks/TNChronology.htm. The most substantial collection of documents related to the case in English can be found in two books published by Red Notes: *Working Class Autonomy and the Crisis* (1979), pp. 139–66, and *Italy 1980–81: After Marx, Jail! The Attempted Destruction of a Communist Movement*, pp. 1–64.

24. Moss, *The Politics of Left-Wing Violence in Italy 1969–1985*, pp. 250, 305, n. 46; Alessandro Portelli, "Oral Testimony, the Law and the Making of History: The 'April 7' Murder Trial," in *History Workshop: A Journal of Socialist and Feminist Historians*, 20, autumn 1985, pp. 28–29; *Amnesty International Report 1986*, London: Amnesty International Publications, 1986, p. 291, and *Amnesty International Report 1987*, London: Amnesty International Publications, 1987, p. 301.

25. Many of the most interesting and important contributions to the Italian debate over the 7 April case, including Chomsky's and Eco's, can be found in Francesco Leonetti and Enrico Rambaldi, editors, *Il dibattito sul processo dell'autonomia (áprile 1979–fébbraio 1983)*, Milan: Multhipla, 1983.

26. Deleuze, "Lettera aperta ai giudici di Negri," in *La Repubblica*, 10 May 1979, pp. 1, 4 (also in Leonetti and Rambaldi, editors, *Il dibattito sul processo dell'autonomia*, pp. 106–09); English translation: "Open Letter to Negri's Judges," in *Working Class Autonomy and the Crisis*, pp. 148–51. International statements of support can be found in the same volume, pp. 143–44 and 151–55.

27. Foucault, "The Masked Philosopher," in *Politics, Philosophy, Culture: Interviews*

*and Other Writings 1977–1984*, New York: Routledge, 1988, pp. 324–25, edited by Lawrence D. Kritzman and translated by Alan Sheridan.

28. One of Ferrajoli's articles, cited above, is available in English translation in *Italy 1980–81:After Marx, Jail!*, pp. 51–55; others can be found in Italian in Leonetti and Rambaldi, editors, *Il dibattito sul processo dell'autonomia*, pp. 83–84, 129–40, 167–78, 181–91, 267–72, and 427–30.

29. Luigi Ferrajoli, "Il caso '7 Aprile': Lineamenti di un processo inquisitorio," in *Dei delitti e delle pene*, 1, 1983, pp. 167–204. To my knowledge this is the most comprehensive and acute analysis of the pre-trial phase under discussion here. For an in-depth discussion of the "inquisitorial" model in English, see Portelli's essay "Oral Testimony, the Law and the Making of History: The 'April 7' Murder Trial," cited above, reprinted as "The Oral Shape of the Law: The 'April 7' Case" in his book *The Death of Luigi Trastulli and Other Stories: Form and Meaning in Oral History*, Albany: SUNY Press, 1991, pp. 241–69.

30. *The Cheese and the Worms:The Cosmos of a Sixteenth-Century Miller*, Baltimore: Johns Hopkins University Press, 1980, translated by John and Anne Tedeschi; *Ecstasies: Deciphering the Witches' Sabbath*, New York: Random House, 1991, translated by Anne Tedeschi.

31. Ginzburg, *The Judge and the Historian: Marginal Notes on a Late Twentieth-Century Miscarriage of Justice*, New York: Verso, 1999, translated by Anthony Shugaar, pp. 7–12.

32. Apparently Ginzburg himself would not agree with this conclusion, however. Exiled Italian activists Paolo Persichetti and Oreste Scalzone (the latter one of the original 7 April defendants) report that, during an event celebrating the French translation of *The Judge and the Historian* in 1997, "Carlo Ginzburg replied to Toni Negri (who had remarked that he too had 'undergone a witch trial') that there was no question of comparing the two cases because 'Sofri was truly innocent and Negri guilty.' According to judicial truth standards the two are equally guilty, but Ginzburg, having frequented the universe of witches, had learned the magic art that allowed him and him alone to divulge the secret of historical truth." See Persichetti and Scalzone, "Des anges et des sorcières … L'affaire Sofri, l'affaire Negri et les années 70 en Italie," in *Chimères*, 33, printemps 1998, pp. 133–48; citation p. 135, n. 3, my translation. See also their book, *La Révolution et l'État—Insurrections et "contre-insurrection" dans l'Italie de l'après-68: la démocratie pénale, l'État d'urgence*, Paris: Dagorno, 2000, especially pp. 191–204.

33. See *'7 April' Trial—Italy:Amnesty International's Concerns Regarding a Fair Trial Within a Reasonable Time*, London: Amnesty International Publications, 1987, as well as the sections on Italy in *Amnesty International Reports* for 1980–88.

34. *Amnesty International Report 1988*, London: Amnesty International Publications, 1988, pp. 206–07.

35. Jamieson, *The Heart Attacked:Terrorism & Conflict in the Italian State*, London: Marion Boyars, 1989, p. 177.

36. Ginsborg, *A History of Contemporary Italy: Society and Politics 1943–1988*, New York: Penguin, 1990, pp. 386–87.

37. The one significant exception to this tendency among English-language historians is Richard Drake, who in his book *The Revolutionary Mystique and Terrorism in Contemporary Italy*, Bloomington: Indiana University Press, 1989, piously insists that "It is wrong to demonize Negri" (p. 98) after having spent a chapter and a half doing just that (pp. 52–58, 78–99). Drake focuses mostly on the rhetoric and practices of violence in the Italian movements over the course of the seventies; when he does turn briefly (pp. 148–50) to the 7 April trial (which provides the title of his fifth chapter, pp. 78–99), he merely rehearses the prosecution's original arguments and ignores the many abrupt changes of direction as well as the widespread and far-reaching criticisms of the case that I have already noted. Despite the fact that his book appeared in 1989, more than a year after the *pentito* Fioroni was finally brought to court for defense cross-examination and his charges were discredited, Drake offers no criticism at all of Fioroni's testimony—though his use of conditional constructions may barely preserve his historiographic "objectivity" (see pp. 106–07). Despite its very extensive use of a wide variety of relevant sources, his argument here is only a little less crude than Claire Sterling's out-and-out parroting of the prosecution's brief (and worse, her extensive use of wild innuendo from anonymous government "sources") in her book *The Terror Network: The Secret War of International Terrorism*, New York: Holt, Rinehart & Winston, 1981, pp. 202–27. Drake's later book, *The Aldo Moro Murder Case*, Cambridge, MA: Harvard University Press, 1995, tacitly acknowledges his earlier book's limitations by paying far less attention to Negri and his co-defendants and much more to the peculiarities of Italian legal procedure. His turnabout comes to completion in *Apostles and Agitators: Italy's Marxist Revolutionary Tradition*, Cambridge, MA: Harvard University Press, 2003, where he admits that "The extraparliamentary left movement was not always or even mainly terroristic. Not all the movement's leaders can be held personally responsible for acts of Red Brigades terrorism. Tactical differences of the sharpest kind separated [Raniero] Panzieri, Negri and the Red Brigadists. The very real distinctions among these personalities must be duly noted" (p. 226). Still, no list of historical evidence or court verdicts, however complete it may be, will ever be able to prevent the circulation of rumor, innuendo, and slander against Negri and company, which continues to this day.

38. The timeline in this paragraph is, once again, that established by Yann Moulier and published in Negri, *Italie rouge et noire*, pp. 318–21.

39. Gramsci too was only able to take the parliamentary seat to which he had been elected in April 1924 as a result of the same immunity from which Negri benefited, since he was being sought by the Fascist government on charges similar to those later leveled at Negri.

40.   Negri's speech to the Chamber has been published in both *Italie rouge et noire*, pp. 224–33, and the original Italian version of that book, *Diario di un'evasione*, Milan: MBP, 1985, pp. 204–11.

41.   See Ruggiero, "Sentenced to Normality: The Italian Political Refugees in Paris," in *Crime, Law and Social Change*, 19, 1993, pp. 33–50.

42.   Negri, *Marx Beyond Marx: Lessons on the Grundrisse*, Brooklyn: Autonomedia, 1991, translated by Harry Cleaver, Michael Ryan, and Maurizio Viano.

43.   At least two collaborative books emerged from his sociological research: *Des entreprises pas comme les autres: Benetton en Italie, Le Sentier à Paris*, written with Maurizio Lazzarato, Yann Moulier-Boutang, and Giancarlo Santilli, Paris: Published, 1993, and *Le Bassin de travail immatériel dans la métropole parisienne*, written with Maurizio Lazzarato, Antonella Corsani, and Yann Moulier-Boutang, Paris: L'Harmattan, 1996.

44.   For a pre-9/11 examination of this generalized and molecularized "state of emergency" in contemporary Italy, see the Luther Blissett Project, *Nemici dello stato: Criminali, "mostri" e leggi speciali nella società di controllo*, Rome: DeriveApprodi, 1999, especially chapters 1 to 6 of part one; for a post-9/11 account of its globalization, see Michael Hardt and Antonio Negri, *Multitude: War and Democracy in the Age of Empire*, New York: Penguin Press, 2004, part one.

# Editorial Acknowledgements
# and Translators' Note

This translation has taken a long time to find its way to its readers, and it would never have done so if not for the assistance of many generous people. I would like first of all to thank Toni Negri for his patience, aid, and encouragement during this process. My deepest thanks go to my hard-working collaborators in the translation of this volume, Arianna Bove, Ed Emery, and Francesca Novello. I would also like to thank Cesare Casarino and Ron Day for useful general suggestions at the outset of the project, and Michael Hardt, Matteo Mandarini, and Steve Wright for their meticulous suggestions on how to improve the translations. The search engine at the Marxists Internet Archive (www.marxists.org) was a tremendous help in locating obscure quotations from Marx, Engels, and Lenin. Last, and most of all, I am grateful for Julie's love and support and for Blackie's grace and equanimity throughout all the years of this project and so many others.

Some of the editorial work on this project was carried out with the aid of a Faculty Enrichment Grant from the University of Oklahoma College of Arts and Sciences and travel funding from the University of Oklahoma Research Council.

The present translation of *Crisis of the Planner-State* is a revision of the one done by Ed Emery and published in Toni Negri, *Revolution Retrieved: Writings on Marx, Keynes, Capitalist Crisis and New Social Subjects 1967–1983* (London: Red Notes, 1988), pp. 91–148. The present translation of *Domination and Sabotage* is a revision of the one done by Ed Emery and published as *Capitalist Domination and Working Class Sabotage*, in *Working Class Autonomy and the Crisis* (London: Red Notes, 1979), pp. 92–137. Both are revised and reprinted here by permission of Ed Emery and Red Notes.

### TRANSLATORS' NOTE

The pamphlets that comprise this book often shift register from the very concrete to the very abstract, and their meaning can be quite difficult to pin down. In order to be as accurate as possible, we have adopted several conventions in our translation, conventions that deserve some explanation. First, the Italian term *"dominio,"* which appears in the title of the last pamphlet, can mean "domination," "dominion," "dominance" and "domain." We have almost always opted to translate it as "domination" so as to maintain a clear continuity with the associated verb *"dominare"* ["to dominate"], but in a few places "dominance" or "domain" seemed most appropriate. Second, the common Italian term *"scadenza,"* which is widely used throughout these pamphlets, has no single English equivalent; we have translated it variously as "deadline," "appointment," "timetable," and so on, depending on the context, and we have generally included the Italian term in brackets for precision's sake. Third, we believe that in these pamphlets Negri had not yet settled upon the systematic discrimination between the terms *"potere"* and *"potenza,"* both of which mean "power," that he would articulate in *The Savage Anomaly* and his later works; here, he almost always uses *"potere"* for both constituted state power and subversive Workers' Power [*Potere Operaio*]. Thus we have decided to translate both terms as "power," and to mark the very few uses of *"potenza"* by the inclusion of the Italian term in brackets. In connection with this, the conventions of the standard Marx translations have also compelled us to use the word "power" in some places where neither *"potere"* nor *"potenza"* appears in the Italian, that is, in translations of compound terms that Negri invents by analogy with Marx's German term *"Arbeitskraft,"* in Italian *"forza-lavoro"* and in English "labor-power": hence invention-power [*forza-invenzione*], logic-power [*forza-logica*], etc. Finally, the inverse situation: instead of two Italian terms translated by one English one, we have a single Italian term that we have decided to translate in two ways. One of the most frequently used words throughout these pamphlets is *"lavoro,"* which means both "labor" and "work." The first meaning, which refers to the source of workers' power, is generally an affirmative term, while the second, which refers to the capitalist regimentation of that workers' power, is generally a pejorative term. We have based our decisions on whether to use "labor" or "work" on context in each case, but we acknowledge that these decisions are open to debate. In connection with this, we have also regularly used the phrase "Official Labor Movement" to designate the institutionalized left (the unions, the Communist and Socialist Parties) and "workers' movement" to designate the extra-institutional left that Negri theorizes in these pamphlets.

Citations of Martin Nicolaus's English translation of Marx's *Grundrisse: Foundations of the Critique of Political Economy (Rough Draft)* (New York: Penguin, 1973) are noted parenthetically within the pamphlets that follow. All other references have been placed in the endnotes.

# Glossary

**Autonomy of the political [*autonomia del politico*]**: In the seventies, some of the workerists who identified with the Italian Communist Party began to argue that the sphere of party political action had its own cycle of struggle and accommodation distinct from that of the "economic" sphere of production, and that as a consequence of this, the working class must at times concede autonomy to its party (the PCI) to act in the political sphere. Some critics saw this stance as a fundamental break with the precepts of workerism, while others like Negri viewed it as a development of the vanguardist logic already evident in texts such as Mario Tronti's *Operai e capitale* (Turin: Einaudi, 1966) as well as an apology for the PCI's strategy of electoral alliance during the seventies. In 1977 Tronti, who had joined the PCI in 1969, published a book entitled *Sull'autonomia del politico* (Milan: Feltrinelli).

**Class composition [*composizione di classe*]**: One of the defining elements in Italian workerism was its focus on class composition, which is the phenomenological, behavioral and disciplinary organization internal to the working class at a specific historical juncture. Class composition is determined by the interplay of the technical structure of work, the psychological pattern of class needs and desires, the institutional environment in which political and social action takes place, and other variables. An accurate understanding of class composition is a necessary precondition of effective worker organization and activism, and such an understanding can only arise from careful empirical research into the sociology of work. Negri's model of the dynamic evolution of class composition in the twentieth century presents it as developing from the professional worker to the mass worker to the socialized worker.

**Command [*comando*]**: In addition to its standard definition—the uni-directional passage of orders down a chain of subordination, as from officers to enlisted personnel in the military or from bosses to workers in the factory—command in Negri's usage also refers to a significant shift in the means of coercion capital exercises over labor. Whereas in earlier eras economic necessity—the threat of unemployment resulting in starvation—was the main coercive force used to discipline labor-power outside the factory, in the phase of real subsumption this is no longer sufficient because of the successes of the workers' movement in claiming a higher and more stable proportion of social wealth through welfare-state redistribution programs and contractual employment protections. This situation compels capital to make use of direct state command and even physical coercion to strip away those guarantees and re-impose its control through political manipulation, legal sanctions and police action on a mass scale. This aspect of Negri's analysis foreshadows his recent interest in Michael Foucault's concept of biopower, the direct and coercive management of life itself.

**Historic Compromise [*Compromesso storico*]**: The Historic Compromise is the name given to the Italian Communist Party's effort during the seventies to enter into national government through a policy of alliance with the center-right Christian Democratic Party. The implicit terms of the alliance required the PCI to adopt a strict law-and-order stance vis-à-vis the radical movements on its left wing, including Workers' Autonomy, and to collaborate with the right-wing parties on repressive anti-terrorism efforts that undermined civil rights and the judicial system. The rising tide of political violence on the one hand and the PCI's declining electoral strength on the other ultimately prevented the Compromise from taking place.

**Mass worker [*operaio-massa*]**: The decomposition of the professional worker during the Great Depression/New Deal period led to the emergence of the mass worker of the mid-twentieth century. The mass worker's relatively undifferentiated technical and behavioral composition (in comparison with the professional worker) arose from her/his experience of unskilled factory labor on a mass scale and the welfare state's safety net of public services. This composition expressed itself politically through the negotiation-oriented national unions, which emphasized the struggle for higher wages at the expense of struggles for workers' control of production, and the reformist left parties, which emphasized electoral participation and inter-party alliance in government instead of popular revolution, that came to dominate working-class action in the industrialized capitalist countries through the end of the sixties.

**Professional worker [*operaio professionale*]**: At the beginning of the twentieth century, industrial production had to rely on well-trained professional workers to operate and maintain the relatively simple machines that constituted fixed capital. Capital's dependence on their skills gave these workers a certain degree of authority and autonomy, and thus they formed a technical vanguard within the factory hierarchy. In Russia this internal composition of the class led to the organization of factory soviets and ultimately to the vanguard party of classical Leninism, which constituted its highest political expression. The hierarchical structure of the soviets and the party corresponded to the hierarchical composition of the working class itself. The success of the Bolshevik revolution, however, drove capital to reorganize production so as to reduce the need for skilled workers: complex machines replaced the simple ones so that unskilled workers could be used to replace the professional workers. At the same time, the establishment of welfare-state mechanisms of income redistribution reduced the intensity of conflict between labor and capital to a manageable level, thereby muting the working class's demand for revolution. This dismantling or decomposition of the professional workers' technical autonomy within the factory led to the decomposition (though not the elimination) of the vanguard party form in the political sphere.

**Real subsumption [*sussunzione reale*]**: This is Marx's term (in the "Results of the Immediate Process of Production"[1]) for the total subordination of all forms of labor in society to the capitalist logic and relations of production. Real subsumption develops out of formal subsumption, an earlier stage in which capitalist relations operate at the highest levels of social exchange (such as finance and international trade) but do not penetrate into all individual forms of production (such as artisanal manufacture or individual farming) and remake them along rationalized industrial lines. Under real subsumption, however, even the hardiest forms of traditional production are reorganized according to capitalist standards of efficiency, and thus capital's logic infiltrates and transforms every productive situation or relationship. In Negri's elaboration of Marx's conception, which draws on the earlier workerist notion of the social factory or factory-society, real subsumption demolishes the factory walls and disseminates the logic and structure of the factory throughout the entire society, making all activities directly productive in immediately capitalist terms.

**Self-valorization [*autovalorizzazione*]**: Self-valorization is the autonomous generation of needs, demands and values from within working-class experience and composition to supplant the alien and coercive needs and values imposed upon workers by capitalist command, by the ideology of work and by the seductions of consumer society. These new values generally lead to demands for qualitative changes rather than quantitative ones—for example, changes in the nature of work or even its total refusal, rather than simply the reduction of working hours and higher wages.

**Socialized worker [*operaio sociale*]:** The socialized worker is the most recent mutation in class composition, a mutation that Negri and his allies saw emerging in the period following 1968. This new composition arose as a result of the decentralization of production that constituted capital's response to the international wave of struggles by the mass workers during the late sixties. This strategy of restructuring began to break down the large factories and disperse the mass workers throughout the whole space and time of society, thereby effectively decomposing both the technical structure of their work discipline and the political organizations that expressed their demands (the national unions and mass reformist parties). If technical skill and knowledge defined the productive composition of the professional worker and collective discipline defined the composition of the mass worker, then communication and sociability defined the new composition and work discipline of the socialized worker. Many of the debates on the Italian left during the seventies, including the arguments in this book, were focused on debating the validity of the socialized worker as an analytical category and theorizing a political form of expression for the socialized worker, one that could replace the outdated union and party models.

**Tendency [*tendenza*]:** Negri's regular use of this term derives from the centrality to his analyses of Marx's law of the tendency of the rate of profit to fall as capitalism develops to maturity (discussed in *Capital* volume 3, part III, chapters 13 to 15). The method of the tendency refers to the critical effort to identify trends and potentialities within the development of capital and the working class that have not yet come to fruition or realization but will do so in the near future. The correct identification of such tendencies allows the correct (that is, most effective and productive) choices to be made regarding working-class organization, strategy, tactics and timing in the struggle against capital.

**Workerism [*operaismo*]:** Originally a derogatory term applied to radical perspectives and movements that blindly fetishized the industrial working class, workerism in Italy describes a diffuse set of radical groups, including not only Workers' Power but also segments of Workers' Autonomy and The Struggle Goes On [*Lotta continua*], that insisted upon the independence or autonomy of the working class in relation to the ongoing development of capital and indeed the priority of the working class's composition and action in determining the form and direction of that development.

**Workers' Autonomy [*Autonomia operaia*]**: Sometimes known as Organized Autonomy [*Autonomia organizzata*] and even simply as Autonomy, Workers' Autonomy succeeded Workers' Power as one of the most confrontational and violent (though not terrorist) militant movements among the archipelago of social and political movements that emerged in Italy during the early seventies. While Autonomists insisted on the continuing importance of factory workers as revolutionary subjects, they also acknowledged the increasing importance of other areas of struggle, including gender, sexuality and ethnicity, which drew in a new generation of militants around the country. Thus Autonomy was much more theoretically and practically decentered than Workers' Power had been. Negri joined Workers' Autonomy in its early days, after the dissolution of Workers' Power, and wrote the last three pamphlets in this book to help shape the debate over its organization. Over the course of the late seventies, Workers' Autonomy lost ground to the newer movements, but like most of those newer movements it was ultimately destroyed not by attrition but by the state's strategy of direct repression and collective criminalization.

**Workers' inquiry [*inchiesta operaia*]**: This is simply a social or political inquiry or investigation undertaken from the viewpoint of working-class composition, needs and values, rather than the perspective of capitalist control or academic social science.

**Workers' Power [*Potere operaio, Potop*]**: Founded in 1969, Workers' Power was an Italian militant organization made up primarily of radical students, as well as workers in large factories who had become disenchanted with the limited challenges that their official unions offered to capitalist management and with the reformist policies that their political representatives (mainly the Italian Communist and Socialist Parties) pursued in local administration and parliament. Negri was one of the founders and primary theoreticians of Workers' Power throughout its existence, and the first two pamphlets in this book were written as position papers for discussion among its members. The restructuring which Italian factories underwent in the early seventies sharply reduced the social and political leverage of traditional factory workers, and the criticisms and alternatives offered by new social movements—especially the feminist movement—led Workers' Power to dissolve itself in 1973.

### Note

1. This text is appended to the Penguin edition of *Capital* Volume 1, translated by Ben Fowkes, New York: 1976; the passages on real subsumption are on pp. 1023–25, 1034–38.

# Preface to the Italian Edition: 1997—Twenty Years Later

*Translated by Francesca Novello and Timothy S. Murphy*

On 3 September 1977 I concluded *Domination and Sabotage: On the Marxist Method of Social Transformation* by writing: "This pamphlet is like a fifth chapter. The previous four pamphlets are *Crisis of the Planner-State: Communism and Revolutionary Organization* (1974), *Workers' Party Against Work* (1974), *Proletarians and the State* (1976) and *Workers' Self-Valorization and the Party Hypothesis* (in my book *The State-Form*, 1977).[1] A fifth chapter presumes, therefore, that the previous four have already been read."

Twenty years have passed from that September in 1977 to this May in 1997 when these five chapters are being published together, and many things have happened during that time. In the following pages I shall try to retrace this period and outline some of the events tied to these pamphlets that are now becoming a book.

## 1. HOW THESE WORKS CAME TO BE

*Crisis of the Planner-State* was finished on 25 September 1971 and it served as an opening paper at the national conference of Workers' Power [*Potere Operaio*]. *Workers' Party Against Work* is dated 1 June 1973; *Proletarians and the State*, 1 August 1975. *From Extremism to 'What Is To Be Done?'—Toward a Critique of the Material Constitution: Workers' Self-Valorization and the Party Hypothesis* was written at the beginning of 1977 and *Domination and Sabotage* was written in the summer of that same year. These works, then, were written more or less every two years and they are tied to the work of analysis and leadership that the author himself carried out in the seventies, first within Workers' Power and later—mainly through the journal *Rosso*—within the area of Organized Autonomy [*Autonomia organizzata*]. These are books that could never have been written outside the collective climate of theoretical elaboration and political action that characterized the seventies. The language and theoretical atmosphere of these pamphlets are completely tied to the "movement of the seventies."

At that time these pamphlets had three functions. The first function was to assert the theoretical originality and the practical irreducibility of the movement in the face of the Official Labor Movement (that is to say, in the face of the whole set of social and political organizations of "real socialism" in our country). The second function was to summarize and at the same time to further the discussion carried out by the movement on how to construct the organization. The third function—probably the fundamental one—was based on the attempt to legitimize a kind of leadership within the seventies movement.

I believe that the first and second discussions in the pamphlets republished here each had a positive conclusion. The third discussion, however, did not lead to useful results.

As we shall see later, the theoretical discussion developed in these works follows each phase of the movement's development: from the critique of the welfare state and the Fordist organization of work to the definition of the form of the neoliberal state and the post-Fordist organization of work and at the same time from the critique of the traditional organization of the Official Labor Movement (written with capital letters) to the definition of new experiences of organization and centralization of the struggles on the part of the movement of the seventies. This discussion allowed the movement to deepen its consciousness of itself and to oppose itself drastically to the opportunism and Stalinism of the Official Labor Movement.

On the one hand, the theoretical discourse in these pamphlets revises, summarizes, and updates the critique of real socialism (the socialism of Eastern European countries, but above all Italian Stalinism, especially that of Togliatti and Berlinguer), a critique that the theoreticians of *Quaderni Rossi* and the left opposition had already developed by the early seventies. On the other hand, the experiences of struggle gained by important sectors of the Italian proletariat in the sixties and seventies are refined and developed in these pamphlets.

It can also be said that these writings—and perhaps also the experiences of struggle that nourished them and that the writings themselves encouraged—would not have been possible without the reading—or, better, the rereading—of Karl Marx's *Grundrisse* from within the workers' struggles. The *Grundrisse* had been translated into Italian by Enzo Grillo in those years[2] and it immediately became the *livre de chevet* [bedside reading] of the movement of the seventies.

The discussion within the movement, then, intended first of all to establish the theoretical identity of the movement and its autonomous capacity to organize itself. Until about 1979, the two aspects in which we are interested, the self-identification of the movement and its independence from the Official Labor Movement, developed effectively and continuously. The pamphlets presented here contributed to this development.

The third task of these writings was to constitute a group of leaders within the movement of the seventies. Unlike the other two objectives of the movement, this third task had a different fate. As a matter of fact the weapons that the pamphlets offered turned out to be inadequate in the face of the experience gained from the struggle that the armed class conducted at the end of the seventies. The acceleration of the civil war destroyed the relative homogeneity of the political "cadres" of the movement. The violent clash between the old workers' vanguard and the state's repression impeded the constitutive process of a new type of centralization capable of governing the post-communist period and rearticulating itself in the new class composition.

The fact remains that the generation of the movement of the seventies, dispersed between prison, exile, an uneasy *retraite* [retirement] to the "simple life," and more rarely the experimentation with new public practices, could speak and communicate politically only by making use of the linguistic forms and theoretical scenarios outlined in these pamphlets—the products, as I have already said, of a collective political experience.

## 2.  WHAT THESE PAMPHLETS CONTAIN

First of all they contain a realistic description of a passage of class composition that today we see entirely realized. At the beginning of the seventies, when everybody was glorifying the factory working class and the "final struggle" seemed to be close, it was not easy to emphasize the extraordinary transformations that were under way in the social body of the working class. And within this transformation it was not easy to try to raise the issue of the necessary renewal of political forms. In the first three pamphlets, the passage from the "mass worker [*operaio-massa*]" to the "socialized worker [*operaio sociale*]," that is to say, the passage from the hegemony of the Fordist worker to that of the post-Fordist socialized worker, is described carefully and precisely. Rereading these pamphlets today, I do not at all feel that they are extremist—as some have said—or utopian—as others have insisted—in their formulations regarding the transformation of the social constitution of the proletariat. Perhaps they are occasionally too timid, but they are almost always correct.

In the first three pamphlets, the problematic of organization is also clarified with extreme precision. We are continually asking ourselves *which organization* will then be adequate to this new composition—adequate, that is, to the social composition of the intellectual, immaterial, and cooperative productive operator.

In the first three pamphlets, the genealogy of an essential passage of working-class composition is described with striking precision. That passage consisted in the subjectivation, singularization, and socialization of abstract labor. This is a passage that goes decisively "beyond Marx"—in the sense that it recovers a phenomenology of the organization of labor and the workers' struggle that completely exceeds the limits of Marx's predictions.

Consequently, what is proposed here is a thorough revision of the theories and traditional practices of the organization of the Official Labor Movement. In particular, it is an attack on the reformism of the Communist Party, which in that phase was preparing the "Historic Compromise," and at the same time a critical confrontation with the terrorist tendency organizing itself within the Official Labor Movement. And yet, how could a new prospect for organization of the workers' struggle, and the struggles of the new subjects that the historic transformation was producing, be opened up? At first the direction taken consisted in constructing a two-level organization: one level that could be a site of resistance for the traditional working class, and another that could constitute instead (in an aggressive form) the mobility and imagination of the new intellectual strata of the proletariat. That is, one level aimed to give structure to centers of counterpower, while the other meant to represent the new governing functions of the proletariat.

The last two pamphlets, both written in 1977, perfect and enrich this problematic. Here the discussions of proletarian "self-valorization" are particularly important. They originate from the analysis of parts of Marx's *Capital* and *Grundrisse* on social reproduction and the circulation of commodities (and first of all that very special commodity called labor-power). After twenty years of theoretical analysis and above all experiences on this terrain, the paradigm of the Italian workerism of the sixties is substantially modified as a result. In fact, all the tendencies that had taken shape in the Fordist neo-capitalism of the sixties and in the crisis following 1968–69 came to maturity and reached their final configuration in 1977. The social struggles, both those conducted in factories and those conducted on the broader social field, can now be considered in a unified way: the conception that exploitation permeates society and individuals as well, and furthermore that the differences between the union activist and the politician, between the personal and the economic, between the individual and the productive become less and less relevant, were established in terms of *self-valorization*. Individual and collective self-valorization are thus tightly intertwined.

But the concept of self-valorization is important not only because it gathers and unifies the new elements that shape the productive forces in post-Fordism: self-valorization means, in fact, to put "the soul to work," to understand the positive, creative, radically alternative side (of the refusal of work). The concept of self-valorization, as it is expressed in these pamphlets, is also important for two other reasons. The first reason is that in these pamphlets the bad dialectic that connected the development of capital to the development of the struggles is declared to be definitively broken off. The struggles no longer appeared to be a mode of modernization. This was the terrible yet necessary event that had compelled the working class to develop its domination at the very moment that it sabotaged the machine in order to get free of it. Finally, on the basis of the conception of self-valorization, the experience gained from the struggles made us face the possibility of interpreting this development as rupture, and consequently the possibility of interpreting the struggle for liberation as exodus.

The consequences of this rupture were extremely important, particularly those that concerned the objectives of the struggles and their increasingly forceful capacity to influence the structures of administration and society by strategically infiltrating them. The critique of the political economy of administration followed and helped to complete the critique of productive exploitation. And even more importantly, self-valorization could now be seen in its separation, in the breadth of its spectrum of action, as a latent, powerful, and very radical *constituent power*. This is the second reason for the importance of the concept of self-valorization.

It is not by chance, then, that at this point the Marxist method of social transformation comes to be considered as an ontological practice, that is, as a constitutive practice. In this way my political and theoretical work and that of workerism in general linked up with the great revolutionary tendencies of Western philosophy and recovered their sense and flavor. Machiavelli, Spinoza, and Nietzsche could integrate the letter and the application of Marxist and Leninist teaching.

In conclusion, it can be said that these pamphlets develop two sequential orders. The first order proceeds from an intensification of the dialectical development of capital to its rupture. Consequently, it marks the limit of capitalist progress and the connection between struggle and development, but at the same time it shows the universality of the consequences of progress. The second order goes from subjectivity in struggle to constituent subjectivity, from the exercise of counterpower to the insurgence of constituent power. In this way, through the analysis of the new forms of post-Fordist productivity, the second order shows how richly ontological and constituent the concept of self-valorization is.

## 3.  THE LIFE OF THESE PAMPHLETS

So far these pamphlets have had two lives. The first phase was the era when the Feltrinelli publishing house made the publication of the pamphlets possible. Published either independently or as part of a book, each pamphlet went through ten printings in the seventies. All of them have been translated into all the languages of the Western capitalist countries. In addition, these pamphlets have often been translated in editions that were more or less clandestine. The second life of these pamphlets begins after 7 April 1979, when their author, together with about a hundred comrades, was arrested. As a consequence of this, the Feltrinelli publishing house withdrew the pamphlets from circulation and sent them to the pulping plant. It is for this reason that the pamphlets are only now once again public property and can again circulate freely. But these pamphlets continued to exist even though they had disappeared from the market and from the bookstores. In the arrest warrants, in the orders of commital for trial and in the sentences, passages from these pamphlets were endlessly and shamelessly quoted and often— when the judges were particularly reactionary and therefore less hypocritical—even the spirit of the pamphlets was quoted. There is no doubt that these pamphlets were condemned *not* because they had not been read but because they had been. Even the bureaucrats and zombies of the defunct Official Labor Movement read them at that time. Their hatred for the pamphlets generated a sort of neo-Torquemadian literature that was effective enough to imprison some one thousand heretics. Now the readers tied to the Official Labor Movement, both those old readers made wise by the awareness of their own mistakes, by the disaster of their politics and by the new clash with fascism that is now in progress, and the new readers armed with present experience and profoundly disillusioned by the false promises of the old Togliattian or Berlinguerian socialists—all these readers may now verify how little these pamphlets contain of anarcho-syndicalism or the doctrines of D'Annunzio. Readers may instead see how these pamphlets were (and perhaps still are) able to carry on the analysis and critique of the transformation of the mode of production and the mode of command of capitalism; and how these pamphlets suggested political lines that, if they had been followed, would have spared us the hideous regression and corruption of the eighties.

Today the Official Labor Movement is over and done with, as all its participants and spectators know. We had expected it since the sixties and we strongly stressed it in the seventies. By getting rid of us, the gravediggers in the Official Labor Movement believed that they had avoided destruction! Poor fellows. It is understood that the auto-da-fé held over these pamphlets cries out for vengeance and that nobody is willing to forgive—that is, supposing that the possibility for revenge still exists, although I sorely doubt it. As a matter of fact, between 1989 and today that zoological species, the so-called Berlinguerian bureaucracy, seems to have become totally extinct, unless some horrible new beast emerges from its ashes, as happens in bad science-fiction movies.

In any case, these pamphlets had a much richer life than the one that repression intended for them. They lived in the movement, and in the eighties they continued to be read and to form part of the education of those who were still resisting. In relation to this, the pamphlets were subjected to some interesting criticism. Two types of criticism in particular seem worth discussing again. The first criticism emphasizes the excessive "tendentialism" of these works. The second one insists on the impossibility of transferring the theoretical analysis onto the terrain of practice according to linear schemas. Thus these types of criticism charge the pamphlets first with being "deterministic" and second with being "mechanical" in drawing organizational conclusions from their analysis.

It seems to me that these criticisms must be accepted whenever they point out the perils of idealist determinism in the development of the analysis and in its application to reality, but at the same time they should be rejected. In fact today, at a time when there is no longer any reason to polemicize about the leadership of the movement, a close reading makes it clear that the project-oriented insistence that these pamphlets express does not constitute an illusion of organization (or a fantasm of organized spontaneity). On the contrary, it points out the practical necessity and urgency of organization: the threat that if $X$ is not done, not only will $Y$ not follow, but for a long time it will be impossible for $Y$ to occur. The maturation of the objective conditions for the passage to communism does not mean that its subjective realization is immediate. That maturation emphasizes a process, the emergence of a new paradigm, the necessity to look at the world from a new point of view. From the viewpoint of method, I have never attacked the bureaucratic (and/or terrorist) adage that today's opportunists have falsely attributed to Antonio Gramsci, "pessimism of the intellect, optimism of the will," as fiercely as I do in these writings. No, the adage must be reversed: "Optimism of the intellect and pessimism of the will." That is to say, we must realistically recognize the extraordinary possibility for the development of human creativity that the reappropriation of labor in the brain [*lavoro al cervello*] today permits. With equal realism we must also consider the terrible difficulties that our adversary, the collective capitalist, puts in the way of our political endeavors and our will when we face the problem of the organization of struggle. Therefore I agree with the point that we must reject in every way the temptations to turn the realistic consideration of the maturity of communism into an immediate organizational proposal or, worse, a contemplative illusion.

But this is not to deny that communism is mature. In both good and bad moments these pamphlets have always stood opposed to this assertion. In bad moments they were subjected to destructive and repressive criticism that was strong enough to destroy the very intellectual value of the discussion. I saw judges who were usually composed become blind with rage from reading and rereading these pamphlets, and they argued with me in legal terms over sentences in them. I heard the—normally soft—voices of intellectuals choke when they were threatened with the actuality of communism. I read the—normally ironic—writings of ultra-revolutionaries that degenerated into resentful sarcasm, accusing me of having become an idealist in these pamphlets.

Not to mention those—and there were many—who did not want to read these writings in order to avoid being tainted by sin. I read journalists who claimed to be the voices of public opinion state that I was obviously innocent of the crimes for which I was being prosecuted but who believed that I deserved to be flogged for what I had written. I received letters from philosopher colleagues—who proclaimed freedom in the university lecture halls—that accused these writings of irresponsibility. And the list goes on. However, with some self-contradiction they all found solace in pointing out how texts so stuffed with old communist blathering would soon turn out to be absolutely unreadable. In reality what they could not accept was the affirmation that communism was there, present, and that they were not aware of it. Today we can conclude by saying that their disquiet and their guilty fear of this communist reality has thrown them into the arms of Berlusconi (who promotes weak thought) during the eighties and in the nineties into the arms of the Ulivo (which promotes the weakening of their senses).

But these pamphlets have also experienced the positive counterpoint of the assertion that communism is mature. Where does this positivity reveal itself? It reveals itself in the fact that it is only in the practical–political, or I should say ethical, translation of what is said in these pamphlets about capitalism and its subsequent transfigurations (or perhaps simply disguises) that *it will be possible today to confront postmodern fascism.*

These pamphlets are powerful. They are the expression of a mass movement that has anticipated the destruction of socialism Italian style, Togliattism and Berlinguerism. These pamphlets sing of a modern hope for insurrection adequate to the violence of postmodern fascism, a requiem for triumphant opportunism. The positivity of these pamphlets lies in their actuality, their presence.

## 4. WHAT IS MISSING FROM THESE PAMPHLETS

These pamphlets, as I said earlier, have been widely read in European countries and in North America. They have been appreciated and criticized in many different ways. The most important criticism falls into three categories or types.

The first type of criticism concerns the fact that the proposed oppositions are not sufficiently articulated on the "molecular" level—they are instead "molar" oppositions and as such they grow inflexible. This criticism seems to me entirely acceptable. In reality this is not a criticism; rather, it points to a necessary completion of the hypothesis here given. As a matter of fact the category of self-valorization is not at all holistic but instead is open, diffuse, dispersed: it is defined as a molecular surface.

But then it can no longer function as opposition. On the other hand, some object that this category will not be able to be effective within a dual and antagonistic relation. Why not? As a matter of fact, Guattari and Deleuze's *A Thousand Plateaus* has shown how the indefinite insurgence of molecular resistances can become revolutionary. Surely in the pamphlets these dynamic prospects, that today are once again considered elements of strategy, are subjected to the rhythm of the fundamental Marxist and class oppositions, without excluding but instead actually soliciting and insisting upon the formation of individual self-valorizing resistances. Sabotage does not demand molar order: it demands that every individual, in the plurality of her existence and in her irreducible, singular desire, hate the enemy.

A second criticism has insisted on the fact that the issue of communication was absent from this presentation of the problems of the twenty-first century. Now, it is not true that it was absent. It was implicit. It is obvious that, during the seventies, the interest in symbolic and linguistic production still took precedence over the interest in communication and that the linguistic-symbolic horizon was only partially considered central to the analysis of the production of commodities. But note the extent to which these pamphlets, and the political work that accompanied them, show an interest in seeking to establish the physiognomy of a class composition that moved increasingly into the social, and toward the form of abstraction of the processes of social valorization—to the same extent that the attention moved more and more firmly toward the symbolic articulations of production. In this sense, the passage via the analysis of money was fundamental. In fact, in relation to the affirmation of the end of the law of value, money was considered less and less a measure of value (a measure that was subverted and overturned, but nevertheless a measure) and it was increasingly considered an index of a symbolic relationship that organized the hierarchical, disciplinary, and repressive procedures of power.

The laying bare of these procedures of domination forcefully introduced us to the identification of the set of new apparatuses [*dispositivi*] of resistance. In *Domination and Sabotage*, sabotage is revealed as an ontological force that destructures the system of power and dislocates its components, overturning them, appropriating them and gathering them up as offensive weapons into the new body of the socialized proletariat. This pamphlet provides the passage to a new phase of definition, to a new paradigm of the socialized worker, to immaterial labor and communicative production.

A third criticism raised against these pamphlets states that the theoretical passage (a deduction made within Marxism) did not produce a synthesis. In short, the passage to post-Taylorism, post-Fordism, and post-Keynesism was adequately described in the critique of the organization of work, in the theory of the wage and in the critique of the political economy of the state. (On an international level there is widespread recognition of the extraordinary foresight that this thematic presented.) But the set of passages did not construct an overall and unitary figure of the new regime of production. All the conditions were probably given, but we would have to wait for Lyotard's or Baudrillard's ironic and caricatural configuration to get the "postmodern." That's the criticism. And this criticism would be acceptable if it were not for the fact that it misses its object. As a matter of fact, the "postmodern" as we understood it, that is the direction in which our line of research moved, was not the post-Marxism of Lyotard and Baudrillard (just to name a few). It was not simply tied to the *critique of alienation*. It was rooted, instead, in the *critique of production*, of mechanisms for the production of value, and in the subjectivation of the critique. In other words it was rooted in the other way of constructing the postmodern (the ontological way? the materialist way? Of course!) which is found in that long route that goes from Deleuze and Guattari's *Anti-Oedipus* to their *Thousand Plateaus* and from Michel Foucault's works on the disciplinary era to those on the era of control. These were the authors with whose help we made progress in the analysis of the processes that led to the postindustrial civilization of mature capitalism, or if you like to Empire. They helped us in our analysis not only because of the political contiguity and the philosophical habits we shared with them, but also and mainly because for us, the fabric of our analysis and that of the struggles, the fabric of the production of sense and the production of subjectivity were the same, as it also was for them.

We both believed that the new synthesis was possible only by keeping to a Marxist terrain of analysis.

Having said that, we must also emphasize that in this criticism there is something that is profoundly correct. These pamphlets are essentially political. It was not possible, on the terrain of political practice, to do a theoretical analysis as complete as the analysis made in French post-structuralism. As Michael Hardt says, in the seventies French metaphysics theorized the politics that was being practiced at the very same time in Italy, just as in the nineteenth century, as Marx reminds us, the politics practiced in France found its metaphysics in Germany. Thus many things are missing from these pamphlets, and that is because they were not meant to be treatises; instead, they were intended to be tools for intervening immediately in the political struggle.

But even today, after so many years, we are not sorry for what is missing. Indeed, it compels us not only to make French poststructuralist theory our own, as a necessary complement, but also to explore it joyfully, and on the basis of the rich experience that political work (in its victories and its defeats) and the work of inquiry have provided, to move forward. In fact we can say that, as a political group, not only do we have a positive experience of the development of Marxism, but we have also established our own points of reference in order to continue to move forward in the construction of a new strategy that is adequate to the present and the future.

## 5. WHY THESE PAMPHLETS ARE BEING REPUBLISHED

We have already given many reasons that justify the republication of these works, but these are essentially reasons of a historical and philosophical nature. Now the question is whether there are also reasons of a political nature that argue in favor of the republication of these works. In particular, we must answer the following question: are these writings still of any practical use?

Frankly, I do not think that these writings can have a great practical influence today. If they were unable to interpret the construction of a leading group in the seventies, they will certainly not work in that sense today. And then there is the fact that the essential part of what constituted the fascination and the power of the experience of the movement of that time is missing. By that I mean a continuous exchange between theory and practice, between movement and project. And yet, granted that and *mutatis mutandis,* I believe that these pamphlets still contain the essential premises for the refoundation of a practice of the movement.

Today the struggle is developing around the production of sense and consensus. The hegemony won by capital over this terrain is unquestionable.

But in order for it to become hegemonic, the capitalist political class had to learn its lesson from the seventies and to organize itself as a movement. On the capitalist side, then, the mechanisms for the production of sense are closely articulated with the mechanisms for the production of subjectivity. We anticipated this mode of production of public space. And having been able to point out its different levels (offensive actions and actions of organization; destabilization and destructuring; network and movement), we should not be particularly shocked by this new political expression of capital. However, if we just look around we are struck by the inability of the left (or whatever the political representative of those who are exploited wants to call itself) to respond. And this impotence is so great that even we are often dismayed about it. How is it possible that we, we ourselves, are not able to break capitalist hegemony on the terrain of the production of subjectivity?

When I started reading these pamphlets again I felt a kind of pleasant surprise from the very first pages. As a matter of fact, once I got beyond the redundancy typical of a still-strong Marxism, I saw that these pamphlets present the only viable way to reweave the web of insurrection against a new organization of capitalist domination. The actuality of a project of resistance emerged impetuously even from the occasionally atrocious determinations of the past and the even worse ones of the degraded present.

So, how can these pamphlets help us with today's battles?

They can help us rebuild political discourse. They are not constitutive of practices, but they clarify and establish some conditions. The first condition is to grasp the theoretical observation that the social transformation of class relations has definitively been completed. Today, the social figure of immaterial labor rises *against* capital.

The second condition posed here concerns the form in which the social figure of immaterial labor can turn into a political figure. Now, this form can only be constituted *outside* the current political organization of capital. Against contemporary domination, workers' sabotage can only exacerbate its externality by pitting non-work against work for capital, by pitting constituent power against the administration of existing social relations.

These very brief annotations are enough to explain how these old pamphlets are still useful references in the universe of rebellion and the communist need for liberation. It is for this reason that they are being republished.

Antonio Negri
May 1997

## PREFATORY NOTE TO THE ENGLISH TRANSLATION

*Translated by Francesca Novello and Timothy S. Murphy*

The editor of this translation asked for my intervention to situate these writings historically. He also gave me a certain amount of space to do that. At first I agreed, but when I took up these writings again I realized that I had largely answered that question already in my 1997 preface. Certainly, any additional development would have been useful but not essential. As a matter of fact, in the 1997 preface I emphasize how these five pamphlets represented in the first place a reflection internal to the workers' struggles that took place on the extreme margin of the development of Fordism. In the second place, they represented the culmination of a discussion that led "beyond Marx." That is, the discussion proposed to go beyond the law of value and to lay out objectives that began to touch upon the biopolitical context of development. In the third place, these pamphlets represented a debate on the forms of organization that were adequate to the passage that the struggle against exploitation was bringing about and experiencing. I do not think there is much more to add on those points. The five pamphlets were completely internal to the development of the struggles of the seventies in Italy and in Europe. I can only emphasize this internality and confront it with the historical interpretation of that period. It is not up to me to intervene on this terrain.

Perhaps only one thing is missing from my 1997 preface, and that is an emphasis on the extent to which these writings (and the experiences to which they bear witness) served much later as sources of debate among many comrades (and ultimately with Michael Hardt) on the new forms of power [*potere*] at the imperial level. I mean that, in Italy in the seventies, we experimented with some of the fundamental mechanisms of the dialectic of class struggle, on that extreme limit that constitutes the crisis of factory production. By analyzing this crisis and experiencing the resistance struggles of the mass workers, we traversed a global limit. In other words, we were entering a new era. These "books for burning" are important because they offer the key to the periodization of the passage that leads from Fordism to post-Fordism and from the modern set-up of the state to the new imperial configuration of sovereignty. Of course, in order to identify this passage to a new era we could also follow other paths, for example the global South and the anti-colonial struggles. But the great transformation we are experiencing arises precisely from the coincidence of these passages. Therefore the seventies that took place predominantly in Europe correspond to the eighties and nineties of the other zones of class struggle in the world.

This, then, is the other reason why these "books for burning" can usefully be read. Anyone who wants to situate them historically should therefore reread the 1997 preface; in the present note I also indicate a track in these pamphlets that can help to define the Empire that is now constituting itself.

Toni Negri
November 2002

### Notes

1. Italian titles: *Il dominio e il sabotaggio: Sul metodo marxista della trasformazione sociale*, Milan: Feltrinelli, 1977; *Crisi dello Stato-piano: Comunismo e organizzazione rivoluzionaria*, first published in the journal *Potere Operaio* in 1971, book versions published by CLUSF, Florence, 1972, and later by Feltrinelli, Milan, 1974; *Partito operaio contro il lavoro*, in Sergio Bologna, Paolo Carpignano, and Antonio Negri, *Crisi e organizzazione operaia*, Milan: Feltrinelli, 1974, pp. 99–160; *Proletari e stato*, Milan: Feltrinelli, 1976; and "Autovalorizzazione operaia e ipotesi di partito," in *La forma stato*, Milan: Feltrinelli, 1977, pp. 297–342.

2. Published by La Nuova Italia in 1968 (vol. 1) and 1970 (vol. 2)

# I

# Crisis of the Planner-State:
# Communism and Revolutionary Organization
# (1971)

*Translation by Ed Emery revised by Timothy S. Murphy*

## 1. THE ANTAGONISM OF THE TENDENCY ACCORDING TO MARX: ACTUALITY OF HIS ANALYSIS

Toward the end of the "Chapter on Money," which forms the first part of the *Grundrisse* (227–28), Marx lays out the trajectory of his entire project, indicating the necessary order of steps in the argument. This must proceed, he says, from the analysis of money in its role as equivalent to the definition of relations of production and the internal articulations of production; thence to the concentration of these relations in the state; and finally, to the study of the world market, the level at which the dialectic of the parts and the whole allows all the contradictions to come into play, and at which the destructive violence of crisis is manifested—as "the general intimation which points beyond the presupposition, and the urge which drives towards the adoption of a new historic form." This indication of Marx's procedure should be regarded as fundamental for an understanding of his methodology. It allows the analysis to develop correctly on the plane of historical material-ism, and to confront the problems of crisis, the state and most importantly organization in terms of the critique of political economy. Moreover, it enables the analysis to do so from a perspective in which the force of the development of the tendency leads to the identification of certain very general theoretical elements, but also to the definition of particular passages that are very close to those that, little by little, are being presented to the workers' viewpoint by capitalist development today.

Besides, Marx's discussion of the problem of money in the first part of the *Grundrisse* already shows the inextricable link between the critique of the economic category "money" and the revolutionary political proposi-tion. In the genesis of money, the tendency appears from its inception as the development of an irrepressible contradiction. In the first place, as the contradiction implicit in the dual nature of the commodity, which "exists doubly, in one aspect as a specific product whose natural form of existence ideally contains (latently contains) its exchange value, and in the other aspect as manifest exchange value (money), in which all connection with the natural form of the product is stripped away" (*Grundrisse* 147). This logical contradiction becomes an overall historical tendency:

> The need for exchange and for the transformation of the product into a pure exchange value progresses in step with the division of labour, i.e. with the increasingly social character of production. But as the latter grows, so grows the power of *money*, i.e. the exchange relation establishes itself as a power external to and independent of the producers. What originally appeared as a means to promote production becomes a relation alien to the producers. As the producers become more dependent on exchange, exchange appears to become more independent of them, and the gap between the product as product and the product as exchange value appears to widen. (*Grundrisse* 146)

However, "money does not create these antitheses and contradictions; it is, rather, the development of these contradictions and antitheses which creates the seemingly transcendental power of money" (*Grundrisse* 146; also numerous other references in the same chapter). The contradiction that money represents is that between the value of labor as general equivalent in commodity exchange and the conditions of social production under capital's domination. On the one hand, we have money as the specific determination and measure of the value of labor-power sold on the free market; on the other, we have the social character of production which capital has appropriated and turned into its own power [*potenza*] over social labor, over the totality of the independent social movement, as an autonomous power above the individual producers. At this point, we already have the formal condition of crisis:

> By existing outside the commodity as money, the exchangeability of the commodity has become something different from and alien to the commodity, with which it first has to be brought into equation, to which it is therefore at the beginning unequal; while the equation itself becomes dependent on external conditions, hence a matter of chance. (*Grundrisse* 148)

At this point we also have the possibility of the state as the manager of this "matter of chance"—wielding the violence that is necessary to establish the unity and stability of the capitalist project of development over and against the contradictions involved.

Up to this point, the argument may appear too formal. (As Marx puts it: "It will be necessary later, before this question is dropped, to correct the idealist manner of the presentation, which makes it seem as if it were merely a matter of conceptual determinations and the dialectic of these concepts" [*Grundrisse* 151].) In reality, this first framing of Marx's analysis of money is not so much formal as limited in scope. So far, it has touched upon only one determinate moment in the function of money in capitalist society. Behind the "idealist manner" of Marx's presentation, the various ways in which money operates in the face of modifications in the relations of production are presented within a given stage of development, one in which the privatized dialectic between individual costs of production and the general value of social labor has not yet been resolved. Money essentially fulfills the role of mediator between the cost of labor-power and the value of social labor; it acts as an indicator of changes in the balance of capitalist power over this relation; it formally validates the functioning of the law of value in a world in which labor is not yet materially homogeneous. For this reason, money appears at certain points to operate as a function of contradictions which it in fact determines. In spite of everything, circulation seems to have priority over relations of production (hence the one-sided appraisal of the crisis of circulation in certain pages of the *Grundrisse*). And even when Marx goes on to consider "money in its third quality, in which both of the former are included, i.e. that of serving as measure as well as the general medium of exchange and hence the realization of commodity prices" (*Grundrisse* 203), and proceeds to define "money as material representative of wealth" (*Grundrisse* 203–18), his analysis is still fixed precisely within this same framework. It is clear from these passages that Marx is confronting here a world of privatized individual wealth, of pure capitalist competition, in which money plays its role as "the general material of contracts" in the Eden of a bourgeois democracy of property ownership. "Equality and freedom are thus not only respected in exchange based on exchange values but, also, the exchange of exchange values is the productive, real basis of all *equality* and *freedom*" (*Grundrisse* 245).

However, the tendency breaks free of the specificity of this reference to the capitalist epoch upon which Marx's analysis is based. The full radicality of the critique erupts into view. The point is emphasized at the outset and then repeated: from the analysis of the role of money as equivalent in exchange, we must pass on to the definition of relations of production. From this standpoint, the first rupture brought about by the tendency, vis-à-vis the specificity of the capitalist epoch to which Marx refers, can already be detected in his discussion of money as general equivalent and material representative of wealth. How is this presented? "The money relation is itself a relation of production if production is looked at in its totality" (*Grundrisse* 214). Money is a relation of production because the money relation, throughout all the determinations of the cycle of capital, expresses wage labor as the basic and essential element of production; it is a relation of production because the exchange between money and wage labor is total (*Grundrisse* 224–25). "When wage labour is the foundation, money does not have a dissolving effect, but acts productively" (*Grundrisse* 224). But if money presents itself as productive function, then the abstract totality of the existence of money must be articulated in a radical way with the development of the capitalist mode of production. This totality has to emancipate itself gradually from its functions of general measure and mediation of market exchange, and its productive role must now be founded upon a totality of homogeneous, compact, and existing social labor. Money must no longer operate as a function of the mediation between costs of production and the general value of social labor. It must become solely and directly a general function of social production, the means of reproduction of the wage-labor relation in an extended, global dimension. The productive role of money leaves its imprint on the capitalist mode of production in the form of a furious will to liberate itself from its office of mediation in exchange, taking on its true capacity of domination over wage labor outside and beyond the petty transactions of the marketplace and within the dimensions of a general sociality whose call money, from the very beginning of capitalist history, has always heeded.

This, then, is the tendency. But today this tendency has become reality; it is fully present. Finance capital has helped to push labor to close its inherent gap vis-à-vis the general value of social labor; capitalist planning has shown that only on this material basis is capitalist development possible. The social character of production has been imposed within the capitalist mode of production. And yet it remains a fact that "on the basis of exchange values, labour is *posited* as general only through *exchange*," only as wage labor (*Grundrisse* 171). Labor time as an element that is quantitatively and qualitatively determinate, varying both in terms of its time-measure and the given division of labor, is dispersed throughout the social machine of commodity production (*Grundrisse* 171–72 and 704–12). Immediate labor as such ceases to be the basis of production (*Grundrisse* 705). Yet in spite of this, money still opposes the capitalist appropriation of commodities to the sociality of production. Hence the problem of money has merged with the problem of a new and extremely radical kind of crisis of capitalist domination over the mode of production. Money is this form of domination over the mode of production; to the extent that production is socialized and it is, "in a word, the development of the social individual which appears as the great foundation-stone of production and of wealth" (*Grundrisse* 705), its functional rationale is stripped away and reduced to that of class violence. The law of value, as the law governing the social recomposition of labor, now exercises its sway entirely over this terrain of arbitrariness and fortuitousness. Nor can this arbitrariness and fortuitousness be seen any longer as dialectical malfunctions in the circulation of money, explained in terms of its doubly contradictory nature. It can only be understood as a radical antagonism, a function of pure domination, as a powerful and inimical externality that can no longer be brought back to any mere function of mediation. No longer can it be readjusted to the process of development; no longer can it serve as a surrogate for social development. In the form of money, capital, which has created the conditions of social production, reveals itself as the fundamental barrier to any further development of the productive forces.

Hence the problem of the state, in terms of the critique of political economy, must be posed in a new way. The rupture of the relationship between money and development is represented, at the political level, by the obsolescence of bourgeois democracy as a regime of equality and freedom. Since this regime was always functional to the world of exchange, and articulated closely with it, freedom, equality, and democracy remain merely an appearance, a façade—representing not merely the mystification implicit in the world of market exchange, but rather a mystification of the dissolution of real exchange relations—a mystification of a mystification, a façade to the second power. The figure of the despotism of capital is ever more openly glorified with the collapse of money's role in mediating the anarchy of production. And the state more openly glorifies its monstrous role as the technical organ of domination as it presides over the total disarticulation of the rationale of development. It is no longer even the guarantor of bourgeois freedom; it "frees itself," in the sense that its own power becomes more arbitrary, more a matter of random chance. The fetishism of state power becomes more pronounced to the extent that it is based on a belief in functions that no longer exist. All that remains is class hatred, a desperate will to class survival. "What holds for machinery holds likewise for the combination of human activities and the development of human intercourse" (*Grundrisse* 705).

In the "Chapter on Money," we can follow the development of the tendency through to the point where money, from its role in mediating the monopolistic sphere within the general process of production, becomes the index of an antagonism arising dialectically from the exchange relation itself, from its function of general mediation. This insoluble antagonism, caught between the socialization of production and the increasing arbitrariness of the representative functions of money in terms of measure, equivalence, and representation of wealth, becomes progressively more critical and violent. In this process, the very dialectic of the capital relation itself is broken; money ceases to represent a moment in the class relation. It now comes to embody the split in the relation, the unilateral, irresolvable, antagonistic, capitalist will to domination. It comes to represent, in other words, the final result of a relation that, through its historical evolution, leads inevitably to this schism. So much for the utopia of the socialist reformers, who dream that money can become an exact measure and representation of social labor: "It is just as pious as it is stupid to wish that exchange value would not develop into capital, nor labour which produces exchange value into wage labour" (*Grundrisse* 249; also numerous other references in Notebooks 1 and 2).

## 2.  A MYSTIFIED PERSPECTIVE: THE ECONOMISTS AND THE DESTRUCTION OF THE CONCEPT OF CAPITAL

The tendency that Marx describes in his "Chapter on Money" finds certain mystified correspondences on the ideological plane today. In the first place, bourgeois economists have grasped this maturity of the tendency, and have transcribed it into the false consciousness of their theories. But then we also have a series of positions that have emerged in the revolutionary movement which draw inaccurate and dangerous conclusions from a confused perception of capitalist development. In both cases, the tendency is seen as a result, as a situation already consolidated and extreme, rather than as a movement. This method is all too familiar today—a description of development by means of broad, extreme images, which is all the fashion. Let us start with the positions of the economists. The economists today have registered or verified, in the negative sense at least, the realization of the tendency described by Marx of the role of money in capitalist development as a whole. Their work has been prompted by an increasingly sharp experience of the failure of the Keynesian project of planned development. The Keynesian project was an attempt to regulate circulation, the cycle, the overall process of capital, by intervening to control the mediation of the contending elements, even to the point of continuously prefiguring it. This system largely swept away the old assumption of classical economics, which focuses "only on the end results without the process that mediates them; only on the unity without the distinction, the affirmation without the negation" (*Grundrisse* 197). The false appearance of circulation as a "simply infinite process," a "spurious infinity," was broken apart and reassembled in the Keynesian system by controlling the various elements that composed it. This effectively eliminated a number of possibilities of crisis, and also removed the need to have recourse to external violence to reassemble the elements and restore the unity of the cycle. In that system, money was called upon to function as intermediary in the precise manner that Marx outlines: as a driving element pressing for the further socialization of production—assuming a productive role—and at the same time acting as general equivalent, operating both as an instrument to measure labor and as a tool for controlling development. Once again, the contradictory nature of money was harnessed as a positive force for capital. But this "socialist" reconstruction of money has now broken apart. This historical rupture has happened due to the obdurate refusal of the working class to become the subject of this development and the enduring emergence of a "wage labour that wishes to posit itself as independent" and acts that way. The reality of this rupture is given by the realization of the tendency of development insofar as it concerns the constitution of aggregate labor-power into an increasingly compact and unified "social individual" for capitalist development itself.

At this point, the economists' Keynesian project collapses. It was premised on control and incentive for development within certain fixed proportions. Control, in other words, was the other side of the coin of the measure of social labor. As the "Chapter on Money" demonstrates, the socialists, in their search for a perfect measure of labor value, never challenged the rule of proportionality that the law of value imposes on the overall social movement; they could only offer difference in place of unity and qualification in place of equalization. Hence socialism becomes reactionary insofar as it can only produce the conditions of its own existence. As against this, the real movement of the socialization of the proletarian subject denies this unity and opposes the conditions of production to the command of capital. In a parallel way, the apparent successes of the bourgeois economists in eliminating the "irrationality" of circulation crises prove to be a Pyrrhic victory. What we have now is no longer a crisis of disproportion between the various elements in the cycle, but a disproportion pure and simple between the working class and capital. No longer are we faced with a dialectic that brings difference back to unity; we now have antagonistic difference, one unity against another.

The poverty of ideology follows from this crisis. From their experience of the failure of the Keynesian project, the economists have developed a negative and indeed exaggerated consciousness. The emergence of a massified and socialized working class has led them to deny the concept of capital itself. This has become, in their hands, an indeterminate entity; no longer is it seen as a homogeneous structure, but rather as a "parable"—an "indirect representation of reality which does not reproduce the details of the structure" (even though it may still reflect one fundamental property in the classical tradition of capital, namely a determinate relation to labor-power). And perhaps no longer even a "parable," since the elements that make up the concept of capital are not only totally heterogeneous and unconnected to any fixed relation to labor-power, but also contradictory to the organic composition of capital. The rate of profit is no longer presented as a dependent variable of the organic composition. The relation between dead labor and living labor is no longer determined univocally by technology's rhythm, and profit is freed from its conditions.

But, having said this, can we not detect here an implicit admission of the realization of the Marxian tendency? Instead of merely denouncing the practical inadmissibility of the concept of capital in an accountancy sense, our economists would do better to consider the real social process revolutionizing the conditions of production, a process that arises from the relation between workers and capital. The "freedom of capital" could then be seen as only the mystification of the historic defeat that capital has suffered in the class struggle. Capital's "freedom" in the eyes of the economists implies a recognition that the independence of the labor-power variable is irrepressible.

Heterogeneity in the composition of capital; indeterminacy in the technical relation between the extraction of labor value and profit; the crisis of the concept of organic composition. Of course: when we turn to Marx, we find that more than a hundred years ago he wrote:

> To the degree that labour-time—the mere quantity of labour—is posited by capital as the sole determinant element, to that degree does direct labour and its quantity disappear as the determinant principle of production—of the creation of use values—and is reduced, both quantitatively, to a smaller proportion, and qualitatively, as an, of course, indispensable but subordinate moment, compared to general scientific labour, technological application of natural sciences, on one side, and to the general productive forces arising from social combination in total production on the other side—a combination which appears as a natural fruit of social labour ... (*Grundrisse* 700)

Hence it is precisely at the moment when labor becomes materially equalized and socialized that capital is forced to emancipate its command over the process of valorization, to assume its own freedom—in total solitude as it were—in the face of a unified labor-power. But Marx adds: "Capital thus works towards its own dissolution as the form dominating production" (ibid.). Whereas, on the contrary, the economists draw from this an apologia for the freedom of capital. They refurbish the illusion—so effective in serving the needs of repression as to highlight the absurdity of a new fascism—of a new kind of capitalist development entirely freed from any link with the class struggle and unrelated to the behavior of overall labor-power. They argue the overdetermination of capital imposed on the system as the material rule of development. They have suffered the collapse of Keynesianism, but have not understood its causes; and as for the "freedom of capital," they can only grasp its relentless will to survive. From this point of view, the capital relation is seen purely as an external one, a pure relation of force, a project for overall control based on the centralized organs of money supply, a totally subjective design for organization and domination. And this new subjectivism among the economists is backed by a modest but useful contribution from the other social sciences. (In this regard, the Galbraith-style encyclopedic reconstructions of the theory of the capitalist overdetermination of the system do not meet with many difficulties in finding references in order to carry out their dirty business.)

Let us turn now to the interpretation of the crisis. A whole series of passages from Marx could be cited here, each totally relevant to the urgent problems that now face science and the economists directly. Crisis in Marx is seen as a necessity for capital, a means of putting the brakes on development, a limit to the expansion of the productive forces when these begin to upset a certain specificity and proportionality in the relations of force. (See, for example, *Grundrisse* 422–23, 442–46, 747–50.) Through a sort of paradox, "the violent destruction of capital not by relations external to it, but rather as a condition of its self-preservation" *(Grundrisse* 749–50), is not seen by the economists as the result of a dialectical sequence in which the relation between material elements leads to this result. Rather, they insist on seeing crisis as the expression of a will that is as material as it is subjective. In the ideology of the economists, this freedom of capital (which could be seen in terms of a "socialist" project in the Keynesian system) is transformed into a permanent design to block a development of which the only spontaneous outcome would be the triumph of the collective practice of communism, the self-realization of the social individual. Hence the permanent state of crisis and controlled stagnation that becomes the condition for the continued existence of the capitalist system itself.

However, the new economists realize this full well. Despite the radicalism of their ideology, in practice they are concerned to roll back the conflict between the social forces of production and the system. They define and use the crisis as self-destruction on the part of capital—quite contrary to the extreme terms of the ideology with which they are identified. From the Marxian viewpoint, as can be seen in the "Chapter on Money," this concept of crisis is merely an intermediate one, corresponding to a low level in the development of the tendency, which evolves further to a more profound intensity of crisis as rooted in a structural contradiction between the maximum socialization of labor and the maximum externality of capital. At this point, the ideology of the economists, in its desperate blindness, refuses to recognize that what crisis leads to, inevitably, is "the most striking form in which advice is given [to the system] to be gone and to give room to a higher state of social production" (*Grundrisse* 750).

On the one hand it is true that "capital ... cannot confront capital if capital does not confront labour, since capital is only capital as non-labour; in this antithetical relation" (*Grundrisse* 288). But if this is so, then every time that capital attempts, at this level of development, to resolve the contradictions inherent in its process through its own autonomy and within its own confines, retreating from the real terrain of the class struggle, considering this to be closed and finished, transferring to itself the full responsibility for development, then at each point the contradiction is more profoundly recomposed, despite the ideological efforts of the economists to mask it. The contradiction develops the tendency to the point of showing its antagonistic and insoluble nature. It is not resolved within the margins of the so-called "freedom" of capital, nor within the attempt to use the overdetermination of capitalist power to restore a circularity of development, a new dynamic recomposition of the cycle. On the one hand, we may have the totality of the power of capital; but on the other we have the totality of a recomposed proletariat.

From the ideological dissolution by the economists of the concepts of capital, organic composition, and the relation between class struggle and development, we come at last to their definition of the state. Here the totality of power which they attribute to capital finds its most functional embodiment—functional because only the subjective attribution that the state allows for can guarantee the manipulation of development that the economists want to establish in terms that are external to the capital relation. In this way, the risk of a failure of confidence intrinsic to a reliance on the possibility of freedom, on the emptiness [*vuotezza*] of capital's determinations, is averted by shifting this reliance onto a powerful subject. To attribute this power to the state may be functional with regard to expectations, but is it effective? The contradictions that mark the path of capitalist science, which seeks always to eliminate the necessity of its opposite, to release itself from the class struggle, are multiplied as the reference point for its action becomes more abstract.

The state, which they portray as an infinite power [*potenza*], a non-dialectical essence in relation to capitalist development, has, on the contrary, an existence that is as capable of precise intervention as it is subordinated in an overall sense to the innumerable contingencies of class confrontation. Its autonomy and freedom are in reality only means, not a secure basis. This does not diminish the specificity of the state's role, or the extent of its lucidity in action, let alone the solid fact of its repressive functions and their effectiveness in development. Nor should we minimize its wealth of articulations or overlook, above all, the functions of collective consciousness and guidance that the state can, and effectively does, fulfill for capital. But, having said this, the ideology of the economists nevertheless fails to convince. In freeing itself from its organic composition, capital above all shows its precariousness. The subjectivism of the economists only shows their limitations; it registers the course of the Marxian tendency, but only by submitting to it and playing a part in it.

### 3.  A DISTURBING CONSEQUENCE: THE "SUBJECTIVISTS" AND THE CONTRADICTION AS CATASTROPHE

So we come to the core of our problem, the question of workers' revolutionary organization. One immediate and disturbing way of grasping the consequence of the realization of Marx's tendency is evident in current debates on organization. The argument goes like this: since capital has broken the organic links which tied it to class struggle, the positive dialectic (from the point of view of capital) that the state was able to impose on this social conflict is finished. Rather than harnessing conflict to promote development, the state is now productive of crisis. And since the workers' struggle now directly confronts the overdetermined level of a social dialectic which has become, precisely, the state itself, the issue of organization must now break with that tired old tradition which saw organization in terms of a mere transposition from the definition of the organic composition of capital. Organization must now be conceived beyond and outside the connections that link the emergence of the class to the form of the labor process. The organizational task becomes rather a positive commitment to constructing a political vanguard that is outside and beyond any intrinsic relation to the determinate composition of the working class—a vanguard that is entirely political, aimed for a direct assault on the state, and organized for the military preparation of this assault.

One step forward and two steps back, as the old saying goes. And we cannot deny that a positive step forward is implied by these positions, inasmuch as they are premised on a critique of the theory of organization elaborated and practiced, in substantial continuity, from the Second to the Third International. This old theory conceived the problem of organization on the basis of a given composition of capital and of the working class which was specific to that historical period: organization of the "professional worker" as the fundamental axis of the capitalist mode of production, as the essential articulation of the process of valorization and exploitation, and hence as the key element in the revolutionary process. To use the terms developed in the "Chapter on Money" in the *Grundrisse*: this class composition still signified the possibility of making money function in its mediating role between the value of labor individually employed in the production of exchange values and the mechanisms of general equivalence, a situation in which money still functions as the overall control of the system and in which the law of value still functions as a dynamic element of the system. Hence a theory of organization that took as its essential reference point the professional worker, and defined the process of political recomposition of the class as a process essentially framed within the organizational structure of work; which saw the productive role of this working class as paramount; hence also the ideology of work, which was the prime feature of the whole program and the organizational project itself, defining them, precisely, as "socialist."

Whatever the extent of the profound tactical differences between the various positions put forward at the time, between, say, Kautsky and Luxemburg or Lukács and Gramsci, it is difficult to see these differences as significant in terms of the basic socialist program they all share. Indeed, the analysis is always objectively referred to the professional worker; the organizational recomposition of the class prefigured socialism; these aspects, together with the ideology of work, not only reflected (in the Marxian sense, as both overview and transformation) the specificity of a given class composition, but also pointed to the way in which, in that situation, socialism was out of phase with regard to the general conditions of capitalist domination at the time. Seen in this perspective, the model of socialist organization put forward was revolutionary even when it took up the nexus of democracy and socialism as its weapon against a capitalism that was still unplanned, and defined the dictatorship of the workers as the highest form of democracy—and of the political functioning of the law of value.

Hence the critique of this model of political organization, carried forward by "subjectivist" theories of organization today, is quite justified. They grasp, correctly, that the objective basis of that political composition of the proletariat has been swept away—absorbed and destroyed by the new structure of the capitalist state that emerged from the great crisis of 1929.

The capitalist response to the October Revolution of 1917, to the movement of workers' councils, not only eliminated the very possibility of this organizational model by destroying the key role of the professional worker in the labor process; it also set in motion an operation of dynamic containment of the struggles of the new mass worker [operaio-massa] who was then coming to the forefront. This marked the end of any possibility of basing organizational class recomposition on the organic relation between the working class and capital.

However, at this point it seems to me that the step forward (that is, their critique of the old socialist model of organization) starts to take two steps backward, and at a tangent. It is one thing to recognize, correctly, that a given organizational model is outdated, that a certain determinate proportionality and materiality of class composition, with the professional worker as its central element, has been surpassed. It is quite another thing to nullify the very concept of organic composition, and to renounce the infinite number of possibilities for an "updating" of the concept which a determinate class analysis today can offer. While it is true that the concept of organic composition must be re-examined—since its content has changed—this does not mean we should throw the baby out with the bath water by jettisoning the method as a whole.

By doing just this, the "subjectivist" comrades[1] come to resemble the bourgeois economists, in that they draw from the realization of the Marxian tendency catastrophic and exaggerated conclusions which are incorrect.

From a correct criticism of the old socialist model of organization, they make mistaken deductions. This impression is further supported when we turn to another series of problems concerning organization. In the frame of reference of the organizational model of the Second and Third International, the articulation between the leadership and the movement was sustained and justified through analysis of the political composition of the class; the requirement that any organization be modeled on the material basis of class composition was again fulfilled in this respect. The political leadership of the proletariat duplicated in its relation to the mass movement the dualism that existed in the movement itself between a mass of professional workers (managers of the mode of production, imbued with the ideology of work) and the proletarian masses. The question of the greater or lesser degree to which leadership should be external to the movement—the issue of contention between Luxemburg and Lenin, for example—is not to be seen as an alternative to this general model. Indeed, this debate (when not interpreted in ideological terms) only confirmed the model; the greater or lesser externality of political leadership depended essentially on the degree of homogeneity reached by the proletariat of the different nations—in the case in question that of Germany, for example, certainly exceeded that of Russia. Hence the socialist model of organization had a clear basis within the social composition of the proletariat at that time. How do our "subjectivist" comrades react to the eclipse of the general conditions of this model, to the end of any material reference point for these organizational articulations? They react by theorizing the most absolute dichotomy between the spontaneity of the unified proletarian masses and revolutionary subjectivity, between workers' autonomy and the goals of organization. Paradoxically, the concept of the subjective externality of revolutionary organization has been borrowed once again from the most rigorous theories of the old socialist model; this is now justified by the refusal to accept any mediation of the organic capital relation and class political structure. What we have here is a sort of abstract Leninism, divorced from the conditions specified by Lenin in *The Development of Capitalism in Russia,* which were the point of departure for his entire practice.

This is a problem, precisely, of subjectivism, which we can now call "proletarian," whereas formerly it was called "third-worldist" or "studentist." It represents a response to the reality of the socialization of the mode of production on an unprecedented scale, and the extraordinary massification of struggles in recent years. It avoids, however, coming to grips with the material specificity of these historical passages, and hence fails to connect the will to organize with any real and effective program.

At this point, we should go back and shift the whole problem to the theoretical plane. Let us return to the *Grundrisse,* to the tendency, to Marx's definition of the rupture of the dialectic between the maximum socialization of the proletariat as wage labor and the absolute externality of capital as agent of command over work. What does this "realization of the tendency" signify for Marx? Does it mean the simple emergence of an inevitable historical necessity? Or, alternatively, a historical rule of thumb lacking any specific content, a transitory custom of an outdated culture? It is neither. On the contrary: the realization of the tendency in Marx is the emergence of a mass necessity. It is objective in that it is constituted in relation to the mass of subjective agents and articulated in specific determinations that capitalist development itself is forced to accommodate. It means the victory of a dialectical movement, the maturation of a specific historical situation in, and its destruction through, the relationship with a historical subject. The compact unity of Marx's discourse here confirms his own methodological premises; the entire Introduction [*Einleitung*] of the *Grundrisse* spells it out. The tendency is itself a movement, the movement of a specific relation. Only in the specificity of this relation does it arise, and is it destroyed. Capital's tendency toward crisis is only brought about through and within a determinate overall relationship: a crisis of the mode of production in relation to the conditions of labor, a crisis of the totality of command in relation to the totality of the workers' subjection—relations which are determinate and have an immediate prehistory. To break completely out of this dialectic, to pose the problem of the destruction of the existing order outside the movement that creates its fundamental precondition—the appearance of the proletarian social individual—is to remain trapped in a suicidal dualism between subject and object. And where theory ends up empty, practice must remain blind. Let it be clear that we are not here attacking subjectivism on the grounds that it has no place in the Marxist theory of the tendency. On the contrary, we must attack it precisely because it cuts itself off from that embodied, dialectical class subjectivity that pervades the tendency in Marx, as a historical individuality concretely and specifically constituted within this phase of capitalist development. At this point, we could elaborate further on this, if space allowed, by tracing back the recent history of Western Marxism, showing how, through the critique of "diamat," the crude materialism underlying Soviet determinism, it has fallen back into the dualistic alternative, a theoretical impasse equally incapable of reading the tendency within the activity of the class struggle as the class struggle in action. This impasse results in political impotence, and hence in the response of terrorism as the only possible form of struggle; this attitude often recurs as an attempt to oppose a free theory to a subordinated one. Free from what? Subordinate to what? Freedom and subordination, whether in theory or in practice, are only given within the tendency, within the movement, within the specificity of the class struggle that materially prepares the terrain for the destruction of the existing order. As regards the question of organization, therefore, what counts is not the realization of the tendency as a given, a result, or a state. What counts is the process of its realization as activity. Hence all forms of subjectivism are illusory which assume the tendency as a result, and see the task as simply organizing the assault on state power. Lenin's *April Theses,* after all, could only have been written in April 1917.

Hence the need once again to relate analysis, discussion, and practice regarding the problem of organization back to the materiality of the movement. In order to move onto this terrain, to be sure, many traditional solutions will have to be discarded. The old categories of the critique of political economy within which the problem of organization was posed are certainly suffocating. On the other hand, the total change in content and reference points must in turn imply a change in the theoretical progression of the categories that is assumed. But there is no other way. And there are no short cuts.

## 4. (ABSTRACT) LABOR AS REVOLUTIONARY SUBJECT: THE BASIS OF THE COMMUNIST PROGRAM AND PROLETARIAN APPROPRIATION

We want here to show that communism is actual; that any notion of intermediate passages in the revolutionary process now becomes irrelevant; and that the class struggle is now immediately and directly aimed against the state. But we have to show this from within the movement of the tendency, because this method of approach has important implications for defining our model of organization, and for the nexus between organization and the program. This is the essential meaning of dialectical materialism: the ability to understand and nourish the growth of the revolutionary historical subject, through concrete analysis and not just by reference to generalities.

Hence we must refer back again to the tendency as described by Marx in the "Chapter on Money." What is the basic contradiction, and in what direction does its movement unfold? Marx distinguishes two cases. The first is that in which the labor of the individual is posed from the outset as a particular labor: to reach the sphere of money, this labor has to be mediated, to become generalized, and it is precisely money that carries out this operation. Here, then, we have a contradiction between particular labor and the generality of money; a contradiction, however, which is overcome by money itself. Hence money here plays a productive role. In the second case, which Marx distinguishes from the first, "the *presupposition is itself mediated*; i.e. a communal production, communality, is presupposed as the basis of production. The labour of the individual is posited from the outset as social labour." Therefore "his product is *not an exchange value*" and "participation in the world of products, in consumption, is not mediated by the exchange of mutually independent labours or products of labour. It is mediated, rather, by the social conditions of production within which the individual is active" (*Grundrisse* 172). This is where the fundamental contradiction becomes evident: the function of money becomes antagonistic; its mediating or real or productive role is overdetermined with respect to the development of the productive forces. Hence:

> Those who want to make the labour of the individual directly into *money*, into *realized exchange value* (i.e. his product as well), want therefore to determine that labour *directly* as general labour, i.e. to negate precisely the conditions under which it must be made into money and exchange values, and under which it depends on private exchange. This demand can be satisfied only under conditions where it can no longer be raised. Labour on the basis of exchange values presupposes, precisely, that neither the labour of the individual nor his product are *directly* general; that the product attains this general form only by passing through an *objective mediation*, by means of a form of *money* distinct from itself. (Ibid.)

We have seen how capital, through the long history of its development from manufacture to large-scale industry, advanced through and out the other side of the first phase or case that Marx describes. After the great crisis of 1929, the second phase opens; from this point, we see the ambiguous, equivocal attempt on the part of capital to make money, as capitalist control over general exchange value, function within a contradictory relationship that is openly recognized.

Today, finally, we are witnessing the full unfolding of this second phase, in which the mystifications of the contradiction, the elements of continuity in relation to the past, are exhausted. "This economic relation—the character which capitalist and worker have as the extremes of a single relation of production—therefore develops more purely and adequately in proportion as labour loses all the characteristics of art" (*Grundrisse* 297).

And today, not only is labor materially constituted as the general basis of social production, but it is explicitly revealed as such:

> As *the* use value that confronts money posited as capital, labour is not this or another labour, but *labour pure and simple*, abstract labour; absolutely indifferent to its particular *specificity*, but capable of all specificities. Of course, the particularity of labour must correspond to the particular substance of which a given capital consists; but since capital *as such* is indifferent to every particularity of its substance, and exists not only as the totality of the same but also as the abstraction from all its particularities, the labour which confronts it likewise subjectively has the same totality and abstraction in itself. (*Grundrisse* 296)

We must emphasize the passage that we have reached today, within this second phase as described by Marx. It has a number of crucial consequences as regards the movement of the tendency. Specifically, the crisis of 1929, or perhaps it would be better to say the moment at which, in response to the revolutionary socialist challenge and the October Revolution, the tendency passed to mass production as a means of destroying the conditions for worker organization (the crisis of 1929 led to the recognition and assumption of this real movement on the part of the state): from this point, production becomes based on a general labor. The social character of production makes the product, from the outset, a general, social product. But in the passage we have reached today, the mystifications of this recomposition of capital and the state after 1929 are exhausted. The relationship between the working class and money as the horizon of control, newly established by planning, and hence the role of money as the general equivalent of exchange values, is now recognized from the workers' viewpoint for what it is: a pure semblance, a hoax. Marx foresaw this latest decisive passage in the following terms:

> When competition permits the worker to bargain and to argue with the capitalists, he measures his demands against the capitalists' profit and demands a certain share of the surplus value created by him; so that the *proportion* itself becomes a real moment of economic life itself. Further, in the struggle

between the two classes—which necessarily arises with the development of the working class—the measurement of the distance between them, which, precisely, is measured by wages itself as a proportion, becomes decisively important. The *semblance of exchange* vanishes in the course of the mode of production founded on capital. (*Grundrisse* 597)

This means that the tendency already includes the movement of a revolutionary historical subject; with the disappearance of the mystification of exchange value, the antagonism of the tendency points to a passage from wage struggle to the struggle over appropriation. (We shall return to this later.) Moreover, if this recognition has come about, then the mystification of socialism also collapses. Socialism is not possible, just as any relation that is not merely antagonistic between labor and exchange value is impossible. Or, to put it more precisely, the socialists' utopia can only serve (as it did for a brief period after the 1929 crisis) as an ideological smokescreen for capitalist control over the antagonism that has emerged.

In this new context, on this unified basis of wage labor, and now that the infamous semblance of exchange has been shown up for what it is, communism has become necessary, both as the product and the subversion of the present state of things. The tendency creates the terms of this opposition: to "the universal prostitution, [which] appears as a necessary phase in the development of the social character of personal talents, capacities, abilities, activities" (*Grundrisse* 163), the tendency opposes "free individuality, based on the universal development of individuals and on their subordination of their communal, social productivity as their social wealth," their patrimony (*Grundrisse* 158).

This analysis of the fundamental contradiction that arises from and finds its resolution in the tendency, however, concerns not just the qualitative aspects of labor—that is, the collapse of any qualitative differentiation within social labor. This constitution of the unity of wage labor also involves the quantitative aspects of labor performance, dissolving them; and this in turn introduces a further series of antagonisms. Marx's analysis of labor time is obviously fundamental in this regard—as we have already noted—but his observations should also be read in relation to the dissolution of the division of labor (to which he refers both implicitly and explicitly).

To the degree that large-scale industry develops, the creation of real wealth comes to depend less on labour time and on the amount of labour employed than on the power of the agencies set in motion during labour time, whose "powerful effectiveness" is itself in turn out of all proportion to the direct labour time spent on their production, but depends rather on the general state of science and on the progress of technology, or the application of this science to production. (*Grundrisse* 704–05)

According to the rhythm of the reduction of labor time, science is incorporated into immediately productive labor: "Invention then becomes a business, and the application of science to direct production itself becomes a prospect which determines it" (*Grundrisse* 704). It is on the basis of these conditions that "Real wealth manifests itself, rather—and large-scale industry reveals this—in the monstrous disproportion between the labour time applied, and its product, as well as in the qualitative imbalance between labour, reduced to a pure abstraction, and the power of the production process it superintends" (*Grundrisse* 705). The contradiction that follows is both general and specific. It is general, firstly, in that capital, faced with this process, "presses to reduce labour time to a minimum, while it posits labour time, on the other hand, as sole measure and source of wealth." Secondly, and more specifically, we have the law of labor productivity: capital "diminishes labour time in the necessary form so as to increase it in the superfluous form; hence posits the superfluous in growing measure as a condition—question of life or death—for the necessary" (*Grundrisse* 706). This contradiction, then, is if anything even more pregnant in its consequences than the contradiction above, brought about by the process of abstraction of labor. Here again, the contradiction reveals the working class as the historical subject of the tendency. Not only is it revealed in all its antagonistic activity, as the active possibility of subversion of the system; it is also shown as representing a new world, a new subjectivity, which is being constructed in a social, communist way. In the first place, this is an antagonistic activity:

On the one side, [capital] calls to life all the powers of science and of nature, as of social combination and of social intercourse, in order to make the creation of wealth independent (relatively) of the labour time employed on it. On the other side, it wants to use labour time as the measuring rod for the giant social forces thereby created, and to confine them within the limits required to maintain the already created value as value. Forces of production and social relations—two different sides of the development of the social individual—appear to capital as mere means, and are merely means for it to produce on its limited foundation. In fact, however, they are the material conditions to blow this foundation sky-high. (*Grundrisse* 706)

In the second place, it is an activity of reconstruction, as the real and present possibility of communism:

No longer does the worker insert a modified natural thing [*Naturgegenstand*] as middle link between the object [*Objekt*] and himself; rather, he inserts the process of nature, transformed into an industrial process, as a means between himself and inorganic nature, mastering it. He steps to the side of the production process instead of being its chief actor. In this transformation, it is neither the direct human labour he himself performs, nor the time during which he works, but rather the appropriation of his own general productive power, his understanding of nature and his mastery over it by virtue of his presence as a social body—it is, in a word, the development of the social individual which appears as the great foundation-stone of production and of wealth. The *theft of alien labour time, on which the present wealth is based*, appears a miserable foundation in face of this new one, created by large-scale industry itself. As soon as labour in the direct form has ceased to be the great wellspring of wealth, labour time ceases and must cease to be its measure, and hence exchange value must cease to be the measure of use value. The *surplus labour of the mass* has ceased to be the condition for the development of general wealth, just as the *non-labour of the few*, for the development of the general powers of the human head. With that, production based on exchange value breaks down, and the direct, material production process is stripped of the form of penury and antithesis. The free development of individualities, and hence not the reduction of necessary labour time so as to posit surplus labour, but rather the general reduction of the necessary labour of society to a minimum, which then corresponds to the artistic, scientific etc. development of the individuals in the time set free, and with the means created, for all of them. (*Grundrisse* 705–06)

At this point, at this level of maturation and expansion of the tendency which we must recognize as real, we are compelled to draw a first conclusion as regards the problems of revolutionary organization in relation to the determinacy of class composition, in the Marxist and Leninist theoretical sense. The exchange of labor-power is no longer something that occurs, with quantitative determinations and a specific quality, within the process of capital; rather, an interchange of activities determined by social needs and goals is now the presupposition of social production as such; and sociality is the basis of production. The labor of the single producer is posited from the outset as social labor. Hence the product of this overall social labor cannot be represented as exchange value, not even in the form of the proportional mediation of general labor and general control over it, nor in the form of capitalist planning. Work is already an immediate participation in the world of wealth. Recognition of this provides a necessary programmatic content to organization. It establishes the theoretical and practical tasks we have to develop on the terrain of direct appropriation, as the recognition in practice of these social conditions of production. The mass content of the project of worker organization today, inasmuch as it extends to the whole figure of abstract labor, can only be based on a program of direct social appropriation of the wealth that is socially produced.

Worker appropriation represents the practical recognition of this. It is a practical revelation that the development of the productive forces faces a barrier in the capitalist appropriation of wealth; and that a new historical revolutionary social subject can now take upon itself the task of making communism flourish through its struggles, through the characteristics of its own existence.

## 5. THE CRISIS OF THE PLANNER-STATE: THE LARGE ENTERPRISE AS ARTICULATION OF THE TENDENCY AND SUBJECT OF THE ANTAGONISM FROM CAPITAL'S POINT OF VIEW

The tendency promotes a development that is at first contradictory and then becomes antagonistic. Contradiction and antagonism imply the existence of subjects in a given relation, and we have seen how the historical proletarian subject emerges with increasing clarity. We must now turn our attention to the other subject, to capital, in order to see how it moves within the tendency, and how its activity develops with a view to closing down the tendency, as opposed to opening it up. Class activity is progressive, that of capital regressive, in the development of the tendency. Both are marked by the fact that they have entered a new and original phase in the class struggle—a fact that qualifies the strategic horizon of the struggle. But at the same time it is only in the determinacy of the actual confrontation that we can grasp the tactical passages, the specificity and the determinations that must be present in any discourse on organization.

At this level of development of the tendency, what then is the response of capital?

We have already highlighted the position of the "economists." In their eyes, the crisis of the Keynesian State constructed post-1929—the breakdown of the proportionality determining the division of social wealth set against the great power [*prepotenza*] of the new class figure—means the end of any possible organic relation between the working class and the state as the collective representative of capital. The crisis of this "Planner-State [*Stato-piano*]" can only lead to a relation totally freed of any determination of the general equivalent of value, completely disarticulated from the organic composition of capital, and hence premised on non-intervention in the process of social production. The schism between labor and command over labor is complete; the state can only take the form of a "Crisis-State [*Stato-crisi*]," in which it manages its own freedom of command for the survival of capital. "A *general devaluation* or *destruction of capital* ... in general crises, this devaluation extends even to living labour power itself" (*Grundrisse* 446). Such perspectives, according to the economists, are unavoidable—relations of force permitting—if one takes for granted a permanent state of crisis as the normal condition of capitalist development and of an adequate functioning of the state. As we have seen, this theoretical line is also the basis of subjectivist tendencies with respect to revolutionary organization, which insist consequently on the need to dissociate organizational projects from any definition of the political composition of the class. Both these positions, we have suggested, represent at best only partial truths. It is immediately certain that this use of crisis as a devaluation that extends to the value of labor-power itself is the royal road that capital must follow. No one would deny this. Equally undeniable, in a less immediate sense, is the affirmation of the tendency according to which "labour itself progressively extends and gives an ever wider and fuller existence to the objective world of wealth as a power alien to labour, so that, relative to the values created or to the real conditions of value-creation, the penurious subjectivity of living labour-power forms an ever more glaring contrast" (*Grundrisse* 455). But emphasizing this does not mean giving up the even more powerful drive of communism as an active force in the real movement. Nor, on the other hand, should the capitalist mechanism of crisis be seen unilaterally in terms of the devaluation of capital and ultimately the devaluation of the value of labor-power. On the contrary, "the destruction of value and capital which takes place in a crisis coincides with— or means the same thing as—a general growth of the *productive forces*" (*Grundrisse* 446). Hence crisis and restructuring must be seen as simultaneous, as an attempt, at the same time as the proportions of necessary labor to surplus labor ("or, if you like, of the different moments of objectified to living labour" [*Grundrisse* 444]) are altered, to re-establish a different relation, to propose new levels of organic composition that are favorable to capital. It might be objected that to argue such a simultaneity of crisis and restructuring, given the present level of the tendency and the relations of force determining the present crisis, can only serve as a mystification. But even if it is a mystification brought about by capital, this does not mean that it is any less efficacious! The answer to the subjectivist comrades who argue along these lines can be found in Lenin's aphorism: "You include in the 'semblance' [*Schein*] all the wealth of the world and you deny the objectivity of the 'semblance'!"[2] In reality, it is precisely within the efficacy of the capitalist response, or if you please that of its mystification, that the tendential antagonism becomes more or less explosive. It is only by confronting this path of capital (however mystified) that the communist instance of the pro-letarian masses can assume a subversive power [*potenza*]. Only within the determinacy of this relation, within its contingency and specificity, can the bosses find their own new concept of capital and the proletariat discover its own new practice of the party.

And indeed the bosses are constructing for themselves a new concept of capital, based, as usual, on the broadest experience offered to theory, the workers' struggles. Only on this basis (as the consciousness, if not the science, of capital recognizes) can theoretical innovation and renewal of political domination be possible: to "capitalize the revolution," as a *Times* headline recently put it. Reflection and the practice corresponding to it focus on the causes of the present crisis in order to overcome and contain them—in order to utilize and repress them in the same way that capital's domination over the relation always has. How then, broadly speaking, has the crisis of the Keynesian State arisen since 1929? The state of determinate proportionality has broken down in the face of the massification of struggles and the exten-sion of wage demands which confronted the state with a unification of abstract labor in the form of collective practice that demanded an increase in the value of necessary labor. This produced a rejection of the determinate proportion between necessary labor and surplus labor which, translated into exchange-value terms, is called inflation. With inflation, the crisis of the system becomes first and foremost a crisis of the state, since the Keynesian State has the hegemonic role of balancing and promoting development in the sequence that runs from the enterprise to the plan to the state. The factory was subordinate to the state, which guaranteed the basic conditions for the functioning of the system—and of the factory system itself in the first place. Through the action of the state, exchange value was guaranteed in its operation as the general law governing the reproduction of the productive conditions. But this mechanism has failed to function. The law that the state had to guarantee has been broken apart, starting from the factory itself and extending to the whole society. In the massified struggles of the mass worker, work has been disconnected from labor value. In this situation, the state could guarantee a relation of general proportionality, and thereby the enforcement of the law of labor value, only by means of a dynamic process of reformism, commensurate with the proportions that it was to guarantee. But under the workers' pressure that had overflowed its fixed bounds, reformism only becomes a further element of dissolution of the mechanism, one that upsets the correct functioning of the law of exchange value.

At this point, capital is forced to accept the situation brought about by the disconnection between work and the general law of value. The capitalist will to re-establish a hegemonic relation follows from this awareness. Here the final determination of the tendency is immediately subsumed under capital; the separation implicit in exchange value is made explicit in the most extreme terms. Capital becomes immediately and exclusively command over the labor of others (see *Grundrisse* 238). The disconnection between work and labor value/exchange value, once it is accepted and appropriated by capital, leads to this conclusion: command as such, generalized command over labor, becomes not just what it has always been, the qualifying general motive of capital, but the element required for its existence, for its very survival. It becomes in short the specific determination of capital for the historical period in question. A second consequence that follows from this premise is also becoming apparent, namely the reversal of the sequence state–plan–enterprise. Whereas the state previously fulfilled a hegemonic role, representing and guaranteeing the equivalence of all the factors in the movement of production–reproduction, the collapse of the norm of equivalence now makes the function of the state subordinate to that of the enterprise—in the dominant form it assumes today, the multinational enterprise. At the level of the world market, the "Crisis-State" thus also represents a crisis of "nation-states" in relation to the multinational enterprise as the form of capitalist command. Whereas hitherto the state was the organizer of all the conditions of social production, the workers' offensive has now disrupted all that and forced capitalist consciousness to fall back on the one condition that remains paramount: command by the enterprise over the extraction of surplus labor. This shift is already registered by the new American economists who, following the demise of neo-mercantilist and Keynesian theories, now openly attack reformist traditions and push for policies of selective incentivization. *Chez nous*, the end of reformist themes can be measured in the striking affirmation that—in a phrase that Marx would have liked—"the enterprise is the basis of the state" (Glisenti), while at the international level, parallel to the end of Keynesian domestic policies, we have the collapse of the Bretton Woods system and of agreements between states on general equivalence. This clears the way for the multinational enterprise fully to take over the functions of motivation and general command over development.

Paradoxically, in this phase of profound crisis, capital is forced to relive the heroism of its own genesis:

The highest development of capital exists when the general conditions of the process of social production are not paid out of *deductions from the social revenue*, the state's taxes—where revenue and not capital appears as the labour fund, and where the worker, although a free wage worker like any other, nevertheless stands economically in a different relation—but rather out of *capital as capital*. (*Grundrisse* 532)

But the capitalist project today is not merely a response to the workers' impact on the structure of the Planner-State. It also seeks to interpret the form or figure in which this impact develops, which is the mass worker. It seeks to interpret the mass-worker phenomenon in order both to recuperate it and to reshape it. The *fluidification* of all moments of the productive cycle, and the concomitant increase in the productivity of both individual and collective social labor, is the positive side of the capitalist project, restructuring in the true sense of the word. Then there is the negative, reactionary side: the attempt to decompose the mass worker by inserting new mechanisms of division of labor now entirely linked to participation in the command of the enterprise. In this way the overall political horizon of capital reaches the level of the labor process, and the urgent need for general domination over development is articulated in attempts to determine the organic composition of capital in a new form. This is now a purely political concept, one that articulates the relation between massification of production and the functions of command within it. The superabundance of capital, as a result of the emergence of the massified worker, has eliminated the possibility of an organic composition determined by labor time and by varying productivities in different sectors of the division of labor. The leveling of work to generic, abstract labor requires as its corollary the continued existence of the value form of labor, of capitalist command, of factory command extended over the entire society. From this point of view, the enterprise—as factory—is the key concept for capital today, produced by the bosses as a concept and category of capital to meet their needs in the specific phase of class relations of force through which we are passing at present. The combination of overall fluidification of work throughout the entire productive cycle and selectivity in the functions of rule within that same cycle—and hence the significance of automation—has now won a role in the history of capitalist development comparable to that of Taylorism and Fordism during the twenties. Then, it was massification that was introduced to undermine the professional basis of the workers' organization; today, it is selective participation in command that is employed against the massified basis of the workers' organization.

We can now draw some general conclusions from this discussion. We have seen that capital—as an alternative to, or better still as part of, its overall use of the crisis—at this level of the tendency, attempts to "capitalize the revolution," mystifying the emergence of abstract labor as massified subject, in a fluid and leveled composition of productive labor. What emerges as the single directing and qualifying element in this is the enterprise, in the sense that it extends the norms of command over factory labor to all social labor. This is the path upon which capital is now embarking, through its awareness of the causes that brought about the fragmentation of the Planner-State, through its attempt to interpret and control the class movement that has destroyed the Keynesian State. If this, in broad terms, defines the line imposed on capital through the dialectic of the relation between classes in struggle, then the rationale for our polemic against all the subjectivist definitions of the problem of revolutionary worker organization is confirmed. The need for communist political organization of workers and proletarians geared to insurrection is too urgent, and, as we have shown, it is made all too obvious by analysis of the tendency, to be left to "voluntarist" choices. To subvert the capitalist articulation of command over social labor, which is exercised by and through the enterprise, constitutes the primary tactical task of revolutionary organization. Failure to take up this specific subversive function would mean running the risk of the communist drive of the masses being nullified by repression—not by judges, but by the materiality of the system. At any rate, it would mean that there could be no immediate organizational effects.

I began this chapter by saying that it was not enough to consider the destructive capacity of the tendency; that it was necessary to grasp the specific behaviors and project of the subjects of the antagonism. Now that we have analyzed the behavior of the class adversary, we can begin to define the problem and the determinate passage to be confronted by revolutionary workers' organization. The issues are: the management of social appropriation by the masses, but at the same time the rupture of the political support, the theoretical symbol of capital's dominant vehicle today—in other words, the enterprise. The problem lies in the fact that these are not two issues, but one. To mobilize all the mass workers against the factory system, and to unleash the whole of abstract labor against the form of exchange value—both struggles are against the factory. Here lies the key issue for workers' organization today, and it is related to the problem of the organic composition of capital.

## 6. PRELIMINARY INTERVENTIONS ON SOME OBJECTIONS REGARDING METHOD: TENDENCY, SCIENCE, AND PRACTICE

At this point, a brief digression on questions of method is required. In the past, two major objections have been raised against the kind of argument I have advanced thus far. The first is the accusation of *economism:* that is, of relying on a deterministic view of the tendency, postulating an immediate translation of this tendency into reality (in other words, overlooking the determinate specificity of any given reality, and the specific ways in which that reality must be mastered [*dominarle*]). The second accusation, complementary to the first, is that of *idealism:* that of subjectivizing the polar articulation of the tendency, of individualizing contradictions and antagonisms, isolating them from the series of practical operations that follow from any determinate, organized individualization. In that case, clearly, idealism leads to spontaneism.

Practice has given these petty objections their due. There would be no need to dwell on them, were it not for the fact that answering them gives us a chance to examine our own point of view in greater depth. Let us take the first objection. In order to answer it, we have to clarify what we mean by "the tendency." The tendency is in no sense a necessary and inevitable law governing reality. The tendency is a general schema that takes as its starting point an analysis of the elements that make up a given historical situation. On the basis of that analysis, it defines a method, an orientation, a direction for mass political action.

The tendency gives us a determinate forecast, specified by a material dialectic that develops the factors comprising it. The tendency is the practical/theoretical process whereby the workers' point of view becomes explicit in a determinate historical epoch. This means that to posit the tendency, to describe it and define its contradictions is a far cry from economic determinism. Quite the opposite: to posit the tendency is to rise from the simple to the complex, from the concrete to the abstract, in order to achieve an adequate overall theoretical horizon within which the simplicity and concreteness of the elements which were our initial starting point may then acquire meaning.

> The concrete is concrete because it is the concentration of many determinations, hence unity of the diverse. It appears in the process of thinking, therefore, as a process of concentration, as a result, not as a point of departure, even though it is the point of departure in reality and hence also the point of departure for observation [*Anschauung*] and conception. Along the first path the full conception was evaporated to yield an abstract determination; along the second, the abstract determinations lead towards a reproduction of the concrete by way of thought. (*Grundrisse* 101)

Thus the procedure of the tendency is far from being rigid or deterministic. Instead, it represents an adventure of reason as it comes to encounter the complexities of reality, an adventure of reason that is prepared to accept risks: in fact, the truth of the tendency lies in its verification. You can hardly call this economism! Mao Tse-Tung describes this method, and then notes: "This does not go against materialism; on the contrary, it avoids mechanical materialism and firmly upholds dialectical materialism."[3] In fact, if we look at the ways in which classical writers like Marx, Lenin, and Mao overturned the

Hegelian dialectic, we see that they were based on a process of decomposing the deterministic horizon in an attempt to reintroduce into the critique of political economy an analysis of the complexities of concrete reality. Their aim was to translate theoretical foresight into politics and practice—and, in the last instance, to pose the problem of organization at this level. So if we are to stand accused, let us be accused not of economism but of our persistent backwardness in finding a new solution to the problem of organization. We would accept such an accusation critically and set to work to resolve it within the movement.

But if proof of the validity of this method is to be found in organizational practice, then the second objection often leveled against us—that of idealism and spontaneism—vanishes.

Our assumption of the tendency's polarity, its contradictory character and the possibility of transforming it into antagonism, into revolutionary process and insurrectional initiative, in no way constitutes a hypostasis of the reality being analyzed; rather, it is a presupposition of any analysis that seeks to be meaningful. There is no such thing as objective truth given at the outset: truth has to be constructed in the struggle, through the struggle, through the transformation of practice. Marxist analysis determines the reality with which it is concerned by imposing a class point of view from the start; this is its operative schema, which takes the side of the worker, and its intentions are revolutionary. It is an act of force in relation to reality. Its truth lies in the result; analysis takes as its starting point the political will to achieve this result. Thus "human anatomy contains a key to the anatomy of the ape" (*Grundrisse* 105). Only a practice thus determined can allow us to constitute an objectivity that is meaningful for us: "Truth is a process. From the subjective idea, man advances towards objective truth *through* 'practice.'"[4] Nor is this an indeterminate process; it is a determinate practice. Lenin writes (and is echoed by Mao): "Practice is higher than (theoretical) knowledge, for it has not only the dignity of universality, but also of immediate actuality."[5] So if this theory stands accused, let it not be accused of sectarian subjectivism—after all, this is a characteristic of dialectical materialism, which "openly avows that it is in the service of the proletariat."[6] If there is a genuine accusation to be made, it is that of not having yet brought to bear on our practice the weight of immediate reality that is needed to constitute an organization. And this is precisely the goal toward which we are now working on this terrain.

On the basis of these presuppositions, analysis of the tendency can uncover in the past (precisely as their presupposition) those objective antagonisms that today the class standpoint wants to extol. Thus we can confirm in the past the changing mechanisms of control and the recomposition of the dialectic of capital which today the class viewpoint seeks to destroy. The existence of the working class has continually produced determinate antagonisms.

The various epochs in the history of the working class are marked by the emergence of specific antagonisms around which the struggle has developed and around which organizations have been built in response to these revolutionary explosions. The specific antagonism in the period of the Second International was that between the workers' control of the labor process and the capitalist ownership of the mode of production. In the period between the two world wars—and right up to the sixties—we had the specific antagonism between the massification of labor-power on the one hand and the dynamic and precisely proportioned control of that massification within capital's plan on the other—that is, the wage contradiction. Today's specific antagonism is that between the overall constitution of the working class into a political individuality and the factory form of capitalist domination, between command by the enterprise [*comando d'impresa*] and a communist will on the part of the masses.

This point of view once again illustrates the fruitfully paradoxical character of our method. This means that, in following through the contradictions and specificity of the antagonism present within the tendency, the result is far from being deterministic and economistic. On the contrary, in the framework of the dialectic between the command of the enterprise and the communist will of the masses, any merely sociological moment in the definition of the elements in question, any merely economic definition in terms of value dissolves. The political dominates and subordinates the social. And this dominance [*dominio*] of the political is brought about precisely through the tendential process that characterizes and is produced by the ceaseless dialectic of the struggle between classes. This dominance [*dominio*] of the political over the social can in turn both be verified by and provide the basis for a redefinition—to which we have already alluded—of several fundamental categories of Marxist analysis: first, that of capital, which, by means of the enterprise form of command, is dissociated from value and operates on the plane of relations of force; second, that of organic composition, which, correspondingly, no longer consists of a relation of intrinsic factors, but is politically overdetermined. Here, in other words, we have a good example of how the new content gives a new form to the scientific categories of Marxist analysis. And this procedure follows the indications of method given by the classics of Marxism:

> The activity of man, who has constructed an objective picture of the world for himself, changes external actuality, abolishes its determinateness (= alters some sides or other, qualities, of it), and thus removes from it the features of

Semblance, externality and nullity, and makes it as being in and for itself
(= objectively true).[7]

The tendency, therefore, is the horizon of a subject who produces himself
within a determinate framework; he places himself in relation to this determinate framework, and above all in this process transforms himself and
thereby alters the frame of reference itself. The working-class struggle is the
means and motive force of this transformation, a process which constitutes
both the objectivity against which the struggle is applied and the subjectivity of class agency itself:

> The struggle of the proletariat and the revolutionary people to change the
> world comprises the fulfillment of the following tasks: to change the objec-
> tive world and, at the same time, their own subjective world—to change
> their cognitive ability and change the relations between the subjective and
> the objective world.[8]

Being within this process is a fundamental precondition for being able to
pose the problem of organization, to develop the tendency to the point of
being able to proclaim it in the first person, and to ensure the victory of the
project contained in the tendency. This method, in other words, enables us
to resolve the problem of organization, to organize ourselves.

One final note. What I have said so far serves to clarify our initial starting
point, but it does not resolve the problem that is posed. That would be
idealism pure and simple! However, while not actually resolving the problem,
it does serve to provide the correct terms of its resolution, and suggests a
style of work which will straight away be capable of meeting a fundamental requirement: namely that of developing issues of organization and its
program—as well as tougher and stronger programs and initiatives—in
contact and symbiosis with the mass movement. A correct method of
working is particularly important as regards the pace [*tempi*] of revolutionary work. Given what I have said, it is obvious that the problem of pacing
[*tempi*] can certainly not be entrusted to a theoretical forecast of some predetermined timeframe [*scadenza*], the wait for some expected result, or a
conjuncture that depends on forces external to the class relation. The pace
of the revolutionary process and of the process of organization can be identified within the relationship with the mass movement that one may or may
not succeed in bringing about. To expect or believe otherwise is mere opportunism. To speed up or slow down the pace is a revolutionary responsibility
and that is enough.

## 7. AGAINST ENTERPRISE-COMMAND: THE ORGANIZATION OF INSURRECTION WITHIN THE NEW COMPOSITION OF THE WORKING CLASS

Let us now turn to the problem of organization in light of the results of our earlier investigation of the new composition of capital. I have said several times that for us it is fundamental—fundamental in order to verify the "objectivity" of our arguments—that we find ways of discussing organization that are capable of opening up programmatic possibilities—in other words, that are able to determine the relationship between the will to subversion and the reality of that which is to be subverted. For this we need to go much further than the traditional positions normally taken on the problem of organization among Marxists. We shall not, however, abandon the key relationship between organization and the composition of capital, first because this provides theory with a negative support, in the sense of a real foundation to be overthrown (the determination of capital as direct adversary, as subject of the antagonism); and second, with a positive support, since it provides us with a referent constructed by capitalist development itself and located within the composition of capital—the support of the proletariat, as a revolutionary subject, with respect to the determination of the material relation.

Now, as regards the program, we have already insisted upon the issue of the mass management of appropriation. Appropriation is a defining characteristic of class behavior against the state of un-value [*disvalore*], of enterprise command [*comando d'impresa*], just as autonomy was the defining characteristic of class behavior against the Planner-State, the state based on determinate general proportions between necessary labor and the surplus labor produced. Appropriation is the process whereby a new figure of the historical revolutionary subject reveals itself; it is abstract labor transformed into both generality and individuality; it is the recognition that the forms of production are increasingly moving from a state of *contradiction* with the social forces of production into a state of *antagonism*. Thus the program (within this composition of capital and therefore of the class) must necessarily be developed on the terrain of generalized appropriation, the mass management of an assault on social wealth as something that should be regarded as our own. In this way the social individual of production can recognize the present mode of production as a straitjacket constraining his own possibilities, and communism as the only reality that is adequate to his own emergence. From this point of view, we can consider as cadres of revolutionary organization all those who have reached this level of consciousness and who promote, provoke, and lead mass actions of appropriation on that basis. Activity oriented toward appropriation must now be seen as the normal, continuous, and immediate terrain on which the program operates; this is a horizon dotted with tactical actions that bring about the recomposition of a general and massified revolt.

However, having said this, we have touched on only one element of the argument. As we have seen, the specificity of the situation consists not only in the emergence of the massified proletarian figure but also in the relationship that is established between that emergence and the enterprise form of exploitation. If organization confines itself merely to the former level, then it is strategically blind and bound to fail; more importantly—as always, when the dialectic is unsteady—organization is exposed to all the pitfalls of reformism and consequently of opportunism. Certainly, appropriation is in itself contradictory to the capitalist form of domination over the mode of production; but haven't we already seen how this enterprise form of capital develops precisely as an ability to render insignificant, to dilute over time, to recuperate within its own circular and mediating dialectic—and at the limit to destroy, within the crisis—the proletarian social individual? Nowadays, in certain cases, the reformism of the Official Labor Movement is open to accusations of this kind of "good faith"—that is, in Marxist terms, false consciousness.

Thus, the second fundamental problem of the revolutionary program is that of a correct assessment of the relationship between proletarianization and the enterprise form of capital's domination over the mode of production. Within this nexus, within this interplay of motifs, capital projects and maintains by force its own survival; only on this political composition of capital can the will to revolution be exercised. If we do not confront this political overdetermination that connotes control over the unified movements of the proletariat, and the specificity of that overdetermination, then organization cannot be said to be revolutionary organization. To say this is once again to recognize the nature of the enterprise as the guiding force behind the capitalist mode of production, in a situation in which there is no longer a general equivalence between labor-power supplied and surplus-value extorted. This relationship—which nonetheless remains effective—can no longer stick to determinate proportions: it is a relationship based on the violence of enterprise-command, on the use of crisis, on a continuous and commensurate restructuring.

Let us be clear: violence constitutes the normal state of relations between men; it also constitutes the key to progress of the productive forces. This denunciation is not therefore directed against that normality of violence, but against the fact that in the enterprise form of capitalist domination, violence has lost all intrinsic, "natural" rationale ("naturalness" being always a product of historical forces), and any relation whatsoever with a progressive project. If anything, the enterprise form of violence is precisely the opposite: it is an irrational form within which exchange value continues to be imposed on social relations in which the conditions of the exchange relation no longer exist. It is the intelligent form of this irrationality, simultaneously desperate in its content and rational in the form of its effectiveness.

The enterprise and its intelligent movements—this is the enemy to be fought, this is the adversary against which, in every single moment, in every single operation, all the class rage of the proletariat and all our hopes for communism should be brought to bear. The attack on the Enterprise-State [*Stato-impresa*] must be carried forward, following the same forms in which the enterprise develops its control over the class: in forms that are intelligent and precise, that repeat within revolutionary organization the effectiveness of the factory form of capitalist initiative. Every action of appropriation, whether spontaneous, semi-spontaneous or organized, should therefore be transformed into an action of militant attack against the domination which capital reproduces through precise and determinate responses. In order to bring the organizational process to maturity in this sense, this is the programmatic passage required by the present political composition of the proletariat. The old perspectives that were based on portraying and constituting workers' action within the cycle—such as the theoretical experiments developed in relation to the Planner-State form—must now be replaced by action aimed at drawing out every proletarian foray against the key moments of capitalist repression that now take the form of the enterprise. The cycle is no more, because it is incompatible with development in the enterprise form. Control is exercised, so to speak, no longer on the horizon of the set of movements of the class that have been brought, in all their continuity and complexity, to a point of dynamic mediation; rather, control is exercised vertically and at precise points against any emergence of the movement. Thus, from the workers' point of view, the program cannot have an extensive horizon on which to develop; it can no longer rely on an organic growth. Rather, the program must make up in intensity what it lacks in extension, and in density what it lacks in complexity. To see insurrection not as the final, but as the first step of the revolutionary process is thus not some over-ambitious and intellectualistic reference to the extremist theses of the Third International; rather, it is a correct and lucid theoretical revelation of the new composition of capital; it is the practice of a level of subversion corresponding to the enterprise form of command over the mode of production. Insurrection is the rationality of a materialist and dialectical point of view in the face of the desperate irrationality of repression of exchange value over the recomposed proletarian individual.

At this point we have to confront a new problem. Having examined the contents of the program, we now have to address the closely connected issue of the form of organization. As we have seen, the program, when it is rooted in the political composition of the class, has both a mass and a vanguard pole. The specificity of the program for the revolutionary period through which we are passing consists in the mediation of this polarity, in the encouragement of acts of mass appropriation that can be positively channeled toward moments of insurrection. The form of organization must be responsive to this polarity, this dualism of the elements making up the program. The vanguard has to prove capable of interpreting and directing the mass will to appropriation against the enterprise, against the factory-command over the class. These two moments cannot be separated, nor can they be merged: both of them must be present within the overall movement, playing specific roles and recomposing themselves through insurrectional action led by the vanguards. Any separation of these two moments must prove disastrous. Action by the vanguards alone is empty; action by the mass organisms alone is blind. But it is equally dangerous to attempt to merge the two moments into unified mass vanguards. In the period immediately preceding our present phase, in other words the period which saw working-class struggle directed toward (and winning at) the level of wages, under the sign of the Planner-State— in that instance, the vanguard could hardly avoid being confused with the mass movement in a way that corresponded to the dimensions of capitalist control. Today, however, this duality of functions has become clearly necessary. At the same time, the division of these two functions cannot introduce elements of separation and reciprocal externality—not in the sense of a temporal separation, a chronological "before" and "after," or even a logical separation. The simultaneity of these revolutionary functions is the correlative of the simultaneity of capital's functions of repression and production. So, we have a militant vanguard which is capable of establishing an effective relationship with the new mass organizations and which is capable of centralizing the overall movement and pressing it forward toward insurrectional openings.

Admittedly, within the real process of organization (and above all during the transitional phase through which we are passing), a rigid use of the model runs the risk—as always—of becoming opportunistic. I say "as always," because no model can be richer in content than the class struggle, and the struggle is the only teacher from which we accept instruction. In particular, today, the accelerator of subjective initiative needs to be pressed toward centralization and the organizational formalization of the vanguard; even—in certain cases—toward the liberation of the subjective vanguards from pre-constituted levels of autonomy and class spontaneity which, having been fundamental in the struggle over the wage, now run the risk of becoming suffocating.

A hard and pressing battle now needs to be engaged over these elements, and against all the opportunism to which they may give rise. But I should add at once that the other danger of which we should beware, in the process of organization, is that of subjectivism and the re-emergence of attitudes that burn all bridges linking them to the internal dynamic of the political composition of the proletariat. Within this jungle of the social factory, rather, the vanguards can construct focal points of insurrectional struggle around which the masses of the exploited can reassemble. This possibility will be organized: the vanguard that struggles in an intelligent way, at precise points, against capital's social enterprise has to be capable of finding its reference point and its support within mass organization.

In this sense, we are today reacquiring many of the elements that defined the structure of the Leninist revolutionary party. In particular, we are again moving toward the articulation between vanguard and mass, between party and mass organizations, as a fundamental element of the program and form of organization. We are also rediscovering the simultaneity of these two elements in insurrectionary initiative. For the militia of the new revolutionary cadres, 1917 provides a formidable proof of the truth of the Marxist method in that historical phase. But today our Leninism is something new, in a very profound sense: it is new inasmuch as it seeks to verify a new analysis of a new project, based on our current class composition.

For us today the articulation of organization is posited not within the contradictions of development, but within the antagonism between the proletariat constituted as a unified class and the desperate vitality of the law of value over and against it. The articulation of organization takes place through the alternating rhythm of mass pressure aimed at appropriation, and vanguard assault against the intelligent actions of the enterprise. Not for work, not over the wage, but against work: this constitutes the positive articulation of the new revolutionary organization.

### 8. "WEALTH" AND "POVERTY" OF THE PROLETARIAT WITHIN THE REVOLUTIONARY DIALECTIC

The great historic quality of capital is to *create* this *surplus labour*, superfluous labour from the standpoint of mere use value, mere subsistence; and its historic destiny [*Bestimmung*] is fulfilled as soon as, on one side, there has been such a development of needs that surplus labour above and beyond necessity has itself become a general need arising out of individual needs themselves—and, on the other side, when the severe discipline of capital, acting on succeeding generations [*Geschlechter*], has developed general industriousness as the general property of the new species [*Geschlecht*]—and, finally, when the development of the productive powers of labour, which capital incessantly whips onward with its unlimited mania for wealth, and of the sole conditions in which this mania can be realized, have flourished to the stage where the possession and preservation of general wealth require a lesser labour time of society as a whole, and where the labouring society relates scientifically to the process of its progressive reproduction, its reproduction in a constantly greater abundance; hence where labour in which a human being does what a thing could do has ceased. Accordingly, capital and labour relate to each other here like money and commodity; the former is the general form of wealth, the other only the substance destined for immediate consumption. Capital's ceaseless striving towards the general form of wealth drives labour beyond the limits of its natural paltriness [*Naturbedürftigkeit*], and thus creates the material elements for the development of the rich individuality which is as all-sided in its production as in its consumption, and whose labour also therefore appears no longer as labour, but as the full development of activity itself, in which natural necessity in its direct form has disappeared; because a historically created need has taken the place of the natural one. This is why *capital is productive; i.e. an essential relation for the development of the social productive forces.* It ceases to exist as such only where the development of these productive forces themselves encounters its barrier in capital itself. (*Grundrisse* 325)

This page of the *Grundrisse* is a fairly comprehensive summary of the results of Marx's arguments regarding the tendency. Here we find all the elements that we have examined thus far: from the direct allusion to money's role in production, to his definition of the antagonism produced by capitalist development; from his description of the emergence of the new historical proletarian subject, to his conclusions regarding the necessity of revolution and communism. But there is also something more, which would repay closer scrutiny: namely, his qualitative definition of the new historical subject. This is important because a number of significant concepts in the debate over organization are based, precisely, on the quality of the proletarian subject.

Now, in defining the quality of the new proletarian subject, Marx pursues two axes of analysis: (a) the expansion of needs, which leads to a requalification of the subject in terms of consumption; (b) the increase in the productivity of labor, which leads to a new concept of productive labor.

(a) As regards the first line of analysis, Marx paints a very broad picture of the expansion of historical needs and the way in which natural limits of consumption are surpassed via the development of the content of real social wealth (*Grundrisse* 526–28). From a material point of view, capital's production of wealth induces "the universal development of the productive forces" via a "constant overthrow of its prevailing presuppositions" (*Grundrisse* 541): "capital has subjugated historical progress to the service of wealth" (*Grundrisse* 590). "The result is: the tendentially and potentially general development of the forces of production—of wealth as such—as a basis [....] The basis as the possibility of the universal development of the individual, and the real development of the individuals from this basis ..." (*Grundrisse* 542). Thus the new definition of wealth becomes not simply a result, but rather a basis for new results: the contradictory nature of the process reaches new heights that necessarily bring with them the possibility of its overturning. For this, however, it is "necessary above all that the full development of the forces of production has become the *condition of production;* and not that specific *conditions of production* are posited as a limit to the development of the productive forces" (*Grundrisse* 542).

(b) The second set of arguments, regarding increases in the productivity of human labor, provides an even clearer view of the new characterization of the historical subject, its fundamental importance, and the way in which (as an active force of production) it manifests a tendency to appropriation when confronted with all the wealth produced. "Not an ideal or imagined universality of the individual, but the universality of his real and ideal relations. Hence also the grasping of his own history as a *process*, and the recognition of nature (equally present as practical power over nature) as his real body. The process of development itself posited and known as the presupposition of the same" (*Grundrisse* 542). It is on this basis—which emerges so powerfully as to require the dissociation of the capitalist constraint to work from labor as free activity, "as the *living source* of value" (*Grundrisse* 296; see also 613), and to require the abolition of the capitalist organization of work, and of work itself inasmuch as it is wholly tied to the former—that wealth (that is, the development of the productive forces) becomes the greatest potentiality of development—but now as a revolutionary inversion. One final, wonderful page, to illustrate all this:

Real economy—saving—consists of the saving of labour-time (minimum (and minimization) of production costs); but this saving identical with the development of the productive force. Hence in no way *abstinence from consumption*, but rather the development of power, of capabilities of production, and hence both of the capabilities as well as the means of consumption. The capability to consume is a condition of consumption, hence its primary means, and this capability is the development of an individual potential, a force of production. The saving of labour-time [is] equal to an increase of free time, i.e. time for the full development of the individual, which in turn reacts back upon the productive power of labour as itself the greatest productive power. From the standpoint of the direct production process it can be regarded as the production of *fixed capital*, this fixed capital being man himself. It goes without saying, by the way, that direct labour-time itself cannot remain in the abstract antithesis to free time in which it appears from the perspective of bourgeois economy. Labour cannot become play, as Fourier would like, although it remains his great contribution to have expressed the suspension not of distribution, but of the mode of production itself, in a higher form, as the ultimate object. Free time—which is both idle time and time for higher activity—has naturally transformed its possessor into a different subject, and he then enters into the direct production process as this different subject. This process is then both discipline, as regards the human being in the process of becoming; and, at the same time, practice [*Ausübung*], experimental science, materially creative and objectifying science, as regards the human being who has become, in whose head exists the accumulated knowledge of society ...

As the system of bourgeois economy has developed for us only by degrees, so too its negation, which is its ultimate result. We are still concerned now with the direct production process. When we consider bourgeois society in the long view and as a whole, then the final result of the process of social production always appears as the society itself, i.e. the human being itself in its social relations. Everything that has a fixed form, such as the product etc., appears as merely a moment, a vanishing moment, in this movement. The direct production process itself here appears only as a moment. The conditions and objectifications of the process are themselves equally moments of it, and its only subjects are the individuals, but individuals in mutual relationships, which they equally reproduce and produce anew. The constant process of their own movement, in which they renew themselves even as they renew the world of wealth they create. (*Grundrisse* 711–12)

Now we must ask ourselves in what form and to what extent this characterization of the new historical subject plays—and must play—a role in our prospects for revolutionary organization. It is important that we be able to answer this question, particularly since the mass experience of the emergence and assertion of the new historical subject has already given rise to some alternative propositions. In short, in some quarters the revelation of the new quality of this historical subject has given rise to forms of prefigurative behavior and individual experiences of liberation—even a mass propaganda along the lines of "living out communism," with specious populist and subcultural consequences. Such attitudes are very far removed from Marx's hypotheses regarding the tendency. In positions such as these, the antagonistic specificity of the emerging proletarian subject is lost: they take an idealist view of the emergence of this wealth of productive forces, seeing it as an already-existing, organic realization, and not—to use Marxist terminology—as a power [*potenza*] that springs from the terrible and contemporary "poverty [*indigenza*]" of the proletariat. In fact such positions tend to imply the prospect of individual happiness in the liberation struggle or gaiety in the revolutionary struggle, which only shows their ignorance of the real dialectical dimensions of the project. This is the point that we made earlier: if the awareness of the growth of this new revolutionary subject is not accompanied by an awareness of the monstrosity of the continuing vitality of the law of exchange value—a law that is abstract, devoid of motivation—against the real movement, then there can be no concept of revolutionary organization. This is why "joyful prefigurations" of this kind are necessarily accompanied by opportunism, and smug reliance on the organic growth of the mass movement as sufficient for the self-development of the new historical subject leads necessarily to reformism. Once again, as so often in the history of Marxist thought, we find society being privileged over the state, the sociological over the political, and the ideal over the real. Such proceedings are incorrect in general terms, and if populism is in general (as it always has been) the harbinger of reformism, then today, in the specificity of the current political domination by capital, they become doubly dangerous: they act to mystify both the program and the form of the new organization.

The only way to understand the emergence of this new historical subject and all the richness of its mass experience is to place it within the real dialectic of organization, beyond any attempt at prefiguration and any individual "liberation" of the escapist sort. Certainly, this mass experience has contributed enormously to organizational debate and practice, in the sense that this new element of working-class composition brings out a revolutionary productivity which is constantly held down and always capable of new explosions. When he defines the characteristics of this new class figure, Marx repeatedly emphasizes its potentiality: the working class is seen as a power [*potenza*], as a continuous possibility of revolt, as a capacity for unceasing and repeated attacks on power. The working class has this revolutionary productivity for itself, but after centuries of capitalist exploitation, it is not prepared to sell itself for a bowl of porridge, or for the obscene suggestion that it should delude itself into feeling free within the domination of capital. The satisfaction [*godimento*] that the class seeks is the satisfaction of power, not the gratification of an illusion. Thus the class knows itself to be infinitely productive, in the only sense in which labor can be productive, not for capital—not as a power [*potenza*] of capital, but as a class power [*potenza*], as non-capital (= revolutionary labor, continual repetition), taking as its starting point that true power—the power of attack against capital, and the ongoing invention of forms of organization and struggle. It is in this sense and only in this sense that the revelation of this new quality of the proletarian historical subject becomes valuable in terms of organization: what is "prefigured" is the living pulse of the relationship between organization and the masses; it is the ever-open possibility—a possibility continually promoted by organization—of advancing the insurrectional conflict. It is in this way that the organization must qualify the flow of information and pressure that passes through its articulations. Today the class's only real "satisfaction" lies in its relationship with its organization and in the confrontation with the hateful apparatus of capitalist power. Thus organization from now on must be defined—at a determinate and mature class level—as living through the historical period of the destruction of capital and of work, the period of the creation of communism.

One final note: at this point it would be opportune to return to Marx's concept of productive labor, in order to see how, in the course of capitalist development and the maturation of the tendency, it must undergo the very same metamorphosis as many other concepts; in order to see whether—as seems probable—this concept too should now be given an entirely political definition. In other words, productive labor can be defined, no longer in terms of its immediate determination in the labor process, but rather within the capitalist overdetermination of the cycle and its unfolding into antagonism at that level.

## 9. OUR IMMEDIATE TASK

At this stage of the argument, posing the problem of how the institutional levels (unions, nation-state, etc.) function in the relationship between workers and capital would mean opening up an extremely broad range of questions. I shall limit myself to a passing (but nonetheless necessary) reference to the new role taken on by these institutional levels, and the structural changes taking place within them.

One specific and fundamental change must be emphasized right away—namely the definitive collapse of any relationship of relative autonomy of the institutions in relation to the enterprise and its form of command. We should examine how and why this has happened, concentrating on the two cases most readily at hand—the union and the nation-state. Both these institutions are significantly implicated in the crisis of the Planner-State. In both cases, the collapse of the possibility of maintaining the ordered and proportionate relationship between struggles and development has ended any semblance of relative autonomy that they previously had in relation to individual enterprises. In mystified but nonetheless effective ways, these institutions had previously functioned as mediators between factors. This now comes to an end. In the case of the union, first its mediating function in the sale of labor-power disappears, to be followed by its function as an institutional agent of the plan in managing the overall distribution of wealth; in the case of the nation-state, even the partial or relative possibility that, within its national boundaries, it will be able to guarantee development on the basis of the invariability of the relationship between factors disappears.

The overdetermination of the enterprise form of command destroys any relative basis of stability, continuity or coherence in the functioning of state and union mediation. It destroys it inasmuch as it removes any effective basis for the measurement of the factors other than that of overdetermination by enterprise command itself. The very existence of these institutions is dogged by political crisis; their role becomes marked by a precariousness that can shape and permit the most diverse and contradictory of outcomes. This is the price that capital has to pay for gaining freedom of disposal over the overall movement—a freedom that, in this perspective, becomes an uncertainty principle as regards the stable aspect of capitalist existence.

We can pursue this line of argument still further. This precariousness threatening the functioning of the state's institutions highlights the extremity of the relationship into which capital has been driven by working-class struggle. The process that initially saw the working class wholly within capital today sees capital wholly within the working class. The precarious existence of capital's institutions and the exhaustion of their mediating functions derive precisely from this situation. The gap between capital's tactics and its strategy, hitherto evident only in situations of acute crisis, tends to become the normal condition of capital's existence. It is tied to tactics as the rationale of the enterprise in the crisis of "socialism" and its strategic project. This passage from the Planner-State to the Crisis-State—which, given the simultaneity of crisis and restructuring, also takes the form of the Enterprise-State— is now a fact; this is the situation within which class organization now has to move.

It is obvious that at this point we must plainly reject the theses advanced by certain incurable optimists of the class point of view.[9] They maintain that, if it is true that the relationship between capital and the working class has been inverted, then in the longer term we can expect to see the invention of new forms of the workers' use of capital. This is to argue as if capital's subordination to working-class struggles does not also take the form of a will to overdetermine that reality; as if capital's violence were not expressing itself with increasing freedom and ferocity as the independence of the class becomes increasingly evident. When we refer to the Crisis-State, and crisis-capital, the accent falls correctly on *crisis,* on the weakness of the bosses, on the definitive rupture between strategy and tactics; but we must also remember that capital and the state remain true to their nature, and that their function is to distort an apparently irremediable relationship of forces by means of repression and destruction. A Kornilov can always be found to oppose the revolution—and it is not inevitable that he will always be defeated.

Nor should our insistence on the urgency of our organizational tasks in this situation be seen as impatience or subjective wish-fulfillment. It is not so, for three reasons: partly because the urgent capitalist will to revenge is becoming more pressing; partly because the tendency itself reveals within its structure the emergence of a confrontation which is intentionally violent and irresolvable, for all that it may be containable; and particularly because the mechanism of struggle reveals in the workers' will an eagerness to possess an instrument of subversion adequate to capital's desperate will to survive. So let us take another look at these worker and proletarian struggles, as we have seen them during the years of the growth of autonomy: we shall see that it is not resignation that grows out of defeat, but rather a growing hatred for the bosses and the whole apparatus that represents them. But this hatred, this positive will to appropriation, this complementary and continuous reassertion of actions increasingly centered on and directed against the capitalist organization of society as an irrational factory—all this requires (in fact posits as a necessity within the very composition of the class) organization, that is, the capacity to oppose the workers' articulation of subversion to the capitalist organization of power. The relationship between vanguard and masses is prefigured in the repeated, differentiated, and violent self-expression of the very actions of the masses themselves. The mass movement of the class struggle indicates to us not only the urgency, but also the very model of organization, that is, the possibility of the vanguard channeling the movement toward effective pivot-points of power.

Within this process, insurrection is the order of the day. We say "insurrection" and not "revolution": what is important today is continually to combat the precise initiatives which capital sets in motion in order to rupture the unified front of the proletariat. There is no place here for ideologies of defeat or the liberatory sacrifice of the vanguards. Rather, there is an awareness of the effective structures of capital, and of the true needs of the working class. Revolution is a process in which a *permanent* series of violent and violently organized responses against the bosses' state is realized. Organization has to be capable of working on the precariousness of capitalist domination based on the structure of the enterprise, in order to make the relationship unsustainable; in order to dissolve capital's capacity for political initiative; in order really and truly to circumvent a capitalist power that is now not only irrational, but is fast becoming ridiculous. This is why we say "insurrection" and not "revolution," because revolution is the recomposition of a process that has destroyed, with its own force, an entire apparatus of power. We also use the word in order to counter all those ideologies which developed in a backward and mass phase of the movement—particularly the theories of "factory guerrilla warfare":[10] they stand in relation to the tasks of the moment as manufacture stood in relation to large-scale industry.

So our immediate task is to set in motion all the mechanisms that will enable organization to realize these aims. The analysis on which we base ourselves is classical in its method—the works of Marx, Lenin, and Mao. There is no space in our organization for impatience or wish-fulfillment; we are within the mass movement, developing a scientific (and thus practical) understanding of its composition and its will. Facing us, we have the state and its violence, we have the irrationality of a power which extols its essence as exchange value, as exploitation and as crisis. We have immediately at hand the complex ways in which the revolutionary process moves, and the modifications within the class that sustain and define the nature of that process. For the second time, "Lenin in England"[11] is real for us.

## POSTSCRIPT (1974)

It would be opportune to add to the new edition of this book some indications as to useful sources, and to propose a number of issues on which further consideration is already long overdue. These indications will be elementary and minimal, both as regards bibliographical material and as regards the elaboration of the issues discussed. They are essentially personal readings assembled around those problems, but we nonetheless consider them useful for starting a discussion on the theses put forward in this essay. These observations are summarily listed under two main headings:

(a) a critique of neo-Marxism;

(b) theoretical development of the arguments concerning organization.

### (a) Critique of neo-Marxism

Our arguments about the crisis of the Planner-State set out in part from observations regarding the historical and political phenomena related to this crisis.[12] They also derive from observations of the relationship linking the historical crisis of capitalist development with the theoretical crisis of the bourgeois science of capital. In order to define these nexuses, it is necessary to present a preliminary review of several important moments in the scientific discussion that has taken place in what we consider to be the most renowned school of revisionist thinking now in existence: the Cambridge school.

The work of the Cambridge school takes as its starting point economic development and an internal critique of Keynesian premises. It bases itself on a revival of classical economic thought and a "Ricardian" rereading of the work of Marx. Its aim has essentially been to demolish two fundamental moments of Marx's theory: the concept of capital and the concept of the wage. Along the way, it also attacks the concept of the organic composition of capital, and it dissolves the problem of the transformation of value into prices.[13]

In all these cases, the operation has been carried out in the same way: it involves conceiving a relationship that is devoid of any value linkage, and dissolving in theoretical terms the internal nexus linking exploitation and the production of capital.[14] The indeterminacy that derives from this view, as regards the material definition of the power relationship (both technical and political) inherent in the concept of capital, finds its surrogate solution in a definition of relations of "exploitation" taking place within the sphere of distribution. Having correctly observed the tendency for the historical barrier of value to collapse by reason of the offensive efforts of the working class, they then mystify it. The theoretical and strategic problems deriving from this situation, the dramatic paradox of exploitation existing in the absence of any "rational" measure of its degree, and the unleashing of capitalist fetishism as irrational power [*potenza*] *tout court*, are calmly denied. In their place we have a political alternative aimed at restoring a "socialist" equilibrium purely at the level of distribution, outside and beyond the proletarian urgency of destroying capital's relation of production. That which is a terminal condition brought about through the development of the working-class struggles—that which, at the extreme limits of the real subsumption of labor within capital, one might call "the formal suppression of labor within capital"—is made to pass for real suppression. The truth, rather, is that capitalist exploitation is accentuated in the world of production by the extinguishing of the law of value; it is rendered even more irrational and implacable. But this is a fact that our lucid Cambridge theoreticians, closed off in their placid "Lorianism,"[15] cannot and will not see. For them, the elimination of capitalist exploitation is a problem devoid of meaning, because the law of value, as a law of exploitation, is not, in their opinion, in the continuity of its domination, being extinguished; it simply does not exist. As a result, capitalist exploitation is seen at most as a disparity of incomes [*redditi*] between various parts of the social body: thus socialism becomes simply a question of redistribution of income, fair shares in development. But at this point—as has been emphasized by the academic synthesizers of political economy—such revisions of Marxism in reality merely prolong (albeit with important methodological and sociological variations) the old equilibrism expounded by Marshall:[16] whereas in Marshall the mechanism was seen as simply automatic, today the notion is that equilibrium can be "willed" and brought about through democratic order. The customary good will and good sense of all Proudhonists! Behind it we can recognize a mystification of the motives on which capital's political "will" is really based, an alignment along a line of command that increasingly emancipates itself from residual progressive margins of economic development. The crisis of economic development and the collapse, under the pressure of the working-class struggle, of the barrier of value increasingly leave economic theory suspended in a void of apologetics.

Obviously, it would be very good to see more research done in these areas. On the one hand, we have to reconstruct in its entirety the trajectory of economic thought from marginalism to Cambridge neo-Marxism; on the other, we have to show how a good part of "socialist" theory (from the late nineteenth-century German professorial revisionists to the likes of Lange and Dobb[17]) is reabsorbed within this line of development. In other words, within the critique of political economy, we have to elaborate a thoroughgoing "critique of socialism." Finally, we have to understand the various passages in economic theory as bourgeois functions of the struggle against the working class, and as designs for stability based on the destruction of the revolutionary class.

### (b) Theoretical development of the arguments concerning organization

The more interesting and fruitful task would be to pursue further our discussions on the theory of organization. In particular we believe that some of the points raised in this essay should be taken up and developed further.

1. As we see it, it is time that the theory of organization be referred back, in the most precise and direct terms, to the critique of political economy, via an analysis of the political composition of the working class. Once again, we have to pose the problem of what changes have taken place within the working class; we have to understand the effects brought about within the political composition of the working class by the tendential collapse of the historical barrier of value. The analysis of classes (particularly of the working class) that was developed during the struggles of the sixties must be subjected to fresh scrutiny by revolutionary Marxists. This working class needs to be studied and analyzed, with a view to grasping its new being and the new structure of needs brought about by the fact of being proletarian within capital's *Zivilisation*. The new structure of needs is a determinate ontological level within the dialectic of the wage; today it is essential that we succeed

in grasping this determinate level—in its formal and real dimensions, in its temporal and spatial dimensions, and in its dimensions of consciousness and consumption. The fixing of determinate quantities of the wage has provoked changes in the quality of life of the proletariat and thus changes in mass needs and forms of behavior. The accumulation of experiences of struggle has redefined the workers' interest in subversion. Once we begin to pursue this study, it will become apparent how much the composition of the class has changed during the struggles of the sixties, and how the tensions between the workers' spontaneity and the provocations of capitalist command are being played out in absolutely new terms. Without this ontological and dialectical analysis of the structure of the working class, it will be impossible to produce adequate levels of organization. The theory of proletarian organization must always move within a continual re-elaboration of the phenomenological analysis of the structure of the workers' needs. Whenever the party has won victories, these have been made possible by the formidable ability of its vanguards to grasp the real nervous system of proletarian interests at that given time. On the other hand, when, as in the twenties, the party ideologically froze working-class consciousness at some level (however victorious, however revolutionary it may have been), while capital, working from similar levels of awareness, was inventing new and better adapted technological, consumerist, and political tools for imposing its command—then the overall movement suffered extremely bitter defeats.

The literature on these issues is very sparse indeed. For some strange reason, interest in modifications in the composition of the working class seems to be entirely the province of reformism. The lessons deriving from Lenin's polemical and scientific activities in the 1890s seem to have been largely forgotten.

One of the tasks of revolutionary Marxism must be to return to the teachings of Lenin, and to change the sign of class phenomenology: the new reality is always revolutionary.[18]

2. An analysis which bases itself on the determinate composition of the class and which builds its organizational project from within that composition can immediately find, in the period of class struggle marked by the collapse of the barrier of value, other criteria for redefinition. There are two issues that seem fundamental: the issue of "appropriation" and the issue of "invention-power [*forza-invenzione*]." The former involves an ability to understand the workers' behavior as tending to bring about, in opposition to the functioning of the law of value, a direct relationship with the social wealth that is produced. Capitalist development itself, having reached this level of class struggle, destroys the "objective" parameters of social exchange. The proletariat can thus only recompose itself, within this level, through the

agency of a material will to reappropriate to itself in real terms what capital has formally reconfigured. But at the same time, within this horizon, the situation is also, and principally, characterized by the fact that the real subsumption of labor within capital no longer involves the social forces of production in the scientific process, but separates them from it, in the most extreme terms. The result is to propose again the possibility of revealing the entire creative potential of labor as a free social activity of the working class, and to pose it against the scientific organization that capital imposes on society. Invention-power, insofar as it is the perfecting of labor-power, is the term we give to the insubordinate presence of the working class within the formal capitalist suppression of labor. Freeing this invention-power is a moment and an aspect of the struggle for appropriation.

But that is not all. Viewed from this perspective, the actuality of communism presents itself perhaps for the first time not as a matter of prefiguration, but as a material practice visible within the development of the struggles. Certainly, there exist extremely dangerous and mystifying positions which interpret these new developments in a way that leads to a conception of the party as *Gemeinschaft* [community], denying the need for discipline and the bitter necessity of organization, and pursuing instead the sweet taste of utopia and the privilege of experiments in living which always come to nothing. All this notwithstanding, the communist experience of the proletarian masses enriches reality, and is forever constituting through struggle new possibilities of organization and subversion. This deserves more attention. In this regard, a return to certain basic Marxian texts is fundamental.[19]

3. The third area in which we should deepen our analysis is that of organization in the strict and direct sense. The relationship between class and capital, in the period of the formal suppression of labor by capital, sees the gradual disappearance of any possibility of struggle that is not an immediate revolt against capitalist command over the extinction of value. If the law of value functions only as command, as arbitrariness in the availability of surplus-value on the part of total capital and its state, then violence is the fundamental characteristic of this management; the state presents itself as mere violence and arbitrariness. The organization of the mass worker, in the period of real subsumption of labor within capital, has played a determining role in the crisis through the continuous upheaval it created in the equilibrium of incomes (wages) within the system. Today, in the new tendency that extends from within the class struggle, the mechanism of re-equilibration—in opposition to the appropriative pressure of the proletariat and the force of the alternative now being lived as a revolutionary need—can now only be entrusted to a relation of domination. Thus the countersign of revolutionary class organization today is the struggle against the relationship of domination in its

entirety. The problem of organization unfolds between two tasks that are equally fundamental: to ensure the effectiveness of instances of reappropriation of social wealth by the masses and—at the same time—to strike with vanguard violence, in equal and opposing measure, at the bosses' mechanisms of command. The law of value, in the process of its extinction, is replaced by the rule of exploitation according to the will of capital; it entrusts the rule of subversion to the will of the vanguards. The theory of organization today entails the material definition of the levels upon which there must be consolidated, and of the forms within which there must interact, on the one hand, instances of appropriation by the masses and the invention-power that the process of the struggles brings about, and on the other, the urgency of an armed force of the proletariat that will attack and destroy capitalist command—the precise, voluntary and subjective command over the extinction of value.

Finding bibliographical references in this area is not just difficult—it is impossible. This is a new world through which we have to travel, and in order for us to get our bearings, neither Blanquism nor its critique, neither the insurrectional theories of the Third International nor their opposite, neither Clausewitz nor Mao will help. Only experience, courage and true revolutionary militancy can untie the theoretical knots that face us.

### Notes

1. TN: Here Negri is probably referring to clandestine paramilitary groups such as the Red Brigades and Giangiacomo Feltrinelli's Partisan Action Group (GAP), which abandoned the attempt to grasp the changing internal composition of the working class in favor of vanguard strategies of violent direct confrontation with the state.

2. Lenin, *Collected Works*, vol. 38: *Philosophical Notebooks*, Moscow: Progress Publishers, 1961, p. 131, translated by Clemence Dutt and edited by Stewart Smith.

3. Mao Tse-Tung, "On Contradiction," in *Selected Works*, vol. 1, Peking: Foreign Languages Press, 1965, p. 336.

4. Lenin, *Philosophical Notebooks*, p. 201.

5. Lenin, *Philosophical Notebooks*, p. 213.

6. Mao Tse-Tung, "On Practice," in *Selected Works*, vol. 1, p. 297.

7. Lenin, *Philosophical Notebooks*, pp. 217–18.

8. Mao Tse-Tung, "On Practice," in *Selected Works*, vol. 1, p. 308.

9. TN: Here Negri is probably referring to Mario Tronti and other PCI-oriented theorists who were still promoting a "working-class use of capital."

10. TN: Here Negri is probably referring to older (and in his view out-of-date) theories of workers' self-organization in the workplace that were still being

espoused by members of *Il Manifesto* and some moderates in *Potere Operaio*.

11.  TN: Reference to an article of that title by Mario Tronti, originally published in the journal *Classe Operaia* (1964) and later incorporated into Tronti's influential volume *Operai e capitale*, Turin: Einaudi, 1966.

12.  See Sergio Bologna, Luciano Ferrari Bravo, Mauro Gobbini, Antonio Negri, and George Rawick, *Operai e Stato*, Milan: Feltrinelli, 1972 [TN: Negri's two essays from this book are included in the Red Notes volume *Revolution Retrieved,* London, 1988]; see also Luciano Ferrari Bravo and Sandro Serafini, *Stato e sottosviluppo*, Milan: Feltrinelli, 1972, and *Scienze politiche 1: Stato e politica*, edited by Antonio Negri, vol. 27 of the *Enciclopedia Feltrinelli–Fischer*, Milan: Feltrinelli, 1970.

13.  See Piero Sraffa, *Production of Commodities by Means of Commodities,* Cambridge: Cambridge University Press, 1960; G.C. Harcourt, *Some Cambridge Controversies in the Theory of Capital*, Cambridge: Cambridge University Press, 1969, translated into Italian as *Teoria dello sviluppo economico*, Milan: Etas Kompass, 1971, especially  pp. 329–70 (an excellent bibliography); and M. Arcelli, "La controversia sul capitale e la teoria neo-classica," in *L'Industria*, 3, 1970, pp. 299–314.

14.  For a paradoxical simplification of this, see C. Napoleoni, *Smith, Ricardo, Marx*, Oxford: Blackwell, 1975; C. Napoleoni, *Lezioni sul capitolo VI inedito di Marx*, Turin: Boringhieri, 1972; and the harsh criticism contained in A. Ginzburg, "Dal capitalismo borghese al capitalismo proletario," in *Quaderni Piacentini* Year X, no. 44–5, Ottobre 1971, pp. 2–46.

15.  TN: Achille Loria (1857–1943) was an Italian economist who criticized Marx's theories on the rate of profit and proposed his own theory of "historical economism" in a series of articles and books between 1883 and 1895; Engels rebutted Loria's attacks in his editorial preface and supplement (pp. 105–09, 1028–30) to *Capital* Volume 3, New York: Penguin, 1981, translated by David Fernbach. In his *Prison Notebooks*, Gramsci coined the term "Lorianism [*lorianismo*]" to refer to "certain degenerate and bizarre aspects of the mentality of a group of Italian intellectuals and therefore of the national culture" (*Selections from the Prison Notebooks*, New York: International Publishers, 1971, edited by Quintin Hoare and Geoffrey Nowell Smith, p. 458, n. 108).

16.  TN: Alfred Marshall (1842–1924) was a leading figure in late nineteenth- and early twentieth-century British economics, a professor at Cambridge and the teacher of J.M. Keynes; his signal contribution to economics was the quantification of supply–demand equilibrium in terms of consumer income and production costs.

17.  TN: A number of German university professors, sometimes called the "academic socialists" [*Kathedersozialisten*], made unfounded charges of plagiarism against Marx or claimed to offer "corrections" or "improvements" to his critique of political economy during the last quarter of the nineteenth century; Engels rebuts some of them in his editorial prefaces to *Capital* Volumes 2 and 3 and in

the pamphlet *Socialism: Utopian and Scientific* that was excerpted from his *Anti-Dühring* (1877). Oskar Lange (1904–1965) was a Polish socialist economist who attempted to reconcile Marxist and Keynesian conceptions of political economy through a controversial theory of market socialism; Maurice Dobb (1900–1976) was a Cambridge school economist who also focused on problems of the market in relation to socialist planning.

18. As regards the methodology of this approach, in addition to the articles contained in *Operai e Stato*, see the following works: Mario Tronti, *Operai e capitale*, first edition, Turin: Einaudi, 1966; Massimo Cacciari, "Qualificazione e composizione di classe," in *Contropiano*, 2, 1970, La Nuova Italia, Florence; Massimo Cacciari, *Introduzione a G. Lukács: Kommunismus 1920–21*, Padua: Marsilio Editore, 1972, pp. 7–66. The phenomenological analysis of class composition and the structure of needs is also becoming important today in the new currents of German Marxism. For different—but nonetheless meaningful—points of attack on the problem, see Peter Brückner, *Zur Sozialpsychologie des Kapitalismus*, Frankfurt: Europaische Verlagsanstalt, 1971; Oskar Negt and Alexander Kluge, *Public Sphere and Experience: Toward an Analysis of the Bourgeois and Proletarian Public Sphere*, German edition 1972; English edition Minneapolis: University of Minnesota Press, 1993, translated by Peter Labanyi, Jamie Owen Daniel, and Assenka Oksiloff. (The point of view from which these authors set out is quite the reverse of a worker and communist perspective; however, their analysis is interesting for the wealth of motifs advanced.) Finally, a particularly important area of investigation is that concerned with the new reality of the proletarianization of women. (See Maria Rosa Dalla Costa, *Potere femminile e sovversione sociale*, Padua: Marsilio Editore, 1972; English translation: *The Power of Women and Subversion of the Community*, Bristol: Falling Wall Press, 1975.) On the multinational dimensions of the new working class in the countries of advanced capitalist development, we know of no general text that contains a sufficiently revolutionary approach.

19. See Marx, *Grundrisse: Foundations of a Critique of Political Economy*, translated by Martin Nicolaus, New York: Penguin, 1973; Marx, "Results of the Immediate Process of Production" [the unpublished sixth chapter of *Capital* Volume 1, included in the appendix to the Penguin edition, New York, 1976, translated by Ben Fowkes]. For commentary on these, see Roman Rosdolsky, *The Making of Marx's "Capital,"* London: Pluto, 1977, translated by Pete Burgess. In general, the following are worth reading for the ways they deal with a number of these problems, particularly the question of productive intelligence and its relationship with invention-power: Hans-Jürgen Krahl, *Konstitution und Klassenkampf*, Frankfurt: Neue Kritik, 1971; Karl-Heinz Roth and E. Kanzow, *Unwissen als Ohnmacht: Zum Wechselverhältnis von Kapital und Wissenschaft*, second edition, Berlin: Editions Voltaire, 1971; Alfred Sohn-Rethel, *Intellectual and Manual Labour*, Atlantic Highlands: Humanities Press, 1978.

# II

# Workers' Party Against Work
## (1973)

*Translated by Francesca Novello and Timothy S. Murphy*

## 1. FROM THE CRITIQUE OF POLITICAL ECONOMY TO THE THEORY OF ORGANIZATION, AND VICE-VERSA

The problem here is to take up the offensive again on the basis of a communist program of appropriation and armed struggle, and to give an organizational response to the mass demand for counterattack by tracing the line that goes from workers' autonomy to the political organization of the proletariat. Workers' party against work—this is the slogan we must make sense of. We must do so by identifying the specificity of the problem within the crisis that we are experiencing: from workers' autonomy to class organization by beating the crisis that is the weapon of the collective boss and his vendetta against autonomy.

Now, in the history of the workers' movement, and more frequently in the most recent period, the presuppositions of a theory of the offensive have sometimes been rooted in a mechanistic theory of catastrophe. The overturning of the negative totality of capital's social system to transform it into a subjective totality of subversion is an organizational project based on exemplarity and the theory of the revolutionary detonator, which are the most recent additions to the old hold-over of catastrophic mechanism. None of this has anything to do with the worker. This is not theory, but at best a populist allusion to despair or to eschatological enthusiasm; it is always an existential suspension of theory and its organizational mass mediation—a pitiful artisanal experiment. The model on which these attempts are based is that of the alternation between the most rigid objectivism of analysis and an extreme subjectivism of the practical conclusions. This model is a mere leap in the dark and not a theoretical passage through the reality of working-class forms of behavior. The nexus between premise and deduction can only be rhetorical, indeterminate, and impractical in mass organizational work.

When a practice is forced upon it, the result will inevitably be terroristic. The dialectic of liberation reveals a false path. It is not opportunistic to assert that the bosses can use this failure against the working class.

At other moments in the history of the workers' movement, during the phases of global reconstruction of its offensive capacity, we found ourselves facing analogous problems. How do we go about solving them? How do we go about it without dispersing the wealth and generosity of the initial cues for offensive reconstruction? Marx and Lenin experienced these problems. What was their response?

Even in Marx there is a catastrophic prognosis for the capitalist system of production. The theory of the tendency of the rate of profit to fall ends up in catastrophism. Roman Rosdolsky has recently emphasized this strongly. He also adds the following note to the reconstruction of the Marxian model: "The assertion that Marx did not propose a 'theory of catastrophe' is primarily attributable to the revisionist interpretation of Marx before and after the First World War. Rosa Luxemburg and Henryk Grossmann both rendered inestimable theoretical services by insisting, as against the revisionists, on the theory of catastrophe."[1]

But *Marx's "catastrophism" has nothing to do with the mechanism of the epigones.* In fact, as the contradictory and antagonistic complex of the tendential trend of the rate of profit implies, *Marx's theory of the revolutionary crisis refers in its immediacy to the relation of force between the classes in struggle* represented in the magnitudes that constitute capital. *From this perspective, the theory thus refers to a determinate and developed composition of the working class,*

> hence it is evident that the material productive power already present, already worked out, existing in the form of fixed capital, together with the population etc., in short all conditions of wealth, that the greatest conditions for the reproduction of wealth, i.e. the abundant development of the social individual—that the development of the productive forces brought about by the historical development of capital itself, when it reaches a certain point, suspends the self-valorization of capital, instead of positing it. (*Grundrisse* 749, translation slightly modified)

From the perspective of Marx and later Marxists, the capitalist catastrophe is the working class, not in generic terms but rather specifically—that is, the working class at a given level of productive organization and at a certain degree of subjective domination over the general conditions of the social reproduction of capital. The analysis must be reversed when this situation is close at hand and when the non-valorizing identity of the forms of working-class behavior becomes central in the crisis of the society of capital. The analysis must give priority to the task of determining exactly the characteristics of technical and political class composition.

Conversely, the mechanistic interpretation of Marxian catastrophism evades this aspect of analysis and the tasks of close examination that derive from it,[2] or else this interpretation develops these points in precisely the mystified terms discussed earlier. That is to say, it does not make the theory of crisis the premonitory sign of a theory of class composition, but rather it turns it into the unresolved pole of an alternative that at best sees in the opposing pole individualistic despair and, in general, finds there all the conditions of the most discredited utopianism.[3] No one should underestimate the damage that these distortions have caused in the course of a century of Marxian interpretations. These distortions have damaged the workers' movement by indirectly helping dogmatism to re-emerge repeatedly and by directly impeding the inquiry into what the working class is, the foundation of its science.

And yet it was not so difficult to find in Marx *the relationship between the theory of crisis and the theory of working-class political composition.*[4] Actually, Marx not only determines that relationship within the description of a tendential development of the workers' struggles, resulting ultimately in the overthrow of the system. Throughout his work Marx also poses the question of that relationship from other angles and in relation to the analysis and the necessity of individual moments of struggle, rather than in relation to the functioning of the fundamental laws of the system. In reality, Marx's historical writings are cases of privileged application of the relationship between the theory of crisis and the theory of class composition. It is the making of the struggle, the incessant internal modification in the relationship between classes, the continuity of the process of recomposition of the proletariat that determines the pace and forms of the crisis. Moreover, at this point the analysis of crisis falls back upon the analysis of working-class composition as the *only* explanation of the crisis itself. In the second place, this analytical explanation becomes a prescription of forms of behavior and an indication and definition of tasks. The point of view of the analysis becomes that of the party. The project of subversion is centered upon the capacity to bring about the crisis, in that determinate phase, by expressing all the potential implicit in that class relation.

But the revolution is thorough. It is still on its journey through purgatory. It goes about its business methodically. By 2 December 1851 it had completed one half of its preparatory work; it is now completing the other half. First of all it perfected the parliamentary power, in order to be able to overthrow it. Now, having attained this, it is perfecting the *executive power*, reducing it to its purest expression, isolating it, and pitting itself against it as the sole object of attack, in order to concentrate all its forces of destruction against it. And when it has completed this, the second half of its preliminary work, Europe will leap from its seat and exultantly exclaim, "Well worked, old mole!"[5]

If we want to talk about "epistemological breaks [*cesure*]" in Marx, let's talk about them not only from the moment the definition of a structure demonstrates the relationship between the existence of capitalist crisis and working-class movements, but above all when the analysis emancipates itself from existing reality to become a program and when the given relation of force turns into an organizational proposition. The *epistemological break is the birth of organization*, which turns the scientific point of view on existing reality into a set of technical tools for a process of destruction of the present state of things.[6]

Only Lenin knows how to read the relationship between political class composition and organization in adequate Marxian terms, or more precisely, only he knows how to move from the definition of crisis to that relationship. In his writings from the 1890s to the revolutionary period, the category of "determinate social formation"[7] predominates and, as a matter of fact, it embraces the problematic fabric in its entirety. The particular phase of the development of capitalism in Russia, the spontaneous consolidation of proletarian unity, the awareness of the limitations of working-class hegemony and consequently the necessary externality of its functions of political command and organization with regard to the people as revolutionary agent in that phase are the links, entirely contained within the notion of "determinate social formation," of the Leninist theory of organization and of the program for the passage leading from democracy to socialism. The analytical gaze is turned toward the entire fabric of the relationship between classes only in order to work back to the definition of the position of the working class and to its capacity to command the process of proletarian recomposition—necessarily—"from above." The analysis becomes the viewpoint of organization to the extent that it succeeds in thoroughly penetrating the relation between the working class, the proletariat, and the popular classes. Working-class isolation is then turned into an organized vanguard force that possesses the capacity for political agitation and that mediates the relations between classes in an increasingly urgent design of insurrectionary initiative.

But all of this has been forgotten. Now the epigones, having turned Leninism into a key to open every door, thus obviously a false key, having imposed the identity of the revolutionary model and the quality of the social formation described by Lenin as a scheme applicable at all times and all places, are afraid of the consequences of these actions and they are now finally trying to assimilate the category "determinate social formation" to the spectral scientificity of bourgeois sociology.[8]

Let us return to the point in question, that is, to the critique of political economy that leads, as we mentioned earlier, through the theory of class composition to the theory of organization. Marx revisits this path over and over again. We should follow the path that goes from the current relevance of the crisis to a determinate definition of working-class composition in order to found the theory of organization on this definition. This is the privileged path, the urgent path, because today we are moving on Marx's terrain as never before. *Marx's final prediction relative to the historical collapse of the value barrier is beginning to come true.* The capitalist crisis is beginning to be catastrophic. But what do we know of the working class in crisis? What determinations does the crisis establish in the very body of the working class? What is the significance, for the working class, of the diffuse awareness of the demise of the capitalist mode of production, the fact that the working-class presence is not an element of valorization but rather one of growing, implacable destruction of the system? The working class has a history of political organization that is centuries old. What is the workers' political organization within the crisis—within this specific crisis that impairs the very function of accumulation as the rationale for capitalist control of the entire society?

The "catastrophism" that Rosdolsky defined as an essential moment of Marx's discourse must then be seen as the paradoxical key to raising the question of class composition that determines the contemporaneity and the form of organization corresponding to the current needs of the class. Because only when catastrophism refers to active working-class subjectivity, that is, only when the critique of political economy refers to the theory of class composition and to a consequent systematization of the organizational proposition, only then is the workers' point of view represented. And it is represented *as the point of view of a workers' power that, by presenting itself as the capacity to destroy the valorization of capital, defines both the crisis of the bosses and, at the same time, the political quality of the workers' struggles.* Only by intervening on this terrain can we obtain the political mediation between the workers' condition in the crisis and the figure of the workers' organization for the revolution. Mechanistic catastrophism, in its powerlessness [*impotenza*] in the face of the given problem, always risks being transformed by the bosses into an anti-worker slogan that is thus excluded from the debate. In this way, every revisionist alternative is struck down because the critique of political economy, despite all the revisionists' assertions, shows us a terrain of class composition and therefore of organization that is immediately the terrain of the management of workers' power which is meant to destroy the development and political equilibrium of the bosses' state. In any case, catastrophe is not the slow modification of the convoluted tangle of power relations that capital extends over the class. Catastrophe is the determinate moment when existing reality is overturned. If we carefully follow Marx's prediction for the development of capital and insist upon his peculiar catastrophism, we have the chance to posit the theory of organization as part of the critique of political economy, as the complement of his very important specification which is the theory of working-class political composition.

A so-called *Leninist objection* can be made to the persistent need to base the presuppositions of the theory of organization on the analysis of working-class composition. According to this objection, what characterizes the theory of organization is not so much the reference to the analysis of class composition as it is the definition of the weak links in the system of domination, the identification of the margins of proletarian action, which is to say tactics. This objection contains some elements of truth, but only on condition, as we have already seen in Lenin, that the reference to the determinate social formation, that is to working-class composition, has priority. Without this prior theoretical foundation, there will always be a risk that the voluntaristic, mechanically catastrophic reduction of the problem of organization, which as we know survives in some of the most recent positions in the movement, will be reintroduced in more or less surreptitious terms. And the risk is even higher today. When the crisis manifests itself in the shape of a qualitative crisis that is substantially new and that weighs heavily on deeper and more essential mechanisms of capitalist accumulation, and when the collapse of the historical barrier of value defines the epoch we are entering, the first question we ask ourselves must be: *what is the working class*, today, within this specific crisis, *no longer solely as object of exploitation but as subject of power?* Only the answer to this fundamental question that, as such, legitimizes the referral of the theory of organization to the analysis of composition, can then reopen the debate over the contents of the Leninist objection. Because here, as in Lenin, such questions of tactics are in fact complements and conclusions rather than presuppositions of the theory of organization.

The last section (5, a–b) of this discussion will be dedicated to problems of tactics. First, within Marx's analysis and as its complement, we shall try to define the character of today's crisis as a specific expression of workers' power (2, a–b). Second, on the basis of the analysis of class composition we shall try to put a new concept of revolutionary workers' organization to the test (3, a–b). Finally, we shall try to verify it in comparison with the historical succession of communist organizations, thus proposing some current criteria for a workers' conception of organization (4, a–b).

There is one last introductory, or methodological, observation to be made that has already arisen frequently throughout the Leninist discussion of the problem of organization, namely that the degree of historical class organization now and then leaves traces in the class composition. Great revolutionary epochs modify not only the relations between classes in struggle, but above all they modify the working class. In moments of generalized revolutionary struggle, organizational behavior has often become the very characteristic, the highest characteristic, of class composition. The path from class composition to the theory of organization is accompanied by another path that goes instead in the opposite direction, from determinate degrees of organization to internal class composition. In general, these two viewpoints, these two paths form a whole and complete each other. In the history of the working class, the superimposition of the ferocious impact of capitalist constraint on overall labor-power usually represents the normal condition. It is this superimposition that shapes and reshapes labor-power in the capitalist mode of production, in the singular forms of the labor process and, at the same time, in every experience of organization and struggle within the class. Why then do we today privilege the path that goes from class composition to the theory of organization? This happens because, *even if modern revisionism has not been able to break the continuity of the organizational process within the class, it has nevertheless blocked the continuity of its coherent manifestation*, and consequently it has suppressed the expression of one of the most profound political needs of the class. Therefore all that remains is to take the route of direct class analysis. But this does not mean that our hope has died. The moment is near when the new organization will be able to live the life of the class once again in an adequate and profound manner. Once again, then, we will be able not only to proclaim as our program "from the analysis of class composition to the theory of organization," but we will also be able to add forcefully: "*and vice-versa*"!

## 2. CRISIS OF THE PLANNER-STATE: PRODUCTION OF COMMODITIES BY MEANS OF COMMAND?

(a) In the unpublished sixth chapter of the first book of *Capital,* "Results of the Immediate Process of Production," Marx generalizes the distinction between absolute and relative surplus-value to the point of describing two important phases in the subsumption of labor under capital.[9] It is through these phases, the first "formal" and the second "real," that we can witness a progressive subordination of the labor process to capital's command. We all know the course of the process (see above all *Grundrisse* 584 and following pages). To sum up with Marx the salient figure of the phases to which the process leads:

> The general features of the *formal subsumption* remain, viz. the direct *subordination of the labour process to capital*, irrespective of the state of its technological development. But on this foundation there now arises a technologically and otherwise *specific mode of production—capitalist production—* which transforms the nature *of the labour process and its actual conditions*. Only when that happens do we witness the *real subsumption of labour under capital* ...
>
> The real subsumption of labour under capital is developed in all the forms evolved by relative, as opposed to absolute surplus-value.
>
> With the real subsumption of labour under capital a complete (and constantly repeated) revolution takes place in the mode of production, in the productivity of the workers and in the relations between workers and capitalists.
>
> With the real subsumption of labour under capital, all the changes in the labour process already discussed now become reality. The *social forces of production* of labour are now developed, and with large-scale production comes the direct application of science and technology. On the one hand, *capitalist production* now establishes itself as a mode of production *sui generis* and brings into being a new mode of material production. On the other hand, the latter itself forms the basis for the development of capitalist relations whose adequate form, therefore, presupposes a definite stage in the evolution of the productive forces of labour.[10]

We must immediately stress that, to the capitalist mode of production based exclusively on relative surplus-value and on adequate instruments for its extraction, there corresponds a new determinate composition of the social productive forces. But we must also stress the significance that the real subsumption of labor within capital assumes in this phase:

> (1) although labour is an *expression of labour-power*, although it represents the effort of the *individual worker*, and so belongs to him (it is the substance with which he pays the capitalist for what he receives from him), it nevertheless objectifies itself in the product and so belongs to the capitalist.—Even worse, the *social configuration* in which the individual workers exist, and within which they function only as the particular organs of the total labour-power

that makes up the workshop as a whole, does not belong to them either. On the contrary, it confronts them as a *capitalist arrangement* that is *imposed* on them;

(2) these *social productive forces of labour*, or *productive forces of social labour*, came into being historically only with the advent of the specifically capitalist mode of production. That is to say, they appeared as something intrinsic to the relations of capitalism and inseparable from them;

(3) with the development of the capitalist mode of production the *objective conditions of labour* take on a different form owing to the scale on which, and the economy with which, they are employed (quite apart from the machinery itself). As they develop they become increasingly concentrated; they represent social wealth and, to put the matter in a nutshell, their scope and their effect is that of the *conditions of production* of labour *socially* combined. And quite apart from the combination of labour, the *social character of the conditions of labour*—and this includes machinery and *capital fixe* of every kind —appears to be entirely autonomous and independent of the worker. It appears to be a *mode of existence of capital* itself, and therefore as something ordered by *capitalists* without reference to the workers. Like the *social character* of their own labour, but to a far greater extent, the *social character* with which the conditions of production are endowed, as the conditions of production of the combined labour of the *community*, appears as *capitalistic*, as something independent of the workers and intrinsic to the conditions of production themselves.[11]

Therefore capital portrays the process of socialization of labor given in this phase as its own, as foreign, independent, and hostile to labor. The process of socialization of labor is a development that capital itself has completely preordained and controlled, not a process that capital has appropriated. But that is not enough. As the process advances, capital must increase the mystification of its power to the same extent that associated labor-power more and more strongly constitutes itself as independent sociality. Associated labor-power appears increasingly to become a hindrance to capital's development. Capital seems to believe in its own mystification. The process must be drained of labor:

And since society is marked by the exploitation of labour by capital, its development appears to be the productive force of capital as opposed to labour. It therefore appears to be the *development of capital*, and all the more so since, for the great majority, it is a process with which the *drawing-off of labour-power* keeps pace.[12]

We are approaching our central argument, which consists in the attempt to give a Marxian definition of the current crisis and consequently to introduce an analysis of class composition into the crisis. Let us ask ourselves first of all: *to what extent is the devaluation of labor-power important for the advancement and perfecting of the process of real subsumption of labor within capital,* which is typical of capitalist development in this phase? *Within this process, is there a moment of qualitative differentiation such that in the development of the capitalist mode of production we go from the completion of real subsumption to a phase in which the valorizing function of labor is suppressed?* To what extent does this new figure of the mode of production characterize the present crisis?

In order to answer these questions, we must return to the issue of the devalorization of labor.

Now, as we know, the key determinant and the most fundamental tendency of the development of the capitalist mode of production is the shortening of the part of the working day that is necessary for the reproduction of the value of labor-power. This law governs the very same passage from formal to real subsumption. This tendency also generates the perfecting of the labor process from cooperation through manufacture to mechanization. But there is a moment in which the progress of the law, its capacity to function (albeit in a contradictory manner), is impeded.

But to the degree that large industry develops, the creation of real wealth comes to depend less on labour time and on the amount of labour employed than on the power of the agencies set in motion during labour time, whose "powerful effectiveness" is itself in turn out of all proportion to the direct labour time spent on their production, but depends rather on the general state of science and on the progress of technology, or the application of this science to production ... Real wealth manifests itself, rather—and large industry reveals this—in the monstrous disproportion between the labour time applied, and its product, as well as in the qualitative imbalance between labour, reduced to a pure abstraction, and the power of the production process it superintends. Labour no longer appears so much to be included within the production process; rather, the human being comes to relate more as watchman and regulator to the production process itself. (What holds for machinery holds likewise for the combination of human activities and the development of human intercourse.) No longer does the worker insert a modified natural thing as middle link between the object and himself; rather, he inserts the process of nature, transformed into an industrial process, as a means between himself and inorganic nature, mastering it. He steps to the side of the production process instead of being its chief actor. In this transformation, it is neither the direct human labour he himself performs, nor the time during which he works, but rather the appropriation of his own general productive power, his understanding of nature and his mastery over it by virtue of his presence as a social body—it is, in a word, the development of the social individual which appears as the great foundation-stone of production and of wealth. The *theft of alien labour time, on which the present wealth is based*, appears as a miserable foundation in face of this new one, created by large-scale industry itself. As soon as labour in the direct form has ceased to be the great well-spring of wealth, labour time ceases and must cease to be its measure, and hence exchange-value [must cease to be the measure] of use-value. The *surplus labour of the mass* has ceased to be the condition for the development of general wealth, just as the *non-labour of the few*, for the development of the general powers of the human head. (*Grundrisse* 704-05)

That is, the development of large-scale industry makes *the proportion of necessary labor to surplus-value produced* (that is, the degree of productivity of necessary labor) *an insignificant relation because of the small amount of necessary labor and the mass of capital, of dead labor, that is accumulated against it*. As the capitalist mode of production progresses, the qualitative leap is not only internal to the further reduction of necessary labor time (that is, an increase in the productivity of labor), but rather it is above all internal to the radical devaluation of labor time as an essential component of the production process (political control and crushing of the working class).

However, we are presented with a contradiction which is already observable throughout the process of development of the capitalist mode of production. It is possible to see this contradiction even before the process itself alludes to the passage to a more advanced form of the organization of labor, that is, to the suppression (and to the *control* of this suppression) of its immediate capacity to produce valorization. As the mode of production and its consequent difficulties progress, the contradiction develops little by little as necessary labor is compressed and nears its lower limit.

Marx expresses this contradiction as follows:

The larger the surplus value of capital *before the increase of productive force*, the larger the amount of presupposed surplus labour or surplus value of capital; or, the smaller the fractional part of the working day which forms the equivalent of the worker, which expresses necessary labour, the smaller is the increase in surplus value which capital obtains from the increase of productive force. Its surplus value rises, but in an ever smaller relation to the development of the productive force. Thus the more developed capital already is, the more surplus labour it has created, the more terribly must it develop the productive force in order to valorize itself in only smaller proportions, i.e. to add surplus value—because its barrier always remains the relation between the fractional part of the day which expresses *necessary labour*, and the entire working day. It can move only within these boundaries. The smaller already the fractional part falling to *necessary labour*, the greater the *surplus labour*, the less can any increase in productive force perceptibly diminish necessary labour; since the denominator has grown enormously. The self-valorization of capital becomes more difficult to the extent that it has already been valorized. (*Grundrisse* 340, translation slightly modified)

Capital's infinite impulse to the increase of wealth through an infinite increase in the productive capacity of labor thus finds its first formidable limitation within the confines of the relation between necessary labor and surplus labor. But all of this is only a first approach to the definition of the problem. Its generalization *"actually already belongs in the doctrine of profit"* (*Grundrisse* 341). *As a matter of fact, the theory of the tendency of the rate of profit to fall is nothing but the historical extension of this first fundamental consideration of the inevitable contradiction that pits living labor against dead labor within that elementary unit of analysis (and exploitation) which is the working day.*

The second great law[13] is that the rate of profit declines to the degree that capital has already appropriated living labour in the form of objectified labour, hence to the degree that labour is already capitalized and hence also acts increasingly in the form of fixed capital in the production process, or to the degree that the productive power of labour grows. The growth of the productive power of labour is identical in meaning with (a) the growth of relative surplus value or of the relative surplus labour time which the worker gives to capital; (b) the decline of the labour time necessary for the reproduction of labour power; (c) the decline of the part of capital which exchanges at all for living labour relative to the parts of it which participate in the production process as objectified labour and as presupposed value. The profit rate is therefore inversely related to the growth of relative surplus value or of relative surplus labour, to the development of the powers of production, and to the magnitude of the capital employed as [constant] capital within production. In other words, the second law is the *tendency of the profit rate to fall* with the development of capital, both of its productive power and of the extent in which it has already posited itself as objectified value; of the extent within which labour as well as productive power is capitalized. (*Grundrisse* 763, translation slightly modified)

Consequently, the law of the tendency of the rate of profit to fall expresses the generalization of the contradiction determined by the capitalist quest to devalorize labor in the production process. The proportion of surplus labor extracted in relation to necessary labor, that is, the ratio according to which objectified labor is exchanged for living labor, is translated into the general dimensions characteristic of the functioning of the rate of profit. It becomes the general proportion between living labor employed and objectified labor. Both proportions fall to the extent that surplus labor increases compared to necessary labor, to the extent that capital can no longer suck the blood of living labor. The contradiction that was previously observed becomes a law, the harsh prescription of the necessary outcome, for capital.

In spite of whatever counter-tendencies there may be, the law works, and capital suffers from this contradiction that continually re-emerges within itself. But then, why does capital press forward the process of devalorization? Why does capital push this process forward to the point of glimpsing the completion and overcoming of the phase of the real subsumption of labor within capital, toward a phase in which labor as valorizing element is suppressed?

Once again Marx gives us the answer to these questions. We can begin to answer them by recalling another element of the theory of profit:

> The *gross profit*, i.e. the surplus value, regarded apart from its formal relation, not as a proportion but rather as a simple magnitude of value without con-
> nection with any other, will grow on the average *not as does the rate of profit,
> but as does the size of the capital*. Thus, while the rate of profit will be inversely
> related to the value of the capital, the *sum of profit* will be directly related to
> it. (*Grundrisse* 748)

But what is this *sum of profit* [*massa del profitto*]? It is both the generality of labor incorporated into capital and the generality of labor presented to capital, at a specific stage of capitalist accumulation and organization of labor.

> It is quite correct, as regards the production process as a whole, that the
> capital acting as material and as fixed capital not only is objectified labour,
> but must also be reproduced, and continuously reproduced, by new labour.
> Its presence assumes, therefore,—the extent which its presence has attained
> assumes, therefore, the extent of the labouring population, population on a
> large scale, which in and for itself is the condition of all productive power—
> but this reproduction everywhere proceeds on the presupposition of the
> action of fixed capital and of raw material and of scientific power, both as

such, and as appropriated within production and already realized within it. (*Grundrisse* 763–64)

*Therefore the sum of profit is, first of all, the sum of capital, and capital is a relation of exploitation: it is the class relation* in the production and reproduction of capital, and in circulation.

But if this is so, the contemporaneity of the divergence and inversion of the relation between the sum total [*massificazione*] of profit and the trend of its rate must have specific presuppositions in the class relations that determine the present figure of capital and the degree of its development, both from the point of view of production and from that of circulation.

Let us examine this from the standpoint of production and reproduction. Marx says that the law of the tendency of the rate of profit to fall

is in every respect the most important law of modern political economy, and the most essential for understanding the most difficult relations. It is the most important law from the historical standpoint. It is a law which, despite its simplicity, has never before been grasped and, even less, consciously articulated. Since this decline in the rate of profit is identical in meaning (1) with the productive power already produced, and the foundation formed by it for new production; this simultaneously presupposing an enormous development of scientific powers; (2) with the decline of the part of the capital already produced which must be exchanged for immediate labour, i.e. with the decline in the immediate labour required for the reproduction of an immense value, expressing itself in a great mass of products, great mass of products with low prices ... (3) [with] the dimension of capital generally, including the portion of it which is not fixed capital; hence intercourse on a magnificent scale, immense sum of exchange operations, large size of the market and all-sidedness of simultaneous labour; means of communication etc., presence of the necessary consumption fund to undertake this gigantic process (workers' food, housing etc.); hence it is evident that the material productive power already present, already worked out, existing in the form of fixed capital, together with the population etc., in short all conditions of wealth, that the greatest conditions for the reproduction of wealth, i.e. the abundant development of the social individual—that the development of the productive forces brought about by the historical development of capital itself, when it reaches a certain point, suspends the self-valorization of capital, instead of positing it. (*Grundrisse* 748–49, translation slightly modified)

The role that capital plays as sum of profit also characterizes profit from the viewpoint of circulation and realization.[14] "Looked at precisely ... the *valorization process* of capital ... appears at the same time as its *devaluation process*, its demonetization" (*Grundrisse* 402). This is so not only because, every time capital enters into reproduction, it modifies the terms of reproduction itself through the reduction of living labor (since this still involves the mechanisms of accumulation). On the contrary, strictly in relation to circulation, it happens because every time capital enters into circulation (and this happens not in terms of value but in terms of commodities, goods) it must realize itself in order to regain its own value. But capital wants to realize itself within altered terms of production, altered in the sense that they reduce (to the most compressed form) necessary labor and they also augment surplus–value more and more intensively. In order for these two aspects to arise, the productive capacity of labor (tied to all the social conditions determining it) must expand simultaneously. That is, there must be the most extreme expansion of the social productive forces, and consequently an extraordinary increase in the mass of products. The antithesis between production and valorization presented here is once again the antithesis between rate and sum, between the process of the devalorization of labor on the one hand and the massification of production and the necessity of realizing it on the other. It is the antithesis between relations of domination and conditions of socialization (of the social massification of labor) that makes the devalorization of labor possible.[15]

At this point we can begin to answer the questions asked earlier. Why does capital push the process of devalorization of labor to extreme limits in spite of the increase in its inner contradictions? Why are we beginning to witness the qualitative passage to a phase in which the subsumption of labor within capital does not assume a valorizing form?

The answer must be based upon the series of elements examined so far. Within the mode of production, the fall of the rate of profit, i.e. the devalorization of labor, is accompanied by a massification of the forces of social production that, because it inheres deeply both in the process of production and in the process of circulation, now presents itself in the unified figure of a subject, of a social individual. Therefore, for the simple reason that the fall takes this form, it presents itself as a power that breaks with the solution attempted by the mechanics of the capitalist process (crisis of overproduction) and instead poses an alternative to the reappropriation of the mass of products in increasingly drastic terms. *Thus on this decisive point Marx's description of the mechanism must be corrected, in his own terms. The relation between rate of profit and massification of production takes shape within new relations of force on a social foundation that capitalist development itself has determined, and that the struggle has defined and constituted as a subject.* The divergence between the devalorization of labor and the massification of the productive social forces becomes the only path for capital to follow at this point. But *since massification can neither be eliminated,* because capital would thereby destroy its new social foundation, nor can it be restructured each time through a destructive crisis of traditional character—because the relations of force between classes would not allow it[16]—then capital insists that *this new social foundation can only be isolated from the production process.* However, this is possible only when the new social foundation presents itself not so much as the subject of exploitation, but rather as the motive force of an increasingly profound instability and uncertainty. Then the present figure of the *capitalist crisis* begins to take shape *as a figure combining the fall of the rate of profit and the mass offensive* on behalf of that social reality of production that capital is compelled to construct in order to valorize itself. As happens with all economic laws, the fact that the process is tendential does not prevent it from being real and actual. Now the working class, the new associated working class, is no longer just an independent variable here but a *radical obstacle* to development. The capitalist response must succeed in striking back fully by devaluing the entire process of production. But it cannot go that far. Admitting a profound precariousness into itself, capital must restrain itself in its operation of isolating and devaluing labor, not destroying the mass of products but rather trying to control, through the operation of redistribution, the precariousness from which it suffers.

(b) Reaching this point of our argument actually means posing the problem of the *crisis of the Planner-State.* It is the crisis of that form of state in which the capitalist project had glimpsed—and begun to put into practice—the possibility of using the massification of social productive forces and the new social productive foundation (new in qualitative terms) in order to make the rate of profit grow by means of a well-balanced redistribution of the sum of profit among the various participants in the reformist design, or more precisely in the cooperative "social peace."

The workers' wage offensive has shattered this capitalist illusion, stimulating again the tendencies toward imbalance that are implicit in this stage of capitalist development. Their offensive has encouraged those tendencies again in a dramatic manner, confronting the bosses with the urgent need for a new form of control and domination. The history of the post-Second World War years has shown them to be a period of impetuous development characterized by high and medium rates of development, erected on the possibility of utilizing an extremely broad and mobile labor-power market. But this stage passed very rapidly. To the extent that the system was reconstructed and living labor was comprehensively reorganized at the highest level of productivity, the fall of the rate of profit (that Carli,[17] together with his buddies, calls "historical") is re-established. *Stagflation* shatters the reformist dream with its accumulation of mechanisms of stagnation (that is, leveling-out of the rate of profit) and inflation pressures, wage pressures, demands for appropriation of gross profit made by the new mass of proletarians reunited as a subject that is productive and potentially subversive in equal measure.[18]

The question is no longer why this happened, although as a response to that question we have offered some theoretical elements to which we will have to return when we deal with the problems of definition of the current political composition of the working class. What we want to know is how the bosses plan to deal with this new phase of the crisis. In other words, we want to know *what is the specific (general and governmental) form through which capital can manage the extinction of the law of value*, that is, the end of labor as a valorizing function in the production process. We want to raise this issue because, as with the analysis of causes, the analysis of effects and of capitalist forms of behavior in crisis can also offer valuable suggestions and complements to the central point of our investigation, that is, to the definition of class composition.

Now, as we all know, in chapter 14 (part III) of Book III of *Capital* Marx analyzes the antagonistic influences that contrast and neutralize the action of the law of the tendency of the rate of profit to fall. It would be possible to document the effectiveness of such policies in capital's current initiative. But if we have followed the argument developed so far, and therefore have situated ourselves within this process, a specific analysis of the counter-tendencies turns out to be outdated at this point because the present crisis proves to be real and effective despite the functioning of the counter-tendencies. And, bearing in mind the effectiveness of the counter-tendencies, the analysis records and describes the crisis. The fall of the rate of profit within the massification of the workers' offensive includes the counter-tendencies and sees them neutralized, checked in some way and rendered strategically irrelevant, in the present action of the fundamental tendency.

What is strategically fundamental, rather, is the divergence of the rate of profit and the massification of the subject of exploitation. The two magnitudes tend to take shape in an alternation so profound, so critical, that the capitalist brain itself is as it were shattered by this schizophrenia. Since the destructive crisis is no longer possible due to the working-class presence that is always materially and sometimes politically organized, there is no way to block a process that is posited as necessary. We must get used to considering the current state of capitalist management of development, or better, of stagnation, *after* the planning stage. *Planning has definitively absorbed the working class into the process of production and distribution,* at least as long as the capitalist mode of production lasts. At this level of development it becomes absolutely impossible to interrupt violently, by means of ferocious crises, the mechanism for the realization of gross profit. In other words, it is impossible to think of repression of the fascist sort and crisis of the disruptive sort as suitable means to interrupt the mechanism. At this level of the fall of the rate of profit, *stagnant capital is, nevertheless, planned capital.* It is the dynamic regulation of conflictuality and therefore of a relation between classes. This relation cannot be annulled. We must get used to *separating planning from development.* The terms are not homogeneous at all. Only reformist utopianism and socialism have tried to overlap them by identifying them. So how can capital try to check, to isolate, to devalorize labor within the overall plan? And how can it maintain itself as capital?

What is profit? Marx says,

> As this supposed derivative of the total capital advanced, the surplus-value takes on the transformed form of *profit.* A sum of value is therefore capital if it is invested in order to produce a profit, or alternately profit arises because a sum of value is employed as capital ... Profit, as we are originally faced with it, is thus the same thing as surplus-value, save in a mystified form, though one that necessarily arises from the capitalist mode of production. Because no distinction between constant capital and variable capital can be recognized in the apparent formation of the cost price, the origin of the change in value that occurs in the course of the production process is shifted from the variable capital to the capital as a whole. Because the price of labour-power appears at one pole in the transformed form of wages, surplus-value appears at the other pole in the transformed form of profit.[19]

What is the (general) average rate of profit?

> As a result of the differing organic composition of capitals applied in different branches of production, as a result therefore of the circumstance that according to the different percentage that the variable part forms in a total capital of a given size, very different amounts of labour are set in motion by capitals of equal size, so too very different amounts of surplus labour are appropriated by these capitals, or very different amounts of surplus-value are produced by them. The rates of profit prevailing in the different branches of production are accordingly originally very different. These different rates of profit are balanced out by competition to give a general rate of profit which

is the average of all these different rates. The profit that falls to a capital of given size according to this general rate of profit, whatever its organic composition might be, we call the average profit.[20]

The general average rate of profit is constituted, therefore, at a limit that the competitive dialectic contributes to determining. The rate tends to level itself out on this limit, on this average determination.

It is here that the mystified process of profit and competition begins to be overturned. In fact the rate of profit levels itself out in those spheres of average composition in which "surplus-value and profit coincide."

The sum of the profits for all the different spheres of production must accordingly be equal to the sum of surplus-values, and the sum of prices of production for the total social product must be equal to the sum of its values.[21]

In conclusion,

It can also be added here, firstly, that wherever an average profit is established, i.e. a general rate of profit, and however this result may have been brought about, this average profit can be nothing other than the profit on the average social capital, the total sum of profit being equal to the total sum of surplus-value, and secondly that the prices produced by adding this average profit onto the cost prices can be nothing other than the values which have been transformed into prices of production.[22]

When does all of this happen in a planning regime? Can we conclude at this point by saying that the rate of profit and the rate of surplus-value in general—"as a tendency, like all economic laws"—tend to coincide here? Can we consider the overturning of the mystified process of profit definitive? And can we consider the equalization of the process of profit with that of the general rate of surplus-value to be given, outside the competitive dialectic? All reformism has acted on the basis of this hypothesis, and all revisionists utilizing the mechanisms of the law of planned value have acted upon that basis. In fact, *in the Planner-State the rate of surplus-value and the rate of profit were seen as tendentially merging [unificantisi]*. This was precisely the new society founded on labor!

But the problem we are faced with is a different one. As we have already said, it is the problem of the *crisis of the Planner-State*. Here, *surplus-value and profit are still given as a single unified rate, but the quantitative determination of the rate tends to be null*. The rate of profit tends to annul itself insofar as labor is expelled from the production process as value and as capacity for struggle, as a new productive foundation and as a new subversive subject. How does capital manage this passage? How does capital save itself once labor is expelled? When, in stagnation, the rate of profit tends toward zero, what is the law of profit then?

Once again Marx shows us the way to the solution of the problem.

> [P]rofit is…a transformed form of surplus-value, a form in which its origin and the secret of its existence are veiled and obliterated. In point of fact, profit is the form of appearance of surplus-value…In surplus-value, the relationship between capital and labour is laid bare. In the relationship between capital and profit … *capital appears as a relationship to itself,* a relationship in which it is distinguished, as an original sum of value, from another new value that it posits. It appears to consciousness as if capital creates this new value in the course of its movement through the production and circulation processes. But how this happens is now mystified, and appears to derive from hidden qualities that are inherent in capital itself.[23]

Here, in the quantitative flattening of the rate of profit and the expulsion of value from the process, the persistence of the horizon of profit reveals its secret: it is only the *persistence of the power of capital.* It is only the exacerbation of its irrational face of *command.*

The Marxian definition of the profit category finds its confirmation at the moment in which all material determinations, all the "natural" screens of mystification, are set at zero. In profit, capital

> relates to itself as positing new value, as producer of value. It relates as the foundation to surplus value as that which it founded. Its movement consists of relating to itself, while it produces itself, at the same time as the foundation of what it has founded, as value presupposed to itself as surplus value, or to the surplus value as posited by it. (*Grundrisse* 745)

And if surplus-value is set at zero, it does not matter because all the conditions for the continuity of determination are given.

> Proceeding from itself as the active subject, the subject of the process … capital relates to itself as self-increasing value; i.e. it relates to surplus value as something posited and founded by it; it relates as well-spring of production, to itself as product; it relates as producing value to itself as produced value. It therefore no longer measures the newly produced value by its real measure, the relation of surplus labour to necessary labour, but rather by itself as its presupposition. (*Grundrisse* 746)

Nor is the mystification of a capital that has expelled labor from itself compelled to reflection.

> After it has distinguished the profit, as newly reproduced value, from itself as presupposed, self-valorizing value, and has posited profit as the measure of its valorization, it suspends the separation again, and posits it in its identity to itself as capital which, grown by the amount of the profit, now begins the same process anew in larger dimensions. By describing its circle it expands itself as the subject of the circle and thus describes a self-expanded circle, a spiral. (*Grundrisse* 746, translation slightly modified)

> I am, by the way, discovering some nice arguments. E.g. I have completely demolished the theory of profit as hitherto propounded. What was of great use to me as regards *method* of treatment was Hegel's *Logic* at which I had taken another look *by mere accident* ... [24]

That is what Marx says. He glanced back through the logic of mystification, which is the logic of state power. When the logic of the relation between profit and surplus-value, between power over the process of production and organization of the production process is broken; when there is no more "virtuous" coincidence of exploitation and progress because the working class has destroyed any possibility of it; when instead there is a "vicious" coincidence of permanent conflict and the stagnation of profit, then capital can only live through mystification. Hegel has clearly taught us the mechanisms of power that make mystification real. It accompanies power. It is the figure and legitimation of command. Surely, an *extreme crisis of the historical motivation of capital*, which is no less effective, is at the root of this situation.

Insofar as the working class annuls profit, in other words insofar as the average formula of the development of capital, based on extraction of surplus-value, on the exploitation of living labor, is annulled—insofar as this rupture is given—*capital, as total capital, as the state, must exalt its function of command*. We have already seen[25] how the alternation between command over labor and organization of labor is typical of a series of fundamental figures of the process of capital, first of all money. We have also seen how the autonomy of the political and the exaltation of the state-function emerge above all in moments when the mystified mediations imposed upon and integrated into development by capital are in crisis. Now, when the historical crisis of class relations reaches its climax, the logic of command must try to express itself alone.

By *production of commodities by means of command* we mean that *every relation between value and price, between production and circulation, fails*. Our economists have a great deal to figure out in the tangled transformation of values into prices. The only thing they will be able to figure out is not so much the difference between the problem of value and that of price (which in planned regimes could be relative) as it is the disproportion between declining value and increasing prices—and this is only the final phenomenon of a process of struggle. The problem of the transformation of values into prices can only be understood, but not resolved, by descending into the struggles, into the determination of the fall of the rate of profit in the presence of class massification.

How, then, does capital manage this dramatic situation? Through the production of commodities by means of command, i.e. through the mystification of value in the decline of surplus-value, through capital's legitimation of itself as value while all the conditions of surplus-value collapse, or rather must collapse. Capital knows that exploitation is legitimized and that it has "reason" to exist only insofar as the rate of profit grows and with it capitalist development and capital's progressive force. *The capitalist management of this crisis must then pass by way of a search for a new form of legitimation*, by anchoring the power of capital in the sources of living labor. If capital does not derive wealth from it, then capital will legitimately derive the delusion of being still capable of exploitation.

Now capital can recuperate this idea of value only where productive labor, that is, labor that produces surplus-value, expresses itself in its highest form, i.e. *in the factory*, in the most advanced capitalist enterprise. But in the factory the working class contests at the highest level—objectively as the lower limit of necessary labor, subjectively as struggle—the production of surplus-value. *Value, then, can be found once again only by making the enterprise the moment of overall recuperation for all of social production, the moment in which the minimum limit of necessary labor valorizes all of social production.* Production of commodities by means of command is the total subordination imposed by capital on the relationship of society with the factory. *The entire society is drawn into subordination to enterprise-command, and the form of enterprise production becomes the hegemonic form of the overall social relation.* The massification of productive social forces, the scientific quantification of the social and its reduction to a general productive base, must be made to leap, in terms of profit, toward the enterprise decision. The state as the representative of total capital places itself at the service of this new relation that sees enterprise-profit, that is, the capacity to use living labor, as an agent valorizing the entire network of massified social relations that stands behind it. The state guarantees the enterprise, it socializes capital in order to guarantee it and it moves within a practice of the plan that has nothing to do with

WORKERS' PARTY AGAINST WORK   **73**

socialist utopianism but is only the projection of the rationale for the renewed conquest of a horizon of value.

But is all this not illusory? Does it not repeat the general contradiction and crisis of the capitalist relation up to this point? Of course. Capital achieves its own intentions as agent of development *in a merely formal manner*, by submitting the social to the factory, which does not change the foundation of the mode of production but instead only confirms its own crisis. *The suppression of the law of value in capital's command is merely formal.*

But, politically, this mystification lives on! It does so because this is the only way for total capital to succeed in reproposing a rule of domination and power as a "relation with itself," to posit itself as "subject of the circle of profit." By accepting the fall of the rate of profit and by formally reactivating the law of value in the subordination of society to the factory, capital continues to control and command all the valences of the unification of exploitation even while asserting their separation. Despite the collapse of every motivation for its own existence, capital nevertheless penetrates the entire social articulation of labor, asserting the law of value in the form of command as an image of profit, toward which surplus-value leans. The *Enterprise-State* [*Stato-impresa*] is total capital that can exist and propose itself again as an infinite articulation of itself, and consequently of its components, in a game of domination that sees the composition and dissolution of the overall mass of labor only in reference to the necessity of its persistence as command. The Enterprise-State accepts the crisis, and on the basis of its peculiar quality, it reconfigures itself as subject. Within all the components and the spaces of social connection, the Enterprise-State acts out its power as a final image of itself. Even if the rate of profit flattens out, the massification of the subject of exploitation is nevertheless irreducible. The Enterprise-State knows that these conditions of crisis do not mean destruction, fascism, and the unrestrained revival of exploitation. These conditions can only mean internal, continuous regulation of the general social relation and mystification of the rule of command on the basis of this control. The only form of commodity production left to capital is the form of production in accordance with an empty logic of the persistence of its domination.

### 3. WORKING-CLASS POLITICAL COMPOSITION AND ARMED ORGANIZATION OF THE STRUGGLE FOR COMMUNISM

(a) Given these characteristics of the crisis, if we now turn to the question of organization we must first ask ourselves two questions. That is, we must ask *what if any modifications this type of* capitalist *crisis*—or, better, of overall historical situation of capitalist development—*will make in the composition of the working class*. Second, it will be necessary to consider the nature of the modifications that may have taken place and the degree of radicality they present. Consequently, in light of this we must pose *the problem of the relation between class composition and revolutionary worker organization*.

We have already insisted on the first point at length, if only in part. We saw how, in the process of the production of capital, the completion of real ·subsumption and the complete socialization of labor as well as the recuperation of all the social productive forces, including most prominently science, together determine the formation of an overall social individual equipped with all the attributes necessary to create wealth. Then, with the disappearance of the historical barrier of the law of value, the process of the fall of the rate of profit extols associated labor as the sole productive force. At the same time it shows how capital, which has used and abused this force, at the very moment when it completes the construction of this foundation, simultaneously sets up the conditions that will "blow sky-high" its control over it (*Grundrisse* 706). Marx describes the characteristics of this new foundation of the production process in general, in other words, the new class composition (when the productive forces have fully developed in such a way that their development is a "*condition of production*; and not that specific *conditions of production* are posited as a limit of the development of the productive forces" [*Grundrisse* 542]), as follows:

> the tendentially and potentially general development of the forces of production—of wealth as such—as a basis; likewise, the universality of inter-course ... The basis as the possibility of the universal development of the individual, and the real development of the individuals from this basis as a constant suspension of its *barrier*, which is recognized as a barrier, not taken for a *sacred limit*. Not an ideal or imagined universality of the individual, but the universality of his real and ideal relations. Hence also the grasping of his own history as a *process*, and the recognition of nature (equally present as practical power over nature) as his real body. (*Grundrisse* 542, translation slightly modified)

Today, the proletariat and the working class express their material needs on this terrain; *the waves of workers' struggles have turned the generality of abstract labor into a subject* whose autonomous forms of behavior present themselves as irreducible. The high quality of this recomposition, and the wealth of dialectical relations between class strata that it displays, constitutes the fundamental characteristic of working-class material composition.

Moreover the unity and the very high quality, the highest degree of articulation and social generality of this working class are not only an objective condition. If that were the case, the working class would belong entirely to capital. Yet this is not so. It is in the very same spontaneous forms of behavior of this unified and associated working class that we read *the refusal of work* as a condition of the relationship with capitalist development.

Let us be clear: we are not talking about the general tendencies that the compression of necessary labor imposes upon capitalist development in terms of the collapse of surplus-value. We are talking about a surplus of refusal to directly valorize capital that today can be generally identified (in the framework of this description) within the forms of class behavior. We are talking about the fact that once workers have reached this level of productivity and "refinement of their talents" (that, after all, is what productivity actually consists in), they "want to enjoy it." That is, they no longer imagine work as a discipline but rather as satisfaction [*godimento*]. Workers imagine their life not as work but as the absence of it, their activity as free and creative exercise (*Grundrisse* 708). We are talking about the massive flight of productive labor from factory work toward the tertiary or service sectors. We are talking about the spontaneous refusal to accept the rules of training for abstract labor and apprenticeship to unmediated labor. All of this is displayed at the level of spontaneity, as an implicitly subjective characteristic, as a general tendency toward the workers' refusal of work, toward the demystification of its formal suppression and as an incipient will and consciousness of the necessity of its real suppression. Capital is so well aware of this situation that it is forced to leave the metropolitan countries and seek labor that is still willing to valorize it in countries that are further and further away. Even as capital expands its "civilizing mission," it thus opens up the possibility of revolutionary recomposition!

There is another modification in working-class composition that must briefly be indicated. This is a substantial modification that concerns the political and, more explicitly, the subjective levels of working-class composition.

Let us look at the premises. In the capitalist crisis of the law of value, the possibility of making the theory of the reserve army function as a way to regulate the labor market collapses. *The theory of the reserve army does not function.* Not only is the wage rigid toward the bottom, but it also tends to become a stable condition, a "guarantee" within capitalist *Zivilisation* itself. The theory of the complete devaluation of existing wealth through a disastrous crisis functions even less; its political consequences are terrifying.[26] Besides, what collapses in the crisis of planning is the possibility of bringing the major proportions of the system back into equilibrium according to a model of development based on the social redistribution of surplus-value. Consequently, the entire institutional system geared to regulating the labor-power market fails in its function. If it continues to exist, if the unions continue to assert their competence, if the reformist parties continue to propose programs for the redistribution of wealth, then we must conclude that we are dealing with filthy mystifiers, with shady operators who are reproposing the law of value in mystified ways.

Let us draw some conclusions concerning class composition, and thus concerning the forms of behavior currently existing and tending to develop among the workers. Since labor presents itself as a power that blows up the conditions of the production of surplus-value and that by means of the rule of value takes every mystified rationale away from capital's domination, we are consequently led to the conclusion that "the growth of the forces of production can no longer be bound up with the appropriation of alien surplus labour, but ... the mass of workers must themselves appropriate their own surplus labour" (*Grundrisse* 708, translation slightly modified). The nonexistence of this bond is the very same nonexistence of capital's rationale of command. It is its consequence and its overturning. The nonexistence of this bond extends to all the modalities of redistribution. *Appropriation is the revelation that the working class, reunited on a new basis of production and materially on its way to emancipating itself through the refusal of work, represents as such an inextinguishable power.* The fall of the rate of profit, in other words the crisis of capital, finds its true origin here, in appropriation as class behavior. It is not simply that "labour-power relates to its labour as to an alien, and if capital were willing to pay it *without* making it labour it would enter the bargain with pleasure" (*Grundrisse* 462).

Here we are further ahead than that:

> The recognition of the products as its own, and the judgement that its sep-aration from the conditions of its realization is improper—forcibly imposed—is an enormous advance in awareness, itself the product of the mode of production resting on capital, and as much the knell to its doom as, with the slave's awareness that he *cannot be the property of another*, with his consciousness of himself as a person, the existence of slavery becomes a merely artificial, vegetative existence, and ceases to be able to prevail as the basis of production. (*Grundrisse* 463)

At this point we can begin to reverse the course of the analysis. We began with the theory of crises in order to arrive at our investigation into working-class composition. Now we know that the reality that dominates and determines the capitalist mechanism of the crisis and all its different forms is the political composition of this working class, reunified as a social class that spontaneously takes up a position at the level of the refusal of work and that turns politically to the practice of appropriation. Now, therefore, we can begin to answer the second question posed at the beginning of this chapter. Given the likely modifications of working-class composition, we asked ourselves, what is their character, what is the degree of radicality that they present? We can answer by saying that it is a character of *extreme radicality*. The overall social formation in which we move, the political class composition to which we refer presents *characteristics that are entirely new compared to the class struggle's recent past*. For this working class, the theory of alliances, the ideology of work, the distinction made between different stages of (economic and political, democratic and socialist) struggle are now nothing more than so much scrap metal, even as we bow down before the epic of these class struggles and of the heroic proletarians "storming heaven." But today heaven is near. Work, the absurd effort that is daily given for free to the boss, has erected a huge quantity of dead labor that we are preparing to appropriate. We are not afraid of the crisis or of violence. We draw our reason to hate the bosses and our inflexibility in struggle not from despair but, rather, from desire, from satisfaction, from wealth. Class unity, the destruction of wage labor, the political struggle for appropriation, in other words *communism as minimum program*, are the political needs—and the tendency being realized—that emerge from the class composition in which we situate ourselves.

Before we go any further, however, we must raise another problem. When we considered the form in which capital manages the process of the formal suppression of labor as a moment of valorization, we noticed a specific— though mystified—dialectical practice. This practice consists in the fact that *two equally powerful processes* have been set in motion and overlap each other. One process is the *maximum socialization* of the productive forces, and the other is the *insistence on the enterprise* as the guiding, intensive moment of the entire social organization. On the one hand, capital has diffused the process of valorization to the point of submerging it in the complexity of social relations. On the other hand, capital feels nostalgia for the immediate extraction of value and wishes to re-establish its centrality. *Capital sets the factory, as the point of valorization of the social circuit of production, against society as the area of devalorization and the site of massification. At the same time capital sets society, as the image of the social machine of production, against the factory since the factory is the privileged site of the refusal of work and the offensive against the rate of profit.* Now given the principal characteristics that we have defined, what are the effects that this particular form of capitalist management of the process of the suppression of labor has on the composition of the working class?

In order to answer this question, we should return to some themes of Marx's discussion on *productive and unproductive labor*.[27] It is well known how firmly Marx distinguishes productive from unproductive labor:

> Since the immediate purpose and the *authentic product* of capitalist production is *surplus-value, labour is only productive*, and an exponent of labour-power is only a *productive worker*, if it or he creates *surplus-value* directly, i.e. the only productive labour is that which is directly *consumed* in the course of production for the valorization of capital.[28]

By insisting on this specificity, Marx puts us on guard against the danger of overextending the category of productive labor. "Every productive worker is a wage-labourer, but not every wage-labourer is a productive worker."[29] It is clear that by insisting strictly on the specificity of productive labor, Marx responds to the necessity of putting the working class as such at the center of scientific and revolutionary considerations, and to the equally urgent need to answer those "apologists of capital" who present

> the productive worker, simply because he is a wage-labourer, as a worker who only exchanges his *services* (i.e. his labour as a use-value) for *money*. This makes it easy for them to gloss over the specific nature of this "productive worker" and of capitalist production—as the production of surplus-value, as the self-valorization of capital in which living labour is no more than the agency it has embodied in itself. A soldier is a wage-labourer, a mercenary, but this does not make a productive worker of him.[30]

However, this *distinction* and definition of the productive laborer is *relative to the degree of advancement of the process of subsumption* of labor within capital. In particular,

> with the development of the *real subsumption of labour under capital*, or the *strictly capitalist mode of production*, the *real lever* of the overall labour process is increasingly not the individual worker. Instead, *labour-power socially combined* and the various competing labour-powers which together form the entire production machine participate in very different ways in the immediate process of making commodities, or, more accurately in this context, creating the product. Some work better with their hands, others with their heads, one as a manager, engineer, technologist, etc., the other as overseer, the third as manual labourer or even drudge. An ever increasing number of types of labour are included in the immediate concept of *productive labour*, and those who perform it are classed as *productive workers*, workers directly exploited by

capital and *subordinated* to its process of production and valorization. If we consider the *aggregate worker*, i.e. if we take all the members comprising the workshop together, then we see that their *combined activity* results materially in an *aggregate* product which is at the same time a *quantity of goods*. And here it is quite immaterial whether the job of a particular worker, who is merely a limb of this aggregate worker, is at a greater or smaller distance from the actual manual labour.[31]

This survey of what is included in productive labor can be extended—following the order Marx gives in these pages—to the point of including the scientific laborer himself.[32] And, on the basis of what we demonstrated previously, we can now state that the concept of the waged worker and the concept of the productive worker tend toward homogeneity.

But this result of our analysis does not solve the specific problem we were faced with earlier, because if the generalization of the assumption according to which the working class today is immediately given as a unity and as the fundamental subject of exploitation (which is why, consequently, every attempt to divide this unity is immediately capitalist) is confirmed, this conclusion does not determine the specificity of the situation within the crisis either.

Let us take a step back for a moment. On the one hand, capital tries to separate and at the same time to unite the factory and society in the generalization of enterprise-command. On the other hand, a socially unified working class is objectively capable of imposing the fall of the rate of profit and subjectively aiming to determine the levels of struggle over appropriation. The unity of productive labor has gone beyond the unification that capital has determined in order to reach its own objectives. It is at the center of this dialectic, then, that we can still specify in its historical concreteness the figure in which *the vanguard of the proletariat* is represented within the current political class composition. This vanguard must influence the fall of the rate of profit in the most determinate manner, and for that reason it must be capable of predetermining the processes of class reunification in terms of timeframes [*scadenze*], pacing and objectives. In other words, this vanguard must be able to forcibly turn the massified presence in production (the product and fate of capitalist development) from the objective representation of a new economic foundation into a subject (itself a mass of indirect producers) that has been recomposed in order to attack the rate of profit. But the vanguard that is capable of doing this is once again the *working class of the large factories,* which is the privileged subject of exploitation and at the same time the effective agent of the devalorization of labor and profit. It is against this vanguard that capital turns its mystifications and its fiercest anger. It is around this vanguard that the whole proletariat comes together in an identity of interests that cries out for an interpreter, in a unity of goals that cries out for direction and with a cargo of anti-capitalist violence that cries out for a detonator.

The workers of the large factories, at the cutting edge of social class unification, display an *absolutely hegemonic political and theoretical configuration* within the current class composition. Politically speaking, they are hegemonic because they can attack the last mystifications of labor value in the factory where the boss tries to reproduce the mythology of living labor as valorization of capital. In this way, the workers strike the capitalist enterprise's command over society at its root, shattering the rhythm to which the boss would like to make all wage labor dance. But the theoretical figure that the workers of large factories express is even more important. They show how productive labor, that is, labor producing surplus-value, is not only annulled in its quality of exploitation rendered to the boss. *Productive labor can also be freed.* It can appear and emerge as creativity and freedom. The infinite fantasy of liberated productive labor is revealed *in the struggles, from sabotage to mass strike, from street fighting to armed struggle.* Here the workers of the large factories recompose their vanguard political task into the theoretical task of liberation.

In this way, the division between factory and society that the boss tries to achieve is ruptured internally. That is, the higher degree of exploitation in the factory, symbol of the boss's power over society, is overturned into the hegemony of workers' unity in the shape of the refusal of work and appropriation over the social class of producers. The workers' process of liberating society from the associated producers of capital comes completely into view. This process finds both its basis and its agents in the current political class composition.

In this way, the Marxian rationale and the worker standpoint that form the basis of the rigorous class definition of the concept of productive labor are preserved and emphasized in the evolution of the subsumption of labor within capital. Through the refusal of work and the urgency of appropriation the working class, the vanguards of the large factories, manifest a coherent definition of productive labor in the passage from the phase of the real subsumption of labor within capital to the phase of the real suppression of labor and capital.

(b) From a general point of view, what has been said so far in relation to the crisis and to working-class composition in the crisis can be referred to several elements that may be briefly summarized as follows. (1) The capitalist line of restructuring must pass by way of the attempt to isolate the fall of the rate of profit in the factory (and its agents) from the process of the socialization of productive labor taking place in society as a whole. All prospects of reformism have failed. By means of the extension and omnipotence of enterprise-command, the plan means to assert, on the social level, the rationale for the isolation and (on that basis) the revenge of the bosses upon the factory workers in an attempt to go back to a mechanism of direct valorization. (2) The workers' point of view is, conversely, that of unification in the massification of the social proletariat's struggles around the fundamental nodal points of the fall of the rate of profit; it is that of the domination of the fundamental rationale of the crisis—the fall of the rate of profit caused by the workers' offensive—over the general conditions of anti-capitalist insubordination and urgency of communism, that is, over the new social figure of a unified proletariat. (3) The fact that a dialectical relation (of separation for the bosses and of unification for the workers) between the factory moment and the social moment exists cannot blur the relation into an undifferentiated identity. From the class viewpoint, this relation must lead to the firm reassertion of the workers' leadership over the struggle as a whole. (4) The depth of the crisis and the relevance and dimensions of the realization of the law of the tendency of the rate of profit to fall, the fact that the law of value—as a condition and a rule for the management of the plan—does not function and is replaced by a rule of enterprise functioning in terms of division and command *puts on the agenda, within the workers' viewpoint, the question of managing a power of command, a capacity for violence that is equal and opposed to that of the bosses.* The relation between the struggle over the wage (that is, to maintain general levels of autonomy and mass offensive against capitalist wealth) and the struggle for appropriation (that is, to develop the struggle against the capitalist attempt to rectify the course of the rate of profit and against the rule of the enterprise) is posed today as the central issue of the "party" program, or better, of the organizational program of the working class.[33]

It is on the basis of these assumptions that the problem of organization is posed today. We prefer initially to speak of the problem of organization rather than the problem of the party because we believe that the very word "party" can be equivocal. That is, out of linguistic habit, we run the risk of attributing improper contents to it. Therefore, let us clarify what we mean before we start using the word "party" again.

For non-revisionist communists, the word "party" immediately refers to the Leninist concept, explained in *What Is To Be Done?*, of a centralized (theoretical and practical) organization capable of leading the workers' vanguards "from above" in the passage from the struggle over progressive democracy to the struggle for socialism (it being understood that this passage is revolutionary and based on the independence of the proletariat's vanguard). As we noted, the Leninist concept of the party is correctly based on the analysis of a determinate class composition, the Russian class composition of the beginning of the twentieth century. Subjectively, the Leninist concept hastens this real relation "from above" and views the revolutionary recomposition of the class as working-class domination of the dialectic between different classes.

But today we have very little to do with this idea of the party. All the contents bearing upon the political composition of the working class have been modified. The objective basis that motivates our discussion of worker organization has been radically modified. We spoke of *class unity. The main Leninist themes of alliances and working-class domination over the relations between classes have been transformed into the problem of unification of the proletariat from within.* This process of unification can only take place, *not from "above," but rather from below, from within.* Today, any notion of alliances raises issues that are spurious even from the Leninist point of view (Lenin would never even have raised the question of an alliance with either rich farmers or state officials!). What has changed is the social formation within which the problem of organization is posed. As a class, both peasants and the non-productive petty bourgeoisie no longer exist as such. *Secondly,* we spoke of the *refusal of work.* In this case as well, the Leninist concept of the party as the concept of leadership in the passage to socialism, and therefore of the passage to a different and higher organization of labor, collapses when compared to the current forms of class behavior. Because today, as we have often pointed out, communism, the use of accumulated wealth, is immediately, outside and against every logic of the labor process, what workers' power expressly demands. And it is, *a fortiori*, the cause of the capitalist crisis in progress.

But above all, in the third place, the Leninist concept of the party collapses when compared to the theme that is more typical of proletarian organization today, that of appropriation, which is entirely distinct from the theme of insurrection. In Lenin, the concept of insurrection is strictly connected to that of the party. They are the same thing, and it is clear why. If, independently of capitalist reformism, the party conducts the struggle for power in the passage from progressive democracy to socialism, its main point of application will be the construction of the insurrectional moment, as the art of using favorable coincidence in the conjuncture, of deepening a crisis that the bosses, not the workers, have provided. Through insurrection the party makes use of, takes advantage of, and accelerates the bosses' crisis. The Leninist party subjectively takes the route of accelerating a conjunctural situation in order to transform it into a moment of subversion, gambling on the secondary contradictions, crises, etc. But all this is no longer given. Of course, the historical events of the class struggle are charged with an abundance of articulations. The reign of tactics has certainly not come to an end. Of course, the revolutionary leader still has to master the art of seizing the winning moment. The concept of appropriation must include the concept of insurrection. We shall come back to these themes later. What we must insist on now is the fact that *appropriation—the powerful influence of the working class in determining the economic crisis and the elimination of the political channels of capitalist control—is undeniably more scientific than artistic.* It is a power that superimposes itself, that seizes the terrain from the other. The terrain of tactics opens up again, but only on this level. Today organization gambles on the struggle, not on the bosses' mistakes but on its own power.

Least of all will we use the term "party" to recall and propose anew the formal aspects of the Leninist party, such as centralization, discipline, division of labor, etc. As Lenin knew and said, these terms are better taught by the big capitalist enterprise than by the practice of the communist international:

> I am denounced for visualising the Party "as an immense factory" headed by a director in the shape of the Central Committee ... [but] the factory, which seems only a bogey to some, represents that highest form of capitalist cooperation which has united and disciplined the proletariat, taught it to organise, and placed it at the head of all the other strata of the laboring and exploited population.[34]

These are not substantive criteria (and if they are not, they are expressions of the particular conditions in which the Leninist party operated, they are determined by the social formation that the Leninist party interpreted). Rather, these are formal criteria that originate in the need for struggle and knowledge of the enemy.

> But this "factory" discipline, which the proletariat, after defeating the capitalists, after overthrowing the exploiters, will extend to the whole of society, is by no means our ideal, or our ultimate goal. It is only a necessary step for thoroughly cleansing society of all the infamies and abominations of capitalist exploitation, and for further progress.[35]

We are not going to become Leninists just because we have read Max Weber. Like mafiosi and some reformists, we are simply going to become good organizers who know the reality on which we must act.

And yet *we propose to start using the term "party" again.* Because in Marx and in Lenin, in the most profound reality of class composition, "party" basically means two things to the working class. It means *independence of the proletariat as organization and uninterrupted revolution*. These concepts are the flesh and blood of the proletariat. The word "party" is a noun that goes beyond the contents that it now and then includes. The party is the—powerful—overthrow of the bosses' state.

The party is the powerful overthrow of the bosses' state. In this, we are Marxist and Leninist too. But that is what we are today, when the immediate problem is that of a workers' leadership that manages the mass unification of the proletariat in order to perpetuate the bosses' crisis and that at the same time works as a mass detonator for revolt and for proletarian insubordination against enterprise command—today, when the immediate problem is that of interpreting liberated productive labor, the refusal of work and the urgency of appropriation from within, from its foundation. We have seen how the relation between a force that—in the factory and places where surplus-value is extracted—acts to compress the rate of profit and a force that—within the social massification of production that takes place from urban neighborhoods to villages—acts as a pressure on the wage and as a practice of appropriation, can constitute an explosive mixture.

This is what the *"party framework"* must interpret today. These are the tasks to which the workers' political elite [*ceto*] must respond. The quality of this new type of political cadre is located entirely within this relation: in the mobility between the factory and the social territory, articulating wage struggle and subversive action. Their fundamental task is to accept the workers' leadership that moves from the large factories to society, drawing from this leadership the objectives to set against the decisive levels of power, after having socialized their significance. The new cadre must act like fish in water, continuously combining subjective initiative with the directives of proletarian struggle. The fundamental task is *to set up the necessary mediations so that workers' and proletarians' power is firmly established on the terrain of the offensive and on the practice of appropriation.* Today the development of capital's crisis produces and reproduces a class composition within which it constantly tries to bring about new divisions. We must not only stress and theoretically reconstruct the unity of the different fractions of the working class that capital tends to divide. Above all, we must see every effort at division as an opportunity for battle, a chance to turn the terrain of division into an attack on command. *These divisions that capital tries to introduce into the struggles do not originate from functions that are objectively determined. They are not articulations of the law of value, but purely and simply an expedient of command.* These capitalist operations have the intensity of command and not the necessity of an economic mechanism (if it is paradoxically and liminally possible to distinguish these two forms of command). It is for this reason that the new party cadre must be able to grasp these *two levels* and, at the same time, to oppose the use that the bosses make of them in the struggle to organize them in the life of the masses. It is within the contemporaneity of these two moments that the realm of tactics opens up again and the "art" of political action finds room to maneuver.

With this in mind, we can also understand the absurdity of old ideological hold-overs and some theoretical alternatives that are still present in the movement, for example the alternative between external organization (reminiscent of Lenin) and process-organization (reminiscent of Luxemburg). Both of these theoretical models exaggerate functions of working-class composition and conditions of struggle that are no longer present in our current social formation. The first insists on the autonomy and innovative force of the vanguard as such—both outside and inside a passage of democratic struggle aimed at class recomposition. The second insists on a more solid and extensive composition of struggle, and sees the possibility of the very same passage boosted by the conditions of management by the masses. If we really need to go back to the classics, then let us say *Lenin + Luxemburg,* within a different horizon, not the one of a continuity of struggle from democracy to socialism, but rather the horizon of the assertion and persistence of the communist need of the masses that is continuously ruptured on the capitalist side and constantly reproposed on the workers' side. Although capital attacks and pushes this terrain of power toward rupture, it has never succeeded in driving it away permanently. The mass vanguard, *Luxemburg + Lenin,* can exist within these conditions. In its capacity to express these two functions, the new political leadership of the party will be able to consolidate itself.

We must insist on the concept of the *mass vanguard.* As a matter of fact, it is not just on the terrain of the theory of organization that this concept and its complementary concept of the party are determined. We can already find their premises in Marx's critique of political economy.

Let us examine this more closely by going back to the relation between rate of profit and sum of profit. We have seen how the capitalist project is determined in the play between these two magnitudes. Conversely, this relation simultaneously has its workers' side in, on the one hand, the attack on valorization, and, on the other hand, the extension of demand for the goods produced. But this relation is still generic, and tells us little about the wage trend, its determinations and magnitudes. Now, Marx describes the fall of the rate of profit as parallel to a law concerning the wage which we could call *law of the tendency of the rate of the relative wage to fall.*[36] According to this law, we would witness a decrease in the relative wage, that is, a decrease in the ratio between the part of the income that accrues to the workers and the part that accrues to profit, that matches—indeed exceeds—the change in the trend of the rate of profit. The causes of the fall of the rate of the relative wage and the fall of the rate of profit are the same. If the rate of profit is inversely proportional to the increase in the rate of relative surplus-value (that is, to the increase in the productivity of labor, to the development of the productive forces, to the magnitude of constant capital invested in production), the rate of the relative wage is directly proportional to the portion of necessary labor and decreases with its compression. Two consequences result from this. The first is that the increase in the relative wage can represent a counter-tendency to the fall of the rate of profit in cases in which no increases in constant capital occur.[37] If, instead, as historically occurs, the increase in the relative wage presents itself as a stimulus to the magnitude of constant capital, the tendential fall of the rate of profit continues and even increases. *At this point the relative wage appears as a mass— it appears directly as an offensive mass*: "the struggle against the fall in relative wages is no longer a struggle on the basis of the commodity economy, but a revolutionary, subversive attack on the existence of this economy; it is the socialist movement of the proletariat."[38] But when we reach certain dimensions of accumulation, this process is no longer measurable. Its parameters are no longer based on the law of value, but on the pace and forms of its extinction. If, "in the struggle between the two classes—which necessarily arises with the development of the working class—the measurement of the distance between them, which, precisely, is expressed by wages itself as a proportion, becomes decisively important" (*Grundrisse* 597), capital is forced to reduce the proportion to nothing. That is, it is forced to determine it solely through its command. All other "objective" determinations of the wage (conditions connected to the functioning of the labor market, to the quality of labor-power, etc) fail. Only command remains. But *it is within the same trend of the overall wage that the proportional relation between the parts becomes a relation of opposing powers. Once again, the struggle over the wage on the workers' part becomes a power struggle.*

The concept of the mass vanguard is determined on the basis of these considerations. The concept of the party of the mass vanguards is that of *the unification between the struggle for the wage and the revolutionary struggle for power.* There are no longer any distinctions or breaks. The management of this passage is the party.

In order to avoid mistakes, it is necessary to reclaim the extraordinary richness of the use of dialectics in the theory of organization. To connect the terrain of the wage to the terrain of power does not mean to confuse them. To connect the struggle for the wage to the revolutionary struggle means to recognize the dialectical unity between the two, which is the leap from one to the other. The unification of the two levels, which is the terrain of the program, and the centralization of workers' command over them, which is the terrain of organization, must not lead us to forget the distinction of functions between them, which is the terrain of tactics. The overall strategy originates from the articulation of these functions—determinate, continuous unification and articulation.

An uninterrupted line runs between the struggle over the wage, the refusal of work, the question of appropriation and the power struggle, a line that the Marxist science of exploitation teaches us to recognize already in the wage structure.

*The struggle of the mass vanguard—and its party—against command means armed struggle.* Above all, it means armed struggle. The terrain of capitalist command, freed from the heavy mystification of the law of value, is the terrain of violence and mere relations of force. The collapse of the law of value, which is the law of market freedom and the functional horizon of reformist planning, deprives the action of total capital—in the form of the state—of every rationale for command other than violence. Once the bosses' crisis has reached this point, it is typical of their state to increase and perfect the functions of violence without the mystified characteristics of legitimacy. The rights state of the liberal tradition of exploitation and the state of labor of the reformist tradition of exploitation went astray on the basis of the urgent capitalist need to transform the disaster of the rate of profit into a rule that allows the bosses' command to survive and persist. This command tries to insinuate itself into the ranks of the working class as a rationale of division and a new rule of exploitation.

Workers' command must be the powerful overthrow of the bosses' command. Workers' command bases itself on the continuity between the struggle over the wage and the struggle for power that is established within the given class composition. Today, every conquest made on the terrain of the wage that is not organized by the workers in order to preserve their power is doomed to failure. Only armed struggle as the mass, dialectical complement of the struggle over the immediate interest of the proletariat, as expression of the political need of the working class, corresponds to the workers' demand. Only armed struggle is powerful on the plane of the relations of force between the two classes. Only the riposte, the counterattack, the armed offensive represents the distinctiveness of the worker in contrast to the capitalist transfiguration of the consciousness of the disaster of the rate of profit into a rule of command.

The party of the workers' mass vanguard determines its fundamental task on the plane and in the perspective of armed struggle. Only armed struggle transforms the capitalist use of the suppression of the law of value into workers' struggle for the real suppression of the command of capital and of work. *Today, only armed struggle speaks of communism.*

## 4.   THE DIALECTICAL ARTICULATIONS OF PARTY ORGANIZATION AND ITS IMMEDIATE OBJECTIVES

(a) Only a Marxian use of the materialist dialectic can allow us to study in depth and clarify the concept of the mass vanguard, and therefore the concept of a workers' party against work. The problem is indeed complex and the old categories press upon, confuse, limit, and block the workers' capacity to express new organizational functions for new class needs.

We distinguish between *the two levels of the dialectic of the mass vanguard*, between *mass organization of workers' power as subject of the struggle for the wage and for appropriation on the one hand and party organization as subject of the offensive struggle, of aggression against command on the other.* Even if good taste prevents us from basing the distinction between the two organizational levels of the mass vanguard on the antiquated distinction between union and political organization, we understand that distinction, at the very least, in terms of that other old separation between mass and party organisms. Only the latter was the independent bearer of proletarian strategy, whereas the former represented the privileged terrain of tactics. But with the new distinction, the opposite is true: only *the organisms of workers' power represent the level of strategy and program, while the party organization is, instead, the subject of tactics.*

The reason is easily understood. Indeed, our entire argument has endeavored to impute to the emerging communist demand among the masses the continuity and determination not only of the crisis but also of the radical modification of the profit curve. The working class, as such, does not present itself merely as an independent variable of the plan, but as a fundamental obstacle to development. Working-class struggle as such expresses all the contents of the program on this strategic terrain. The militants' task, the direct function of the organisms of workers' power, is to be able to see this position and to read these contents. Appropriation is the synthesis of the workers' needs at a determinate level of composition and the capacity to select and articulate objectives; that is, it is the horizon within which this political recomposition of the proletariat establishes itself. Conversely, on the basis of what we have said so far, we cannot presuppose a traditional figure of the party. In Leninism the party plays its role of interpreter and representative on the basis of a working-class political composition in which that class is a minority constrained to carry out the strategic reunification of the proletariat from above. The party does this on the basis of a technical composition of the working class that sees the working class engaged in the task of imposing work in a socialist form upon the social totality and on the basis of a composition of capital that allows the working class to turn capitalist development into the socialist management of power, but only to the extent that this process is piloted from above. Today, none of these premises are given. *The party presents itself, instead, as the overthrow of the capitalist management of the extinction of the law of value.* The party must break the absurd imposition of an image of surplus-value over and against the real, massified actuality of the flattening of profit and the extinction of value. The party must reveal the given class unity, the recomposition that has taken place within the proletariat, from within and below, not from outside and above. The insurrectionary art of the party is maieutic, it is the capacity to oppose the burden of the bosses' irrational command with equal intensity but in reverse. Just as capital's command in the moment of valorization uses the whole social connectedness of productive labor, so the party tears the totality of productive labor away from capitalist command by attacking and destroying the moment of valorization. The moment the working class presents itself in its objectivity and autonomy as an obstacle to the recovery of profit—and within this autonomy it discovers the world of its own needs, communism and appropriation—the moment the working class presents itself not so much as an independent variable but as a determinate blockage, the task of the party is increasingly to break the mystified image that the bosses' power forces upon the class. *The selection of tasks, of timing, of objectives is up to the class, and it is up to the strength of the party to break capitalist command. This is how the process of subordination of all the institutional forms of power to the working class comes to completion: the party ceases to have the function of representation and divests itself of this last residue of capitalist necessity.*

The specificity of the workers' political need is dispersed, or, worse, is mystified and betrayed when we forget that the power and party functions exercised by the mass vanguard are contemporaneous and when we are unable to use Marx's extraordinary dialectical instrument to understand the unity of the diverse. This happens from different points of view. By turns it is either the offensive or the power function that gets left out and betrayed. It is always the working-class character of mass vanguard organization that is put in parentheses. The novelty of the sociological perception of what is changing in the working class is set against the scientific and dialectical totality of its hegemonic vocation.

In order to exemplify the mystifications, let us start with those who insist on the concept of working-class "hegemony." Most Communist reformism starts precisely from this concept, and on this basis Gramscianism and all the theories of the "new trend" have celebrated and are celebrating their feast days.[39] Here, the more or less socialist objectives the working class proposes are posited as elements of a strategic path that modifies the power relations between classes. It does not claim to modify the class character of society which Communist reformism also confronts, but it hopes that, on the basis of the victory of the structural reforms, it can find the definitive key to the attack on the system.[40] We are not interested here in ascertaining to what extent these good intentions have remained the same or become, instead, refluxes of abhorrent gradualist reformism. Instead, what we dispute is the very possibility of posing the problem in such terms, which overlook the functions of attack and rupture of command that the organization of the mass vanguard must possess in order to allow proletarian independence not only to win, but also to reproduce itself. *There is not one single law of Marxism that distinguishes the growth of workers' power in society from the affirmation of their power against the state.* But today, when every—mystified yet effective— parameter of value collapses, the connection between society and state, between exploitation and command becomes totalitarian. *Only an offensive against command allows workers' power to express itself.* Without this fundamental awareness, the so-called "hegemony" could be brought into play by the bosses to integrate needs into subsystems or delimit worker subculture, thereby confining hegemony to the role of a non-determining element in the process of reproduction of class relations. The correct appreciation of what has changed in the working class, namely the demand for "immediate" results, only finds expression in a violence that stands opposed to that of the bosses, a violence which renders significant and fruitful what capitalist command reduces to a merely irrational function.

On this terrain even the most recent Marxist-inspired sociological theory is happily oblivious to the function of mass vanguard violence.[41] It sets out from the perception of the unity of productive labor and the extraction of surplus from the unified context of the society of capital. But in defining this homogeneous terrain of exploitation, these theorists blur the mechanisms within which the mystified figure of value, and therefore the rule of command, operate. The terrain on which these *Narodnik sociologists* move becomes one of transformation and distribution, from which it is not possible to get back to the articulations of exploitation. In particular, it is the specific working-class terrain—like that on which the mechanisms of exploitation and the mystification of exploitation are established—that is effaced here. This is how the mass vanguard organization presents itself when the time appointed for the redistribution of the surplus, and perhaps also for appropriation, comes. But it will be impossible for the mass vanguard organization to turn the momentum of mass struggle directly against work and against the mechanisms in which value is mystified. The intensification of violence at decisive points does not correspond to offensive massification. *The argument shifts to distribution, exploitation lies in circulation, and the working-class character of mass vanguard strategy is dispersed.*

*Conversely* there are those who, in grasping some characteristics of the new class composition, no longer confuse and dissipate the anti-revisionist dimension of the offensive function of the party. Rather, they confuse and dissipate the function of power, the mass character of the vanguard or the working-class specificity of its political need. *The absence of a determinate use of the dialectic and in particular the dispersal of the power–violence relation is characteristic of all terrorist positions.* Within these positions we certainly do not need to combat the use of violence, the anticipation of capital's moves, the appreciation of the irrational nature of its command or the subjective determination to follow its movements and individual articulations. In terrorism, what we need to combat is the programmatic will that refuses to incarnate the moments of class power and is unable to grasp *an organic relation* between the subjectivity of workers' power and the subjectivism of the use of violence. An ideology of defeat and resistance, the desperate last-ditch image, always takes root in terrorist exemplarism. This results in the radical forgetting of the originality of the workers' struggle's new contents, of communism as minimum program. If the function of capitalist command is then recognized as essential, its nature is defined according to the old models. The scheme upon which the offensive function unravels is the model of fascism as an alternative to socialism, not the regulated extinction of value as the capitalist alternative to the communism of the masses. The forgetting of vanguard action's mass content and the withdrawal over the program are thus identical to the offensive action's loss of working-class characterization. Thus we witness the absurd, ignoble conjunction of socialism and terror, in which mass experience and class composition propose armed struggle for communism. Therefore our criticism is addressed not only to the theories that insist on terrorism as an armed wing, as the separation of the function of offense from the function of workers' power, but also—and above all—to the break within the theories between offensive struggle and the communist contents of struggle—and to the regression that derives from it.

The use of violence is not a quality that eludes or can elude the action of the organisms of workers' power. When workers' power affirms itself in terms of appropriation, the consideration of the use of violence necessarily forms part of the issues involved in the program. What eludes the persistence of the mass movement and the organization of the mass vanguard in its consolidated autonomy is only *the specificity in the organization of the use of violence.* Apart from insurrectional moments, this happens because the autonomous activity of the working class aims above all to satisfy its own material needs.

But to what extent do these material needs become political? To what extent does the struggle for a more "equitable" distribution of income demystify itself and transform itself into political struggle? How do the material motifs of class struggle transform themselves into a weapon of political offense, into the terms of the communist program? Why today, more than ever, is class struggle revolutionary struggle?

Apart from the objective reasons (such as massified class pressure on the rate of profit) which are nevertheless determinant, the answer to these questions lies in the tendency of the refusal of work to become increasingly manifest. Whenever workers' power appears and organizes itself, the refusal of work is already in progress. The programmatic articulation of the refusal of work begins to have a spontaneity that is the obverse of, but just as effective as, the workers' habituation to the constraint of work was. It is for this reason, and beyond this threshold, that the program does not constitute a problem, and that it can be entrusted to the mass movement. From this point of view, the materiality of the workers' refusal of work is more significant than all the erudite attempts to identify its canons in literary form. *The communist contents of the program begin to be expressed from the lowest level of worker behavior* such as absenteeism, sabotage, direct—individual and group—appropriation, etc. The political generalization of these forms of behavior does not come about by means of sermons but, instead, is entirely contained within the working class' political needs. The working class has never so fully revealed what it really is: by refusing to sell itself as labor-power, and refusing to accept the capitalist organization of work, the working class reveals itself immediately to be a political class. It begins to live out its own experience of the destruction of work and of all the means of domination connected to work. *The continuity between spontaneous and political forms of behavior is no longer merely a logical exigency of the theory, but an experience of the practice of the movement.*

*But is the existence of this material continuity,* this political essence of the class, *sufficient* to explain the emergence of its forms of organization? *Of course not,* because—as we have seen—capital responds precisely at that level, on those points of passage. This political continuity of the forms of class behavior is thus a necessary condition, but it is not sufficient. *In order effectively to determine the passage, there must be a force that is at once equal and opposite to the capitalist force that blocks and impedes it.*

Therefore, we have now reached the point of identifying the characteristics of the party function within the complexity of the mass vanguard. As we have seen, this function is as intrinsically linked to the promotion and conservation of the organization of workers' power as the diamond point of its offensive capacity is—so intrinsically linked that it represents an extraordinary case of the dialectical reality of the class struggle. The party is defined within this complexity, within these functions. This definition sweeps away all the more or less sanctified traditions, and strives to correspond to the degree of political intensity of the current working-class composition.

*The party, therefore, is not the consciousness or self-consciousness of the class.* It is not because the mass vanguard already comprises, in the immediacy of its own behavior, the totality of revolutionary consequences resulting from it, and because the organisms of workers' power already express the program of communism. The relation is reversed. *The party is instead, and liminally, the transmission belt, the executive organ of the organization of workers' power.* Least of all, then, is the party the force that represents the working class. This could happen only insofar as the theory of revolution was reduced—due to the objective force of capital—to a theory of revolutionary stages and to a resulting practice of alliances. The doctrine of contradictions among the people, outside the conditions of underdevelopment and instead within the conditions of class and proletarian recomposition—and consequently the theory of the party as vanguard representative in relation to other popular fractions—does not apply when the conditions of communist revolution are given. And not even then will we grant the party the theoretical role of program bearer, or the driver and exemplar of the armed wing, because the conditions of theoretical or practical, doctrinaire or militant prefiguration do not present themselves at this level of massive and lasting unitary class composition. On the contrary, compared to the workers' capacity to struggle against work and therefore to express invention-power, these conditions present themselves as pedagogically pedantic and useless.

Here, then, is the definition of the function of the mass vanguard party. The party is the function of destroying the capitalist mechanisms of command, the capacity to intervene in an offensive form wherever the organisms of worker's power find the limit of capitalist command. The party is a force that overthrows, for the entire proletariat, the relation of domination wherever capital can still exercise it. If the entire society functions by means of the central moment of capitalist valorization and by means of its mystification in the rule of domination, the party is the specular and opposed overthrow of this capitalist function. It is the heightening of the function of antivalorization and destruction. Just as capital, through the management of the historical collapse of the law of value, imposes its domination on unified labor-power, so the party, through its management of offense aimed at the destruction of the law of value and its capitalist mystification, reopens the force of workers' autonomy at a higher level in order to become the communist power of non-work. Against the power of capital's enterprise, the class rediscovers in the party an enterprise power, yet without losing it as an instrument of its autonomy. The party is the enterprise of non-work, and this also constitutes the dialectical specificity of its use of violence.

(b) Those who are bound to tradition may find this concept of the party singularly reductive. As a matter of fact, the determining elements of its figure consist neither in the hegemony of representation and the totality of consciousness, nor in the capacity to define the program. What is determining can only be the dialectical function within the workers' program, within the workers' power, subjectively and tactically to break the fundamental hinges of the capitalist management of the extinction of value, and therefore to be confronted directly with the motivations and articulations of command. Yet despite the reductiveness of this concept, this is the only figure of the organization of the mass vanguard and its distinctiveness in the organization of power and party that corresponds to the specificity of the present working-class political composition. We have already seen and sought to demonstrate this. *But we must add that if there is something irritating in this theoretical process, it is not the deconsecration of the party as a totality, but rather the necessary persistence of its function.* Although we bow to this with Leninist realism, at the same time, with Leninist enthusiasm, we know that the party is nevertheless posited on the level of institutions, of necessity. Therefore, we know that the workers' imagination, while it accepts and insists upon the function, thinks ahead to the phase in which—along with the state and the slavery of work—the party too will be extinguished. Every step forward on this terrain, every direct reassumption of the functions of power on the part of the working class as such, is a step forward in Leninist terms. It is a verification of both *What Is To Be Done?* and *The State and Revolution*.

In order to avoid a harmful resurgence of dogma in working-class thought, *we must insistently reassert the historicity of the concept of the party.* The foundation of the historicity of the party concept is situated in its reference to the category of working-class political composition, when this category is defined in such a way as to allow a correct use of the dialectical method. And Marx himself offers us the set of concepts—that almost constitute a network—with which class composition can be described in a way that directly connects the political dimension to it. This network of concepts defines *class composition:* (1) *with reference to the form of the labor process* and thus in relation to the form of cooperation; (2) *with reference to the contents of the labor process* and thus in relation to the dimensions of the working day, to its subdivision into a part belonging to necessary labor and a part comprising surplus-value; (3) *with reference to the objective level of needs*, historically growing and determined in the historical structure of the wage; (4) *with reference to the level of struggles and organization* that the working class experiences in different phases.

For each historical moment, therefore, we can define the composition of the working class by taking into account these dimensions. So far they have been purely methodological indications, but we saw in the preceding paragraphs how valid and effective these indications are in the definition of the current class composition. However, the problem here is completely different. In fact, it is not a matter of going back over the current definition of working-class composition, but rather of showing how, *in different phases and times, the structure of the working class has turned toward a figure of the party that is itself different and specifically correlated to such a composition. In the second place, it is a matter of showing how the procession of the forms of the workers' party tends increasingly to co-opt the party into the class,* how it tends to squeeze the function of power and that of the party into the concept of class. The party therefore is not merely a historical concept; it is a concept and a reality that is historically and tendentially subordinated [*sottoposti*] to the movement of the working class as such.

In the first place, then, we should ask ourselves whether at this point *a historical typology of the forms of organization* of the working class, in relation to different political compositions, is possible. Surely it is, even though this is not the place to trace the entire trajectory of the figures of the party. It will be sufficient to confirm by means of a few examples how different forms of the party, of mass organisms and proletarian weaponry, must correspond to different phases of the subsumption of labor under capital.

It is beyond doubt that the central hegemonic moment of the traditional figure of the party corresponds to the transition from the phase of formal subsumption to the phase of real subsumption of labor under capital. Here, the process of unification of the social conditions of production is intermittent and interrupted. The extraction of surplus-value takes place by the intensification, uneven in its development, of its relative dimension, but always in a manner conditioned by the persistence of extremely significant class stratifications. Here the professional worker as subject of struggle is the motive force of the passage—both positively (that is, by ceding invention-power to the bosses) and negatively (that is, by imposing a restructuring that encompasses him)—from manufacture to generalized large-scale industry. The traditional figure of the party is founded on this worker. Under the professional worker's control, that figure mediates the passage to large-scale industry. Little by little it drags all the other proletarian strata into capitalist development by means of alliances that extend its base over the production of capital. The traditional figure of the party gains its independence thanks to the lucid consciousness of its project; it possesses the point of view that recomposes the class from above, and it pulls the different class stratifications through various stages of composition, ultimately to socialism, that is, to the recomposition of work and its self-management. Both the mass struggle to reclaim rights conducted by special organisms and the offensive struggle conducted by the red army (with its generals and officials) are naturally situated within the hegemony of the party and its guidance. The attack on work that the working class has always unleashed is organized and systematized within the framework of a work discipline that—from the party to the mass organism to the red army—the professional worker imposes as an image of himself. The law of value is, then as always, a capitalist mystification that is nevertheless imposed on the revolutionary movement as a necessary habit—as form of organization, the content of its program, and the criterion of selection of command. This form of party organization— within which the greater or lesser accent on the centralized moment is absolutely secondary (the different positions depend more on the strength of the enemy than on that of the class)—is hegemonic throughout the period that goes from the Commune to the Great Depression of 1929.

But what about before, and after? What was the form of the party in the period that bore witness to the workers' offensive against the unlimited working day, that period that concluded with the Communards storming heaven? What is the form of party organization in all the passages, in the different moments of struggle the proletariat has experienced? What was the correlative form of armed struggle? We genuinely need a complete typology of the forms of worker organization, because it is both a product and a mirror of the modifications of class composition. What is certain is the fact that the tendentious relativity of the concept and practice of the party is a given. It is not revisionist to acknowledge this, but it would be revisionist not to.

*The centralized socialist party of the qualified worker comes to an end with the Depression of 1929.* Rather, it comes to an end in the consciousness and practice of the masses, but it survives as an element of repression and democratic reconciliation. But within the dramatic solution of continuity that is imposed upon the theory of the party, and within the horrible impoverishment of the subjective composition of the working class, the class movement nevertheless begins little by little to reconstruct itself and develop a new party practice. Class vanguards identify themselves at the mass level. They discover the use of the wage as a term of passage and subsequent identification between the struggle to reclaim rights and the political struggle.

In place of centralization they substitute circulation, mobility, the inexhaustibility of wage objectives, guerrilla warfare in the factories and the streets. All of this is born of and bases itself on the workers' new awareness both of the planned social form in which their exploitation is carried out, and of the new figure of unity that they as workers now constitute: autonomous and integrated subject, mass worker and mass vanguard. All of this demolishes the structures of capitalist power like a sledgehammer; the functioning of the law of value is carried to an extreme and the workers' strength little by little annuls the possibility of its average validity. From the Great Depression through the fifties in the US to the whole of the seventies in Western Europe (and probably also in socialist Europe), *this process of the mass worker* implacably develops.

*But it is precisely on this unitary content of the mass worker, on undifferentiated subjectivity recast within the mass levels, that today the capitalist operation of crisis and restructuring imposes itself once again.* We have seen the aspects of this operation on different occasions. By destroying the law of value, capital attempts an operation of separation and rearticulation of its command within the working class. From the capitalist point of view it is a difficult situation, because it compels the boss to put violence on the front line once again, to select it as an important moment in the arsenal of his means of organization. But this is necessary in order to prevent his margins of power and profit from being slowly, substantively, and continuously eroded by the struggles for autonomy. This is a difficult situation from the workers' viewpoint as well because *the boss imposes an articulation that must be anticipated and overthrown because the indistinct massified class subject must find inside itself a doubling of functions, of power and of party, and it must carry them through in their dialectical mediation.* The maximum simplification of the terrain of struggle, the tendential capitalist reduction of the class clash to a mere relation of force, catches the working class unprepared. But little by little this operation that penetrates the body of the working class intensifies its action. From this day forward the vanguard of the workers' party, the squadron dedicated to offense and defense against the capitalist tendency, must move forcefully against this project. But only the emergence of the articulation of the mass vanguard, organized into workers' power, will blow up the capitalist operation. Only the armed organization of the entire proletariat will win. The number-one priority is to assure this passage, to constitute these first moments of armed organization, to see workers of the party vanguard not as officers of the red army but as a function of the process of workers' power—to see them as sources, not of sermons or orders for the comrades, but of destruction against the most advanced points of the capitalist offensive. We must see workers as gatherers not of money but, instead, of open spaces for the growth of workers' power.

But there is another point to consider, and this is tied to the following question: does the development of the historical forms of party organization in their relation to the class reveal a certain logic, a certain tendentiousness? In this case as well the answer is yes. *The more the working class constitutes itself into a social individual, the more the problem of power, of its direct management, becomes an issue and a fundamental requirement for the class as such; the less that is delegated to the vanguard, the more that is granted to the party.* In the first heroic genesis of the workers' movement (1848–70), the direct management of power on the part of the workers is just an *"interruption"* in the continuity of the bosses' power. It is revolt, insurrection. In the second phase, 1870–1917, in the tradition and figure of the professional workers' party, the direct management of power is conceived as an *"alternative"* to the bosses' command—planned acceleration of development against the crisis, and socialist self-management against private irrationality. At this point mediation becomes central. The reorganization of work—socialist work—presents itself as the condition whereby the class can reunite and carry forward the communist struggle. However, once again, in the third phase that took place after 1917, the capitalist reform of the state and development modifies the structure and the possibility of mediation by 1929. The state anticipates the workers on the terrain of socialism. But for this very reason, within the planned state, working-class management of power becomes continuous within the entire society. Here the delegation of functions of representation fails because the redistribution of the social product must be direct. Consequently, the worker organization formed in the previous period becomes, if not an organization of work, then certainly an institutional moment of the social development of capital. Yet this is already the principle of the crisis of profit, because when the massification of production—that by itself can prop up the fall of the rate of profit—becomes the object of direct redistribution, without collective bargaining, for the working class, every criterion for the persistence of the system and of development disappears or is subject to the most frightening precariousness. At this point, capital is forced to react by attempting to break the mass worker, thus showing how the destruction of the law of value has made every terrain of mediation between classes vanish. But here as well, within the offensive against the mass worker, capital reveals itself to be unable to propose a superior form of enjoyment of income and of the productive recomposition of labor-power. However, if from the capitalist point of view all mediation fails, all working-class mediation in terms of a new work discipline is bound to fail as a consequence of the persistent offensive against the progressive organization of work. Unlike what happened in the previous periods when the capitalist rupture of workers' unity, of the worker body, was always—materially—a condition of restructuring, here, instead, the rupture of the body of the massified worker is merely political, its materiality merely repressive. *Here, even the workers' recomposition will be merely political. It was necessary for capital to reach the point of dissolving itself as development in order for the working class to recognize itself immediately as political power. Here the direct working-class management of power is a horizon that demands no mediations. The working class does not present itself here as a state confronting others, but as a despotic state, as a state that destroys capital completely. Working-class management of power aims at the totality of power. It is entirely and from start to finish "substitution," the refusal of every delegation, the refusal of work, in action.*

Certainly, this passage must be mediated. Workers absorb all the functions of command within the struggle. Mediation must therefore be posited in confrontation with the capitalist anticipation of the clash. On this terrain, the organization of the mass vanguard specifies its party function, a party function that has been totally subordinated to the project of direct management of power, of the destruction of capital and work. Therefore the party function is the organization of struggle of the mass vanguard, of workers' power.

It is important to insist and to continue to insist on these concepts, because too often this tendentiousness in the relation between class and party is not acknowledged. Too often, in defending the traditional concept of the party, we forget that the party is always an institution, that the institution mediates the class struggle, and that the mediation of the class struggle is a necessity for capital. At times, historically, the party mediated as an offensive function, as an agent of development. Today, the working class no longer recognizes the possibility of this function. The party of the refusal of work can therefore be nothing but an organism of labor and struggle linked to the necessity of the clash. *The class can delegate power only to itself.*

We must downplay the polemical reference to the Leninist model of the party. What we have said so far shows how the correct use of a dialectical methodology can situate the problem of the party within the historical dimension of the determinate class composition and thereby lead to its solution. It also shows that workers' struggles tend to bring about the recuperation of the party as a class political need directly within the class. It is neither a matter of bad historicism (and after all, when has historicism ever been a good thing?) nor a matter of teleology. Like all the other tendencies that construct the class struggle, this one is born from the interweaving of worker subjectivity and capitalist necessity, born as the workers' capacity to break and to destroy even the capitalist necessity that the class had to admit into itself. The party is an aspect of this necessity. It is also dead labor—sometimes reactivated by the workers' freedom, often threatening and hostile. The working class can use it only when the class's activity dominates it. This is not the case with regard to the historical parties of the workers' movement. *The real drama of the situation consists in the fact that every continuity between these things and the new political demand of the class has been interrupted, smashed.* The process through which the historical parties of the working class have been drawn into the capitalist mechanism of labor management has gone too far for the refusal of work ever to use these institutions in any case. Conversely, the political liberation of the class as a struggle against work has gone too far for the antiquated and instrumental mediations to be used, even duplicitously! Yet even within this subjective power [*potenza*] of the refusal of work, the class senses that the lack of continuity in the party tradition is a fact that impoverishes it. But there is nothing else to be done! Purely ideological revivals will not satisfy the materiality of the class's political need! Neither will the appeals coming from different and differently developed experiences! The only route to follow is that of reconstructing the articulations of the mass proletarian vanguard: instruments of workers' power and party offensive. Directly and without nostalgia. As always when we lack the support of the past, we must look to the near future with trust, imagination, and commitment. Everything that the class is today, its power and the bosses' crisis, reassures us and pushes us forward.

### 5. HASTENING THE PASSAGE FROM WORKERS' AUTONOMY TO WORKERS' LEADERSHIP: THE WAGE AGAINST WORK, POWER AGAINST COMMAND

(a) We now come to what we initially presented as *(so-called) Leninist objections* to the very type of approach to the discussion developed so far. These objections see organization essentially as a problem of definition of the regime's weak links and identification of the margins of proletarian action. In short, it is a matter of tactics rather than of a specific analysis of working-class composition. Since we believe that the course of discussion to this point has made it clear that this alternative has no reason to exist, we are now prepared, as we were not at the start, to devote ourselves to these questions— which this time are truly Leninist.

Two of these in particular seem to be the specific problems we have to solve. *First of all*, it is a matter of verifying, within the specificity of the individual political passages of the class struggle, the validity of the general argument in terms of theoretical theses and in terms of the passage to organization. *Second*, it is a matter of reconnecting the present needs to the prospects of the revolutionary movement, to the tendency, and consequently of testing it out by forecasting the tactical pace of the movement.

We believe that today the crisis of the movement of the refusal of work, of working-class autonomy, consists essentially in the difficulties the movement faces in building political leadership for itself. Although the material movement of pressure on profit, the tension toward appropriation, and the difficulty of the struggles have not slackened in the least, the movement is not achieving significant levels of leadership, and therefore of promotion and intensification of the general conduct of the struggle. The lack of direction manifests itself in the fragmentation of the organizational moments of struggle and in the absence of a theoretical unification of the offensive. Why does this happen? Those who refer to old conceptions of the party consider this condition inevitable. They believe that the passage from the working class in struggle to the party is external, and therefore that the party must directly take up the task of guidance, substituting itself for the workers' leadership of the movement. On the basis of what we have said so far, we believe instead that we must overcome the stagnation of the organizational level of the working class by putting into operation a positive dialectic between the objective class pressure on profit and against work and an offensive action of the party vanguard, a dialectic that extols and brings to bear upon the fundamental structures of capitalist power the effects of the—perhaps fragmentary, but nevertheless real and massified—persistence of workers' power. The need for organization must pass through the interior of the class, instead of presenting itself as an ideology or function of substitution. Workers' leadership will be an effective and extraordinary hammer to demolish the articulations of capitalist command only if the workers in struggle will constitute it. *The fundamental tasks are to hasten autonomy and to bring to it the function of leadership.*

Is this possible? Won't the proclamation of these tasks be reduced instead to a mere declaration of good intentions? In order to demonstrate how effective the movement of the mass vanguard toward organizational objectives is, we have recalled the quality of the new constitution of the overall proletarian individual and the effects deriving from the capitalist articulation of command in the face of a tendential line of compression of profit. But does this suffice? Is this actual? In reality, we cannot definitively prove that this line will be successful. But a working class that stands before us strong and jealous of its prerogatives will nevertheless assure us that this is the only line that will be successful. So the problem is to successfully consider the tendency as the result of a subjective commitment that plays itself out entirely and justifiably on this terrain that it considers determinant.

In the solitude of the organizational obligation that we assume, only our theoretical awareness of the tendency pushes us forward.

Our project is to hasten autonomy from the inside, to compel it to develop leadership, to transform the existing continuity of workers' struggles in the factory and over territory into a molecular extension of the points of workers' power, their capacity for appropriation and for the construction of comprehensive frameworks. For us, this project is a commitment, a subjective bet based on the awareness of the tendency (but conversely, the tendency will be considered real only if mass subjectivity wins, and does so by moving in this direction). Therefore, if this is our commitment, it must be said that the bosses have unleashed the maximum repressive pressure on this very terrain, precisely around this passage from autonomy to workers' leadership. It can be deceptive to grasp the bosses' moves as proofs of the line, but when the bosses are pushed to the furthest limits of defense, we must admit that their action is often intelligent. Now, what is distinctive about this political moment of theirs is the fact that the bosses have given up hope of crushing autonomy. *In the Keynesian State, the rigidity of the wage toward the bottom constituted the limit of the bosses' action. In the Crisis-State, the acknowledged resistance and persistence of autonomy, that is, a sphere of power and no longer of the wage, are considered limiting. The boss is compelled to accept a sort of dualism of power that cannot be eliminated, and that at the very least imposes stagnation.* But all the boss's strength is turned against this limit. Above all, the boss moves against the translation of workers' power into an offensive force, the translation of stagnation into a total blockage of the mechanism of reproduction and the translation of the action of the workers' vanguard into revolutionary proletarian action. We have seen the *reform of the mode of production* as a way to block, to isolate autonomy and break the proletarian unity in society. But we have also seen a *reform of the state* intended not to crush autonomy (those who speak of fascisization do not understand that it is exactly the opposite that is in fact specific to our time), but rather to contain autonomy, to isolate it through an elevation of the executive and a perfecting of the administrative practice—which is itself dialectical in the most banal terms, that is, instrumental and socialist—of social control. And so, an old workers' adage suggests attacking where the boss reveals himself to be weakest. The arsenal of the working-class science of crisis supports this empirical induction. Let us proceed, therefore, on this terrain. Let us hasten the passage from autonomy to workers' leadership.

But in its crisis, capital does not work merely to block autonomy. The collapse of the law of value and its mystified reproduction in terms of command aim to separate the factory from society. Conversely, in the workers' consciousness the unity of productive labor is articulated as the project of the appropriation of overall social wealth. Is this project actual and possible? What relationship can the workers' leadership establish on this terrain? *A priori* we can only speak of our will and indicate the project— the violent obstinacy of the vanguards—of testing ourselves on this terrain. Theoretically, it is on the basis of this relationship that the class's political need becomes an organizational function. Just as the bosses, despite every mystification, turn to the factory to test the justification of their power, so does *the working class base its capacity for the revolutionary destruction of work in the factory*. But just as the bosses base their capacity to reproduce value on the isolation of the factory from the social unity of productive labor, so the working class will only be able to base the capacity to reproduce, to multiply and consequently to organize the passage from autonomous struggle to the struggle for power on this conjunction. We said in the first place that we need to hasten the passage from autonomy to workers' leadership. But *the content of the workers' leadership* (not the empirical but the substantial content, the struggle over social labor and appropriation) *is the whole social struggle, it is the insubordination of the whole proletariat*. The organizational unit that must extend itself molecularly is *the red base*, the liberated territory on which appropriation becomes a mass practice. The material content of the struggle against work—*the wage against work*— extends to the whole society. The specific form of the struggle against work—*power against command*—expands and translates itself into timetables [*scadenze*] of appropriation. *Therefore, the second fundamental task of the mass vanguard is to go from workers' leadership of autonomy to workers' leadership of the red base*. The objective and material emergence of workers' power— legible in the tendency of the rate of profit to fall—must be grasped in subjective and organizational terms. The subjective initiative is in play throughout the process in which workers' power approaches its completed organizational form. In the present situation, within the wealth of positive indices that everyday events present, the only problem is to pull the movement forward, to draw it ahead.

So much opportunism, so much nostalgia for the past, so much need for pre-established assurances flourish in the movement! But participation in the vanguard movement can be justified neither by referring to illustrious ancestors, nor to one's own—perhaps—great personal past, nor by referring to the movement's capacity to repeat what it once was. Risk, struggle, anticipation are the militant's fundamental qualities. Beyond what we do in and for the working class, nothing justifies us. Theoretical intelligence blurs and dissolves if it does not undergo the daily examination of revolutionary practice. Therefore, when in Marxian terms we relate the tendency to the will of the cadres, we are not repeating subjectivist operations. We have rooted the possible solidly in class composition. Here we have established the tasks and limits of subjective agency, in this harsh school of the materiality of the workers' interest. But today, the workers' interest is communism. It is on this terrain that subjectivity puts itself to the test.

It is here, then, that party action, that chemical—indeed explosive—reagent between autonomy, workers' leadership, and the red base, is rooted. Is this actual and possible? The problem really does exist, and in order to solve it, we must be attentive, courageous, and shrewd. Because an offensive action that at times can and must be one of red terror, or succeeds in being dialectically combined with the emergence of workers' power, runs the risk of being a personal testimony, an isolated fact. It also runs the risk of being provocative, and therefore the risk of not producing organization, when in fact *the only sign that can give positivity to a party action is precisely that: producing organization.* Now, the problem arises from the fact that the relationship between the emergence of workers' power and party action is circular: the overall workers' leadership is not given, party action functions to found the workers' leadership, but at the same time it must be motivated and given orders. Thus the problem is tactical, and often, as in this case, tactics is not a science but an art. Nor is it possible to get a better approximation by examining more closely the two functions of the mass vanguard, because in reality a series of political exigencies and technical levels prescribes a relative (but effective) separation between the action of workers' power and party action. How can we produce organization, overall organization, within this relative separation? Once again, we are compelled to trust in the extraordinary capacity of the cadre of the mass vanguard, in its subjectivity. That means moving within the separation of functions in order to produce the unity of the movement and to build workers' leadership, to centralize its action at each individual level, and to dialecticize that action among the different levels of initiative. The comrades will be able to perform this organizational miracle, and they will do so guided by the awareness of the passage that we must produce.

This leads us to examine the second issue raised at the beginning of this section: *how can we connect the current organizational themes to a perspective and to the specific temporal moments of organizational development?*

We must not delude ourselves about this. The pace of the reunification of workers' power and party organization in a mass action based on a general extension of red bases and supported by an effective homogeneity of the political insurrectional proposition cannot be predetermined. It is all in the hands of the masses. The passage from red bases to the working class in arms is a passage that defines a revolutionary phase close to the final objective of the destruction of power. But, nevertheless, we can permit ourselves to make some observations that might be useful. We can be certain that the moment has passed when the matter of insurrection could be proposed. Insurrection was a hypothesis founded on the incapacity of the Planner-State to readjust its instruments to the pressing pace of the workers' attack, and consequently on the capacity of the existing organization of the working class to put these margins of capitalist irresolution decisively into play. However, the state restructuring of capitalist power has eliminated these margins. The reordering and elevation of the structures of command will henceforth allow it to control these margins. *At this point, the insurrectional thematic shifts its focus from actuality to the process of preparing and determining itself. No margin is conceded to us any longer, and every possibility must be fought for.*

Obviously, this does not mean that capital is to be pictured as the capacity and totality of development. Rather, it means that its action must be configured as the ductility and complexity of command. This does not mean that a contradictory, at times explosive, relation between development and underdevelopment, between wealth and backwardness, cannot exist; indeed, as we have seen, the determination of this relation essentially results in the new capitalist project of command. It means, rather, that the re-emergence of this relationship will be determined now and then by capital in relation to the exigencies of command. This means that *the only possibility for the workers' attack is in terms of offense and the anticipation of the capitalist capacity to intervene on the necessary and intentional imbalances of the system, and therefore in terms of organization.* Only that which is organizationally intended by the class vanguard and constructed by it will come into existence. When we load the term "subjective" with the intensity of a social process of organization of the refusal of work, then the subjective aspect of the timetable [*scadenza*] is fully given here. From now on, every passage in the movement is organizational, every timetable [*scadenza*] is the production of organization. All the experiments conducted thus far that do not consolidate the organization on the mass level have no meaning, they cannot be repeated. Those who repeat these experiments will be reformists who always propose anew the illusion of encompassing and controlling the communist movement of the refusal of work. Let us leave this illusion, without nostalgia, to the reformists. In reality, our problem is completely different: it can be summed up in the fact that the capitalist determinations of command over development and crisis today leave no space for anything other than the offensive against the foundation itself, against the motivation of capital as such, against work and its social organization. Molecularly diffuse offense *in a first phase,* from every emergent point of workers' power; *in a second phase* the reunification of offense: after dissemination, reunification, to the extent that the organisms of workers' power and those of the party succeed in coming together, in quantitatively significant dimensions, to determine the overall command of the movement.

After the period in the sixties that gave birth to and supported autonomy, and after the period of struggles and the generalization of workers' power that took place around 1969, a third period in the action of the mass vanguard of the movement is beginning. This is a period of construction and unification of the instances of workers' power and the offensive instances of the party. It is a period of *construction of a general cycle of armed struggles for appropriation in which the entire potential of productive labor is assembled.* In this phase, an effective dialectic among the various levels of the movement aimed at workers' leadership of autonomy, aimed at leadership of the mass proletarian movement, aimed at the diffusion of red bases, aimed at a general arming of the movement is proposed. The medium-term objective of workers' action is a more advanced level of crisis, not so much in terms of profit (because, for the bosses, it could not get any worse than it already is), but rather in terms of the use that armed, massified workers can make of this crisis, in other words in terms of power. However, even if organization is our fundamental problem, this does not mean that, given the mass character of the referent we are addressing, a hundred flowers will not bloom on this same terrain of organization that is shaken by the tendency.

A very brief appendix: some in the movement defend the thesis of a process of *fascisization of the state* which they have somehow successfully urged and convinced the militant cadres to defend as well. We have already explained that, from a theoretical point of view, this thesis does not seem valid because a probable—or, if you prefer, tendential—progress of the repressive system of capital will not be able to have an impact on the existing levels of autonomy. That is, it will not be able to deny and suppress the fundamental determination of the present class composition. But this theoretical–practical line is also ruinous from the standpoint of organization and the determination of its offensive tasks. In fact, it distorts and destroys the theme of the refusal of work to the extent that it consigns the timetables [*scadenze*] of struggle to the margins of proletarian resistance. On the basis of the issue of fascisization, it is not clear why these comrades' entire stance does not compel them to repeat the political themes of reformism, namely the demand for political and constitutional space. If this is the case, then the thesis of fascisization is not only blind and powerless, but it becomes reactionary and loses sight of the scientific element to which it obscurely alludes: that is, the renewal of capitalist justification of social management by means of command. It is around this issue, instead, that the pace, the urgency and the violence of the movement must be intensified in order to organize a new, generalized armed offensive against work on the social terrain. Nor would searching for a nexus of continuity within the Official Labor Movement be a valid way to justify the thesis of fascisization and its use. This is because the present class recomposition does not accept this nexus, because the themes of appropriation and communism characterize the working class in new terms. It might seem dangerous and distressing to think that there is no continuity, but it has never been our habit to cry when acknowledging reality. It is our habit, instead, to try to change it. Conversely, given the tasks we have to face, perhaps it is necessary that there be such a solution of continuity. Nevertheless, it is our job to construct organization by extending proletarian consciousness of this novelty: that communism is our terrain of struggle, and work our enemy.

(b) The first conclusions we have reached might seem pessimistic: the fact that today, the reality of the organization of the mass vanguard is given only in the movement and in the dialectic between the organisms of workers' power and the instances of the party's offensive capacity, and that this has aroused a capitalist response that has had a profound impact on the deepest structure of the working class itself. We are compelled to move onto this terrain. The workers' spontaneity—that has offered this terrain to us—has also confined us here. Yet this should not be cause for pessimism, because to the extent that we realistically acknowledge this situation and begin to act accordingly, we also begin to overturn the necessary relation that binds us. Conversely, the dualism of the organizational functions that we set in motion is not only the reflection of the problems we must face at the level of class composition. It is at the same time a first overturning of practice, a first attempt to make organization once again an element of the transformation of class composition. This model, which has shaped our discussion of organization, can have a considerable impact—with normative efficacy—on the life and mass behavior of the class. *Today we can stake our revolutionary anxiety on this inversion of the composition–organization relation.*

Perhaps some may think that, at other moments of the overall reconstruction of the proletariat's offensive capacity, things were simpler. We do not think so, and that is the reason why we do not indulge in pessimism. In other situations, within different compositions of the working class, has the relation between party and soviet, or the relation between the mass union struggle and the general political struggle, ever been considered less problematic or less radically divided? The problem is not the intensity of the dualism, which could be extreme, but rather the possibility of surveying and taking possession of the real terms that constitute it. To escape from this situation by following old paths and by clinging to old texts is tiresome and useless.

There is something traditional in our attempt to invert the composition–organization relation, to make organization, and its first steps on the terrain of workers' power and armed struggle, the motive force of a subjective acceleration in the class's political composition. Not only the classics reassure us in this prospect. In reality, we can establish a strict parallelism here—even though from a diametrically opposite position—between our perspective and the project of capital. The overall situation is marked by a precariousness in the relations of force between classes which gives the behavior of the working class and that of capital a homogeneous tinge. Whichever side succeeds in anticipating the other will be the winner. The concentration of the capitalist offensive against the class is shaped by the will to anticipate and the need to identify political spaces in which the reproduction and social diffusion of command, and the offensive capacity which is at the base of everything, succeed in founding themselves effectively. To reach an analogous capacity of concentration of force and anticipation is a parallel necessity for the class. Concentration of force and anticipation: for both, the party is the domain of tactics and organization. There are no margins left which we can occupy and from which we can strike at our opponent. We can only constitute and organize the margins occasionally. At this point, spaces and times derive only from the capacity of the two opposing organizations.

Surely—from the viewpoint of the working class—we are terribly backward. As for capital, it has identified new terrains of control, such as the expansion policy of leading large enterprises, new continental dimensions of political initiative and repression, the determination—at this continental level and within the dimensions of the large multinational enterprise—of new imbalances, the repressive unification of monetary policy, the restructuring of executive, governmental and planning tools. But small class initiatives can still grasp—are still grasping—this initiative of capitalist anticipation as it takes shape. The uninterrupted movement of the workers' offensive, even when merely on the plane of autonomy, and the first symptoms of a higher level of workers' initiative impede the constitution of the new foundation of capital's command. Unfamiliarity with the levels that restructuring and counteroffensive involve gives rise to capitalist uncertainty, which is continuously transformed into the precariousness of control. So does dissatisfaction with the lack of a new justification for exploitation that is not materially based on the development of profit. But in reality, the capitalist reproduction of control will not succeed in establishing itself so long as the workers' reproduction of offensive capacity does not cease. Within this precariousness of the relations of force, the working class can establish the first organizational spaces on the new terrain. In the midst of this alternation of forces, the first red worker and proletarian bases must arise and flourish.

But let us return to the impression of inconclusiveness that this type of proposal gives. It is not enough to respond that this inconclusiveness is just an initial phase, that nevertheless it allows a first political proposal—the organization of red bases—and consequently a first attempt at inversion between the necessity of composition and a program of organization to be made. Conversely—from the point of view of tactics—even the bosses are stuck on this precarious terrain, and therefore this makes the first organizational steps realistic. The mythology of the party, "the Machiavelli of the working class,"[42] and so forth are opposed to these first conclusions. Thus we can say that this inconclusiveness that is forced upon us, in spite of its limitations, alludes to the party, to the organization that the working class needs for the revolution, in a better and more significant way than any allusion to Machiavelli, Moloch, Weberian bureaucratic machines or any other literary expedient ever did. The key to party fetishism lies in the supposed capacity (attributed to the party) to represent the class. In today's weak organizational reality, nobody and nothing represents the class. Nor will it ever be represented. Any single organizational passage made by the class is worth more than all the more or less philologically correct, conventional representations of the hegemonic class's destiny. *Behind the party mythology lies the unexpressed conviction that the party is not only the representation, but also the substitute, the very force of the class. For us it is the opposite: the force of the class is the direct assumption of power and the destruction of every separate function.* The discussion of what is to be done is uncertain and inconclusive: of course, but these are things that the working class is doing. When have you ever seen the impulse of workers' struggles hold up for decades, reproduce itself socially, constitute itself in organisms of power, and verge upon the level of armed struggle? Today, all of this represents the threshold on which the first conscious attempts at generalization, at inversion of the relation between class composition and revolutionary organization, take shape. It might not be much, yet the bosses still tremble. It might not be much, yet it is in the main line of proletarian struggle: to appropriate everything, but first of all *to appropriate its own organization.*

From this point of view the very first organizational proposals that are emerging—like *the red bases of workers' and proletarian power and the red brigades of the workers' and proletarian offensive*—must submit to examination by the workers' analysis and the use of dialectics in the theory of organization. The fundamental problem is to construct these organizational instances without fetishizing the organizational proposal. To construct without fetishism means to prevent the organizational formula from being considered definitive. Yet it must necessarily be constructed. This organizational formula must be played out over the whole range of possibilities of organization and line. It must be seen as the passage to a general level of organization. Generally speaking, even the most correct organizational formulas can be shattered and recuperated by the initiative of capital and reformism if they impose themselves too insistently. This particular danger is multiplied today by the capitalist initiative that, as we have seen, stakes everything on the terrain of command and organization. Capital and the workers are equally attentive to the genesis of the forms of organization on the direct terrain of class struggle. Here, time and again, everything is predisposed toward recuperation. Recuperation always takes place when we lack the capacity to push the terrain of conflict, the organizational formula, forward. There are no moments of rest or reflux in the class struggle; there is no trench warfare—only opportunists preach that. Just as there are no talmudic formulae or eternal organizational verities. For example, free Derry becomes an organization in the struggle, but when capital counterattacks, it maintains itself as a workers' organization only if it transmits its destructive potential to the automobile factories in Liverpool or the shipyards in Glasgow. By merely persisting in itself, Londonderry becomes a ghetto; worse, it is compelled to offer itself again as insurrection, as an act that aims to be conclusive but only begins and then fails, thus ultimately as subjective despair.

Who will keep the process of organization continuously open? Who will insist that all fetishism be regularly burned away and that the process of organizational reproduction be carried out with the necessity and force of a process of accumulation? We are once again back to the central issue of class relation that concerns us: that is, the relation between organisms of workers' power and offensive instances. The fundamental task seems to be to keep this relation open, to deepen it, to make its growth implacable and to rationalize it. This is the essential commitment of the mass vanguard.

The problem thus posed is no more difficult than the one that is posed within the greatest organizational experiments of the workers' movement in its offensive phase—not more difficult, just different. The Bolsheviks solved the problem of the soviets by making them their own. Conversely, the IWW solved the problem of the workers' mobility and the circulation of millions of workers throughout the territory by mingling with them. The former represented the necessary centralization of the workers' initiative in a situation of class non-homogeneity and in light of the need to oppose autocracy, while the latter represented the opportunity to twist capital's fundamental weapon, mobility, territorial and racial division, into a highly integrated society, that is, into an instrument of the workers' recomposition. The work of the IWW was no less profound than that of the Bolsheviks, and it is doubtful that their defeat was worse than that of the Russian workers. Both, however, made class composition the first term of an organizational inversion, of offense. Our problem is no different with regard to the formal modalities of the relation between composition and organization (in this we follow and renew Marx's and Lenin's teaching). Our problem is different, rather, because of the type of class relation with which we must contend, and because of the possibilities that are offered to revolutionary organization today.

Today, capitalist command takes the form of autocracy and the contents of mobility and division. Today, capitalist action is motivated by surplus-value when faced with the collapse of the historical barrier of value. The capitalist state is the unity of opposites against the working class: development and crisis, wealth and its destruction, dictatorship and pluralism. Worker organization must reckon with all of that, just as the Bolsheviks did against the state and the IWW in a situation of working-class mobility. Again, like the Bolsheviks, worker organization has to attack "from above," from working-class positions where the mystification of valorization continues to be proposed, and like the IWW it must remain within the extraordinary unity of productive labor and promote instances of liberation. In these years of extraordinary struggle, when throughout the European and American, democratic and socialist metropolitan terrain, the workers and the proletariat have once again discovered mass insubordination, the experiments we have undertaken make it possible today to look realistically upon the incredible task ahead of us.

*Our task is to destroy in order to construct workers' power, to arm ourselves in order to lay the foundations of mass appropriation, to attack in order to stabilize the powerful development of the mass worker as possessor and manager of all social wealth, to make the capitalist destruction of value, against development, into the key to the passage to communism.*

Little by little, the alternatives and ambiguities of the theory of organization find their foundation at the characteristic level of the working class. Indeed, *everything depends on us, here where the working class is strongest.* We are going to set up an organization for *the dictatorship of the proletariat,* whose content will be not merely *the extinction of the state,* but also the *destruction of work.* Today there are comrades (who claim the titles of militants and leaders) who cry over the fortunes of the movement, who fall back to anti-fascist positions. We are moving onto the terrain of the most terrible precariousness and capitalist violence in the management of power, yet there are people within the movement and intellectuals organically bound to the masses who shrink back in fear when they are faced with the massified use of violence! Enough of these lackeys, enough of these scabs! Our difficulties, the inconclusiveness of the organizational program, do not arise from the bosses' strength, but from the strength of the working class, from the fact that here, today, we are truly struggling for communism. What we have said so far might not be sufficient, but it goes well beyond any reminiscence; it is at the forefront of the awareness that is leading the mass vanguard. When the terrain of reformism is eliminated, when the terrain of tactics itself becomes not a space for craftiness and the art of organization but instead its patient construction, then in all probability to approach the solution to the problem of organization is already to carry out the revolution.

Worker's party against work: we have already begun to prove this slogan right. But at this point we can also say, following Marx, *party "of the workers" against work*. In its collective practice, the working class does not annul the individuals that constitute it, but instead it exalts them. They emerge from the struggle enriched and liberated. Communism is the workers' dictatorship against work, which is intended to liberate individuals from work. And today, in the midst of the path toward reconstructing communist organization, we need to conscript individuals, militants who choose to follow the task we are proposing to the end: a conscription always within the working class and the proletariat, whose members are able to arm themselves and to manage the instances of power, and above all to resolve in and through themselves the dramatic alternatives that the organizational situation presents. We have no doubts that this will happen. Perhaps for the first time, today, aside from utopianism and those extraordinary moments of enthusiasm that are insurrection, the objective that the class proposes—in its intensity and totality—once again includes the needs of individuals as well. *Liberation is not something we must expect from communism.* Liberation can grow, develop, and take place within the process of struggles, within the instances of workers' power, as the form and result of its existence. The reuniting of instances of liberation and communism is characteristic of the high level at which the present recomposition of the working class in struggle is organized. The new needs of the most recent generations of the working class are needs of liberation. *There is nothing more beautiful and more rich than success in situating the immediate needs of individuals within the political needs of the class.* The continuity of organization, its growth, the overcoming of the internal dualism that still characterizes it today will also be guaranteed by the capacity to carry out the training of the conscripted militant cadres who see their work repaid in the revolutionary satisfaction of needs for liberation, including individual ones. This is not utopianism. It is, instead, the opportunity for organization to situate itself on these levels of the emergence of need and to learn to use them in the struggle, to understand how the growth of organization is the growth of the satisfaction of the need for liberation.

But of course we are not relying solely on a call for a new conscription of cadres and for their capacity to mediate the organizational dualisms of this phase. To limit our reading only to this and not to consider what we have been saying all along means to read the appendix and leave out the main point. In recognizing the dualisms and difficulties that the process of reorganization faces, we did nothing but track down the new terrain on which the struggle must be based that is to be found in the class's political need. But the focus of the discussion is certainly not the call—however important it may be—for a new conscription of cadres that we see coming out of the factories armed with the political need for organization. The focus of the discussion is the *material necessity of a new cycle of struggles* that are all now rooted in the revolutionary terrain. Here it is no longer a question of the program— the program and the slogans are immediately given by the class. Here it is no longer a question of external leadership—the class promotes the organization of offensive nuclei. Instead, what only organization can give us is the overall reunification of the movement, and an overall determination of offensive timetables [*scadenze*] that can only be organizational.

The illusions of a heroic period of spontaneous struggles are finished. The time when small groups, with faith in the working class, determined the timetables [*scadenze*] and interpreted the results is over. The wealth of experiences that these groups had must be brought back into the battle for organization within the working class, in preparation for a new cycle of unified struggles of the proletariat against the state, under the leadership and the promotion of the workers of the large factories. We have some building blocks of the new organization: it is a matter of bringing the organisms of workers' power into the offensive on the terrain of appropriation and of bringing the party organisms into the direct offensive against the institutions of command. But their fundamental task is to confirm all of this: unification is a qualitative leap, the working class in arms and communism in action. This is what we are fighting for: the extinction of the state and the destruction of work—the complete subversion of the present state of things.

### Notes

1.  Roman Rosdolsky, *The Making of Marx's Capital* Volume 2, London: Pluto, 1989, p. 382, n. 32, translation by Pete Burgess slightly modified.

2.  Cf. the editors' notes by Lucio Colletti and C. Napoleoni in *Il futuro del capitalismo: Crollo o sviluppo?*, Bari: Laterza, 1970, particularly pp. 113–15.

3. The analysis of one of the most notable commentators on this Marxian theme, C. Napoleoni, goes in this direction: see *Smith, Ricardo, Marx*, Oxford: Blackwell, 1975, chapter 5. On Napoleoni's interpretation of Marxism, see A. Ginzburg, "Dal capitalismo borghese al capitalismo proletario," in *Quaderni Piacentini* anno X, no. 44–45, ottobre 1971, pp. 2–46.

4. Cf. Negri, "Marx on Cycle and Crisis," in *Revolution Retrieved,* London: Red Notes, 1988, pp. 47–90.

5. Marx, *The Eighteenth Brumaire of Louis Bonaparte*, in David Fernbach, editor, *Surveys from Exile: Political Writings*, vol. 2, New York: Penguin, 1973, p. 237.

6. The so-called "epistemological break [*cesura*]" usually traced in Marx by structuralist Marxists consists in extending the understanding of the revolutionary subject. It marks a passage from the humanistic definition of the revolutionary subject as abstract genera to its determination as material, determinate negation that influences and modifies its own existence as it develops. In Marx's thought the passage from youth to maturity certainly represents a transformation of his theoretical horizon (and the moments of this transformation are more or less those that Althusser indicates). However, this passage is not a leap. Historical materialism and the dialectical demand for organization take into consideration, indeed they study in depth the significance and importance of the historical "proletarian" subject. Far from ending up in a "process without a subject," the evolution of Marx's thought instead closely follows the organizational reality of the revolutionary subject. The true result of the critique of political economy is always necessarily this subjective anchoring. "When we consider bourgeois society in the long view and as a whole, then the final result of the process of social production always appears as the society itself, i.e. the human being itself in its social relations. Everything that has a fixed form, such as the product etc., appears as merely a moment, a vanishing moment, in this movement. The direct production process itself here appears only as a moment. The conditions and objectifications of the process are themselves equally moments of it, and its only subjects are the individuals, but individuals in mutual relationships, which they equally reproduce and produce anew. The constant process of their own movement, in which they renew themselves even as they renew the world of wealth they create" (*Grundrisse* 712). Having said that, having stressed Marx's collective humanism (and both humanism and collectivism are equally important terms) against the structuralists, it remains to be said that their experience must nevertheless be drawn upon in its demand to struggle against the reformist subjectivism of the Stalinist tradition (in Italy, Della Volpe's school plays such a role) and above all as a methodology which aims to discover the specificity of roles and spaces of political action. But when these legitimate demands are put into play outside the incidence and presence of working-class subjectivity, they are reduced once again—this damned Minervan philosophy!—to an apology for mere fact (and in the case of a nascent Italian

structuralism—Luporini, Badaloni, Vacca, De Giovanni—they are reduced once again to an apology for the same old Togliattian opportunism). [TN: Galvano Della Volpe (1895–1968) was a neo-Kantian Marxist philosopher who taught at the University of Messina, where Lucio Colletti was his student; he is best known for his books *Logic as a Positive Science* (originally published 1950) and *Critique of Taste* (originally published 1960). Cesare Luporini, Nicola Badaloni, Giuseppe Vacca and Biagio de Giovanni were PCI-affiliated philosophers and historians influenced by Althusserian structuralism; the onetime existentialist Luporini in particular collaborated with Etienne Balibar on the book *Marx et sa critique de la politique*, Paris: Maspero, 1979.

7. Lenin defines this category in his writings of the 1890s, above all in *Who Are the Friends of the People* and *The Development of Capitalism in Russia*.

8. In particular, see C. Luporini's important essay, "Marx secondo Marx," in *Critica Marxista*, vol. 10, nos. 2–3, March–June 1972, pp. 48–118 and pp. 291–95. Even though the internal rigor of this essay distinguishes it from the general tone of the discussion developed in various interventions in the preceding issues of the same journal, it is valuable inasmuch as it confirms how radically insufficient the revisionist approach to the Leninist category is.

9. In the Italian translation, B. Maffi prefers to use the Italian term "*sottomissione*" (submission) instead of "*sussunzione*" (subsumption) to render the German word *Subsumption*. In the note on pp. 51–52 Maffi argues that it was a matter of making the choice in favor of a term that does not have mere conceptual consistency. We don't think that this argument holds up. The term "*sottomissione*" (submission) is every bit as conceptual as the word "*sussunzione*" (subsumption). Besides, it makes the dialectical reality of the passage disappear from view.

10. Marx, "Results of the Immediate Process of Production," included as an appendix to *Capital* Volume 1, New York: Penguin, 1976, pp. 1034–35, translated by Ben Fowkes.

11. Marx, "Results," pp. 1052–53.

12. Marx, "Results," p. 1053.

13. The first fundamental law expresses profit as a proportion smaller than the total amount of surplus-value: cf. *Grundrisse*, p. 762.

14. Here we follow the *Grundrisse*'s pages too (401–23). Rosdolsky rightly points out that, unlike Book II of *Capital*, "the section of the *Rough Draft* which deals with the circulation process of capital opens with an excursus, which, strictly interpreted, goes beyond the limits of the abstract analysis of the process of circulation and the new characteristic forms of capital which arise there. However, this section should be regarded as a welcome complement to the analysis" to the extent that circulation is directly related to the capital process and to the relations that it includes (Rosdolsky, p. 317).

15. In this antithesis Marx sees the basis of the crisis of overproduction (*Grundrisse*

410–12, 415 and following, 423 and following). In the following section we will see how this consideration has become outdated.

16. "Our duty is to have only one God, to worship only one God, that is, monetary stability. This is true, but it is also true that these propositions become increasingly inconsistent when behind them there develops an unemployment rate that society does not accept. And this is a bond that even the priests of monetary stability must respect ...": G. Carli, "Intervento a un'assemblea del Forex Club italiano," in *Mondo economico*, no. 44, 4 novembre 1972, p. 41.

17. TN: Guido Carli (1914–1993) was a director of the International Monetary Fund, Governor of the Bank of Italy from 1960 to 1975, and president of the industrial employers' group Confindustria from 1976 to 1980.

18. An excellent description of this capitalist situation can be found in Paolo Carpignano, "Note su classe operaia e capitale in America negli anni Sessanta," in *Crisi e organizzazione operaia*, Milan: Feltrinelli, 1974.

19. Marx, *Capital* Volume 3, New York: Penguin, 1981, pp. 126–27, translated by David Fernbach.

20. Marx, *Capital* Volume 3, p. 257.

21. Marx, *Capital* Volume 3, p. 273.

22. Marx, *Capital* Volume 3, p. 274.

23. Marx, *Capital* Volume 3, p. 139.

24. Marx, letter to Engels of 16 January 1858 in Marx & Engels, *Collected Works*, vol. 40, New York: International Publishers, 1983, p. 249.

25. Cf. *Crisis of the Planner-State: Communism and Revolutionary Organization* in this volume.

26. See a good documentary account of the overall situation in G. Carli, "Relazione alla giornata del risparmio," in *Mondo Economico*, no. 47, *rapporto mese*, n. 2, novembre 1972, pp. 27 and following.

27. In particular, "Results," pp. 1038–49.

28. Marx, "Results," p. 1038.

29. Marx, "Results," p. 1041.

30. Marx, "Results," p. 1042.

31. Marx, "Results," pp. 1039–40, translation slightly modified.

32. Marx, "Results," p. 1053.

33. For an in-depth study of some points that are only summarized here, see Appendix I at the end of the version of this pamphlet contained in *Crisi e organizzazione operaia*, pp. 161–65 [English translation: "Reformism and Restructuration: Terrorism of the State as Factory Command" in *Working-Class Autonomy and the Crisis,* London: Red Notes, 1979, pp. 33–37].

34. Lenin, *Selected Works*, vol. 1, New York: International Publishers, 1967, p. 419, translation modified.

35. Lenin, *Selected Works*, vol. 2, New York: International Publishers, 1967, p. 345.

36. Rosdolsky, pp. 293 and following.

37. Once more, see the chapter on the counter-tendency to the tendency of the rate of profit to fall: *Capital* Volume 3, part 3.

38. Thus writes Rosa Luxemburg, *Ausgewählte Reden und Schiften*, Berlin, 1951, vol. 1, pp. 719–20 (cited by Roman Rosdolsky, p. 295).

39. TN: The "new trend" probably refers to the emerging notion of a specifically "Italian road to socialism," separate from the Moscow line, that would soon lead to the project of the Historic Compromise and ultimately to Eurocommunism.

40. We believe that we have found the most explicit and clearest definition of this program in Rossana Rossanda's article, "Note sul rapporto riforme–rivoluzione nell'elaborazione del PCI," in *Critica Marxista*, vol. 1, no. 2, March–April 1963, pp. 19–21.

41. More precisely, we are referring to the American theoretical *Narodniks*: Sweezy, Baran, and Gillman [TN: The original Narodniks were members of a Russian populist movement whose opposition to capitalism was predicated on a preference for the peasantry over the industrial working class as the privileged agent of socialist revolution; both Marx and Lenin criticized the movement but also acknowledged its organizational value. Joseph Gillman's empirical studies of US profit rates led him to question the general validity of Marx's law of the falling rate of profit; Paul Sweezy (1910–2004) and Paul Baran (1910–1964) later developed a revisionist theory of monopoly capitalism that dispensed with the law of the falling rate of profit and consequently displaced the industrial working class from its leading role in the struggle against capital.].

42. TN: Negri is alluding to Gramsci's "Brief Notes on Machiavelli's Politics," an examination of Machiavelli's *Prince* in which Gramsci asserts that "The modern prince, the myth-prince, cannot be a real person, a concrete individual. It can only be an organism, a complex element of society in which a collective will, which has already been recognized and has to some extent asserted itself in action, begins to take concrete form. History has already provided this organism, and it is the political party—the first cell in which there come together germs of a collective will tending to become universal and total" (Gramsci, *Selections from the Prison Notebooks*, edited and translated by Quintin Hoare and Geoffrey Nowell Smith [New York: International Publishers, 1971], p. 129).

# III

# Proletarians and the State: Toward a Discussion of Workers' Autonomy and the Historic Compromise (1975)

*Translated by Timothy S. Murphy*

## PREFACE TO THE SECOND EDITION

The publication of this second edition of *Proletarians and the State* a few months after the appearance of the first gives me an opportunity to insert some remarks in response to the reception that the theses set forth here have received.

During these past months, and even more so in the busy year that separates this reprinting from the first composition of the pamphlet, the issues of political debate have changed profoundly: what was once merely anticipated has now become actual. The "Compromise," with its funereal characteristics of "inevitability," has arrived, and the struggle against the crisis and against the workers who "brought it about" is unanimously under way in the realm of the autonomy of the political. From Amendola to Carli,[1] the language is no different. It is all the fault of the workers who have not "sacrificed" themselves, so that today they are "privileged," in relation not only to several million "unemployed" but also to several million more "Balkanized workers"[2] who infest Italy—they will have to pay for their privilege. In short, it has been "discovered" that there is an incurable contradiction between the masses' aspirations (which are more American than European) to consume on a mass scale, aspirations that are present in various forms on the labor market as well as on the goods market, and the productive capacity (or will?) of Italian (and multinational?) capital. The workers in the large factories wanted too much cash, got it, and in return the "ingrates" have worked even less. Not content with that, they have induced their children, parents, friends, and comrades to adopt their levels of consumption. The "productive base" (the boss) has not gone along with this. Instead of responding to this demand for labor and consumption, the capitalists have either hidden themselves in the "black" economy or fled abroad. Hence the crisis and the necessity for a redevelopment that will lower the wages of workers in the large factories and thereby permit an increase in accumulation and a reorganization of the productive base that is adapted, in terms of capitalist profitability, to domination over diffuse labor. Workers, proletarians, sacrifice yourselves!

The economists and politicians who have made this argument certainly don't suspect that they are expressing the highest praise for the Italian working class. That very same praise fills this entire pamphlet, which describes the effects of the mass workers' struggle. Through this struggle, the overall hegemony of the mass workers' needs over the entire proletariat has successfully been established, as has the recomposition of the working class as a social class. There is nothing but contradiction, as the reformist Fuà[3] puts it, between the class's "aspirations" and the "productive capacity" of the system! At this point, the antagonism lies between the new figure of the productive forces and the given relations of production: an old contradiction filled with new contents.

*Proletarians and the State* traces the formation of this antagonism that is universally recognized today, and against the bosses' project of economic redevelopment, against the subordinate and crumbling proposition of the Historic Compromise, it proposes a commitment to the struggle and to the "political" redevelopment of the workers' movement. Hence the perfect contemporaneity of the argument and the intact, unchanged viability of the pamphlet. Hence the possibility of some remarks in response to the critical judgments more or less publicly raised within the movement.

The first criticism is barely worth examining: it insists on the impossibility of proposing the substitution of the term "socialized worker [*operaio sociale*]" for the term "mass worker [*operaio-massa*]." From the point of view of the determinate analysis, it seems to me that there is nothing scandalous in this substitution and that the quantity of data in support of it is impressive. I recall as well that as far back as 1969, during a seminar in Padua, Bruno Trentin[4] had reminded me (who was receptive to the idea) and some other critics (who were obviously recalcitrant) of the importance of this modification that was already foreseeable even then. The analysis of the development of "class composition" in the highly developed countries (*which tends entirely in this direction*), on the other hand, should be well known to the cultists of the concept. Nevertheless, critics of this sort have a rather tiresome and unfortunate attitude that must be rejected more forcefully than the simple exhibition of the facts will permit. Indeed, what is the use of denying the evidence of the social expansion of rebellious forms of worker behavior if not for the purpose of predicting the long march through the institutions or with the (minority) goal of engaging in a relationship of mere ideological influence with the proletariat? The Leninist taste for the insurrectionary hypothesis, that is, the analysis of the tendency from the workers' point of view, is dead at this point, and the repression of all that is new becomes masochistic.

There is a second criticism of this pamphlet, one that it is simply slanderous. Nevertheless, it is worth taking the trouble to linger over it because it exemplifies a method and it is characteristic of intellectual currents that are active today within the Official Labor Movement. This criticism turns on my assertion that the *structural change* in class composition necessarily involves *qualitative characteristics*. That assertion spoke of the *tendency* toward self-configuration of a new *subject*, of a new *quality* of *needs*, of the emergence of *new struggles*, and of the workers' will to *self-management of the struggle*—but stopped short of a *metaphysics* of a new epiphany of being, stopped short of hawking cheap pretexts on the working class's Carnival Thursday.[5] These little brothers and half-brothers of 1968 have really understood nothing. Their anti-Engelsian criticism has been so misleading that they end up once again confusing every accession of novelty and class subjectivity with idealism. Materialism is in no way a historical and political conventionalism, but rather the always new flavor of reality, not sixteenth-century mechanism but rather humanist realism, neither Gassendi nor Descartes but rather Bacon and Rabelais—as Marx, on the other hand, emphasizes several times—yet they seem cut off from this understanding. By what? Organizational formalism or lack of contact with the workers? Nietzschean negativism or nominalism à la Roscelin?[6] Revisionist disgrace is nonetheless the reward of whoever takes the role of fortune-teller. Those who did not know how to read the quality of struggle in 1968 will be even less capable of reading it in 1978, and those who have thought of the "French May" in "wage" terms will be even less capable of understanding the other months of the year: they will forever refuse to recognize "October." Therefore, for these critics, we confirm to the very end the correlation between the new class composition and the new forms of behavior, a correlation that is qualitatively decisive in defining the programmatic and organizational project.

But now we come to the third objection, which is a serious objection, but only insofar as its seriousness is no doubt attributable to the force with which it is declaimed from established positions. Thus the bosses and reformists accept Fuà's analytical remarks in order to transform them into a program of government: Luciano Barca is "grateful for them," while Alberto Ronchey recognizes Fuà's essay as playing "a decisive role."[7] So class composition, expectations, and productive forces have all changed. If the productive base has changed, then the relations of production need to expand so as better to cover—or dominate or exploit—the new proletarian forces. It is utopian to think otherwise. Concretely speaking, ladies and gentlemen, the CMP [capitalist mode of production] is immutable. In reality, as Barca admits, so far the Official Labor Movement as a whole has managed to overlook much of this operation—hence a certain air of decay lingers around the Historic Compromise. But we have high hopes that Barca is worthy of Ronchey's disillusioned futurism!

Thus this criticism does not mystify the new reality, but rather attacks its organizational version, denies its materialist valence, and professes a wholly revisionist position. This position is nevertheless worthy of respect: its effectiveness gives it dignity and—unlike the empty intellectualist ambitions of the first two criticisms—it expresses a position that is taken by a majority in the Official Labor Movement.

A new composition to dominate in redevelopment, control from "below" in the "revolution from above," the rediscovery of the economy: all this is the attitude of a majority in the Official Labor Movement. It may be a majority there, but what about here, at the class level? Here, things are different—neither repression nor conventionalism nor surrender in the face of the concrete [concretezza capitolardo] pays. Here, direct action, sabotage, and armed struggle respond to the repressive force of revisionism, to the demand for complicity, and to the criminalization of the refusal of work. This attitude is not only the start of a new organizational process, for now only the swamp awaits revisionism after years and years of frustrations in the implementation of its project, its stop and go,[8] the English disease [male inglese] of the workers' movement, while the organized alternative grows. In fact, the swamp is the terrain best adapted to proletarian guerrilla warfare.

Thus I fully endorse the theses expounded in this pamphlet, since the force of a theory lies solely in its truth, its verification in the short term, with all the intellectual, moral, and physical risks that the operation entails. But there is something else to add in this regard. A recurrent motif in this pamphlet is the polemic against the so-called "autonomy of the political." This is also a high-risk hypothesis. I believe it will be possible, over the next few months, to find more ample verification of this hypothesis than has occurred in the past few months, since its theoretical core consists precisely in hypothesizing the conditions for a workers' political alternative within the leadership of the Official Labor Movement. Like never before, the intensification of the workers' criticism directed at the revisionist leadership allows this theory to try its strength concretely and to risk proposing ways to settle the issue positively or negatively. Even if I personally consider other sorts of risk more entertaining [più divertenti altri livelli di rischio], I cannot fail to look upon what is at stake at the formal level with sympathy and friendship, provided that this game—beyond the assurances of theory—is effectively played.

But let us turn now to this little book's fundamental meaning, and to the proposition that it contains. This consists in the conviction that the crisis of the mass worker brings about an enlargement of conscious existence and proletarian revolt, and that the project of organization must be set in motion in relation to this new dimension of proletarianization. It consists, moreover, in the conviction that, in this new dimension, the proletarian demand for communism is—here and now—broader and more pressing than ever. All this can only be verified in practice, and the fact that the boss is not winning does not in any way ensure that our forces will do so. That said, nevertheless it must be added that only on this basis, the basis of the new reality presented by the new subject, can the project of workers' dictatorship as a project for the abolition of the state begin: in the current process of proletarianization, the working class in fact begins to negate itself as a class, and its power can only consist in extolling the hatred that it bears toward its adversary and toward itself at the same time. A new social foundation, a new productive force, a new revolutionary organization, proletarian dictatorship, the abolition of the state—only in that order do these steps constitute a sequence that is fundamental to the project and one that we can set in motion.

Antonio Negri
Milan, October 1976

## THESIS 1: REGARDING THE PROLETARIAT: ELEMENTS
## OF THE NEW CLASS COMPOSITION

For the past fifty years or so, in any case since the American crisis of 1937, the unfolding of contemporary capitalist crises clearly appears anomalous in comparison with Marx's description. Marx's analytical tools can still serve, but only if they are focused on the new dynamic of the crisis—focused, that is, in the sense that what presented itself in Marx as a tendency and could only be analyzed as such (whereas Marx describes the crises of his time in terms of the theory of the disproportions of the cycle) has today become actual. The definition of the disproportions of the cycle, even though it is important from a phenomenological point of view, does not go beyond the "appearance" of the development and the crisis, whereas the *actualization of the Marxian tendency* stems not only from the fact that the fall of the rate of profit has become the essential rationale of the critical conjuncture, with new and determinant effects, but also from the fact that the effects of the fall of the rate of profit are multiplied by the subjective—yet also structural and irreversible—insurgence of working-class and proletarian struggle, viewed as a revolt of the exploited mass against the rate of profit, as the initial yet definitive refusal of the proletarian class to fulfill its definition as mere labor-power.[9]

We must now tackle the capitalist project of restructuring and resolution of the crisis such as it is realized today, in order to see if the new analytical proposition holds up even when faced with the concrete maneuvers of the class enemy. We believe that this is hypothetically possible. In fact, in the capitalist countries, taken separately or together, restructuring has not had the effect of rectifying the slope of the rate of profit, even though we find ourselves quite obviously faced with an effective restructuring, and thus with a colossal operation of modification and innovation in the organic composition of capital, which has been obliged to follow a line that responds to the compensatory and critical action of the class. This means that *capital no longer succeeds in setting in motion the counter-tendencies that are capable of opposing the action of the law of the falling rate of profit*, any more than it succeeds in developing factors that are antagonistic to this law by rendering its functioning purely tendential, *even when*, faced with the growth and the quality of workers' and proletarian struggles, *its activity of restructuring is effective*.

Marx's study of the counter-tendency to the fall of the rate of profit rests essentially on the identification of the capitalist attempt to reduce, at the moment of crisis, the density of capital's organic composition. Given that the rate of profit is represented by the relationship between the rate of exploitation and the magnitude of capital (pv/C), activity antagonistic to the fall of the rate of profit tends either to increase the rate of surplus-value or to decrease constant capital: however, given that C = c + v (total capital is equal to constant capital plus variable capital) and pv/C = pv/(c + v), it tends to reduce the components in the denominator in order to protect the numerator, or rather the value of the proportion, which is the overall measure of exploitation. Marx lists a whole series of means to achieve this: increase in the level of exploitation of labor, reduction of the wage below its value, devaluation of constant capital, increase in the relative level of overpopulation, expansion of foreign trade, growth of capital through its own activity.[10] Taken separately or together, these means have all been put to work by capital in the midst of the current crisis. But this has not resulted in a rectification of the profit curve. Why? Because, despite the greater flexibility imposed on labor-power, despite the efforts aimed at the territorial disarticulation of production (at all levels: local, regional, national, multinational), despite the new mobility that capital acquires at the level of the world market, despite the effects provoked by inflation, despite all this and still other efforts, the overall rigidity of the pv/C proportion, which is the rate of profit, has not been dissolved. The antagonistic operations no longer succeed in making the actual effects of the crisis and its historical emphasis once again tendential; on the contrary, *the tendency is really actualized*. Even with inflation and all the other antagonistic operations, at best profit "stagnates."

This does not mean that the capitalist operation of restructuring is powerless. It is powerless in the sense—which must once have been proper to it—of consolidating the bosses' capacity to make class exploitation ever more ferocious and thereby to guarantee profit: here, in fact, the capitalist greed for living labor is blocked when faced with the revolt of living labor and the continuous and cyclical reproduction of struggle. But it is not powerless in its capacity to weigh heavily on the organic composition of capital, and thus on the technical composition of the class.

In his analysis of the law of the falling rate of profit, Marx always noted the innermost contradictoriness of the process. The fall of the rate of profit becomes a "law" of capital, its inescapable destiny, because the contradiction between a permanent increase in accumulated capital and a permanent decrease in living labor is inscribed within it. But what does a decrease in the proportion of living labor mean today? It does not mean a *quantitative decrease*, quite the contrary: the permanent increase, the gigantism of accumulated capital, the urgency of guaranteeing its circulation and realization, the necessity of accelerating its individual and social turnover—all these elements consequently press for a wider and wider *socialization* that conforms to the rhythm of capitalist production, they socialize in a totalitarian manner the relationship between capital and living labor, and thus they lead to a quantitative increase in the labor-power employed. But it is here that the change takes place: the *decrease* in the proportion of living labor is *qualitative*, a decrease in its value. To capital that perseveres in accumulation, there corresponds an increasingly complete socialization of living labor, and the recognition of its exclusive productive force that is henceforth present as a socialized force, in a socialized form; but the fact that living labor is present exclusively in a socialized form is at the same time the source of its overall rigidity, a decrease in its constraint to the extortion of value for accumulation, the re-emergence of struggles and ruptures of command wherever and whenever the process of socialization is extended. Qualitatively modified in this sense, capitalist restructuring is today the prisoner of the fundamental contradiction, which has taken on gigantic proportions throughout its area of determination. On the other hand, to the very extent that restructuring does not succeed in restoring the rate of profit's "correct" dimensions in a new configuration of productive forces, as a result of the workers' opposition that materializes along a front of permanent struggle, to that same extent capital is constrained in every way to press this socialization forward; that means increasing constant capital, overseeing circulation, furthering the process of socialization and thus, once again, exposing itself all the more to the workers' struggle.

The law of the falling rate of profit thus assumes a paradoxical form: on the one hand, capital is constrained to press forward the process of socialization, because it is only in this way that capitalist command over production can be maintained today, only on the condition of mystifying the role of living labor by way of this socialization, and bringing about such a high degree of organizational interpenetration between production and society that the role of command therein becomes necessary and socially legitimate. But at the same time, within this capitalist socialization, the proportion of extorted living labor and its value decreases, since the process of socialization and the process of workers' struggles (of the offensive against command) develop together. From this perspective, capital finds itself enclosed in a contradiction that grows ever more acute as the process advances. For in fact, materially speaking, command adds little or nothing on the side of profit; on the contrary, restructuring creates conditions that are increasingly favorable to the workers' revolt against profit. Every increase, every social extension of the power [*potenza*] of constant capital brings about an intensification of the potentially revolutionary unity of living labor. One can hypothesize that, even without the emergence of counter-positions of this revolutionary sort, restructuring today has the unilateral effect of revealing the contradictory situation into which capital has been driven. Instead of increasing profit, restructuring consolidates the crisis in the presence of a further massification of abstract labor, socially diffused living labor, which is predisposed to struggle.

This is not a conclusion, but rather the point of departure for Marxist investigation today. It is a matter of comprehending *what the working class is today*, faced with and within this restructuring. All the elements of analysis that we have established lead us to propose the following specific hypothesis: faced with modifications imposed and provoked—or in the process of being brought about—by restructuring, the body of the working class expands and articulates itself into the body of the social class, into the proletariat. But this expansion and articulation are not unarmed. The negativity of the capitalist response to the struggle of the mass worker finds itself overturned in the synthesis of the socialization of living labor as growing struggle and insubordination. An overwhelming hypothesis then begins to take shape: *the category of the "working class" goes into crisis, but as the proletariat it continues to produce all the effects that are proper to it on the social terrain as a whole.*

In fact, the red guiding thread of the abstraction of labor is increasingly realized. The proletarian once made himself into the worker, but now the process is inverted: the worker makes himself into the tertiary worker, the socialized worker, the proletarian worker. But this figure is *aufgehoben*,[11] because here, for this new proletariat, it is no longer exclusion from the extortion of capitalist work that is specific, but on the contrary inclusion within the totality of the productive social process and within the twists and turns of its conditions that is fundamental. We have seen the mass worker (the first massive concretization of the capitalist abstraction of labor) produce the crisis. Now we see restructuring, far from overcoming the crisis, unfolding and lengthening its shadow over the whole of society, not on its surface but in its heart, all the way into the depths of class composition, where it attempts to defend capitalist command from the activity of the mass worker and seeks at the same time to destroy the latter's composition and, in general, to mystify socially the origin and role of living labor. With quite contradictory results: for at this level of the class struggle, the capitalist devastation of the mass worker results only in the spread of the conditions of reproduction (but here, capitalist reproduction is also reproduction of the conditions of struggle) to all the living labor diffused throughout society.

*Proletariat—working class—proletarian worker.* To dissolve the concept of the working class produced by the Second International is to respond to the theoretical imperative, which is to discern the proper characteristics of a subject that results from the combined apparatus of workers' struggles and capitalist restructuring in this historical period. The struggle against work that characterizes workers' behavior in our current phase is in itself the dissolution of the capitalist effort to subjugate the whole body of the proletariat entirely within the social cage of exploitation. But today it is necessary to extend the investigation to the struggle against work, against the social mediation of abstract labor, against the state configuration (the state as collective capitalist) of the social organization of labor, and to test Marx's hypothesis regarding the proletariat on this terrain.

### THESIS 2: CAPITAL'S COMMAND AND THE NEW COMPOSITION: CONCERNING MONEY

There is one element in the capitalist point of view that deserves to be strongly emphasized. Command over the crisis can henceforth be defined only as *command in crisis*. If the blockage of profit recurs even in the face of innovation, if the modification of the organic composition of capital reproduces and massifies the "class" pressure of the proletariat at the social level, if therefore the capitalist planning of development becomes *the planning of crisis*, then these are the parameters within which the figure of command must be defined.

In Marx, this role is played by the category of money—by money as capital, not as currency. Or rather, by money insofar as it emancipates itself from the financial system so as to confront directly the material levels of the organic composition of capital and the political composition of the class, to confront production as well as the wage.

Through *money*, capital tends today to win back a force of *mediation between crisis and restructuring*, posing itself in this figure as *a selective rule that functions in the definition of command*, that is to say as *rationality and project with respect to the organic composition* and as *terrorism with respect to the political composition of the proletariat*. Here as well, therefore, a historical path is inverted: having been unfailingly defined as currency, as a calculable fetish that transcends class relations and—above and beyond that—as a political term of pacification and mediation for the (eventual) conflicts between bourgeois strata, money must be redefined as capital and therefore as the determinate function of the crisis-restructuring relationship, as a lever shifting inside the organic composition of capital, between its different parts, as a selective, indeed a rigidly selective rule adapted to command as terrorism for and over the new class composition.

Thus, when we have recourse here to the category "money," we tend to interpret it and make use of it not only as a category of mediation between the costs of production and the general value of social labor (the same goes for money as currency within the conditions of competitive capitalism), but also as a category of the material and political mediation of these elements. Whenever we say "money," we could just as well say "Keynesian State" or "Planner-State"; in fact money no longer exists outside of these determinations. But despite this, the category doesn't disappear: it persists as a category of mediation, changing its contents in order to confirm its proper function. Therefore "state-money" is substituted for "currency-money": it is thus confirmed as the mediating category of commodity exchange. Its materiality changes—in an "exogenous" manner, the apologists of bourgeois economy would say, while we would say politically—whenever the materiality of mediated elements changes. But the category of money remains fundamental, and around it all the elements of the altered situation are interwoven anew. Beyond the historical success of Keynesian techniques of control and development, the reformist work of capitalism provides us with this renewed functioning of the category "money" as a theoretical scaffolding for the new functions of the capitalist state. This is also valid in the extreme tension imposed by the change in relations of force between the two classes: this means that, in the new functioning of the category "money," mediation can submit to the redoubling of its own image and be presented either as the pure image of mediation, without object, or as pure command, as violence. Faced with the dialectically opposed pole of the workers' struggle, the objectivity of capitalist function has in itself the possibility of transforming itself into a totally subjective function—"zero development," crisis in the rate of profit, and therefore "command-money."[12]

We must be careful here: the fact that capital tolerates currency badly is an old point. Rather, the productive boss is constrained to currency by the class struggle, not by any innate predisposition: in fact, absolute surplus-value and primitive accumulation despise currency, even when they are subjected to its uncertain horizon. The phase in which finance capital predominates represents a phase of relative distortion for capitalist development. Rosa [Luxemburg] and Lenin have clearly emphasized this. In currency there is something fictive and fortuitous, something subjective and maneuverable, that capital's righteous feelings detest. In fact, from the financial phase of development onward, capital returns to the large enterprise, to self-financing, to the subordination of the wage (as a social category) to its own capacity productively (and directly) to command all the segments of its organic composition. The economic science of the bosses no longer tolerates currency: the search for value corresponds in the classics to the attempt to escape this determination, and even in Marshall—if not in the whole marginalist school—this tension is perceptible. Today it explodes. Sraffa translates the material algebra of the Menshevik Leontiev into theoretical terms[13]—not the monetary quantities but the material dimensions of the productive process: recognizing them, weighing heavily on them, commanding them after the monetary terrain of capitalist control had been swallowed up in *stagflation*—such is the fundamental task for all those able to see since at least 1937, and for everyone today.

Capital thus follows a paradoxical trajectory and undergoes a radical inversion. Posing as money in the phase of its first glorious revolution, then constrained to dominate the value-producing emergence of the working class via the dictatorship of the subjective abstraction of currency, it must today turn into money-capital—but now *aufgehoben* in its turn. That is, it must return to a transfigured role, to the extent that what money now *does* [*fare*], while it reproduces the ancient contact with production, is introduced into the new universality of monetary fetishism. Today, money as capital has the materiality of the productive relationship of early revolutionary capital *along with* the generality of the monetary function. At the same time that it once again becomes material calculation, a continual scrutiny of the organic composition, money has subsumed the universality of the monetary standard. Emblematically, this means passing from gold to oil, to energy, to a material and dynamic equivalent (that one can call whatever one wants, until the special drawing rights are authorized). This consciousness is the capitalist key to a sufficiently radical management of the crisis imposed by the working-class struggle.

Thus today, *money is the general equivalent* (it presents itself again as general equivalent and tends somehow to define the conditions for resolving the monetary crisis) *solely to the extent that it is immediately capital's organization and command*. It functions in the first sense only if it succeeds in materializing itself in the second sense. It is interesting and important to emphasize this characteristic of money, because this is the very thing that—in outline—scientifically defines the new modality of the fall of the rate of profit: the capitalist theory of money is complementary (and must be so if capitalist awareness is to be scientific) to the determination of the new characteristics of the rate of profit's trend, which constitutes the terrain that reveals the crisis.

In a word, the rate of profit falls, the counter-tendencies no longer act, but the c variable of the overall relationship (which designates constant capital in the equation for the rate of profit) is modified. We have already said it: the fact that profit stagnates does not mean that restructuring is powerless or less imposing; if the rate of profit doesn't rise, nevertheless the organic composition of capital and the political composition of the working class are affected. But if the rate of profit stagnates, whence comes the continual perfecting of c? And on what is this perfecting of capitalist intelligence, which does not give in when confronted with the fall of the rate of profit, based? A quantitative analysis does not get to the bottom of this problem; if we agree to privilege the monetary standard, our horizon will remain opaque and meaningless. Never more than in this situation has the universality of value needed to materialize itself in concrete, qualitative operations—which propose anew the particularity of money and only later the universality of its function. Only a capacity to recast value as command, only a power of selection internal to wealth and capitalist society that is developed in such a direction can permit the re-assertion of a general project at this point. The c variable improves, even in the presence of the fall of the rate of profit, solely because, within it, a new materiality of capitalist command is gathered together and organized.

How is this done? The selection is articulated on the basis of the necessity of command as well as on the radical requirement of the persistence of capital's system. It is articulated and organized, first of all, *against* the specific points of emergence of the workers' struggle and its organizational manifestations.

Taylor and Ford destroyed the professional worker of the workers' council movement by means of the selection of a corps of capitalists who extolled a new specificity of the c variable. Even in this case it was not a matter of a new accumulation, but (at least in its entire initial phase) of a selection and monopolizing of capitalist alliances and initiatives adapted to that goal. *Today, capital must destroy the mass worker of the social wage;* therefore it selects, on the basis of the new c value, a new conglomeration of will, projects, and money. It anticipates and destroys the political composition of the mass worker, and goes so far as to push the tension that it exerts to a maximum of socialization of the struggle in order to bring that struggle back into the social organization of production. In the poverty of general equivalence, it carries innovation to its highest point and seeks to define a new existence for itself that would stem from a constant capital that is unassailable by the mass worker. It accepts defiance on the social plane with the aim of anticipating the density of the workers' project and organizing its foresight into a repressive force.

Naturally, the task is difficult. The game is played out in its entirety between monetary devaluation and the extolling of money as a material, organized, and repressive function. To put it another way, it is as if the game was entirely played out between an attempt to destroy the given working class, its technical and political composition, and the project of organizing the results of that destruction. Constant capital is constructed *despite and because of* the continual fall of the rate of profit, by means of monetary devaluation as the selective weapon that coalesces the capitalist will. On the other hand, in the medium term c seeks to present itself as a new C, as the proposition of the overall organization of capital. The particularity of the operation lies exclusively in the negative movement of the capitalist project's dialectical totality.

The analysis will have to delve much further into this difficulty and attempt to untangle its forms, modes, and pacing. To this end we propose the following plans:

(a) To view in broad outline the ideal and typical characteristics of the new materialization of the "money" function (thesis 3).

(b) To describe the political determinations and contradictions that the capitalist project assumes today here in Italy (thesis 4).

(c) To consider, again abstractly, the political and institutional relations in which these new relationships arise (thesis 5).

(d) Once again to confront the crisis, restructuring and political development in the form that they take here (theses 6 and 7).

(e) From there, on the basis of the distortion and the crisis that the capitalist and reformist project encounters, to reformulate a discourse on the workers' and proletarian struggle (theses 8 and following).

The original conditions of the revolutionary process in Italy arose within this web of theoretical problems and practical expectation.

### THESIS 3:  THE ENTERPRISE AND THE TERRORISM OF SOCIAL DEMOCRACY

The commentators and politicians of the capitalist economy agree on the definition of the *characteristics of restructuring*: it is centered on the reorganization of the raw-materials market—particularly (but not exclusively) energy sources—and on an enormous innovation in the instruments and processes for the control of the circulation—and reproduction—of the factors of capital. This second objective also means automation. From the point of view of its contents, capitalist restructuring thus tends toward a seizure and reform of the world market within which the organizational power [*potenza*] and integration under the capitalist mode of production and its highest levels of organic composition are defined. From the formal point of view, this further progression of the subsumption of labor within capital requires the most complete mobility of all the elements of the organic composition, and emphasizes and exacerbates their dynamic complementarity. Automation is the scientific and operational armature of this form of subsumption. The first age of capitalism lived on tar and iron, and the maturity of its development on carbon and steel; today, oil and automation constitute the ideal type of the capitalist form and its project of reform.

Money in its dual form—capitalist equivalent of social productivity and materially organizational referent—itself submits to these materialized idealities of the process. Everything is destroyed, selected, and reconstructed according to this rhythm. The internal dialectic of capital tends on the one hand to reorder the relationship between the capitalist command over labor and the working class, in terms of the (materially transformed) adequate proportion between constant capital and variable capital; on the other hand it tries—to the extent that the dialectic between the two active elements is solidly anchored—to intensify the internal mobility of the elements so that any rigidity in the nexus is dissolved. The capitalist process imposes increasingly elevated levels of fluidity—to the point of configuring constant capital as a "form" (organization of fluidity, its calculation and control)—in a direct relation to the force and overall power [*potenza*] of the working class (which presents itself on the immediate plane as rigidity that is local, intersecting, international, etc.). Let us be clear—we are speaking in code, but this does not necessarily mean vague allusions: this Bergsonian capital is called Kissinger and company, MIT and IBM ... Above all, we call it a determinate reflection and restructuring on the basis of the uninterrupted struggle of the metropolitan workers and the anti-imperialist victory of the global proletariat. We call it a new and radical definition of money as the determinate—and always renewed—mediation of capital's inner relationship in terms of the relations of force established between itself and the proletariat: in this case *as mediation between the function of productive restructuring* (energy, automation) *and the function of political reorganization* (social democracy, terrorism).

Here our examination of the process takes a step forward: the modification of the base [*struttura*] falls within the modification of the superstructure.

(Speaking of this, now would be the time to verify a tendency defined by Marxist thought which *argues that the relationship between base and superstructure becomes increasingly organic the more the organic composition of capital intensifies*, which is to say the more complete the formal subsumption of labor within capital becomes. This amounts to saying two things: (1) a growing lack of differentiation of the two levels; (2) a sublimated, *aufgehoben*, subtle restatement of the struggle between the two classes to the point of maximum synthesis. As we will see, in this case the fundamental contradiction comes to be inscribed little by little at the level of the state. We note this tendency here in order to verify it.)

Thus the modification of the base falls within the modification of the superstructure. Consequently, the condensation of command around issues of energy control and automation is articulated hierarchically with the structure of the world market along domestic lines. Centralized organization of mediation between circulation and production, centralization of points from which the quality of money derives: in the current situation, faced with this determinate materiality of restructuring, all this signifies the fluidity of the hierarchical articulation of control, its capacity for anticipatory intervention, its terrorism against antagonistic elements to the extent that they cannot be anticipated, the provocation and destruction of the very possibility of antagonism. The reasons for this development of the superstructure are immediately obvious: the fragility of each point of the system (the efficient cause of the crisis) must be diluted in the fluidity of the totality of the system: the general axis of the legitimation of command is shifted onto the totality of the system, so its junctures, disarticulations, and secondary contradictions can only be evaluated with reference to the logic of the general consistency of the system. Conversely, capitalist anticipation of the possible contradictions is pushed to the maximum, either by the effectiveness of the capacity for control over an integrated system or by the knowledge of the disintegrative power of singular, particular ruptures of the integrated system in its totality. It becomes possible and indeed indispensable to anticipate forms of behavior that are deviant in relation to the logic of the system, and anticipatory repressive terrorism is legitimated by the expectation of the terrible incidence that defines each subversive form of behavior in its particularity. In this framework, *the old institutional categories of the enterprise and the state go into crisis, and their conceptual and effective legitimacy must be measured by new parameters of the centralization of the world market*: and it is on the basis of the new materialization of money that they count what they have in their pockets!

A new parenthesis, before we return to the definition of institutional categories, to mark several distances, namely those that separate us from the traditional concept of state monopoly capitalism[14] and from the terms that follow from and are complementary to that concept: monopolism, imperialism, dualism of development (third-worldism etc.). It is nevertheless worthwhile to emphasize strongly that these fastidiously repeated concepts have nothing to do with reality. Where do we still find a monopoly that independently determines prices and costs? Where do we still find a nation-state gripped by the will to superprofit of enterprises that have been guaranteed monopolistic privileges? Where do we still find a state whose political elite is saturated [*compenetrato*] by the will to national monopoly to the point that this determines the material constitution (legitimation, government, power politics)? Imperialism, inter-imperialist contradictions, local dualisms and controversies, etc., are terms utterly lacking in meaning. Listen: we are not contesting the designation of phenomena here, nor are we denying their importance as phenomena. It is not a problem of designation but one of definition, not a problem of name but one of substance. In sum, we touch here on the second definition of money, that is, no longer merely on the quality of mediation between production and circulation defined today, but also on its form—the form that it assumes on the world market in the universal power [*potenza*] of its sublimated role. From the highest levels of capitalist management, the multinational enterprise gathers up the passages of the dialectic of capitalist control, of the role of money, dismantling the pre-existing unities, be they economic and/or political, at the institutional level.

*The productive and/or social legitimation of institutions must therefore be examined in relation to these new parameters*—and not merely abstractly, but first and foremost materially, since this is where the unity and the fluidity of the productive process arises and the homogeneity of command is inscribed on the basis of the control of energy sources and the international mobility of labor-power, that is, on the basis of the power of response and counterattack of the struggle of metropolitan workers and the Third World proletariat. The capitalist legitimation of production and/or command means an adaptation to this frame of reference. It means that the capitalist enterprise today exists only as an entrepreneurial reality overdetermined by this validating frame of reference [*quadro di validità*], and that the mature capitalist state, insofar as it is a microcosm, reinterprets the rules, articulations, and nervous system of this macrocosm that is the centralized and hierarchized order of the world market. We could talk at length about the dialectic that is deployed between multinational enterprises and nation-states, about the crisis in the concept of sovereignty and its role, about the multiplication of separate bodies and the distinct levels of legitimacy from which their current roles and constitutions derive, but what must be said, to start with, is that the frame of reference must be completely recast, and thus brought to light according to the tendencies that we have delineated.[15]

We have thus implicitly returned to what was already defined in thesis 1. The analysis of the effects of restructuring outlined here refers back to the definition of the subject of the crisis. The direction [*senso*] of the development of capital is in general determined by the fact that it is a relationship, a dialectical, reciprocal relationship whose overdetermination is enforced by and thus depends upon the relationship of force between the two classes in struggle. *Restructuring tends to entail a capitalist use of the socialized workers' political reality and the tremendous achievement of the mass workers' struggle.* The deeper capitalist restructuring goes, the more obvious this presupposition becomes, but also the more obvious it appears that the capitalist will [*volontà*] despairs of anticipating, and in anticipating disrupting, the inevitable advance of the proletarian subject. Whoever is unable or unwilling to measure this process in practical terms is lost: here, pacing [*tempi*] is as important as knowledge and foresight. The enterprise and social-democratic terrorism must increase the interpenetration of their project before the reality of the socially proletarian worker explodes: the capitalist project must accept this form and reduce it to variable capital before the accumulation of the subversive forms of behavior that comprise it causes a new subversive emergence of the working class—a new class consciousness—to arise.

## THESIS 4: THE HYPOTHESIS OF THE HISTORIC COMPROMISE

At first sight, confronting the "Historic Compromise" from the class point of view might seem a serious regression. On the scale of the capitalist project of restructuring the relations of production, the Historic Compromise seems indeed to be a subaltern and ineffective project. In relation to the reality of the proletarian worker, the socialization of the mass worker and the need for communism that the mass struggle expresses on this terrain, to speak of the Historic Compromise seems in reality to mark a withdrawal from *history into prehistory*. As another version of the "Salerno turnabout," an internalization of the order of Yalta, a refinement of Togliatti's *Risorgimento* ideology,[16] the Historic Compromise seems to be a classic version of revisionist themes.

And there can be no doubt that it is, in large part. If national-popular ideology ever had a history, it was this. What are the avowed political goals of the Historic Compromise? The peaceful passage to socialism via an insertion of popular forces into the state, forces capable of guaranteeing a number of the fundamental objectives of productive development. This means first of all guaranteeing quantitative and qualitative control over class movements—and in this a fundamental role is assigned to the union as the transmission belt of reformism, as guard dog and veritable "state union," conditioned by the rhythms of the legitimation of planning (restructuring). The second objective consists in rationalizing the mechanisms of reproduction and distribution of labor-power by means of the planning of social institutions (local and territorial boards etc.) that attain a relentlessly growing homogeneity in the form of the Planner-State: here the role of the party as "union of the social" (and even in this case, obviously, as "state union") is fundamental. In the third place, the Historic Compromise proposes a (future and partial) redistribution of productive potential—more than just incomes [*redditi*]—within the framework of the system by preparing to offer future advantages to the public sector and the politico-economic elites who administer it (on the assumption that the state represents "all the people").

But this conception of the control of the working class in production, the reproduction of the market for labor-power and the redistribution of power is contradictory in the first place, since it takes as its object a working-class composition that is in fact anachronistic: the linearity of the socialist project refers to the professional worker and his productive logic, every dimension of which the Historic Compromise coherently adopts and re-emphasizes. But this form of worker no longer exists, nor does this possibility of program-building. "Socialism," if it were possible today, would be the inheritance of the bosses, the blessing of the social productivity of capital. In fact, socialism has been destroyed *as a possibility* of capitalist development in the latter's violent exchange with working-class struggle; it has therefore been withdrawn from the panoply of possible restructurings because of the *effectiveness* of the new extension and character of the forms of behavior, because of the assertion of the refusal of work and the recognition of the actuality of the communist alternative. On this basis, all the propositions of the Historic Compromise explode into contradictions. A guarantee of control over the movements of the class? But this control, defined in the crisis by the massified movement of the refusal of work, can only present itself in terms of repression and certainly not in terms of participation. Rationalization of the mechanisms of reproduction of labor-power? But this rationalization is, under these conditions, necessarily manipulative and repressive when it is exercised, as it must be exercised in its ultimate consequences, at the limits of a labor market that has become rigid—the employment/unemployment relationship, schooling, tertiarization, exclusion, and marginalization. As for the heart of the problem, we find ourselves faced here with another mystification: that of an independent and sovereign state, a neutral machine on which one need only lay a hand in order to command it ("after having driven out the four bad monopolists who had manipulated it earlier"). In fact, such a project of state reform, conducted in terms of a socialist use of state monopoly capitalism, forgets that at least two conditions have disappeared: on the one hand the state is organic—it is neither an accessory nor an empty receptacle—to capitalist development and its determinate disarticulations (crises, manipulations along domestic lines, control and command as conditions of profit); on the other, this interpenetration of the state and capital is not produced on the national level, but within the new dimensions of the world market. Reductive by definition and adventurist in its proposals, the ideology of the Historic Compromise in its first traditional version simultaneously mystifies the analysis of the crisis (and the subjects who define it) and the effects of the crisis (and the state-form that once again undertakes them). *It proposes the same model of the Planner-State*, the model of the workers' co-participation in the exploitation of workers and the apology for work as a proposition of socialism—the same model, we are saying, *that has been defeated by the workers' struggles in all the countries of advanced capitalism these last forty years*. From this point of view, the Historic Compromise is not a reformist project, but rather the faltering reprise and revenge of its prehistory. Consequently, in its absolute lack of reference to money and capitalist restructuring, the ideological and superstructural foundation of the politics of the Historic Compromise (the Catholic–Communist alliance and the legitimation—beyond 51 percent—of a socialist government) collapses into meaninglessness in the face of Marxist analysis.

The politics of the Historic Compromise are no less effective for all that. Alongside its first version, completely anchored in ideology, another version presents itself, one that gets passed over in silence but is even more efficacious. This version strives to present itself *as the political form of the capitalist overcoming of the crisis.* This means that, alongside the necessary repetition of social-reformist litanies, a radical spirit occasionally appears among the forces of the Historic Compromise and in the voices of its most effective managers, one that radically confronts the capitalist project without fishing for alibis or justifications, in short putting itself forward as a candidate for a direct and responsible insertion into capitalist strategy. In the first place this means, in the specificity of the Italian situation, overcoming the delays and confusions of state management of the cycle so as to pass through this phase of the crisis, shaking up and renovating the washed-out structures of the state by using every possible deterrent and rationalizing the set of control structures, but in appropriately repressive and determinate terms. This means, in the second place, bringing the Italian structure of production back up to the level of the international organization of capital by destroying the force of the Italian proletariat's struggles, and therefore the specificity of the crisis and the delays in development of our capitalist sector and its institutions, until that c begins to function again, until total capital has been reconstituted. In this way, the apologists of the Historic Compromise maintain, we will have made a long march through the institutions and put the social hegemony of the mass worker's behavior into play within and against the institutional mechanisms of the bourgeois state!

Let us leave to one side the definition of the character of the bourgeois state (so that we can come back to it later). Let us leave to the other side this curious conception of hegemony (to which we will return as well). Already this single reference to the massified behavior of workers' autonomy seriously weakens the hypothesis. A form of behavior linked to the overall rigidity of labor-power in its qualitative and quantitative elements (relative to the organization of work and the quantity of the wage) tends to be irrepressible within the political form of socialism; indeed, it is socialism's opposite, an alternative dynamically aimed at communism. Let us suppose that the Historic Compromise goes all the way, with stubborn will, in its effort to insert itself into the capitalist mechanism of restructuring. What means does it have at its disposal? Upon what class strata will it attempt to force its project?

It is beyond doubt that the sole space in which the Historic Compromise can attempt to assert itself and effectively mystify the effects of restructuring against the mass workers' struggle is the space that extends between the ideology of work and the new reality of the proletariat and the socialized worker. It reaffirms the ideology of work and puts into play the blackmail threat of employment in a professional and productivist sense. It attempts to intermingle its actions with those of the hegemonic forces of restructuring, *hastening the passage to tertiarization in terms of division*—that is, productivist professionalization and requalification—rather than in terms of proletarian unity. Here its tendency reaches a maximum. The orthodoxy of "alliances" and "leadership" and "the conquest of middle strata" has little to do with its illustrious [Gramscian] tradition: here this politics is remodeled as an intent to bear down on the unitary potential of the class, to break it up and divide up the process of political recomposition defined by restructuring.

The hypothesis of the Historic Compromise thus incorporates itself into that of capitalist restructuring according to two versions. The first, of an ideological and socialist character, is purely subordinate and completely "prehistoric": it is an old-fashioned reproposal of the laborist ideology of the Planner-State. The second, on the contrary, is a version that tends toward an adaptive mystification of the capitalist operation that is already at work. From this point of view, it functions in the immediate effects of restructuring wherever the latter acts and just as it acts, in the sense of defining a new structure of control over the movements of an overall labor-power that was becoming unified, and bases its project on an adequate requalification of constant capital. To break the potential unity of the socialized worker by isolating the factory from society and playing the latter off against the former in terms of employment, by simultaneously demanding from society levels of productivity analogous to those defined in the factory; to render the workers' struggle incommunicable and the socialized workers' struggle headless at the same time; to prevent by any means the mass workers' ongoing recognition of the identity and social generality of proletarian interests—while its characteristics are exaggerated out of all proportion by the very mechanism of the restructuring that is constrained to receive and transmute into itself the tension and rhythm of the working-class struggle: these could well be the effects of the realization of the Historic Compromise.

Whatever the prescribed passage might be, it is by means of the state and its full instrumentality that the Historic Compromise proposes its hypothesis of dividing the working class in the name of the ideology of work. And this is the issue upon which our analysis must now come to bear.

## THESIS 5: ON THE AUTONOMY OF THE POLITICAL: THE STATE TODAY

Nevertheless, let us examine this contemporary state in which so much confidence is placed.

Reformism stakes every one of its possibilities on the hypothesis—which belongs to the theory of state monopoly capitalism—that there remains in the state a pure, autonomous sphere of the political, the result of all the social-control mechanisms ascribed to the state. This is the sphere of political mediation, the mediation of command over *civil society*.

But what was civil society? It was the domain within which the repro-duction of capital was articulated with the density of bourgeois and proletarian interests that were not "immediately" reduced, or even capable of being reduced, to the rule of profit: interests derived from revenue [*rendita*] on the one side, poverty and the proletarian industrial reserve army on the other. Ideology, charitable associations, police and army, state of law versus the proletariat; banks, clubs, universities, priests, and once again the state of law versus the bourgeoisie: in civil society these were some of the institu-tions that organized the hegemony of profit. And when necessary, dictatorship—*extrema ratio*—and Bonapartism as the always lively spirit of the autonomy of the political. In its good bourgeois substance, civil society finally ended up being the site of the exclusive intermingling of revenue and profit: the other interests, in this case the proletarian ones, were not subal-tern or subordinate, but rather repressed and marginalized. The autonomy of the political was this division of mediation of the overall hegemonic bour-geois interest.

But what remains of civil society today? Profit is constrained instead to the mediation of other forms of revenue: but the latter are neither simple bourgeois revenue nor the mere existence of the proletariat in the form of indigence and employment blackmail. To the extent that the realization of profit devolves upon the state, civil society disappears. It dissolves not because the categories of revenue and unemployment disappear, but because their characterization is referred directly to the state. It dissolves because the rules of the market, even if they subsist and seem now and then to be strength-ened, can *only* exist (and this constitutes the novelty of the situation) through the defining mediation of the state. *The autonomy of the political is crushed and reduced to a pure technical fact, without any material class rationale, when the inter-mingling of other forms of social revenue with profit passes from the moment in which it found an autonomous foundation in the social to the moment characterized by state action.* This proved to be necessary in the Planner-State phase, in the face of the mass workers' offensive; it has now become a fundamental norm, to the exclusion of every alternative, in the presence of restructuring and the for-mation—already implacable and threatening to the process of restructuring—of the socialized worker, the proletarian.

The autonomy of the political: this condition of reformism loses its impor-tance with the realization of the Planner-State, and even more so with the Planner-State's maturation and reconfiguration in the course of restructur-ing. At this level of capitalist development—and the workers' struggles that determine it—civil society comes *after* the state; the autonomy of the political is thus only the ideological reproduction of a dead order. On the contrary, the reality of the state is extolled, not as the site of impossible mediations, but rather as the center of the total ascription of social action and as the moment of the predetermined characterization of this action.

As a consequence, the working-class struggle shifts to this level. *The contemporary state knows no working-class struggle that is not a struggle against the state*—against the state as boss insofar as it has had to comprise within itself the totality of modes of development and the crisis as well. The class struggle is transported inside the state. As working-class struggle, it appears as a struggle against the state. Capital identifies itself with the state: from capital's point of view, the state carries on the class struggle directly. The working class therefore recognizes in the state its direct adversary, its essential enemy. Here civil society, as the domain in which the different interests in the order of the reproduction of labor-power present themselves as intermingled, is only a product of the state's will, that is, of a kind of state-imposed resolution of the struggle between classes.

Be careful: at this level of the class struggle and the perfecting of the subordination of every other domain of conflictuality to the center of state decision, *capitalist command is marked by specific new contradictions.* Let us consider the most important of these, the ones related to the control of prices and costs in the face of a massified presence of workers' struggles, or the "fiscal" ones, that is, those characterized by the constantly growing disproportion between the means of financing and the necessity for social intervention in the form of a generalization of the guaranteed wage and in the form of an ever more broadly extended welfare regime. None of that will restore the fetish of "civil society"! "Workers' income [*rendita*]"—by this term we designate the monetary quantity distributed by the state to the working class in "civil society"—has nothing to do with bourgeois revenue; while the latter in essence implies a connection to the spontaneity of the market, workers' income is based on the maximum rigidity of the market and on the direct intervention of the state. The constant extension and diffusion of this type of income does not demonstrate the autonomy of the political, but rather the opposite: namely, that the contradiction between the relations of production and the productive forces takes shape today as an *antagonism between the state* (as overall center of ascription of command for production) and *the proletarian forces of social production. In relation to the state, this constitutes the new form of the fundamental Marxian contradiction.*

But then, once again, what is the autonomy of the political if not the illusory and vain movement between a civil society that no longer exists and a radically different state? And what space is left for reformism, when the margins

of mediation which once existed between civil society and the state have necessarily been annihilated by the unification of collective capital and its state?

Nevertheless, reformism doesn't merely demand that a space for the
autonomy of the political based in civil society should be allotted to it; it
further imagines a state that offers a possibility of "revolution from above"
as a totalizing, rational, and powerful function of political will. Let us pose
the question again: is such a condition fulfilled? No, it seems, insofar as the
overturning of the mystification of civil society opens up a terrain of
struggle in which the state fully represents the capitalist pole as a pole of
conflict. When the mediation of the class struggle shifts directly and irreversibly into the state, then the figure of the state is convulsed under the
effect of the dualism of power and tends to assume one face and one face
only of this dualism. It is still possible to speak of revolution from above,
so long as we understand that today, every reform of the state, every revolutionizing of the state is only an antagonistic function in relation to the
other pole of the real process, the one that is represented by the power of
the proletarian and working class (and this would be equally valid—as the
Chinese Revolution teaches us from afar—in the case of a proletarian
conquest of power).

Still, let us specify this reality of the contemporary state a bit further. We
have seen how the fact that it is placed in a relationship of pure and simple
domination in its confrontations with civil society forestalls any possibility
of maneuvering a reformist perspective in a revolutionary direction [senso].
There is another side to this situation, however, that is still weightier in consequences, as follows: in this framework, the state necessarily develops an
impact on social existence that, in its totalitarian character, comes to be
increasingly compact and functionally congruent. *The overturning of the civil
society–state relationship opens up the possibility of a broad description of the manipulative role of the state in its confrontations with society.* The state bloc must take
apart every potentially hostile social aggregation and reassemble it according to capital's overall, planned schema of functioning. The manipulation
may be conflictual and democratic, or it may not and instead once again
bring about the insurgence of terroristic scenarios for the development of
command (this can increasingly be recognized today); in any case, such is
the figure of the state and its pre-eminent role. It is illusory to speak (in
juridical terms) of legitimation by consensus for this type of state, because
the dialectical terms of the process of democratic legitimation have dissolved.

On another level, a number of the old characteristics of the state have disappeared as well. We have already mentioned one: *the consolidation of total
capital in the figure of the state occurs within the reorganization of the world market.*
There, the authentic and original foundation of the sovereign power of the

state declines markedly, to the same extent that the bloc of sovereign power asserts itself feverishly in domestic relationships, to the detriment of even traditional legitimacy and its processes of validation of power—in international relations, this bloc is diluted and submits to the intersecting and filtering play of the multinational structures of capital. The figure of the state emerges from this turned upside down. The action of the multinationals infiltrates the nation-state, objectively innervating (here it is not a question of deceptive games or manipulation) the components of sovereignty, elevating and shifting the reference points of state action as well as the sources of legitimation.

The state bloc—in the combined operation of capitalist integration on the inside and the multinational dimension on the outside—seems increasingly to configure itself as a resultant of numerous segments that have an overall impact, but which on the other hand take distinct routes. From this point of view, the state bloc articulates in a new way the unitary structure and the multiplied figure of the bodies that comprise it.

In this overall framework, faced with the essential overdetermination of the figure of the contemporary state, the reformist crisis of perspective is accentuated. It is drained of its reality, so to speak, not only with respect to its essence (the modification of the civil society–state relationship) but also with respect to the historical and individual overdeterminations that act on the essence of the phenomenon (the modification of the processes of legitimation and the role of sovereignty).

In the face of all this, the artificial character of the proposals put forward by the project of the Historic Compromise stands out.

## THESIS 6: IN GENERAL: RESTRUCTURING AND ITS EFFECTS

In Italy, the restructuring of production has been under way at least since 1963. In its first phase and following the wave of struggles of the late fifties, the process of restructuring, essentially based on labor-saving[17] machinery, underwent a rapid acceleration and an overall intensification after the wave of struggles of 1969. In the driving sectors, *the process of restructuring* at work in Italy takes up once again the principal characteristics of the capitalist restructuring operating on the world market, namely the fact that it tends *to institute a greater force of capitalist command through maximum flexibility in the use of labor-power*, and against worker organization—that is, against its political mobility and its wage rigidity. This objective is approached via modifications that involve the articulation of production in sectors (reorganization with a heavy emphasis on sectors producing tools: machinery, cybernetics, telecommunications, etc., and consequently the diffuse instrumentality of "technological control" over the socialization of industrial labor), the integration between industry and collateral sectors (above all credit and distribution, which is just another way of saying the "tertiarization" of industrial labor) and finally the internal reorganization of industry (the process of decentralization of manufacture, etc.). *Socialization, tertiarization, and flexibility* (decentralization etc.) of industrial labor, therefore, are the three fundamental objectives that are added to and articulated with the permanent objectives of control and labor-cost reduction in the ongoing restructuring.

It is useless to point out that the quality and intensity of the process of restructuring are determined by the struggles: never before has Marx's expression that "machines rush in wherever there are strikes" been so true. Instead, what is interesting to note here is the other side of the material dialectic of restructuring: that is, to see what direct impact its effects have on the composition of the working class, to see in short what consequences restructuring induces in the body of the working class—such as further progress in the socialization of productive labor, such as its tertiarization and the command that is exercised over the flexibility of labor-power and against the political mobility of the working class.

We have already seen and said it: the political goal of restructuring consists in socially mystifying the sources of surplus-value, in concealing the origin of the workers' offensive. The productive unification of the social and the fluidity of control tend to render the factory workers' struggle incommunicable and the socialized workers' struggle headless. The political goal of the process of restructuring, therefore, consists in *destroying the image, constructed by the struggle of the mass worker, of the identity and generality of the particular interests of workers.* In the crisis, we begin to see the effects of this political project engraved in fiery letters on the worker's body: the separation of employed from unemployed workers, of those in large factories from those in small factories, then a savage proletarianization of the social strata of labor—until then considered unproductive but now reintegrated into productive labor, tertiarized but separated in their classification and function— followed by a territorial decentralization of massified production and the infiltration of the nervous system of direct capitalist production into all the compartments of society, along with the destruction of every worker concentration and reformist intervention that aims to render this destructive passage fluid (from this point of view, the true paradigms of the ongoing operation are the "Uncle Toms" put in place to govern the ghetto cities ravaged by the "racial" revolts of the American and European mass worker). And this is only the beginning: never before have we seen the capitalist will to destroy both the heritage of struggles and the reformist vocation gather itself together in such a homogeneous and harsh manner to smooth this passage and support an adequate reorganization of social labor. *The blackmail and obligation of industrial labor are articulated in a terrorist form*: a homogeneous bloc of political forces proposes once again, by means of restructuring, *the coercion of wage labor.*

As always, however, every capitalist process has its opposite. Or better, it bears in itself an antagonistic potential that we must now grasp, not only as the cause of the overall project, but also as a new presence of the working class—a presence modified by the very development of the relations of force implicitly contained in restructuring. The question is this: to what extent and in what way does restructuring modify the political composition of the class? As we have always emphasized, it seems that this restructuring tends to bring about *an enormous increase in intensity of the political composition of the class.* We have spoken of the emergence of a socialized worker, a new pro-letariat that reabsorbs into itself the power [*potenza*] of the mass workers' struggle and expands its dimensions and social impact enormously. We have repeatedly stressed that this new social reality, by its mere emergence, leads to a series of new contradictions in the apparatus of capitalist domination. What is more, at these levels of capitalist development, the particular workers' interest that reveals this immense revolutionary potential acquires a social generality that cannot be contained.

This new unity of workers' interest, this new revolutionary tension, this potential for political unity, is born of the crisis, of the intensity of terror and poverty that workers endure. It is born of the critique that millions of wage earners carry out every day, on the basis of the inhuman suffering to which capital—in its more or less repressive cycle—condemns wage labor; it is born of the practical recognition that only rebellion can strip away the horrible rationality of the system. Above all, it is born of the everyday discovery that restructuring sometimes makes the old forms of struggle impossible (but only insofar as they are separate), even though it raises the workers' fantasies of struggle to new dimensions and orients them around the globality and cen-trality of the workers' interest. To fail to recognize this is to comprehend neither the dialectic nor the working class: it is to ignore the dialectic of the capital relation, since capitalist development has always—from its first appear-ance—led to these kinds of consequences, and one must follow their insubordinate materiality and take part in them, because the reality of cap-italist development requires it. What is more, it is to ignore the working class, because the dialectical overturning of the tendency of restructuring always represents the fundamental aspect of its definition.

Thus to so-called worker (and Marxian) triumphalism are habitually opposed long catalogs enumerating membership in social classes, litanies of classes, subclasses, sectors and subsectors, and all this climaxes in a hymn to alliances, to compromises, to contortions of the workers' program: as always, the false objectivism of the analysis is accompanied by a completely subjective arbitrariness in the proposal.

Today, if we travel through the network of class composition, we can instead catch sight of a process of recomposition that is extraordinary in its breadth and intensity. Restructuring and the crisis act as moments in which the process of proletarian autonomy explodes. The "layoff fund"[18] teaches the worker his/her identity of interest with the unemployed, and decentralization shows the worker in the large factory that she/he has the same immediate interest as the worker in the small factory. The tertiarization of production shows the agent in the tertiary sector that her/his condition is directly proletarianized from the point of view of her/his place in the productive process and in the wage system. The exclusion of vast strata from production, the marginalization of schooling, etc., reveal the presence of one single law of exploitation over the entire planning process of capitalist society, based on inclusion in and/or exclusion from production; division by sex, age, and race show women, the young, and all minorities the deceptive far-sightedness of the capitalist project for the division and organization of society, and push to rebellion whoever can find a material base in the unity of proletarian exploitation. And so on! To be able to travel through the network of class interests, therefore, it is necessary to see *in restructuring the formation of a unitary potential of struggle*, one that is constantly getting larger.

But this is not merely a quantitative process that begins to reveal itself in restructuring and in the dialectical overturning of its tendency by the working class. The quantitative process has quite specific qualitative aspects. For in fact, if the capitalist objective in restructuring essentially consists in mystifying the sources of surplus-value, in disorganizing the class poles, in destroying the unitary capacity for working-class struggle, the proletarian reconquest of the unity of class interest posits itself immediately in political terms. A huge leap forward is thus accomplished: the struggle must unfold against the unity of the capitalist project, whose tensions and articulations have no other source than pure and simple domination. The relationship with profit—and thus with the utopia of a state planned according to the rhythms of production and the growth of profit—has collapsed under the blows of that fundamental weapon, the savage wage struggle of the mass worker. Today, the proletarian struggle tends instead to become entirely political: a struggle against the state as the political form of command for production.

But this must be correctly understood. To speak of political struggle today, within these processes of restructuring, is not to revive the old Leninist categories or ultimately to distinguish political struggle from economic struggle. This distinction provided for a double definition of struggle, the unmediated (the economic) and the mediated (the political). The mass workers' struggle had already recovered the unity of a political project in the wage struggle against the determinations imposed by the Planner-State. Today, the objective is raised as high, dialectically speaking, as the objectives of the Crisis-State that are being transformed in the present restructuring. As we have said, these are not objectives that seek satisfaction—in commodity form, if you like, but nonetheless real—for the workers' needs, but a radical annihilation, by means of command, of the potentially insubordinate unity of the workers' needs. Here, then, the proletarian and workers' struggle takes a step forward: *from the wage to the use value of the wage, from the struggle over the wage as controllable entity of exploitation to the struggle against command over production, from struggle within the system to the struggle for power.* This is because, while capitalist restructuring squashes a purely mystified expression of the unity of the workers' needs, it gives rise to the conditions for the broader social unification of the proletariat. So the political consciousness of the class is no longer simply a consequence of assuming an antagonistic stance, but is born rather of the demand for liberation. It no longer arises only from the consciousness of the monstrosity of wage labor, but directly from the refusal of work, not from the necessity of production but from the urgency of invention. It is born of the destruction of the wage relation insofar as the latter is a law of destruction that is now completely irrational and no longer linked to any given proportion of development—it seeks to destroy every proletarian need, every instance of class autonomy.

*Finally, the working-class struggle appears more and more clearly as a struggle for liberation.*

## THESIS 7: IN PARTICULAR: THE CRISIS OF THE HISTORIC COMPROMISE

At this point, restructuring clearly appears to be a proposition and practice of power that contradicts the political form to which the Historic Compromise alludes. Neither at the productive level, nor at the state level, nor in the overall tendency of the capitalist project is the possibility of compromise present, least of all in reformist terms. The socialism of the Official Labor Movement reveals itself to be a *pure and simple ideology* with respect to the material impact of capitalist restructuring prompted by the Planner-State's awareness of crisis. It is nothing but ideology and utopia, when it is not simply justification, betrayal, and deception, as it has always been in the history of the "great" European social democracies.

It is indeed unthinkable that socialist good faith could endure in the face of the constantly renewed verification of restructuring's effects. Insofar as these effects emerge from the body of the working class, they are radically opposed to any practice whatsoever of the ideological pacification of class antagonisms—even the old ones, that re-emerge with sublimated intensity from the new order of relations of force between classes. "The great Communist reformism" cannot withstand the simplest confrontation with the reality of restructuring: all the *class* effects of the latter are forcibly inserted into a schema of *class collaboration*, the new needs forcibly reduced to the old, the analysis of the state tediously repeated in terms of monopoly capitalism, the new occasions of struggle obliterated, suppressed in a manner that is half sentimental and half brutal. If capital marches imperiously toward command over and disarticulation of the class's movements, the Historic Compromise intends to legitimate all that by means of the workers' participation; if, in the crisis phase, capital does not consider the attainment of satisfactory levels of profit to be its pre-eminent concern, the Historic Compromise urges work for socialist profit; if capital considers the instruments of its plan to be essential to the management of a critical long-term conjuncture, the Historic Compromise raves about sectorial, global, and international planning—beyond any formation of consensus. *Even from capital's point of view, the Historic Compromise presents a shabby political form of restructuring.* From the point of view of the working class, the Historic Compromise has a purely reactionary essence.

But then, why does capital's economic elite press decisively for the Historic Compromise? From a tactical point of view, certainly, the Historic Compromise has launched a renewed challenge to the old, abusive, and corrupt capitalist political elite. From a strategic point of view, capital instead is attempting to impose a colossal repressive operation on the working class and the proletariat as a whole. The form of the institutional conclusion of the crisis, in terms of the Historic Compromise, is necessarily repressive: this capitalist awareness is centered on a thorough knowledge of base [*struttura*] and superstructure, and it is the mature expression of capitalist hegemony today. The functional limits of the project of the Historic Compromise, as they are understood on the capitalist side, concern a new nature of the state, the organic character of the interpenetration of state and capital, the potency [*potenza*] of the economic and political power of the multinationals, and the disintegration of the traditional sources of sovereignty and legitimacy. At this point, every transformist[19] operation, whatever it may be at the level of the "autonomy of the political," runs up against the unreality of this category, its mere adaptation to the mystifying ideology and practice of capital. *Today, the workers' utilization of state institutions is inconceivable:* the tendency toward dual power can only result in a class dictatorship. Thus capital gambles with this terrain, while remaining aware that the political form (the Historic

Compromise) of restructuring can only take on a completely ideological aspect and an essentially repressive role. Every bourgeois-institutional political conclusion of the crisis can only oppose itself repressively to the needs induced by restructuring in the body of the working class and thereafter reproduced and remodeled in the struggle.

But the workers' poverty, the proletarian division induced by restructuring, cannot be enclosed again in any formula, ideology or delegation: it carries in itself the need for worker unity and workers' power. This is not the first time that we have seen the Official Labor Movement play a repressive role when confronted with the needs of the class. This was already the case when, after the Resistance, the workers were "disarmed" and subjected to the ideology of reconstruction and thus of planning. In 1968, when this ideology was defeated and the new worker weapons were called councils, assemblies, continuous struggle and workers' power, the Official Labor Movement at first "rode the tiger"[20] but ended up controlling and repressing the workers. But despite the proverbs, there will be no third time: in relation to its predecessors, the new repression incorporated into the Historic Compromise no longer has even the dignity of diplomatic prudence, Keynesian utopianism, and camouflaged bureaucratic opportunism. *Here, the schism between proletarian needs, workers' struggles and capitalist institutional repression reaches its maximum size.* The crisis of the Historic Compromise is coterminous and consubstantial with the advance of restructuring and its effects.

Clearly, if this crisis had to develop in the absence of an organized proletarian alternative, it would be a tragedy; but if the bureaucratic control of workers' and proletarian autonomy and the need for communism demanded by the Historic Compromise came to pass, it would be worse than a tragedy— far worse, because the structural and ideological elements of social-democratic repression are accompanied by a deadly instrumentality. Arrogance is the quality of the new repression, mass manipulation is its means and a dark will to destruction is its goal. The political elite of the Historic Compromise is in reality no less outworn than that of capital. It is perhaps only one small step ahead of capital: capital expects from its representatives the ferocious coherence and sullen efficiency that the managers of reformism have already demonstrated. But in reality, both are united in the arrogance that is characteristic of the totalities that they express, in the domination of the "autonomy of the political" that they experience [*soffrono*]. The use values, the radical simplicity of the workers' needs, the direct management of power are illusions to them: they live the commodified reality of exchange value, deal-making and political compromise, delegation. For them, political invention is nothing, and tradition is everything: the filthy requirement of specialized skills [*mestiere*], the hypocrisy of global, or national, in any case physiological representation. Arrogance is their fundamental quality. All this is the opposite of what proletarian needs reveal to us. It is therefore not by chance that every time the real movement wins, these Moscow functionaries are rapidly liquidated, like the Escalantes and Cunhals,[21] not because they are more or less close to Moscow, but on the contrary because these bureaucratic "micro-factions" are close to the state's interest in centralization for profit and far from the political composition of the proletariat struggling everywhere for communism. They believe in transition via the capitalist technocracy of Indira Gandhi instead of via the desperate struggles of proletarians: instead of "storming heaven," they "descend" upon the disinherited! The Communist Parties that more or less follow the Moscow line have become parties of order and work. Occasional moments of dissidence do not modify but rather confirm this vocation.

The Historic Compromise certainly has a social base too, albeit one that lacks the characteristics of a social class. As we have seen, this includes public managers and bourgeois intelligentsia who demand a "socialism with a human face"—meaning a humanization and rationalization of the relationships of planned exploitation—but who refuse to discuss the "professional," "technological" legitimacy of those who command. Here, there is also an ideological continuity between the technocratic utopianism of (post-1956) socialism and the Historic Compromise: following the frustrations of the first period of planning, today the political elite of the Historic Compromise is trying to strengthen itself and offer its candidacy by organizing social-reformist *hothouses*. From this point of view, *the party of the Historic Compromise is a state party*, even before it gets its hands on the state.

But conceding this, how can a party that finds itself within such critical antagonisms think of a socialist and governmental management of its policies? In critical situations no party, insofar as it is traditionally rooted in the masses, can be permitted so dramatically to exaggerate its organic functions of top-down mediation of the masses' expectations. This is valid in general, but it is even more true today when these nephews of Giolitti[22] oppose the immediately revolutionary needs of the proletariat. And all this is only to regard the problem from a simple political-science point of view: even now, in fact, while the Historic Compromise is barely stirring, the historic party is already constrained to leave political spaces all over the place—not only for workers' autonomy but even for the bourgeois radicalism of the struggle over civil rights.

If we pass now from the political to the substantive point of view, then the organic character of the Historic Compromise appears still more precarious. It is not a function but a mystification of capitalist restructuring. It is a function of the latter *only insofar as* it is mystification. How long can this image last? Only as long as the capitalist recovery. Therefore, the Historic Compromise adds adventurism to its characteristics. It is an impossible proposal that is credible enough in the short term to be passed off as strategy.

The Historic Compromise would like to be a form of capitalist command over the social organization of living labor; it would like to be the "socialist form" of command, but the economic crisis and restructuring are already preventing this from happening. Therefore, it finds itself in crisis as well: in this one can see, from an *objective* standpoint, that wherever socialism is impossible, the specter of communism begins once again to haunt the world.

### THESIS 8: THE SUBJECT OF THE CRISIS OF THE HISTORIC COMPROMISE

When the assumption of the proletariat into capitalist valorization is total—directly or indirectly, in any case not merely on the terrain of distribution but also on that of production and realization/circulation—the passage from the "mass worker" to the "socialized worker" is a passage to a new horizon of needs. *But it is not only that.* It is the passage to a new dialectical stage of the process of the technical and political composition of the working class and proletariat; and this passage unfolds with unusual intensity. What, then, is this passage? What does it represent among the successive moments of the proletariat's formation?

When we speak of needs, obviously we are speaking of that system of use values which wage earners aim to acquire in order to satisfy themselves [*realizzarne un godimento*]. But in capitalist development, use value—and even more the overall system of needs—is always given as the reflex of exchange value. The dialectical process of class composition does not escape this. It is certainly true, as Marx says, that there are "times when business is good" during which the worker can succeed in "widening the sphere of his pleasures" (and in this situation it is possible for the worker to construct an organization, which is to say his "participation in the higher, even cultural satisfactions, the agitation for his own interests, newspaper subscriptions, attending lectures, educating his children, developing his taste etc., his only share of civilization which distinguishes him from the slave ..." [*Grundrisse* 287])—but it is also true that this relationship between composition and satisfaction is immediately utilized, transformed by capital into an increase in the productivity of labor. The intensification of class composition is always redirected by capital toward an intensification of the organic composition of capital. The widening of the horizon of needs and satisfactions is gathered up into an ever-broader subordination to the command of exchange value. In this context, the rule of exchange increases and enriches the productive forces of labor but also reproduces them as such, in a nexus of necessary subordination, as a moment of the capital relation.

Nevertheless this does not exhaust the complexity of the relations that constitute the relationship of class composition, for in fact another relation exists that must be taken into consideration. Not all use value presents itself as a mere reflex of exchange value; there is a use value that is no such thing, that is instead the general potentiality of wealth, *id est* labor. Certainly "labour, such as it exists *for itself* in the worker in opposition to capital, that is, labour in its *immediate being*, separated from capital, is *not productive*" (*Grundrisse* 308). *But it is the total power* [potenza] *of all wealth, the only potentiality of production, the sole productive force*. The opposite of exchange value, therefore, is not use value, which on the contrary presents itself as the reflex of exchange value—whatever the class composition (the level of relationship between the "poverty" and the "satisfaction" of the worker) may be. *The opposite of exchange value is instead the use value of labor, labor as activity, as pure creative force of production and invention.*

Let us backtrack a moment. Is it possible to assert that the *indefinite* dialectical process of working-class and proletarian composition tends to resolve itself within the passage of class composition (from the mass worker to the socialized worker) currently under way?

To answer this question, we must recall a further series of concepts. Every system of needs has a content and a sense. Marx speaks particularly of a "positive" content (the simple relation between commodities and consumption) and an "irrational" content (the capitalist relation between commodities and money): as capitalist production develops, the first content is absorbed into the second, to the point that we can speak of a single sense of the systematic relation, the capitalist sense. Now, from the moment when—as in the current phase of totalization of the capitalist system of needs—the subordination of use values to exchange values is total, when the emergence of use values is mere "indifference," sometimes "chaos" and sometimes "utopia," and when the sense of the system and its totalizing seizure preclude any possibility of a simple relation in any moment of the development of needs—at this point everything that remains human rebels, and labor is the sole terrain of rebellion, the sole terrain on which use value resists and condenses around itself the possibility of a different, alternative, revolutionary system. Because here labor, in the triumph of the capitalist system of exchange value, remains the sole use value that can deprive the capitalist of the command that is exercised over itself, and therefore make itself worker use value, which is to say the refusal of work and the development of labor's own creative value.

The passage from the composition of the mass worker to that of the socialized worker does not mean merely a further perfecting of the productive force of labor, nor merely the proposition of a new system of needs; rather, it means that, when the dialectic of composition is exhausted in a totality of subordination to capital, proletarian rebellion assails the entire fabric of the composition and the system of needs. *Ranged against exchange value appears its opposite, labor as creativity and liberation; on the basis of this liberated polarity, the possibility of a system of struggles defines itself against the system of needs.*

Let it be clearly understood that we are not engaged in metaphysics! We are only seeking to understand why insubordination reaches a maximum at the precise moment when the old contradiction between relations of production and productive forces ("science, general social knowledge, the quality and sociality of labor, nature, machinery, labor organization," etc.) seems to fade away, once the organic functioning of the latter in the exploitation of living labor is complete. We understand it because we see—necessarily—the full force of insubordination coagulating along this last front that is the antagonistic and general persistence of living social labor, a front along which productive force, this *sole* productive force that is living labor, opposes itself as struggle to the "relations of production" *and* to the "productive forces" that are incorporated into them. Against the dictatorship of exchange value, this front of insubordination does not oppose a project for the restoration of use value and the utilization of a particular system of needs, but rather a project of the *hegemony of this completely particularized utility that belongs to living labor, namely its creativity,* and the hegemony of the latter over every use value and against exchange value.

At this point a question begins to arise, the question of whether there is a "possibility that the working class could use the productive forces to valorize itself against capital as an antagonistic class. Whether an alternative use of highly developed productive forces is possible."[23] But this question can only be posed if we recall, in Marxian fashion, that living labor in itself, in its independence, is not productive, but rather it is creativity struggling against the system of needs produced by capital, against the universality of exchange value and its persistence, against the state as the site of the general determination and the mature (and increasingly exclusive) mediation of the system of needs as a rigid and obligatory system that is monstrous and oppressive.

At this turning point in the historical process of the dialectic of class composition, everything changes. This implies that henceforth the particular utility that belongs to living labor can consolidate itself in a social class composition, and verify its own intensity, only in the struggle. *The system of needs is replaced by the system of struggles*: an alternative system of struggles that the proletarian subject, as living social labor, knows to be an antagonistic reappropriation of the productive forces.

The very concept of *class composition* must henceforth be modified to become a *category*—the only fundamental category—*of communist transition*. Detaching itself from its poverty, class composition at this point becomes *the subject of the subsequent reappropriation of productive forces by the class*. The bad dialectic under which the class suffered, the dialectic of ferocious capitalist restructuring, must be broken and regenerated: here, radical antagonism founds a constructive dialectic. After the repressive dissolution that capital continuously imposed on the class composition comes a phase in which the processes of recomposition are defined solely as processes of class antagonism, and in which the proletarian class turns itself into the complete, independent revolutionary subject. *Here, composition tends toward organization, reappropriation becomes program, and the system of needs is a system of transitional struggles.*

Thus we are confronted with a qualitative passage in the class struggle. In the era opened up by the mass workers' struggle and defined by the most profound crisis capital has ever known, the sequence of class compositions has prepared and left room for the *qualitative leap* that we have described. We are beginning to experience this new era of class struggle. It has already shown what revolutionary wealth it contains.

For in fact, only the wealth of revolutionary behavior belongs to the class. There is no qualitative change in this—history repeats itself: Marx teaches us that, had the workers taken as their goal wealth and not immediate satisfaction, not only would they not have acquired wealth, but they would have totally lost the use values—"the most [the worker] can achieve on the average with his self-denial is to be able better to endure the fluctuations of prices— high and low, their cycle—that is, he can only distribute his consumption better, but never attain wealth" (*Grundrisse* 286). But then, in what does this qualitative leap consist? It consists in the fact that the real conditions based on the quality of the class composition and the intensity of capital's crisis are added to the formal possibility of the wealth of struggles today. Possible consciousness and immediate satisfaction today contain, in themselves, the revolution.

Furthermore, at this turning point in the process of class composition, the concept of the revolutionary organization of the proletariat arises and is rediscovered. We must return to this concept, but it is important here to note its birthplace—along with all the novelty that distinguishes it. "The party," if one still wishes to call it that, is in this case something other than a vanguard on the march: *it is the motive force of the transformation of a system of mass struggles, it is the organ of the mass political reappropriation of power, against wage labor, as an invention of communism.*

## THESIS 9:  BETWEEN WORKER STRATEGY
## AND WORKER TACTICS

When faced with this class composition, capitalist reformism and especially its new figure, the Historic Compromise, cannot imagine class relationships in any form other than the wage. Whether this is conceded directly or indirectly, it is nevertheless the fundamental element of the reconstitution of consensus and domination, and at the same time the keystone of the system's development. From this viewpoint, the state of mature capitalism, which is implicated in the economic crisis, seems to be some sort of enormous social machine that is understood to be the instrument of pressure of a "union of society"; but it only appears thus, because in reality none of this is given, and this machine necessarily functions to control, dominate, and manipulate within margins of consensus and agreement rendered ridiculous by the crisis and the structural complexity of the contemporary state (that is, the extinction of civil society).

In appearance, therefore, the capitalist reform of the state stakes itself on the wage. But it confronts a social composition of the proletariat that allows no space for this ploy. The irrationality of using individualized categories of wage differentiation to divide the proletariat internally emerges rapidly in the class point of view: all the forms of behavior, objectives, struggles of the working class press, at the very least, for a *social realignment of the wage* at these middle levels of socially necessary labor with which the whole range of individual wages must be aligned and according to which every indirect wage must be measured. But even this is not enough, because this realignment of necessary labor exists only within capitalist command, and itself appears as irrationality and domination, compression and negation of the antagonistic emergence of the proletariat's productive force. In short, faced with the appearance of a state that uses the wage to mediate and establish consensus, not only does a line of struggle appear, one that tends to stake itself on a realignment of wages by appealing to socially necessary labor, but consequently *a coherent offensive line against that very same necessary labor*—as necessarily capitalist labor—also appears!

Revolutionary action against capitalist reformism and the Historic Compromise situates itself within this tangle of determinations. Yet what may appear to be a contradiction must be shown to be dialectically necessary, from the workers' point of view; the tangle must be unraveled. This comes down to saying that tactics must allow us to *expand the dimensions of the struggle over the average social wage in order to begin to attain the strategic level of the struggle against necessary labor.* They must increase the tension of the struggle over exchange values in order to reach the point of breaking open this particular working-class utility that is living labor as struggle, as communist potentiality. As always, the proletarian forms of behavior show the way. The wage struggle in fact tends to transform itself into a struggle for appropriation, a class struggle that includes within itself all the motifs of the struggle for liberation.

It is necessary to emphasize the complexity and at the same time the radicality of this passage from the terrain of tactics to the terrain of strategy. Today, it is no longer possible to envision any tactical proposition that does not firmly refer to strategy (and from this point of view, the old organizational conception of the Third International is a total loss). From the workers' point of view, therefore, every wage struggle is increasingly evaluated in relation to the contents of power and liberation to which it gives rise. Only when the wage struggle transforms itself into a *struggle for appropriation*—and be careful: it is not necessarily a struggle for appropriation in the strict sense of the term, instead it suffices for the wage to be seen as the immediate possibility of acceding to new human possibilities—only then does this wage struggle become credible. But this is not enough: for in turn, the distinction between collective bargaining and the struggle for power is extolled in the radicality of this passage. Collective bargaining is always the definition of a new system of needs that is opposed to the struggle, and the struggle for power is an assertion of the continuity between struggles and needs. To destroy collective bargaining is to destroy the final level of the capitalist manipulation of needs, and therefore, on that basis, to rise once again to the discovery of the struggle against the system as such, the discovery of the terrain of antagonistic revolutionary appropriation that today signals the existence of the proletariat and its hope.

Clearly this insistence on the strategic contents of the project does not mean the devaluation of tactical passages. That which is always valid in general for Marxist political science is even more important in our particular situation. It is certainly difficult to distinguish between strategic and tactical, mediated and unmediated interests in a political and social situation as repressed and desperate as ours. The bureaucratic mediocrities who rule the policies of the Historic Compromise wanted to be able to make such distinctions right away and in a rigid manner; yet the failure of their project must not give credibility to an Anabaptist emphasis on immediate salvation. Here, the situation is "between the tactics and the strategy of the proletariat," or better, "between strategy and tactics." The continuity, the interests, the unresolved alternatives make up the proletarian gamble. But the problem is to resolve them little by little from the inside. This is once again a characteristic of the "party," if that is what we want to call the revolutionary organization.

The intermingling of the struggle against the false pretence of the wage and the struggle for appropriation also refers to the *issue of organization*. In fact, we have seen how the concept of the "party" is born within this qualitative leap that materially transforms—for the new class composition that tends toward total participation in productive mechanisms—a system of proletarian needs into a single need, that of struggle, and hence into a system of struggles. But these passages of possible consciousness, rooted as they are in the confused context of strategic emergences and tactical occasions, are likewise confronted with the whole body of enemy power. The struggle, setting out from the level of the wage and rising up against the commodification of every value, tends toward appropriation and ventures to test itself in the dialectic of liberation, but each of these passages finds itself confronted with the full power of the class enemy. How, then, is the maximum space established for the self-constitution of proletarian collective practice, against the blocs of capitalist power and the state's command for profit? On this terrain, the experience of the class grows in density and we must refer to it in order to proceed, or rather to specify the functions of organization. These functions do not claim to split this mass terrain on which revolutionary organization reformulates itself today, but simply—and fundamentally—to articulate it in reference to the density of the clash, to the intensity of the relations of force between the classes.

Therefore, wherever the overall mass movement shows itself capable of maintaining the very highest levels of struggle against work and at the same time of articulating in progressive succession the struggle for appropriation and communist liberation, revolutionary organization must assume the tasks of *rupturing capitalist restructuring, command, and stabilization*. This virtuous unification of strategy and tactics at the mass level as a continual fermentation of new levels of the mass offensive must be differentiated and articulated as offensive functions wherever capitalist response and repression weigh most heavily. The party can sustain the complexity of immediate functions that the mass articulation defines between appropriation and struggle for power only to the extent that it articulates adequate anti-capitalist offensive functions. It is not a matter of extolling the "separation" of these functions. In fact, they are separate only to the extent (and this may be considerable) that capitalist repression imposes separation: in fact, the process tends toward unity, the mass level tends to arm itself and no longer leaves its weapons in just anybody's hands. Communism is the construction of an armed workers' society that extinguishes the power of the state by destroying it.

But that said, it is necessary once again to emphasize the fact that, in the face of the capitalist offensive, the role of the vanguard is essential and fundamental, and it can be well articulated with the mass movement at every moment. Nevertheless, it is dangerous to surrender to linear conceptions of the relationship between mass struggle and militant struggle. Such dualisms are necessary only when the movement is so rich that it includes them dialectically within itself.

Is this not the original condition of the movement in Italy today, this formidable and continuous movement of struggle that advances toward its strategic goals, and in advancing destroys every institutional mediation, this movement that has interwoven tactics and strategy in singular combinations, constructed and emancipated itself, appropriated the highest political levels, and above all utilized *all* the tools of struggle? Within this continuity and originality of experience, the party process moves forward.

## THESIS 10:  GENERAL PROSPECT OF
## THE REVOLUTIONARY PASSAGE

When the problem of the revolutionary passage is posed in general, on the basis of this new class composition, it is necessary first of all to get to the bottom of the analysis of what concepts like workers' and proletarian reappropriation of the productive forces, the system of struggle and its relation to the advance of power (in the conquest of power) mean.

The problem is entirely Marxian. Indeed, wherever Marx's analysis of the problems of transition is most advanced, in the *Grundrisse* and the writings ancillary to *Capital*, these issues are posed with extreme clarity in pages that contain one of the most courageous visions that the human mind has ever produced. In fact, Marx proceeds from the definition of a proletarian composition determined at the level of capitalism's maturity, in which a collective human individuality capable of communism has fully developed, to the determination of the material preconditions (the development of automation, use of machines, and invention–power in the law of value's tendency to lose significance) for such collective human individuality, in order to conclude that, on these bases, the proletarian reappropriation of social productive force is necessary, and that it is simultaneously the metamorphosis of labor and the extinction of the law of labor-value as the law of development of communist society.

This series of passages alludes to and announces the struggle of the "socialized worker," and the sense of the workers' proposals leaves no doubt: the communist transition, the revolutionary passage must *simultaneously* signify the destruction of both capitalist command *and* worker poverty, and thus the direct reappropriation of the productive forces of social wealth. *Direct reappropriation* is not a vague appendage to the communist program, but rather its essence. The fundamental concept of dictatorship of the proletariat is completely deprived of meaning and utterly mystified if it is removed from the nexus that defines it, namely its relationship to direct reappropriation. The classics of Marxism never denied or omitted this problematic sense: thus, after the long oblivion of the Second International, this sense regains its centrality and is thrown into extremely high relief in the work of Lenin, where the whole analysis is centered on the simultaneity of the transition and the extinction of the state. Nothing is more false than confusing the dictatorship of the proletariat with state capitalism (and it is not by chance that this confusion coincides with the Stalinist program, without having the historical rationale of Russian Stalinism).

What a difference we see when we compare this to the discussions of the Historic Compromise! Here, the alternative is between "pluralist democracy" and "popular democracy," the fundamental goal consists in the state-organized expropriation of the proletariat, and the mediation of the so-called transition unfolds in the form of the division of labor, in this case that of the autonomy of the political. Here, all the Marxist terminology is forgotten and mistakenly referred back to its reactionary interpretations, not merely because of the refusal of dictatorship (on the contrary, too many of these pluralists have had much to do with "totalitarianisms"—to speak like they do—first corporativism and then Stalinism, with which most of them have collaborated), but because of the refusal of the *dictatorship of the proletariat*, that is, the direct appropriation of the productive forces by the workers, the destruction of the capitalist mediation of the socialization of the productive forces, and the transfer of the material legitimation of the management of power from the parties to the organs of proletarian democracy.

But this refusal of the dictatorship of the proletariat is what so vigorously sets the forces of the Historic Compromise in opposition to the proletarian forces, the forces of workers' autonomy. Let us be clearly understood: after that season of struggles, after the first great mass experiences of self-management of the revolutionary process, after 1968–69, this will to re-appropriation has become a necessary component of mass behavior, one that cannot be eliminated. It has become an objective structure of proletarian subjectivity. At this level of the struggle, and of the composition induced by the struggles, "*workers' autonomy*"—which is to say, the refusal of work, the will to reappropriation, etc.—*is a category of the productive forces*. From this fundamental point of view, the general prospect of the revolutionary passage can no longer be envisioned except from within the advance of proletarian power, from within the struggles and moments of the reappropriation of social wealth and the productive forces. To imagine a different passage is pure illusion, it risks defeat, when it is not simply mystification and betrayal. It is social fascism pure and simple, in which the expropriating will—which is abstract, but no less harmful for all that—of Soarès[24] and Cunhal comes together in the face of the insurgence and diffusion of this true pluralism, which is not that of the party but belongs instead to the organisms of worker and proletarian power. Diffidence before the force of the masses, dismay that the "irrationality" of the masses is out of control, confidence in bureaucratic mediation and the vertical integration of the process—all this is an insult to the class struggle and a desperate resistance to its powerful advance. On this terrain the Historic Compromise moves in a direction [*senso*] that is opposed and antagonistic to the predictions of the classics and the experiences, demands, and struggles of the socialized worker and the contemporary proletariat.

Above all, it is a terrain on which the Historic Compromise, in proposing its own theory of transition, claims to rediscover credibility and efficacy. This is the terrain of ideological mediation. Up until now, the terrain of ideology has been too undervalued, or so they insist, so we must instead go back to an examination of its density, the effects of superstructures on their bases, and the record of the defeats we have suffered when we have refused, or not known how, to develop mediation on this terrain and in the face of these problems. Which comes down to saying, by the way, that here a heavy price is paid for the errors that have been committed. Because only someone with an already abstract and mechanical perspective on the relationship between base and superstructure could be astonished hereafter by their intertwining! But the recourse to external and bureaucratic mediation is not allowed, because if mediation is going to come into being, it will be objective or it won't exist at all. This amounts to saying that the discourse must once again make contact with the discussion of class composition in order to verify the role and place of mediation. This correct observation must be neither an alibi for revisionism, nor a mechanical subterfuge to reverse the relationship between base and superstructure and to consider the latter exclusively, just as the former was once exaggerated. In this way, the method does not change. Once again, we are moving into the filthy heaven of politics and delegation.

Nevertheless, the whole development of class composition implies *a fundamental reshaping of the issue of mediation*. The class composition of Lenin's day, on which he exercised his political will, objectively demanded external political mediation. The externality of the mediation was characteristic of this composition and was based on counterposing the professional stratum of the class, in its project for the recomposition of labor and the totalization of functioning of the law of value, to the great majority of the proletariat. It is not a matter of chance, then, that the professional workers' *theory of knowledge* alternated between an encyclopedic schema and a projective one, and tended toward the dynamic recomposition of knowledge and the mediation of the complex of scientific elements that constituted the society of labor, because it wanted to impose its command on these things too. This totality, commanded by the professional worker, then counterposed itself *as ideology* to the ideology of capital, and projected itself as an alternative schema of social management; and polemics open up and mediations develop on the path that goes from the political intention of the project to the set of elements that compose its ideology. A delegation of knowledge and mediation, one that is functional in the political project and adapted to the contents of the projected totality, is permissible and necessary in this case. But the same cognitive project, faced with the new composition of the socialized worker, becomes completely different. Here, *knowledge is reorganized not as an ideological recomposition of reality, but as a tendency toward the recomposition of homogeneous forms of behavior*: the antagonism is not entrusted to representation, the totality of the project does not pass by way of mediations or delegations, and communism is not consigned to the future. A directly practical and collective knowledge, linked to the material construction of a collective alternative to the capitalist mode of production—such is the terrain of workers' knowledge: a savage terrain of reappropriation, invention, and destruction of the adversary. Mediation does not pay because there is no objective space for it, while ideology is obsolete or at least is not manageable by others, and the totality is presupposed and measured according to the rhythm of the set of collective needs and desires. Here, knowledge insinuates itself materially and corporeally into reality, differentiating it from within, denying any dignity to abstract and external theoretical mediation, thus reducing mediation to a mere tendency and ultimately negating it. A new materialism that extols the continuity between theory and practice, and subordinates and reduces every passage to its internal movement: such is the socialized workers' "philosophy of knowledge." It is nothing other than the discovery, on the plane of knowledge, of this "uniqueness" of the particular utility of labor when it is opposed to exchange value and grasped in its creativity and insubordination—in this case as invention-power freed from capital and completely subject to the collective human individual of communism.

The poverty of the Historic Compromise casts curses and exorcisms against the new proletarian reality, while singing the praises of mediation. This may displease some, but it must inevitably be said: the Historic Compromise is a reactionary project, and it certainly cannot easily be relieved of this burdensome definition. But on this terrain, it pushes the mediocrity that characterizes itself to the limit, if that is possible, because here all the refinements of reformism and transformism—stop and go,[25] personal articulations, diplomatic skirmishes, double-crosses—find their philosophical glorification: everything becomes a function of the ideological totality and "delegated mediation" resolves everything into the project!

Yet someone could object: there is a political richness in that, whereas this conception of class composition tends toward linear and organic solutions to the problems of transition. In reality, it may be objected, the conception of mediation is a conception of politics, history, and dynamics. But good God, how can we remove all these stereotypes from the heads of intellectuals? And make them understand that the materialism of composition is *dialectical materialism*! Nothing is further from the dialectic of the socialized worker than the conception of a linear and organic passage to communism, if for no other reason than that dialectic's negation of external and superstructural mediation and its assertion of the role the proletariat plays in the destruction of this mediating horizon. At this point, the position of the issue relative to the revolutionary passage cannot progress; it is stabilized and confirmed around these first moments: the definition of the internal, practical, and theoretical axis of recomposition, the assertion of the material dialectic of destruction and invention, the progressive reappropriation—enunciated according to these rhythms—of struggle in the construction of tools of power.

At this point, it is certainly not possible to construct scenarios of transition. The only lesson that can be learned from the analysis concerns the concreteness of the dialectic that the passage implies; it imposes a capacity to measure the steps in relation to the unfolding of the "party's" action, that is, in relation to the articulation between the terms of destruction and the terms of reappropriation that the advance of the socialized worker defines. The center of revolutionary action shifts to the center of gravity of proletarian action.

## THESIS 11:  HERE AND NOW: NOTES ON THE PROGRAM

But we can go further in this analysis. The problem of the revolutionary passage, beyond the formal conditions imposed by the composition of the socialized worker, must be related to the real conditions of the class struggle in Italy, that is, the formidable and original conditions which we have mentioned in passing. In fact, the Italian working class has for some time carried out a continuous process of struggle that, through the systematic and violent overturning of the sequences of directly capitalist reformism and institutional reformism (the Historic Compromise), has not only deepened capital's crisis but also begun to prefigure—*materially*, and not just in the sense of "setting future pots to boil"—the contents of the revolutionary passage.

To begin with, let us see how the workers' overturning of the sequences of restructuring has functioned. These sequences have aimed for an intensification of worker mobility within direct production, a division (and eventually a marginalization) of the compact parts of labor-power over the social terrain, and overall a flexible definition of command made rigid by a higher composition of capital (and a social totalization of its existence). The different passages of the crisis, the alternation of offensives against employment and the instruments that guarantee the wage, the insistence on mobility and agreements for "a new form of production," have all been organically bound to the general goals of the project. But what was unexpected was the fact that these sequences of restructuring would be systematically overturned and used, from the workers' point of view, for the establishment of a vaster front of struggle and a more advanced pursuit of objectives. Thus on the one hand, the layoff fund [*cassa integrazione*] is used by the workers to guarantee their behavior of refusal of work, and at the same time the guaranteed wage is used for the recomposition of a social front of struggle. Therefore, the attempts to divide the proletariat over the wage induce a constantly growing demand for a social wage for women and students, beyond even the social wage demanded by the adult male unemployed. Paradoxically (but not so much so that these forms of behavior are excluded from a new composition), the social extension of productive labor is recognized and asserted by the class on the basis of the practice of the refusal of work.

Here a fundamental law of the transition to communism is clarified: *the transition is possible when the working class, instead of being moved by capital, moves itself and subordinates capital to its own forms of behavior.* This material and objective dictatorship of the class over capital is the first fundamental passage of transition, most obviously when the relationship does not result in the capitalist mediation of development, but rather in the workers' mediation of capital's crisis.

Faced with the institutional sequences of capitalist restructuring, the workers' overturning has had an even more profound role to play, if that is possible. The class forms of behavior defined here look like an act of devastation. The state mediations of the plan, and then the dynamic mediations managed by the unions in order to guide the relationship between the mass of wage earners and investment, unfold one by one. *The control that the state must exercise over itself in using the imposing means of reproduction that capital is constrained to put at its disposal diminishes at the same rate that consensus collapses!* Less consensus, less control, less legitimacy, and it is crucial to insist upon this last point because the mechanism of overturning, opened up and prolonged by the workers' struggles in their confrontation with the instruments of control that the state tries intermittently to deploy, has not simply brought about the collapse of any single majority or formula of government, but rather the collapse of the very legitimacy of the state to guarantee the reproduction of capital. The more the urgent needs of command accumulate at the highest level of the state, the more fully does an opposing sequence develop at the class level—a sequence of forms of behavior that denounces the abstract and despotic character of capitalist command as managed by the state, and indicates its structural extraneousness to the material and political needs of the masses. At this point, the final attempt on the part of the Historic Compromise to give legitimacy back to the state's action crumbles. This is not what the proletarian masses need; they need to intensify the struggle for spaces of effective counterpower.

In the accumulation of workers' overturnings of direct capitalist sequences and institutional sequences, the second character of the process of transition as it unfolds on the basis of the new class composition can be discerned: here we find not only the class dictatorship over capital in material and objective terms, but also *a first fundamental impetus of struggle against the state*. The materiality of this transition begins to reveal itself subjectively. In the disaster of legitimation that the state experiences, in the void of rationality over which the capitalist economy extends, all the workers' objectives unfold into the dimensions of the program, into elements of the struggle for power. The offensive against work, against the time of enslavement under the boss's command, the offensive against the wage, that is, the demand for a socially unifying wage that can recompose the struggle, the manifestation of the recomposed unity of productive social labor against the social extraction of profit and the state guarantee of capitalist reproduction: at this turning point in the struggle, the workers know that these objectives cannot be attained in union or party contract negotiation, but only in the form of decrees, or rather in the conquest and destruction of the bosses' state as the first act of dictatorship. *The drastic reduction of labor time, equal social wages for all, the end of the division of labor and the obligation to productive labor, and the liberation of invention-power* are the workers' and proletarian objectives that are growing in the continuous everyday struggle, that are necessarily transforming themselves into a political program of proletarian dictatorship against the state.

Once again, however, the framework becomes abstract and shifting if we merely imagine that the process is continuous and organic. No, the revolution—whatever the level of the productive forces—is not a tea party. Right now, we have said, there is a struggle over the program; and we have seen how the contents of the program and the tensions of the revolutionary passage exist in the concrete relations of force. But whatever the extent to which the proletariat tends to exacerbate and break the chains of reformist mediation, to that same extent the violence of the bosses gets it in range [*aggiusta in tiro*] and prepares its salvo. Repression is organic to capital, even more so with the decomposition of the reformist capacity to control. By now history is full of butchers like Noske![26] And yet, in the moment when the illusion of the Historic Compromise sweeps away the old equilibria without the possibility of reopening an effective reformist process, it is to be expected that a series of mechanisms of violence, destruction and blind class hatred would be set in motion, with processes of acceleration that are as unknown as they are certain. No one can truthfully accuse us of ever having cried wolf; nevertheless, today, for the first time, the analysis of the relations of force between classes seems to open up the *material possibility of a vigorous capitalist "reaction."* Within the working class and the proletariat exist adequate possibilities of resistance and counterattack; they must not be considered as external to the program that resides and expresses itself in the new class composition, but on the contrary as completely complementary to it.

Having emphasized the necessity of the existence of a material class dictatorship over capital, and the emergence of a revolutionary mass consciousness that leads from the program to its contention with the state, we now must clarify a third characteristic of the process of transition, one in no way subordinate to the others: *the necessity of a militant vanguard force capable of violently and continuously deepening the crisis and blunting the violence of the bosses in equal measure.* What once seemed to be a formal condition now becomes fundamental and materially determinant: as always, the theory of organization finds itself verified only at the highest level of analysis, and in the approach to the most elevated political objective. Here and now, therefore, this function of the program of transition must be able to develop itself within the limits of the original conditions of the revolutionary process in Italy.

## THESIS 12: THE CRISIS ON THE INTERNATIONAL LEVEL

With thesis 11, we have arrived at the heart of the most burning political issue. In the very short term, the failure of the reformist prospect launches another round of the most brutal repressive action against the class. This may come from inside or outside the bloc of reformist forces: only a series of worker provocations can permit us to identify which of the two domains is better prepared to counterattack. This action is taken particularly against those spaces and forces that the critical self-realization of the Historic Compromise sees forming on its left wing, and thus against the party of workers' and proletarian autonomy.

But the critical situation is accentuated by the unfolding of the crisis on the international level. This critical international situation has had and will have extremely grave consequences for the domestic situation.

If we look, therefore, at the situation of the crisis on the international level, what is most striking, beyond the repetition of domestic elements of crisis in each of the mature capitalist countries, is the *failure*—or rather the extreme precariousness—*of the project of restructuring on the international level.* Elsewhere we have maintained that the elevation of capitalist top management, the reorganization of the structure of command over the unification of the world market, and the new hierarchical structure and organization of the international division of labor by zones must, in short, cause a rupture in the cumulative series of struggles by workers in the capitalist metropolises and by the Third World proletariat.[27] The capitalist objective consists in reinforcing the top management of capitalist command over the world market (through the policy of higher oil prices) and at the same time in defining a new flexibility of productive factors—energy sources and labor-power—to underpin the new money, which is to say the new criterion of equivalence and hierarchy, on the basis of restructuring. And we have seen in the first theses of this document that this project is still alive, and still influences the new class composition. But nevertheless, after addressing the effects that restructuring has on the body of the class and on the new composition, showing the persistence and renewal of proletarian action at the highest levels, at this point it is necessary to carry the analysis even further and try to foresee what will come next. For in fact, the capitalist project does not hold up.

It must be said that, after several years of extreme tension, the capitalist project of a new form of control over the world market—despite the acceleration of the pace of restructuring—finds itself in a profound crisis. Flexibility in the use of productive forces, far from having been consolidated, is in reality still a mirage. The attempt at restructuring in fact finds itself faced with a set of absolutely resistant and contradictory rigidities. The intent to disarticulate the cumulative series of struggles by metropolitan and Third World workers has failed. The consequences of this failure can be very grave, to the point of prompting new precipitations of antagonism on every level.

Let us take another step forward and try to grasp the core of the problem. How can the preceding situation, which has been defined by a formidable cumulative series of struggles on every side of capitalist control, be unblocked? Only by playing one series of levels of struggle against another: that is, by increasing the capacity for domestic containment of the socialized workers' continuous pressure through energy prices, and the setting up of a form of money adapted to the productive and technological capacities of the leading imperialist countries; by re-establishing unfavorable terms of exchange for the secondary countries of the capitalist zone (Europe and Japan); by imposing a heavily punitive crisis management on class confrontations; by opening up reformist spaces in the petroleum-producing countries and thus permitting a policy of the dynamic containment of proletarian struggles; and finally, by isolating the poor countries that lack raw materials. The new differences in level that have been established in this way will have to take shape within a linear organization, without sudden changes, and thus in a project of flexibility for all restructured factors. In fact, the scheme has not worked. In the leading capitalist countries, the utilization of the crisis against the workers has not been sufficient to bring the state's balance sheet back into the black, and thereby create the conditions for recovery. In the intermediate capitalist countries, the crisis has been an even bigger failure from the capitalist point of view: in fact, it has often given rise to situations in which the uncontainability of worker and proletarian pressure has led to the attempt to violate the terms of loyalty in the confrontation with the imperialist hierarchy (it no longer pays to stay in the system!). In the leading countries of the Third World, the proletarian push not only shows no sign of being placated, but it also continually insists on the rupture of reformist moderation. Lastly, in the marginalized countries, not only has this sentence not been accepted—as is obvious—but a way out has also urgently been sought, by means of a continual reassertion of revolutionary hypotheses and political agreements that render precarious, if not the economic order, then at least the political order of whole continents; here, the only response is dictatorship, destruction and starvation. In short, once again, *what should be a flexible model of compatibilities and proportions is transformed into a rigid and chaotic model of incompatibilities and disproportions.*

It is so rigid that the pessimistic predictions of the Chinese often seem to take on an extremely realistic tone when they see—in this unmediated fixation on the interests of states—the danger again arising of imperialist contradictions of the classical, i.e. inter-imperialist, type, including flashpoints [*scadenze*] on the path to war.

In reality, the dramatic nature of the situation cannot be underestimated. At the limits of Kissinger's reformism, in the presence of the crisis and the generalized fall of the rate of profit, and in a situation where capital fails to reimpose adequate rhythms of development on the whole world market, all that remains is *the alternative between a catastrophic solution and a revolutionary solution.* A catastrophic solution not only means war, but also starvation, the impoverishment and bestial exploitation of broad sections of the globe, and disaster through the organization of the most unbridled mobility of labor-power. A revolutionary solution, through the definitive destruction of the rule of profit, sets out to destroy the rule of the international division of labor.

All this, nevertheless, remains the case so long as capital fails to impose, by whatever means, rhythms adequate to the dimensions of its project of control over the world market, rhythms of development that legitimate the role of command in a new way. Such is the capitalist hypothesis today, and with a desperate will, capital stakes everything on it. It is disposed to respond with maximum violence in order to constrain labor. And this capitalist will, organized in response to the international requirements of command, reverberates within every single country, accumulating and exacerbating the will of national capital to destroy the workers' resistance to work.

To be confronted with the framework that we have defined implies, on the proletarian side and in every single capitalist country, a formidable forward leap of consciousness. *Faced with these problems, a party consciousness is not something added on but rather something prior and fundamental* that no longer appears as an external and superimposed ideology, as a form of internationalist solidarity, but becomes the necessary condition of the class struggle. If the problem of the transition includes, as it must, this series of problems, then we must emphasize here a fourth characteristic of transition, to complement the three indicated in thesis 11: *the foundation of a theory of the international conditions of the revolutionary passage* and the articulation of a series of tactical passages in reference to it.

Making headway on this terrain obviously entails a general exploration of political propositions. Suffice it to say at this point that the capitalist provocation that originates at the international level must be accepted—accepted and overturned. Only by accepting the terrain to which capital wants to reduce us can we attempt to overturn the sequences to which capital wants to constrain not only us, but the world proletariat as well. Capital says, either you accept reformism or there will be a catastrophe. Conversely, the workers' point of view, based on the last decade's experience of struggle, poses the problem from the inside: only by pursuing capitalist reformism closely from the inside, only by combating it at the highest levels of development, will the blackmail end and the road open up to the revolutionary process, its spread and the circulation of its objectives on the world level. It is only by combating reformism, by keeping open—in the heart of the class enemy's battle formations—the reality of a movement for communism, that we can prevent all the contradictions, rigidities and antagonisms of the world market from leading to catastrophe. Of course, positioning oneself on this terrain— and it is the terrain on which the refusal of the Historic Compromise positions itself—means facing the height of domestic and international capitalist violence; but for the proletarian movement, for communism, there is no alternative. How is it possible to think, in the face of this level of proletarian struggle, that a different road exists in Italy? All the contradictions registered in the whole set of the world market's political structures resound here with too much intensity. The specificity of Italy is that of being *a large capitalist country with an irreducible working class.* From capital's standpoint, neither the exclusion of Italy from the camp of advanced capitalist countries nor the political integration of the class is immediately imaginable.

Hence the vicissitudes, the comings and goings, the perplexities of judgment of the international bourgeoisie on the subject of Italy, a judgment that is quite different and more attentive than that of the last wretched remnants of the national political class. Hence the feeling of drama, the obscure powerlessness that the leadership of international capital feels whenever the Italian problem moves to the center of the discussion. Some of the most drastic judgments are more the expression of this malaise than of a lack of attention.

What does this situation mean from the workers' viewpoint? It means that *the Italian working class represents a midpoint,* one of extraordinary force and fascination, that is positioned *at the center* of two concomitant movements of struggle: *struggles in development and struggles in underdevelopment.* At the level of the productive forces that the working class represents, it constitutes a fundamental point of attraction for the revolution of the underdeveloped countries, just as the Italian working class's objectives and capacity for struggle constitute a constant reference point for working-class struggles in the advanced countries because of their insistence on appropriation and the refusal of work. From this class midpoint, the revolution is possible—with reference to these international class conditions—to the extent that the refusal of work and the liberation of the Italian working class's enormous productive, scientific, and political forces advance together. In the first place, the productive potential of a liberated working class, capable of self-managing the suppression of its own exploitation, can provide enormous openings to the rising proletariat in the underdeveloped countries. Consequently, the revolutionary force of the Italian working class's struggle against work, which ultimately turns itself into a revolutionary offensive against the state, is able to gather around itself the active solidarity of the advanced working class and reconstruct a workers' mechanism for the international defense of the revolution, a mechanism that is highly advanced because it is based on that struggle's capacity to be a dynamic motive center for the active proposal of objectives that are wholly linked, and belong, to the most advanced working class.

From this point of view the Historic Compromise is the most deeply contradictory and mystifying element in existence. It accepts the imbalance of the international relationships of domination, and "realistically" (*sic!*) and passively agrees to settle there. The demands for restructuring, conversion, etc. advanced by the Historic Compromise all forecast an acceptance of the stabilization of the Italian system of production at an intermediate rank in the international chain. Furthermore, such a subaltern position is accentuated and suffers the blackmail of the international terms of capitalist productivity to its fullest extent. The structural danger of such a dependence on the outside, the danger of the continual reproduction of a model of development that has an exorbitant dependence on the export market, is certainly well known: and it will be even more so in the future when the forces of the Historic Compromise will be increasingly hemmed in between workers' struggles, the expression of proletarian needs, and the demand for communism on one side and the blackmail of the imperialist market on the other. Within this play of forces, in the unified world market, it is unthinkable that the Historic Compromise should succeed in taking hold. But nevertheless, up to that point it will have further aggravated the situation by introducing additional elements of organic dependence into restructuring.

## THESIS 13: TO BEGIN THE INQUIRY INTO WORKERS' AND PROLETARIAN AUTONOMY

Against the Historic Compromise, against all the institutional entanglements of the proletarian class movement, it is possible today to begin a *mass inquiry*[28] *into workers' and proletarian autonomy.* It is not only possible but necessary. This inquiry must proceed from the following three fundamental points: (a) the social level of autonomy; (b) the dialectical domain within which autonomy confronts institutions; (c) autonomy's timetables [*scadenze*]. Let us examine these points one by one.

In the first place, *the social level of autonomy.* To carry the analysis onto this terrain is to tackle fully the problem of the definition of the new technical and political composition of the working class and proletariat, that is, to determine the political density of the new social composition of productive forces. But first we must provide a complete description of three fundamental processes: the further proletarian unification and the *marginal disarticulation of the proletariat* (a, 1), the *maximum socialization of productive living labor* (a, 2), and the *tertiarization of direct production* and thus its automatic control (a, 3). The first issue (a, 1) requires an intervention able to clarify, in every single aspect (related above all to the youth proletariat and schooling, to the female proletariat and domestic labor, and to unemployed labor-power and the mechanisms of marginalization), the inherent nature of the disarticulations of the unitary process of proletarianization and their necessity from the standpoint of accumulation. But here, perhaps the most important element of the inquiry consists in the political characteristic of the process: out of proletarian marginalization emerge new needs that are irreducible to the demands of wage labor. The analysis must grasp this power [*potenza*] of marginalization as the extreme limit—and radical force—of the refusal of work. The "lumpen" today establish, in and for the movement, a yearning for political liberation in which the proletarian class struggle seeks to establish itself: the "lumpen" are the true bearers of those "human values" that fill the mouths of socialism and revisionism. With this difference: they are not bearers of values that take the form of an "originary and generic essence," but rather *Träger*, the bearers and transmitters of struggle. Here, at the limits of marginalization and its extreme negation, the human sense of the class struggle is regained: to rediscover it means to struggle in the most radical manner. By facing the issues of the socialization and tertiarization of living labor (a, 2 and 3), we move forward onto better-known terrain: here, the quantity and quality of constant capital come directly into play, and thus social labor can be considered as a productive force, faced not only with the labor market but also with the social organization of labor, the social articulations of command, social knowledge, applied science, etc. *The problem is to weigh the wealth of issues and problems that must be faced,* to do so politically according to the goals of struggle and political organization. From this point of view, then, rather than insisting on the relative decline of the mass worker, the analysis will bear on the identification of the territorial disarticulations of the factory, on the formal articulations of these disarticulations (how command is exercised and how profits are realized), and in parallel fashion on the direct integration of functions that are otherwise separate (tertiary, administrative, scientific, etc.) into the mechanism of production and control. From the political point of view, the problem is that of radically overturning the capitalist organization of living social labor in its potential for struggle, not by indulging in formal schematics or functions of continuity [*funzioni continue*], but by insisting on the content of exploitation in every form of the process, and at the same time by demystifying the capitalist image of its division and separation. Here too the political contents come to the forefront, because in this unity of social exploitation and capital's drive against intellectual labor (in order to render it absolutely homogeneous to the regulation of living social labor), the innovative and liberatory function, elusive and mystified by work at this level of abstraction, can begin to redeem itself. To work in order to liberate, to carry the struggle not only against surplus-value but also against necessary labor: this insistence resides and reproduces itself as an elementary need in the behavior of this new (*aufgehoben*) proletariat. The analysis must—and can—begin here to express the very particular creative utility of labor (insofar as it is incarnated in its enormous social diffusion) against the domination of exchange value and the dictatorship of money.

In the second place, the inquiry must face the *dialectical framework within which autonomy clashes with institutions.* It is then a matter of determining what contradictions and antagonisms have been opened up by autonomy's impact on the institutions of capitalist command. If, in the first *tranche* [installment] of the inquiry, the analysis shifted between technical composition and political composition, forcing upon it an originary objective indistinctness, here the subjective component is made much stronger and the tendency to pose the problem of organization is actualized. The fundamental issues on which we propose to base the research are the following: (b, 1) the *contradictions between* collective *processes of accumulation and the legitimation of command*; (b, 2) the definition of the proletarian class's *levels of struggle*. On the first issue, the analysis of all the articulations of the political system must be overturned: it is, in fact, on the basis of the state's inability materially to guarantee and ideologically to legitimate the collective mechanism of accumulation that the fundamental contradiction opens up and expands. On different levels, from the union level to that of relationships between (private, public, etc.) enterprises to that of local and territorial entities, the contradiction is held open by the emergence of proletarian needs. On this tightrope, the various currents of capitalist reformism balance themselves, split up and come together again. The task of the inquiry is to transform these contradictions systematically into antagonisms, to show how any state solution to the problem of legitimation anticipates an intensification of social exploitation, and to demystify the alternatives offered by reformism. On this terrain, the developing analysis of the processes of legitimation intersects with and is completed through the analysis of levels of proletarian struggle. Here, the richness of the framework becomes immense, and the subjective dimension widens and imposes itself. Never before this moment has the analysis been able to satisfy itself. At this point it doesn't register or grasp already completed processes, or recount past struggles and constituted figures, but rather *traverses* a completely new phase; it undergoes a biological mutation, or a change from one state of matter to another. In the end, the workers' point of view in the sixties only reached the point of expressing itself when everything was over and done, since the mass worker was already constituted; now, on the other hand, critique coexists with the expansion of a new revolutionary figure of the proletariat. At this point, therefore, political need truly becomes desire. Nevertheless, what an extraordinary complex of "things over and done" the class presents! Appropriation is a diffuse revolutionary practice, and the relationships between the struggle for appropriation and the exercise of proletarian power by *every* means are developing radically. Now the analysis must fully encompass this field of possibilities, return to the initial concepts, and take up once again, on the basis of the definition of forms of behavior, the inquiry into the social level of proletarian autonomy.

The third point of the inquiry concerns *autonomy's timeframes* [*scadenze*]. Here, research develops fully into political practice. As usual, political practice must be a practice of discussions and debates: on institutional timeframes, on the political program, on aggregation, on the party. The problem is nevertheless one of posing these issues for discussion in a homogeneous manner, within a network of relevant concepts and sufficiently developed theoretical approximations, and above all within determinate timeframes and levels of struggle. Thus, it is not a simple problem of method that is posed at this turning point in the inquiry: instead, a material approach to organization and definition is required. In what sense? In the sense that here, in this regard, the theoretical and practical experience of Marxism-Leninism regains all its importance. Here the subjective tension toward organization, and with it the battle over political lines, becomes fundamental. The whole development of the inquiry so far has avoided the introduction of unrealistic ideological schemas: the path goes from practice to theory and back to practice. We can follow it through, from cognitive practice situated on the terrain of the demand for power by the new proletariat, to the theory of the program, and back to the practice of the revolutionary party of the proletariat. In Marxist fashion, the analysis has made the tendency its own, and in Leninist fashion, the tendency is now actualized, founded again on the subjective will to organization.

### THESIS 14: MORE ON THIS ISSUE: THE SUBJECT OF WORKERS' INQUIRY

If the class composition of the socialized worker does not allow delegated knowledge, if at the current level of the revolutionary process of autonomy there is no knowledge that is not both theoretical and practical, *then conducting workers' inquiry today*, in these conditions, *means describing in practical terms the possible consciousness of an ongoing party process.* Workers' inquiry is a political battle right from the start: it is a political battle on the side of theory as well as that of practice. On the side of theory, workers' inquiry is a battle against all the mystifications, delays, illusions, and tricks of the lingering ideological images of a reality that has been destroyed (or is in the process of being destroyed) through the violence of restructuring. It is a battle for the construction of a new basis for workers' science, defined by the insurgence of the *socialized worker* as the material unification of the social determinations of exploitation and as the potentiality of a fundamental new revolutionary need: that of liberation *from* work as well as the liberation *of* labor. Here the theoretical battle in its turn becomes a practical battle, or, better, it is wholly rediscovered as a political horizon. Indeed, only organization reveals the working class to itself as a unity and at the same time as the development of a fundamental revolutionary project. Organization means the direct self-management by the working class of the simultaneous destruction of ideology and exploitation; organization means the direct reappropriation of existing wealth in order to destroy it or to liberate invention-power. Rebellion, insurgency is the dialectical nexus of every sequence of revolutionary activity. And it is a totalizing nexus: there is no revolutionary consciousness that is not based on this will, and no organization can truly call itself revolutionary unless, far from isolating it in a single moment, it extends this will to its whole reality.

To speak of the subject of workers' inquiry, therefore, means to speak of a totality, of the power [*potenza*] of a totality. It means to speak in a majoritarian way, not in someone's name, but because theory and practice result in an instance of overall organization. Consequently, it means above all to act directly and immediately. Here we touch again upon one of Marxism's great truths: the working class is radically distinct from the bourgeoisie because the latter can recognize itself as a class only through the state, only through ideological mediations, while the working class is the first social force that can destroy every mediation in production and in life, first of all that of the state. In the maturation of the socialized worker, this instance of class reappropriation emerges ever more strongly. The first objective of the socialized worker is to reappropriate its own organization, as knowledge of itself and as direct management of power, and therefore—on this basis—to destroy the state. Today, to forge ahead in workers' inquiry is to define a communist terrain and at the same time to follow a communist path. At this point there is neither neutrality nor mediation.

Beyond the determinations of immediacy and direct reappropriation, the process of possible consciousness presents other characteristics. A fundamental one is defined by the *materiality of the timetables* [*scadenze*] on which the inquiry shows the social figure of the proletariat in conflict with the class adversary. It is important to define these timetables to the extent that they make possible the establishment of an *accumulation of struggles*, a fundamental condition for the opening up of a process of *political aggregation,* and therefore for the rearticulation of the *proletarian front* and a further definition of the *program* and the project of *party organization.*

The inquiry has presented its own determinate articulations regarding timetables [*sulle scadenze*]. The economic crisis is deepening, and it seems that only the economists, *stulta logicalia cacantes*,[29] make a show of not noticing it. In fact, all the sequences of economic development (and the theory that describes them) are confused to the point that only the most extreme simple-mindedness allows them to ignore the situation. What preoccupies the bosses is not so much the fact that the elements of the objective determination of the crisis are accentuated—from the expected new wave of raw-material cost increases, to monetary chaos, to the ineffectiveness of the tools of planning—

as it is the fact that their counter-strategy is producing effects that systematically reactivate the front of struggle. On this terrain, workers' inquiry must allow the seizing of moments of offense defined punctually by the timetables of the crisis and the strategy of restructuring, from the struggle over the wage to the practices of reappropriation, thus establishing class forms of behavior. The political crisis is a second terrain. Here, workers' inquiry shows that it is possible to define an extraordinary continuity of workers' forms of behavior: the struggle over immediate needs, at the very moment it develops, ensnares the levels of state legitimation, confuses the proportions of the balancing mechanisms, and introduces alternatives, frictions, and antagonisms into the political elite. But if the bourgeoisie is divided over the question of how to command the masses, this division is immediately reflected in and manifested as a social crisis of the bourgeoisie, because the only element that socially unifies the bourgeoisie is state command over exploitation. The inquiry must grasp the continuity of the class adversary's crisis and aim at timetables [*scadenze*] of struggle that penetrate—from the levels of immediate proletarian struggle—into the institutional levels of power. This tension is already a given on the proletarian side: it is a matter of accentuating it, making it continuous, articulating it in the alternation between mass action and vanguard action. *If the class adversary seeks in the short term to readjust its power by force*, as well it might—and it is necessary for the first time to insist strongly upon this—*we must develop not only a force capable of responding effectively on the militant plane, but also a mass practice that precludes the "necessity" of alliances that are not adequate to the radically communist alternative that the socialized worker expresses.*

The offensive against the wage and the struggle against wage labor; the destruction of the legitimacy of the class adversary's political restructuring (the Historic Compromise as well as its alternatives); the preparation for militant struggle against the capitalist attempt to force a resolution of the conflict: these are the analytical objectives that, through the inquiry, define the party process. This process has been, is now and will remain the fundamental objective.

To express the possible consciousness of the proletariat and to develop it into an adequate party program is thus a complex process, above all because the subject and the object are identical here. But the inquiry begins to show the maturity of the timetables on the basis of which the accumulation of struggles, political aggregation, the constitution of a front, the definition of the program, and the foundation of the party can move forward. We are conceiving a party that knows how to develop an effective leadership role, but only the struggles and the materiality of a power consolidated among the masses can decide on this leadership capacity. The party process, in the

Marxist-Leninist sense, knows its own possibilities and conditions, and this is the road that we are traveling today. A whole generation of workers' and proletarian political cadres, constituted by the struggles of the last decade, springing either from the experience of "workerist" groups or from metropolitan experiences of Marxist-Leninist inspiration, all renewed today in the basic struggle for proletarian autonomy—that whole generation is available for this effort of inquiry. We have known defeat, disillusion, regression, and yet, through storm and through calm, the path has led onward. To recognize ourselves today as subjects of the party process, therefore, means marching through the new composition of the socialized worker, but it also means insisting on the unity of the subjective situation that the whole process reveals. Then, "armed with a just theory and an inflexible practice," we will perhaps realize that the pain of recognizing ourselves as subjects of the revolutionary process is worthwhile, above all by virtue of the fact that "there is great disorder under heaven, and the situation is excellent."[30]

### Notes

1. TN: Giorgio Amendola (1907–1980) rose to prominence as a representative of the PCI's right wing following the death of Palmiro Togliatti in 1964. Guido Carli (1914–1993) was a director of the International Monetary Fund, Governor of the Bank of Italy from 1960 to 1975, and president of the industrial employers' group Confindustria from 1976 to 1980.

2. TN: By "Balkanized workers," Negri means workers outside the large factories and workers' organizations, workers whose relative isolation (in small factories, doing piecework in their homes, etc.) impeded their participation in the successful workers' struggles of the late sixties and early seventies.

3. TN: Giorgio Fuà (1919–2000) was a statistical economist and policy researcher at the University of Ancona.

4. TN: Bruno Trentin (b.1926) was a Resistance fighter in Italy and France during the Second World War; a member of the PCI from 1950, he served several terms as secretary-general of CGIL (*Confederazione Generale Italiana dei Lavoratori*), the largest Italian union organization, and in the Italian parliament from the Fifties to the Nineties.

5. TN: Carnival Thursday (*giovedì grasso*), also known as Fat Thursday, is the official beginning of the pre-Lenten Carnival in most Italian localities, although the specifics of the celebration vary according to local history and tradition.

6. TN: Roscelin (c.1045–c.1120) was a French Scholastic philosopher who taught a nominalist metaphysics that claimed universals (general concepts) were merely words used to name groups of objects and had no independent existence of their own.

7. TN: Luciano Barca is an Italian political scientist and party bureaucrat; during the sixties and seventies he was a prominent PCI member of the Italian parliament. Alberto Ronchey (b.1926) is a prominent Italian journalist who wrote for the daily newspapers *La Stampa*, *Corriere della sera* and *La Repubblica* as well as the weekly news magazines *L'Espresso* and *Panorama* during the sixties and seventies.

8. TN: In English in the original.

9. For the definition of this approach to the analysis of the crisis and this rereading of Marx, allow me to refer to my essays "Keynes and the Capitalist Theory of the State" and "Marx on Cycle and Crisis" (both in *Revolution Retrieved*); *Workers' Party Against Work* (in this volume); "Communist State Theory" and "The State and Public Spending," in Michael Hardt and Antonio Negri, *Labor of Dionysus: A Critique of the State-Form*, Minneapolis: University of Minnesota Press, 1994.

10. Marx, *Capital* Volume 3, New York: Penguin, 1981, part III, chapter 14.

11. TN: The German word "*aufgehoben*" is a form of the verb *aufheben*, which in Hegelian parlance means "to preserve and abolish in the resolution of a dialectical opposition."

12. On this argument, see Walter Guntherroth, "Kritik der Marxorthodoxie," in *Autonomie: Materialen gegen Fabrikgesellschaft*, Munich: Trikont Verlag, 1 October 1975, pp. 36–58.

13. TN: Piero Sraffa (1898–1983) was an Italian economist and personal friend of Gramsci who came to Cambridge on the invitation of John Maynard Keynes and became a member of Ludwig Wittgenstein's circle; he later became the major figure in the "Cambridge school" of neo-Marxism (see Negri's discussion of this school in the "Postscript" to *Crisis of the Planner-State* above). His most important work is *Production of Commodities by Means of Commodities*, Cambridge: Cambridge University Press, 1960. A. Leontiev, an economist and member of the Soviet Academy of Sciences, originally wrote *Political Economy: A Beginner's Course* (San Francisco: Proletarian Publishers, 1964) in the thirties.

14. TN: The theory of state monopoly capitalism, which originated in the post-Stalin Soviet Union, holds that the most recent stage of capitalist development is characterized by the direct involvement of the state in the accumulation of capital; this generally takes the form of the state's legislative support and protection of a few very large enterprises. These large enterprises constitute effective monopolies that depend upon imperialist expansion of the state to remain profitable, and thus the operation of state monopoly capitalism on a global scale creates a two-tiered system of economic development: overproduction in the industrialized nations and underdevelopment that prevents capital accumulation in the post-colonial "Third World."

15. Certain comrades have expressed some reservations on this subject. It is obvious that our hypothesis anticipates the preliminary discussion and critique of several positions that are present in the movement today, and that are related to the analysis of the reorganization of the world market through multinational

enterprises. We are alluding here to the positions of O'Connor, Nicolaus, Mandel, Neusüss, Hymer, and Poulantzas. [TN: James O'Connor, author of *The Fiscal Crisis of the State*, New York: St. Martin's Press, 1973, and *The Corporations & the State: Essays in the Theory of Capitalism & Imperialism*, New York: Harper & Row, 1974; Martin Nicolaus, translator of Marx's *Grundrisse*, New York: Penguin, 1973; Christel Neusüss, author (with Wolfgang Müller) of "The Illusion of State Socialism and the Contradiction between Wage Labor and Capital" in *Telos* 25, fall 1975; Stephen Hymer, author of *The International Operations of National Firms: A Study of Direct Foreign Investment*, Cambridge: MIT Press, 1976, and *The Multinational Corporation: A Radical Approach*, Cambridge: Cambridge University Press, 1979; Nicos Poulantzas, author of *Political Power and Social Classes*, translated by Timothy O'Hagan, London: New Left Books, 1973, and *Classes in Contemporary Capitalism*, translated by David Fernbach, London: New Left Books, 1975.] A critique of these positions is contained in Luciano Ferrari Bravo's introductory essay in *Imperialismo e classe operaia multinazionale*, Milan: Feltrinelli, 1975, pp. 7–67. We are convinced that the unification of capitalist command, beginning in the leading imperialist countries and exercised through the nervous system of multinational enterprises, does not represent a contradictory tendency (that could perhaps become antagonistic) but rather the reality of a tendency that has been actualized. This assertion allows us to accept, even on the international level, the hypothesis of a "subjective" interpretation (in the manner of Marx) and on this basis to attempt an analysis of the development of the world market according to the rhythm of analysis of the class composition of particular fractions of the global proletariat and the incidence of class struggle. An initial and very important attempt in this direction is Ferrucio Gambino's "Composizione di classe e investimenti diretti statunisenti all'estero," in the volume cited above.

16.  TN: Palmiro Togliatti was the leader of the PCI for nearly forty years (many of them in exile in the USSR), from Gramsci's arrest in 1926 until his own death in 1964. The "Salerno turnabout [*svolta di Salerno*]" was Togliatti's decision, in line with the outcome of the Yalta Conferences regarding the political geography of the postwar world, to lend the PCI's support to the establishment of parliamentary democracy in Italy after the defeat of Fascism instead of fomenting a communist revolution with the help of the communist Resistance brigades. See Togliatti's speech "The Communist Policy of National Unity" (1944) in Togliatti, *On Gramsci and Other Writings*, edited by Donald Sassoon, London: Lawrence & Wishart, 1979, and Alexander De Grand, *The Italian Left in the Twentieth Century*, Bloomington: Indiana University Press, 1989, pp. 87–91.

17.  TN: In English in the original.

18.  TN: The layoff fund or "*cassa integrazione*" is a specifically Italian form of unemployment compensation in which the state pays around 90 percent of laid-off workers' wages for roughly one fiscal year, in order to reduce the financial

burden on private enterprise; see Paul Ginsborg, *A History of Contemporary Italy,* New York: Penguin, 1990, p. 353, and Steve Wright, *Storming Heaven*, London: Pluto Press, 2002, pp. 168–69.

19. TN: "Transformism" [*trasformismo*] is an Italian political term that refers to political co-optation by means of the division and absorption of oppositional parties or groups by the ruling bourgeoisie. See Gramsci, "The Problem of Political Leadership in the Formation and Development of the Nation and the Modern State in Italy," in *Selections from the Prison Notebooks*, New York: International Publishers, 1971, especially pp. 55–59 and the translator's note on p. 58.

20. TN: "Riding the tiger" was Italian slang for the traditional unions' practice of co-opting delegates who had been elected by the workers to non-union representative councils within their factories. See Wright, pp. 128–29.

21. TN: Aníbal Escalante was the Stalinist leader of the Cuban Popular Socialist Party before it merged with Fidel Castro's July 16th Movement in 1961; in 1968 Castro accused Escalante of leading a "treasonous micro-faction" that sought to stage a coup against the Cuban revolutionary government. Álvaro Cunhal (b.1913) was the Stalinist leader of the Portuguese Communist Party following the military coup of 1974, and served as a member of the provisional government for several months thereafter.

22. TN: Giovanni Giolitti (1842–1928) served five terms as Italian prime minister between 1892 and 1921; although he was a pro-labor Liberal, his political methods—which included co-optation of opportunistic opponents (including both Socialists and Fascists) through patronage and open intimidation of intransigent ones—belied his ideological commitment to progressive politics.

23. Romano Alquati, *Sindicato e partito*, Turin: Stampatori, 1974, pp. 165–66.

24. TN: Mário Alberto Nobre Lópes Soarès (b.1924) was the leader of the Portuguese Socialist Party following the military coup of 1974, after which he and his party sided with the center-right parties; he served three terms as prime minister and two as president.

25. TN: In English in the original.

26. TN: Gustav Noske (1868–1946) was a German Social Democratic politician; while in charge of the armed forces following the republican revolution of 1918 and minister of defense in 1919–1920, he violently suppressed radical movements throughout Germany, including the Spartacus group, whose leaders, Rosa Luxemburg and Karl Liebknecht, were murdered after the defeat of their revolt in January 1919.

27. See the "Theses" published as an appendix to my *Worker's Party Against Work*, in *Crisi e organizzazione operaia*, op. cit., pp. 166–83 [English translation, "Theses on the Crisis," in *Working-Class Autonomy and the Crisis*, London: Red Notes, 1979, pp. 38–54].

28. TN: On mass inquiry, see the entry for workers' inquiry in the Glossary.

29. TN: The Latin phrase *"stulta logicalia cacantes"* means "stupid defilers of logic."

30. TN: A well-known aphorism from Mao Tse-Tung.

# IV

# Toward a Critique of the Material Constitution[1] (1977)

### *Translated by Arianna Bove and Timothy S. Murphy*

## 1. MUTATION OF THE MATERIAL CONSTITUTION AND CLASS ANTAGONISM

This essay aims to demonstrate that the political event of the Constitution of 1948 is now over. This is not news: we all know that Constitutions are transient and sticky institutions, and the formal continuity of the Constitution of 1948 will hardly be put into question; but liturgical ceremonies and visits to the temple are probably going to continue, even more often as faith in them fades. However, "Germany is no longer a State,"[2] that is, the (Hegelian) state required by those leaders and administrators who demand the correspondence, in principle, between the formal and the material character of the constitutional process, as required by the system of "certainty" of right [*diritto*]. The Constitution is no longer the law of all laws: laws proceed by themselves, following the pace and coherence of the constitution of a new structure of political power. A *new regime* is taking shape day by day and a *new material constitution* is arising.[3]

Obviously, resistance to this assertion is general and stubborn, so it would be near-suicidal to confront it head on. To begin, let us pretend to agree with it, particularly in order to see whether such resistance is in fact entirely contradictory. Its main claim is that "at the end of the fifth Legislature (1972), despite some open questions that remain, we can consider the implementation of the constitutional design accomplished as a whole and in its most crucial parts,"[4] yet it is also true that the Constitution—because of its "long-sighted" ability to foresee—maintains a promotional role of leadership and guarantor after its realization.[5] But there is more to this. In and beyond its realization, the Constitution is supposed to prefigure a model of democratic socialist, or at least anti-capitalist, society and to establish prescriptive [*ordinante*] criteria for social transformation.[6] Well, *all o'right,*[7] now that we know the *materialis, formalis ac efficiens* cause of the plague, we can rest assured! But as soon as we take hold of the Constitution, our juridical system suddenly becomes a "discontinuous entity traversed by fractures" that can be *used* in a way that is alternative to the domination of the capitalist will, however contradictory its essence.[8] Today, this impression is so predominant that, as the political debate intensifies, it is not unusual to hear the Italian political system described in more dualistic terms: "On the one hand, there is a recovery of the capitalist relation of production; on the other hand, the political economy that conditions economic development derives its features from current relations of force in Parliament, the means at the disposal of the public sector and the constant pressure exerted by the mass movement."[9] One has to admit, for a constitution realized under such difficult conditions, this is the best way to be: prey to immediate political relations that finally result in a dualism of powers!

Constitutionalists and economists fall into a contradiction that can only be explained if we start by analyzing the development of the struggle between the two classes, rather than the Constitution itself. On this basis, we have to assume that constitutionalist reformism is no longer necessarily compatible with the consistent terms of the struggle. *The sixties swept away reformist politics along with the juridical form of its management.* Anyway, did reformists have any reason to be complacent in those years? "The twenty-five years after the war that passed without a major recession has been called the Age of Keynes, but it was not much like his vision. It turned out closer to Kalecki's sardonic description of the regime of the political trade cycle."[10] What was successfully hidden by ideology back then is immediately revealed by practice today: a new relation of force between the classes has emerged and its consistency is increasingly antagonistic; juridical representation (still effective despite its mystifications) must deal with this new relation. But why should we insist on the "*laudatio temporis acti*"?[11] What we are faced with is not a restoration; the situation has moved forward on both sides of the class struggle. Rather than struggling against a restoration, we have to operate within—and, for whomever so desires, against—a capitalist restructuring, and within a new and increased possibility of workers' struggle.

The new material constitution is taking shape around the capitalist attempt to end its crisis. The Constitution of labor of 1948 registered a certain set of relations in order to control them: it accounted for a state of diffuse conflict in the relations of production that was nevertheless not meant to turn into antagonism. *Today the dimensions and quality of conflict are instead immediately antagonistic: the whole circuit of reproduction is involved in such antagonism.* Thus, the new material constitution must be tested against the reality of this antagonism, and more specifically against the new dimensions and quality of workers' struggle, the new composition of the proletarian and working class. Unexpectedly, capital hysterically declares a general interest in production and in the co-management [*cogestione*] of social profit. But the urge to achieve a new state form and a *regime* that denies conflict while heightening co-management corresponds to the realization that class struggle has definitely blown up the proportions of development from both the quantitative and the qualitative points of view.

Now, let us see whether these issues are any clearer if we directly analyze class struggle: "the class struggle as the key into which the movement and the analysis of all the shit [*der ganzen Scheiße*] resolves itself."[12]

"The *semblance of exchange* vanishes in the course [*Prozess*] of the mode of production founded on capital" (*Grundrisse* 597). The overcoming of exchange is part and parcel of the physiology of capital. Exchange is posited as a barrier to the development of the productive forces and as the specific form in which, in a given period, the relationship between necessary and surplus labor must be determined (to the advantage of capital) (*Grundrisse* 415–19). But the exchange form is a barrier: capital has to destroy and abolish exchange as a limit to production. In this case, capital "constantly revolutionizes [production], tearing down all the barriers which hem in the development of the forces of production, the expansion of needs, the all-sided development of production, and the exploitation and exchange of natural and mental forces" (*Grundrisse* 410).

This applies to the form. As for the substance, capitalist consciousness is increasingly aware of two essential issues. *First, the nature of exchange is altered to the extent that the exchange relation is transfigured*: exchange is increasingly posited in collective rather than individual terms, and while capital appropriates the entire productive power of labor and presents it as its own productive power, the labor force borrows the overall socialization of capital and makes it its own irreducible characteristic (*Grundrisse* 585–89). *Second*, at the very moment when capital "has subjugated historical progress to the service of wealth" (*Grundrisse* 590), and for this purpose presents itself "as the condition of the development of the forces of production as long as they require an external spur, which appears at the same time as their bridle," the *productive forces become more emancipated* and their discipline, in this case exchange, "becomes superfluous and burdensome" "just like the guilds etc." (*Grundrisse* 415). Capitalist development needs to overcome two material barriers: the social dimension and the emancipated quality of labor-power, which is to say, of the productive forces at a given level of development. Exchange is inadequate to the possibility for capital to set in motion the collective power of socially cooperative labor: hence, the obsolescence of exchange is total and radical. Capital must overcome this internal barrier.

However, for this to be accomplished, the regime of proportions on which capitalist development has heretofore been based must be overthrown. Obviously, "Capital is just as much the constant positing as the suspension of *proportionate production*" (*Grundrisse* 414; see also 443–47): but what is under discussion here is the *structural function* of the proportion of exchange. The dimension of socially necessary labor and its emancipated quality call into question not only the quantity of the proportionality of exchange, but also proportion and exchange *tout court*. The law of value is in crisis. Hence the capitalist urge to overcome it. But how?

> But from the fact that capital posits every such limit as a barrier and hence gets *ideally* beyond it, it does not by any means follow that it has *really* overcome it, and, since every such barrier contradicts its character, its production moves in contradictions which are constantly overcome but just as constantly posited. Furthermore. The universality towards which it irre-sistibly strives encounters barriers in its own nature, which will, at a certain stage of its development, allow it to be recognized as being itself the greatest barrier to this tendency, and hence will drive towards its own suspension. (*Grundrisse* 410)

Here is the issue: the ideal capitalist overcoming of exchange. The terms of this problem are now posed and they are twofold: its *overcoming* and *its ideal character.*

The Constitution of 1948 attests to a social organization (and its regula-tion) that is founded on conflict, exchange, and the functioning of the law of value (and secondarily on compromise). These conditions are in the process of changing; the Constitution too must be altered materially. But how? "Competition generally, this essential locomotive force of the bour-geois economy, does not establish its laws, but is rather their executor" (*Grundrisse* 552). Therefore, the Constitution has to change, in ideal terms, not the laws of bourgeois economy but rather their executor. The social character and emancipated quality of the movements of labor-power must be subsumed within an ideal form of social organization that, through the elimination of exchange, perpetuates the laws of exploitation. "Unlimited competition is therefore not the presupposition for the truth of the economic laws, but rather the consequence—the form of appearance in which their necessity realizes itself" (*Grundrisse* 552). When the working class, because of its mass movement and the quality of its needs, prevents competition and exchange on the only terrain that is essential for development, i.e., that of the exchange of labor-power against the valorization of commodities, the Constitution must then be overcome in ideal terms. For the capitalist rule of valorization to be realized, the exchange form of labor-power must be overcome. The appearance must be altered while the essence remains. The problems and contradictions of constitutionalists, economists, and political scientists only begin to become clear in light of this.

However, it is not enough to remain within these limits, because we risk falling into a *"residual" conception* in the analysis of the dialectical relationship between working-class struggles (and composition) and capitalist development. The stagnation, blockage, and annihilation of equal and opposing forces, a conception deprived of quality and subjectivity, are "residues" of class activity rather than its real horizon. "Mere negation … creates nothing" (*Grundrisse* 613). On the other hand, in material production, labor assumes a "really free" character under the following conditions: "(1) when its social character is posited, (2) when it is of a scientific and at the same time general character, not merely human exertion as a specifically harnessed natural force, but exertion as subject, which appears in the production process not in a merely natural, spontaneous form, but as an activity regulating all the forces of nature" (*Grundrisse* 612). Now, *at this level of the massification and socialization of labor, these characteristics arise.* The Constitution is obsolete and in crisis not simply because of its failure to constrain the massification of labor within the rule of exchange and the proportions of planning, but especially because of its inability to respond to the *alternative valorization* that the working class carries out on and of itself. The formal overcoming of exchange and the ideal subsumption of the new figure of class composition reproduce a form of development "on a limited basis—the basis of the domination of capital" (*Grundrisse* 652, translation modified). The "objective power" of competition turns into the "overpowering object" of command.[13] However, in saying this we might underestimate the intensity of capitalist crisis, the class strength that brings it about and the specificity of the mystifications that try to contain it; we might fail to understand that working-class struggle (and composition) determines the movements of capital as well as their quality, the dynamics as well as the motions.

This means that the Constitution is failing in the face of the collapse of the law of exchange because the reduction in necessary labor (and its social medium: the wage) is becoming rigid and expanding. But above all, the Constitution is failing when confronted with the quality and articulation that the reproduction of the working class is assuming, according to the rhythm of the rising cost of necessary labor. *The refusal of work (and all the political and social phenomena related to it) assumes a positive connotation:* in pursuit of capitalist development, it shifts the terrain of struggle from production to the totality of social (production and) reproduction; here again, it anticipates capital and determines not only the crisis but also its quality, framing the crisis around its own needs. *The refusal of work defines the modes of working-class self-valorization in reproduction,* it demands differential and/or indirect wages—it no longer seeks to realize itself on the terrain of production—it determines counterpower and proves itself willing to exercise it.

We are entering a new era of class struggle.

> Whatever the social form of production, workers and means of production always remain its factors. But if they are in a state of mutual separation, they are only potentially factors of production. For any production to take place, they must be connected. The particular form and mode in which this connection is effected is what distinguishes the various epochs of the social structure.[14]

In this case, the epochal shift is determined by the particular form of separation—i.e. productive labor-power that refuses its unpaid collective use and demands payment for it—and the particular form of unification that capital wishes to impose—ideal subsumption within capitalist command. Workers' refusal and capitalist command, the irrationality of the latter and the search for an autonomous valorization of the former, are intertwined in an absolutely antagonistic way across the entire realm of the social reproduction of the working class. The Constitution is obsolete when confronted with the new material dimensions of struggle and the impossibility of recuperating the latter into the proportions of planning and exchange; but it is also blind to the emancipated quality of class behavior in reproduction. The new era of class struggle begins where the historical space of the Constitution ends (and conclusively so).

*The new regime is born in the posing of these problems. It perceives that class struggle not only blocks development through its struggles but also intensifies its effects by tormenting the body of organization and social administration with the acuteness of its needs for an alternative self-valorization.* Power does not underestimate the violence of this laceration. The extreme specificity of the expression of proletarian needs for emancipation attests to the impossibility of resolving the contradiction. The violence of the response is and must be adequate to the sustained level of antagonism. The modification of the material constitution follows the rhythm of the destabilizing force of class struggle and the self-valorizing power [*potenza*] of the proletariat: its aim is to destroy them, in order to deliver the exclusive power of command over the valorization and devalorization of labor back to capital.

While we are tackling the terrain of institutions, our analysis ought to concentrate on the manner in which capitalist command tries to re-establish itself in response to the actions of class power. The main focus of the government's actions becomes the repression of this new valorizing quality: without the one, the other would not present itself in its specificity and intensity. The entire front of class struggle has advanced on both sides. *Command* and *co-management* are contradictory terms only for the *laudatores temporis acti:* in fact, in the current situation they are totally complementary—command is only given in the form of co-management, and co-management is defined by its essential function of authority.

Therefore, the capitalist elite and all the forces involved in co-management can only march in the direction of hollowing out the Constitution of 1948. As for constitutional dictates, the sixties were characterized by an attempt at democratic planning that atoned for the gap, the shift, the sometimes repressive dialectic between a planning hypothesis and its economic tools on the one hand and state command and the concrete articulations of its authority on the other, treating the two as "separate bodies".[15] However, behind this gap lies a more decisive factor: the inability of power to respond at the explicitly political levels of struggle other than by means of flexible operations that target large economic aggregates. The Keynesian imperative to implement policies designed to control (and sustain) overall levels of employment remains unquestioned: however, the working class and the proletariat destroy all the possible proportions of planning precisely on this terrain.[16] The backwardness and irrationality of the constitutional structure of the state and the gridlocks and shortcomings of power brought about on the institutional plane are multiplied by the liberation of the class movement. Consequently, the monetary realm, public spending, taxation, and the administrative network are all implicated in this process of crisis and degradation of command. This sequence unfolds in all Western democratic systems.[17]

It is precisely its generality that reveals the radicality of this process. The notion is increasingly being asserted that this process can only be blocked by an intervention that no longer simply bears on the broad dimensions of labor-power, but also affects its internal structure and forms of political behavior.[18] In this respect, co-management becomes essential to what has been called the *Crisis-State*. The system of planning can be rebuilt, the institutional frictions overcome and effectively coordinated within the global function of command only if the functions internal to class stratification are developed and included in this process. The functions of command must be diffuse and convergent. The whole discussion on revisionism today (to keep to the current crisis and its documentation) is moving in this direction.[19] The same goes for capital's more mature levels of political consciousness.[20] The modification that follows from this is necessarily related to the material constitution. The material results of labor effort [*travaglio*], as we have already emphasized, are neither necessarily given in their immediacy, nor are they mirror images [*specchiali*] or even simply congruent: in the letter quoted, Marx mentions to Engels this matter that plays an important role in this relation. The process of the material constitution is much more dramatic and urgent: at times, as in our time, it is even precipitate. The terms of modification must involve the whole set-up of the organizational process of the (production and) reproduction of capital: in other words, the form of command and co-management as well as the administrative articulations.[21]

One term refers to the other: the *material constitution* is by definition the level of *political agreement of the regime that establishes the tendency toward unity of the constitutional project.* Thus the socialized management of the economic process (and/or crisis) of development tends to restore *corporative forms of economic government* on the institutional side, on the side of normative production and, above all, on the plane of political imperatives for administration. Therefore, the administrative articulations of command must be re-established on the basis of a mechanism of *centralization and de-centering* that is entirely dependent on its compatibility with authority and the dynamic needs of the system. Finally, command as a whole tends toward a *general overdetermination of the process of co-management.* As co-management intensifies, so does command. The civil-rights modality[22] of the democratic process must be subordinated to the determinations of the other moments: this subordination can either take the form of the fiction of corporative managerial agreement or present itself through repressive anticipation, functional control and the criminalization of mass movements and their emancipatory power [*potenza*]. The obvious paradox of this system is that it must stretch the arc of recomposition to its maximum point. The recomposition enacted by authority is characterized by a need to reduce to a minimum the organizational options. We shall return to this later: the same radical antagonism that imposes modifications on the material constitution is also present in the institutional sequences set in motion by these modifications.[23]

The illusion of *reformism* is not the belief that socialism can be achieved through a reform of the material constitution: that is just treachery. The illusion consists in its faith in the supposed adequacy of means to ends and in its confidence in the fact that modifications of the material constitution can stabilize the system of capital. We are very far from the communist hypothesis, in whatever formulation: on this terrain any dialogue with reformism is ruled out because while the communist hypothesis exists for us, for them it is already resolved in terms of conventional wisdom and/or theoretical discredit. We are moving onto the terrain of political science pure and simple. In this realm, regarding matters of political science, reformism proves to be illusory, especially on the institutional terrain.

Reformism tries to define its political project positively and actively in terms of ending the crisis and stabilizing the system. The two proposals it puts forward are based on a common acceptance of the modifications of the material constitution and the attempt to situate itself within the regime and "use it." They are: *(a) the properly managerial hypothesis*, and *(b) the innovative hypothesis*.

The first enjoys the support of a large majority in the Official Labor Movement and is organized in terms of *politiques d'abord*. It regards the seizure of power and regime change as in themselves capable of securing stability, whatever their costs. The model of co-management is supposed to be capable of resolving the antagonistic elements of the crisis into a new, contradictory but not explosive synthesis. Co-management is supposed to be able to successfully preserve all the innovations in the constitution—i.e. the corporative regime, the overdetermination of the democratic relation with regard to administration and consensus formation, and the reassertion of the proportions of development imposed by authority. The second hypothesis differs sharply from the first because it demands, as the condition for stabilization, an active involvement in the restructuring of working-class and proletarian composition. The Official Labor Movement, according to this thesis, not only has to secure a necessary role in the network of relations that makes up the new material constitution, it also needs to overturn the latter in the process of innovation attributed to the social brain of production. Stabilization is only conceivable in the framework of the overall innovation of class relations. The current historical phase must register this leap forward. This alone can be the foundation for an effective stabilization. Both these positions are illusory, at the level of mere political science. The first hypothesis fails to take into account all the elements of analysis and is reduced to a cynical celebration of the autonomy of the political; the second one falls into absolute formalism. In other words, the first hypothesis reduces class forms of behavior to a pure and simple wage pressure, while the second acknowledges the valorizing and innovative forms of class behavior, but only in order to draw them back into the fetish of capital's ability to progress.

Thus these two positions engage in reciprocal polemics on partial issues: the party and unions exaggerate a partial point of view and turn it into "politicist" or "economicist" guidelines, so to speak, to use their abused language! In fact, one thesis breaks apart the aggressive unity between the new level of the workers' offensive and its capacity for self-valorization, while the other degrades it and reduces it to a subordinate political role and a formally innovative function. In both cases, the unity of antagonism is broken apart into the contradictory nature of its components.

At this point, the discussion ought to return conclusively to the issue of capital and class struggle within capital for the overthrow of the capital relation. We can now begin to appreciate the extent to which bourgeois constitutional "science" flails about in the confusion of an exhausted task (the realization of the Constitution) and a vaguely perceived need (the modifications in the material constitution). We have begun to catch sight of some of the characteristics of the new era of class struggle—those that impose an adequate modification of the material constitution from the viewpoint of both the dimensions of struggle and the quality and incisiveness of behaviors. We have begun to see how the new regime comes into being, at least in its broad traits and fundamental orientations; lastly, we have looked into the useless mystifying attempts of the Official Labor Movement. We now have to extend the debate and *place the concept of class antagonism in the processes of reproduction at the center of our analysis.*

## 2.  THE FORMAL CONDITIONS OF THE PROCESS OF ANTAGONISM IN REPRODUCTION: ON *CAPITAL* VOLUME 2

"The process of production disappears in the finished commodity."[24] When we read this and many other similar Marxian definitions, the search for the formal conditions of antagonism in reproduction appears difficult. Marx's position is not secondary: his critique of Smith (and Ricardo, who in this regard reproduces Smith's doctrine almost to the letter) represents a grounding moment for the development of and insistence on the conceptualization of the *one-sidedness or univocity [*univocità*]*[25] *of the capitalist process of production and reproduction*:

> (and this is the high point of Smith's stupid blunder:) After he has begun by correctly defining the value components of the commodity and the total value product embodied in them, and then by showing how these components form an equal number of different sources of revenue; thus after he has derived revenues from value, he proceed in the reverse direction—and this remains the predominant idea in his work—and makes these revenues, instead of just "component parts," into "original sources of all exchangeable value," thereby throwing the doors wide open to vulgar economics.[26]

The ambiguity of Marx's method on this issue should be stressed. Marx's interest in a description of the unilaterally constrictive effects of the productive process—which must dominate the whole circuit of the social production of capital—does not reach the level of analytical maturity that would permit him to grasp the dialectical (and/or antagonistic) effects arising from the entire framework of reproduction. The antagonism of the passages (of the mode of production = social form of the labor process) from one phase of the reproductive process to the other is hidden by the insistence on the unitary nature of the process itself (based on the production of surplus-value). The polemic against the "original factors" of Smith's theory destroys the *capitalist articulations* of the process of reproduction. *In our opinion, to seek the formal conditions of antagonism in reproduction means to identify the determinate articulations of the process of surplus-value (of exploitation) within the whole framework of reproduction.* Others have spoken, in this respect, of the "enchantment of method and the blockage of research":[27] and rightly so, because the assumption of the univocity of capitalist action between production and reproduction gave rise to an impotence—motivated by objectivism—to articulate this relation in terms other than those "exogenous" to the mechanism of capital. As we know, the reading and use of the reproductive schemas of Volume 2 of *Capital* have frequently led to the discovery of equilibrium models (mainly mono-causal ones) and, as a consequence, a gap between the political project and the terrain of the critique of political economy: *Luxemburg docet!*[28] So the formal conditions of antagonism on the terrain of reproduction would only be given by transcending or sidestepping the level of analysis of reproduction! This is not true. We shall see later how Marx's particular optic in Volume 2 of *Capital,* far from ruling it out, actually accounts for the development of the internal logic and the recuperation of antagonism that is "endogenous" to the entire process—when these "endogenous" characteristics are loaded with workers' subjectivity and the immediately antagonistic valence of workers' action.

Instead of analyzing Smith's theory, Neo-Ricardianism or the repetition of "original factors," it is a matter of grasping the struggle between two classes exclusively within the univocity of the process of capital and fully appreciating its subjectivity, against any mechanistic view.[29] On the other hand, if the "enchantment of method" were to be accepted as theoretically insoluble, we would be forced to reduce the Marxian approach to the issue of reproduction to a question of circulation: this would be absolutely illegitimate—even though it is common, especially within Italian workerism.[30] These reductive conditions of research and political debate are destroyed by practice. In fact, the constant upheaval of the terms of class struggle from within the workers' struggle and capitalist restructuring demonstrates exactly the opposite: the *terrain of reproduction is dominated by the antagonistic categories of production* and *the process of production does not disappear in the commodity* but re-emerges in all of its elements (as identified by Marx rather than Smith) in the reproduction of capital and workers' struggles. And *this is all the more obvious the deeper we probe the social composition of capital and the working class.* The working class, through its struggles, motivates capital to restructure production as well as reproduction (which is increasingly equivalent to social production). It pushes capital into a collision with surplus-value and toward the antagonistic disarticulation and segmentation of the processes of social formation and the imposition of the command of profit. At the current level of class struggle, worker organization only emerges when the struggle can have an impact on factory production and from there be transferred onto the whole mechanism of reproduction of social capital.

It is not out of philological curiosity that we mean to look in Volume 2 of *Capital* for elements that we can use in the formal analysis of the reproduction of antagonism, but because there we are sure to find active tendencies in that direction.

At first sight, the formula that expresses the figure of the circulation of capital in Volume 2 seems to confirm the impression of rigidity of Marx's schema and its cogent univocity. In the analysis of the M–C–M' formula, where C is composed of L (labor-power as commodity), and mp (means of production, primary matter), Marx contemplates the possibility of articulating the formula as $M-C_1$ and/or $M'-C'_2$, where the apostrophe (') indicates, in the process of circulation–reproduction, the change-increase of value (surplus labor/surplus-value), while the index $_1-_2$ refers to a change in use value.[31] However, when faced with the immediate question of *whether L—as a component of C—can be independently characterized by innovations of use value*, Marx does not answer. He replies negatively on the quantitative aspect: given M'–C' (equal to L + mp), he rules out the possibility that an increment in C as a whole can be indicated by a possible increase of its components, L' and/or mp' (it would be wrong to do so, "as we know that the growth of capital involves a change in its value composition, in the course of which the value of *mp* constantly grows, while that of L always declines relatively, and often even absolutely"[32]). He says nothing about a possible $L_1-L_2$.

Marx's silence is not sufficient to close this question. The unilateral assumption of these passages of reproduction, presented as so strictly dominated by capital and so implacably linked to the organic composition of capital, is likely to devalue any historical or dialectical articulation of the process.[33] In these pages,[34] Marx seems to be aware of the problem and in fact he chases after several dialectical definitions of the M–C relation, always in order to define it in relation to total capital, to the stages of capital and especially to the role of L in relation to total capital. However, the framework changes substantially later on in the analysis, when Marx treats the concept of *total capital* directly as the sum of the individual cycles of individual capitals, and the concept of *social capital* as resulting from (and presupposed by) the social character of capitalist production. Here, unlike the formula M–C which is typical of the first mercantilist variant of capital in the formula P–P' that presents us with the "naturalness of superficial rationalism" of classical economics,[35] the formula C–C' shows that "the transformation is not the result of a merely formal change of position belonging to the circulation process, but rather the real transformation which the use form and the value of the commodity components of the productive capital have undergone in the production process."[36] This means that, in relation to "total capital and its value-product,"

> The transformation of one portion of the product's value back into capital, the entry of another part into the individual consumption of the capitalist and working classes, forms a movement within the value of the product in which the total capital has resulted; and this movement is not only a replacement of values, but a replacement of materials, and is therefore conditioned not just by the mutual relations of the value components of the social product but equally by their use-values, their material shape.[37]

Here, the character of reproduction finally becomes wholly materialist and dialectical.

But this is only a foundation: we must extend the dialectical character and the material conditions to the point of determining *a new mode of exposition*—one that, we insist, does not simply attest to the analytics of the critique of political economy, but that, by destroying any "methodological enchantment," identifies the *terrain of class struggle*. In fact, Marx first of all emphasizes that in this schema C has a double character: first it presents itself as C (L + mp) within the cycle of productive capital, then it reappears as c–m–c, which means the cycle of revenue (i.e. also as c–l and c–sv).[38] This is the small-scale circulation of the *Grundrisse* (673–78) that, as we will shortly see, is of great importance. Second, and this is important because here the double character of the elements tends to become fully dialectical, Marx also emphasizes that the schema of total capital contained in the formula "C–C' ... presupposes C (= L + mp) as other commodities in the hands of others":[39] thus, insofar as L is extraneous to P while being drawn into and changed by it, the movement of separation and/or inclusion of L in P presupposes the total-social cycle of capital, rather than resulting from it.[40] But it *presupposes it as a possibility for antagonism:*

> In this circulation, capital constantly expels itself as objectified labour, in order to assimilate living labour power, its life's breath. Now, as regards the worker's consumption, this reproduces one thing—namely himself, as living labour power. *Because this, his reproduction, is itself a condition for capital,*

*therefore the worker's consumption also appears as the reproduction not of capital directly, but of the relations under which alone it is capital* ... in so far as capital is a relation, and, specifically, a relation to living labour power, [to that extent] the worker's consumption reproduces this relation. (*Grundrisse* 676, translation slightly modified)

It presupposes the inherence to social capital, that is, not only the possibility of a relative independence of working-class consumption, needs, and use values from capitalist development, but also the form of an (antagonistic) dialectic on this overall terrain.

Going back to the question of apexes and indexes, in relation to the functioning of social capital we can now conclude that, for Marx, the material independence of movement (in its genesis as well as in its development) of the L component (and thus also of $L_1$, $L_2$, $L_3$, etc.) is admissible and actually increasingly fundamental (this determines the change in the "form of exposition"). The schema of social capital, i.e. the new mode of exposition, allows for the consideration of the *working class outside of capital*, hence of antagonism in the process of reproduction.

In Volume 2 of *Capital* we find an instance where Marx, from a materialist viewpoint and thus at the level of the commodity, thoroughly investigates the inherence of the process of reproduction in that of circulation. The latter is in fact only the phenomenal side, the "appearance" of a real reproductive process that is realized in its image. *This is the case of the transport industry.*

The "circulating" of commodities, i.e. their actual course in space, can be resolved into the transport of commodities. The transport industry forms on the one hand an independent branch of production, and hence a particular sphere for the investment of productive capital. On the other hand it is distinguished by its appearance as the continuation of a production process *within* the circulation process and *for* the circulation process.[41]

Within the framework of our analysis, why is this case relevant? Because, having shown how the conditions for the antagonistic independence of the forms of behavior of the proletarian subject are given in the process of reproduction (subsuming circulation), we can now begin to see (also *objectively*) that moments of reproduction extend into the sphere of circulation. As a consequence, the conditions for social antagonism are affirmed *not only* on the basis of the needs of workers' subjectivity in social reproduction, *but also* on the basis of the objective weight of the capitalist mystification of circulation. Far from being inevitably resolved in the commodity, the process of production results in the social organization of a new extraction of surplus-value. One term falls out of the formula M–C ... P ... C'–M', the passages are commanded in reproduction without mediation, be it circulation, the *faux frais* of circulation or the reduction of surplus-value, that shatters the process of social reproduction. From the above formula the transport industry extracts the following one: M–C ... P–M'.[42] Production and use value are joined together: use value (the spatial transformation of the commodity and its social mediation) is an immediately productive fact.[43] In the face of this shortening of the formula, the direct and immediate intensification of antag-onism in reproduction emerges at the social level.

*The example of the transport industry* is not important in its singularity; rather, it *reveals a tendency and its realization.* The capitalist tendency with respect to reproduction is to abolish all the *faux frais* imposed by circulation, insofar as the latter is not directly organized in terms of capitalist production.[44] The formal—and costly—metamorphoses of circulation must endure the real—and valorizing—metamorphoses of the productive process. The increasing complexity of the capitalist mode of production relentlessly follows this tendency: *tertiarization and automation* of production are the determinate figures of the verification of this tendency.[45] In this way, the formal condi-tions of antagonism on the whole terrain of social reproduction begin to be realized too.

Marx is not reluctant to speculate on this reality of the tendency: he provides a full interpretation of the formula for the circuit of productive capital.

> Whilst in the first form, $M ... M'$, the production process, the function of P, interrupts the circulation of money capital and appears only as a mediator between its two phases M–C and C'–M', here the entire circulation process of industrial capital, its whole movement within the circulation phase, merely forms an interruption, and hence a mediation, between the productive capital that opens the circuit as the first extreme and closes it in the same form as the last extreme, i.e. in the form of its new beginning. Circulation proper appears only as the mediator of the reproduction that is periodically repeated and made continuous through this repetition.[46]

In this respect, the formal conditions of antagonism in reproduction stand out in high relief: just as we had come across the continuity of "small-scale circulation" and its antagonism in the interruption of M–M', here—rein-forced by the productive tension of the capitalist tendency to overwhelm circulation (as, for instance, in the transport industry)—we find the interrup-tion of circulation reduced to a minimum and continually captured by the innovative rationalization of capital. But this is the very terrain of antagonism itself! No renovation of the capitalist structure fails to follow the tendency toward totality—no renovation fails immediately to entail the innovation of class relations. *The more capital productively innovates on the terrain of circulation, the more it draws into the unity of its process the complementary force of workers' antagonism.*

The further we venture into a reading of Volume 2 of *Capital*, the better we understand that there is nothing more mistaken than seeing the schema of capital in circulation as univocal and rigid. The "enchantment of the Marxian method" is a literary mystification because, as we showed in the last section, this is a terrain on which all enchantments break down and class antagonism emerges in its immediacy, beyond the tensions in Marx that point toward the dialectical unification of the process and even from the standpoint of an analysis of commodities (transport). This is *the terrain of "social capital."* Here everything is overturned and the method of exposition changes because the analysis has followed the tendency until it explicitly revealed its power—power [*potenza*] that is the qualitative leap, theoretically implied and historically effective.

We have already seen that Marx insists on the fact that, at a certain stage of development, the relation of circulation and labor-power to production presupposes social capital, in inclusion and/or separation, in subsumption and/or antagonism.[47] This will help us understand Marx's next strong emphasis:

> The way in which the various components of the total *social capital*, of which the individual capitals are only independently functioning components, alternately replace one another in the circulation process—both with respect to capital and to surplus value—is thus not the result of the simple intertwining of the metamorphoses that occurs in commodity circulation, and which the acts of capital circulation have in common with all other processes of commodity circulation, but rather *requires a different mode of investigation.*[48]

All enchantments are destroyed on this terrain because it offers the greatest power [*potenza*] of capitalist mediation and workers' antagonism, so it is now necessary for our analysis to dwell on the formal conditions of antagonism in reproduction.

Undoubtedly some of the most important Marxian categories, when used at this level of inquiry, radically change. The "different mode of investigation" comes into being: the analysis has hitherto pursued and punished, through demystification, the standpoint of the petty bourgeoisie for whom "commerce is value-producing"; now, it is time to attack the essence from which they and their mystifications emanate: social capital.[49] *The categories must change.*

First, *productive labor*. Marx minutely demystifies all the labor forms that the petty bourgeoisie and their consciousness—vulgar economics—consider to be productive and that in reality constitute mere *faux frais* in capitalist production.[50] This demystification is upset—in the mode of exposition—by the awareness that capitalist development tends toward the unification of labor, and thus toward the annihilation of all the *faux frais* of the integration of production and circulation, in the subsumption of the latter within the former (*Grundrisse* 585–90).

Yet this is not enough. In order to get to the bottom of this tendency toward subsumption from the standpoint of social capital, we need to understand how latent capital operates in circulation. This is a *potential productive capital*:[51] its effects operate entirely in the direction of subsumption, and *"production time" (and reproduction time) is increasingly modeled on (and reduced to) the "working period."* The life of capital is dominated by a tendency toward the effective reduction—and elimination—of the *faux frais* of production and the transformation of every type of labor into productive labor.[52] This means that, as a historically verifiable tendency, the action of potential productive capital that is latent in the structure of circulation presses for the reduction and control of production time, through the centralization of capital and the increasing tertiarization of the productive processes (in this case labor processes).[53] Therefore, the category of "social capital" passes from latency into effectiveness as the operative premise of a mode of social production.

> The result of our digression is, incidentally, that the production of the means of communication, of the physical conditions of circulation, is put into the category of the production of fixed capital, and hence does not constitute a special case. Meanwhile, and incidentally, there opened up for us the prospect … *of a specific relation of capital to the communal, general conditions of social production*, as distinct from the conditions of a *particular capital* and its *particular production* process. (*Grundrisse* 533; see also 524–33)

Yet this is still not enough. This capitalist tendency is always effective in the full complexity of the class relations it registers. In fact, "there is no valorization of the productive capital, as long as this finds itself in that part of its production time that is in excess of the working time, no matter how inseparable these pauses may be from the accomplishment of the valorization process"; hence, "the tendency of capitalist production is therefore to shorten as much as possible the excess of the production time over working time."[54] Therefore, "the more that the circulation metamorphoses of capital are only ideal, i.e. the more the circulation time comes to zero, the more the capital functions, and the greater is its productivity and self-valorization."[55] But what does this mean? It means that *capital is forced, by the dimensions of its centraliza-tion and tertiarization of labor, increasingly to mystify this unification* and to "see only its appearance"[56] in circulation, exalting it against the reality of unification. Why? Because "the intervention of industrial capital [in circulation] every-where promotes this transformation [of capitalist production], and with it too the transformation of all immediate producers into wage-laborers."[57] Again, this is precisely what capital needs to conceal, because the process of realiza-tion of this tendency means class antagonism over the entire terrain of society.[58]

   *The different mode of exposition is thus the revelation that social capital is a relation of antagonism at the social level.*[59] The development of the productive forces does not, at this stage, "condition" production as a limit or obstacle, but is itself the "condition of production": antagonism conceals the concept of social capital by forcing it into a negation that is necessarily determined by the very development of capital (a development that is necessary in the name of surplus-value) toward social conditions of existence (*Grundrisse* 537–43, 548). The necessity of this process is not negated by the fact that capital relentlessly sets *counter-tendencies* into motion. On the contrary, the more capital discov-ers the means to determine "circulation without circulation time" (money, credit, etc.), the more it is forced to "to give *circulation time value*, the value of *production time*, in the various organs which mediate the process of circula-tion time and of circulation; to posit them all as money, and, more broadly, as capital" (*Grundrisse* 659–60; see also 542–44). To summarize, then:

> It is the necessary tendency of capital to strive to equate circulation time to 0; i.e. to suspend itself, since it is capital itself alone which posits circulation time as a determinant moment of production time. It is the same as to suspend the necessity of exchange, of money, and of the division of labour resting on them, hence capital itself. (*Grundrisse* 629)

These are most certainly "enchantments of method"! Here, precisely on the terrain of circulation, Marx comes to the same conclusions he arrived at in the analysis of the labor process in the "Fragment on Machines" (*Grundrisse* 690–712).[60] The higher the level of capitalist integration of production and reproduction, the stronger the formal conditions for class antagonism.

   *The terrain of the reproduction of capital tends to subsume that of circulation. In place of a realm of enchanted equilibria, it is now the open field of struggle between the two classes, exactly like the terrain of production.* Workers' analysis follows the structural development of this tendency and grasps its process of maturation. "The inner laws of capital—which appear merely as tendencies in the preliminary historic stages of its development—are for the first time posited as laws" (*Grundrisse* 650): the victory of legislation external to capital is not the victory of the individual freedoms that the capitalist tendency flaunts as fundamental; on the contrary, the victory entails "the most complete suspension of all individual freedom, and the most complete subjugation of individuality under social conditions which assume the form of objective powers, even of overpowering objects—of things independent of the relations among individuals themselves" (*Grundrisse* 652). Thus the greater the development, the greater the antagonism and its formal possibility. This is the result of Marx's investigation in Volume 2 of *Capital*; this is the result of the structural investigation carried out from the standpoint of the workers.

But *the possibility* for antagonism in reproduction *is not its reality*. The material constitution of the developed capitalist state organizes its command over and within the reproduction of capital on the presumption that this possibility would not result in an effective insurrection. Therefore, on this inflection point, workers' analysis must assume the opposite standpoint and follow the restructuring of the material constitution—modeled on the mediation of increasingly contradictory contents of class relations—in order to perceive the effectiveness of a revolutionary rupture. This happens every day on the terrain of class struggle. If the constitution of the capitalist state changes materially, this is due to the fact that the state, faced with this impending struggle, must nevertheless always take on a corresponding process of the *constitution of the insubordinate proletarian subject*.

Up to this point, the analysis has led us to a completely objective understanding of the formal possibility of antagonism; thus, it has helped us to comprehend the need for a constitutional modification of capital. From now on, our analysis will be interested in the other aspect: how the subversive subject constitutes itself by constantly reshaping itself in the course of this. The formal possibilities of antagonism in the reproduction–circulation of capital refer us to the effective consideration of the expression of workers' antagonism within and against the reproduction of capital. Let us examine some of the key points in the analysis of the passage from the anatomy of reproduction to the physiology of workers' struggle.

### 3. THE PROCESS OF WORKERS' SELF-VALORIZATION: THE REAL CONDITIONS OF ANTAGONISM

Capitalist development (and/or its crisis) consists in the continuous attempt to devalue labor-power. Workers' struggle breaks the mediating mechanisms of development, blocks them, and in so doing it blocks the process of devalorization: what is supposed to be united is split in the here and now. Onto the mediation of the law of value are superimposed its metamorphoses, its functioning as law of command.[61] However, command is a withdrawal of the political force of capital: the latter can only triumph in the unfettered development of competition and the full functioning of the law of value. The fact that the law of value must transform itself into command shows that the capitalist siphoning-off of labor-power is already faced with a limit— an obstacle to the further intensification of exploitation and of devalorization as a whole. *The opposite process, the valorization of the proletarian and working class against capital and its circuits of valorization, is the obstacle.* Workers' labor begins to take shape as liberated labor, as *refusal of work* in the form of capitalist social subsumption. *Antagonism is the keystone of the liberation of labor:* to this end, any means other than the intensification of antagonism is unthinkable. The liberation of labor starts taking shape when, at a given level of capitalist development, the capitalist mediation of productive and reproductive relations systematically goes into crisis: mediation, i.e. the capital relation, cannot put an end to it. But life goes on here: what the working class refuses to capital is developed as self-valorization, as self-liberation. It enriches its own composition, i.e. the value of necessary labor, its capacity for struggle, its force of resistance and invention-power. The refusal of work is a rich and constructive category. The maximum level of negation is also the maximum level of synthesis. The process of workers' self-valorization and the transformation of the workings of the law of value play a crucial role in revealing the qualitative change in the productive forces (the proletariat) with respect to productive relations. As Marx recalls (*Grundrisse* 548, but especially the "Fragment on Machines," 690–712), workers' labor enters into production, is pitted against production while taking on irreducibly collective and scientific characteristics: workers' labor, i.e. the refusal of work, is an innovative force against productive relations. Invention is inextricably linked to the capacity to valorize the body of the working class and its reproductive processes, as well as to attack and destroy its adversary.

Today, this antagonistic contradiction lies before us. Every capitalist attempt to put an end to the crisis and recompose the tendency of profit into a rising curve ends up making the profit rate jerk up and down. As capital tries to understand the contradiction through its own categories of equilibrium, the boss's economic science *becomes jammed.* But this is not a sufficient explanation of the complexity of the framework or of the specificity of the processes of self-valorization. In fact, the existence of a crisis and the sudden blockage of the capitalist ability to develop are not the peculiarities of this situation. Instead, what characterizes it is the fact that *the very reproduction of capitalist command is forced to conform itself to the articulations of the processes of class self-valorization.* Capital has no possibility of setting development in motion again, or even simply exercising command, other than that dictated by the class offensive, the process of self-valorization and the refusal of work. The paradox of the crisis of capital consists in its being determined by struggles precisely when these struggles impel capital to endure class self-valorization.

But this is hardly a paradox! It is as paradoxical as the radical and ontological positivity of the refusal of work. Instead of the logical rules of paradox, perhaps this is the application of the practices and techniques of the art of war. The spaces opened up in the war between bosses and workers are new and singular: they are liberated spaces where material seized from the enemy gets rearranged, transformed into new offensive weapons, and accumulated as a wealth that destroys the enemy. These spaces open and close in their reciprocal relation of antagonism: but revolutionary force imposes its own rules on the enemy, just as the Vietcong guerrillas do on the US Marines. This is the capital relation today.

Let us insist upon another aspect that is crucial for us. The system of capital, in its antagonism, acts in dialectical rather than organic terms and dimensions. It continually proposes antagonism, and this system of contradictory relations continually shifts within the capitalist mode of production. *Workers' self-valorization is not immediately satisfaction [godimento]: it is rather a struggle and unfulfilled tension toward satisfaction.* "[I]n production based on capital, consumption is mediated at all points by exchange, and labour never has a *direct* use value for those who are working" (*Grundrisse* 419).

> Indeed, living labour itself appears as *alien vis-à-vis* living labour power, whose labour it is, whose own life's expression [*Lebensäußerung*] it is, for it has been surrendered to capital in exchange for objectified labour, for the product of labour itself. Labour power relates to its labour as to an alien, and if capital were willing to pay it *without* making it labour it would enter the bargain with pleasure. (*Grundrisse* 462)

But the system operates precisely within the relation on which the antagonism of development is based:

> the *most extreme form of alienation*, wherein labour appears in the relation of capital and wage labour, and labour, productive activity appears in relation to its own conditions and its own product, is a necessary point of transition —and therefore already contains in *itself*, in a still only inverted form, turned on its head, the dissolution of all *limited presuppositions of production*, and moreover creates and produces the unconditional presuppositions of production, and therewith the full material conditions for the total, universal development of the productive forces of the individual. (*Grundrisse* 515)

Now, in a given relation of antagonism, workers' processes of self-valorization operate alongside capitalist coercion, both intensively and extensively, so to speak. We have already seen this from the intensive point of view: "an enormous [advance in] awareness" of liberation is born out of alienation (*Grundrisse* 463).[62] No less impressive is their historical dimension, whereby the workers create needs, free time, and civilization: only insofar as "the capitalist usurps the *free time* created by the workers for society, i.e. civilization" is the economist "again correct in this sense, in so far as he posits capital = civilization" (*Grundrisse* 634). *In reality, these functions are separate and capitalist command can only be constructed on the basis of the forced unification and overcoming of this separation.* Such is their actual separation that the greater the complexity of the entire mechanism of capitalist reproduction, the greater the need to analyze the form of interweaving and simultaneity (rather than superimposition) of different systems of circulation. In particular, "The circulation of the part of capital which is posited as wages accompanies the production process, appears as an economic form-relation alongside it, and is simultaneous and interwoven with it" (*Grundrisse* 674–75, but see also 673–78). In bourgeois economy, "*The simultaneity of the different orbits of capital*" is posited in circulation "in specific distinctions and specific unities. The point is to understand precisely these specific, distinguishing characteristics. Nothing is accomplished by the [assertions of] Mr Proudhon or of the social sentimentalists that they are *the same*" (*Grundrisse* 639, 647). We must therefore probe more deeply the *differentia specifica* that comes to be determined in the course of the development of capital's system. *In the historical period analyzed by Marx, the relation inevitably results in capitalist command:*

> The production process, as containing within itself the conditions of its renewal, is a reproduction process whose speed is determined by various relations developed above, which all arise from differences of circulation. The reproduction of capital also contains the reproduction of the use values in which it is realized—or the constant renewal and reproduction by human labour of the use values which enter human consumption and are themselves perishable. The change of substance and of form subordinated to human need through human labour appears from the viewpoint of capital as its own reproduction. It is at bottom the constant reproduction of labour itself. (*Grundrisse* 741–42)

*But this historical closure can be overcome in the very logical conditions of the model.* The phenomenology of class struggle in late capitalism is characterized by an intensification of antagonism and a diffraction of the circuits of realization of capital and the reproduction of labor-power that are all the more radical, the more substantial the subjective strength of the working-class.

It is not by chance that Marx's treatment of the explosion of contradictions and of the subversive "transition"—in the famous "Fragment on Machines" in the *Grundrisse*—is placed right at the center of his analysis of circulation. The reason for this is that "the development of the social individual which appears as the great foundation-stone of production and of wealth" is the explosive element that will "blow this foundation sky-high", i.e. the capitalist ability to simultaneously bring back to unity and regulate the antagonistic development of the cycles of the working class and capital (*Grundrisse* 704–06). "The more this contradiction develops, the more does it become evident that the growth of the forces of production can no longer be bound up with the appropriation of alien labour, but that the mass of workers must themselves appropriate their own surplus labour" (*Grundrisse* 708).

*Reformists in the working-class movement emphasize the mechanisms of reproduction in order to describe and adopt them as the site of mediation of capitalist development.* This emphasis grasps the dialectic of the process of workers' valorization in reproduction against capitalist command only in order to flatten it onto the dimension of collaboration. However valid they may be, the union initiatives of the Official Labor Movement are in this respect merely bills of sale that confirm its betrayal of the expression of the class's objectives and actions. They are unable and unwilling to grasp the mass character of antagonism that these processes manifest on the terrain of reproduction. This necessarily leads to an organicist conception of the development of the dialectic of class, an open and continuous conception that systematically takes the path of mystification and ideological containment and thus often leads to the harshest repression.

As far as the second aspect is concerned, we need only mention the recent analyses of the notion of *the "other" workers' movement*.[63] The striking element that emerges out of these analyses is the power [*potenza*] that capital and its union and party functionaries have been forced to use against the workers' offensive in different eras of class struggle. Repression, the organization of a ferocious system of containment and systematic terrorism are complementary to the organized liberation of the processes of workers' self-valorization. When confronted with the *quality* of class subjectivity, capital loses the opportunity to use the neutral and quantitative weapons of containment (democracy and wages); given the situation, the action of containment must become repressive, must impose a rupture, a blockage or an overturning of the valorizing quality of workers' behavior. *The organizational convention of the workers' movement cannot withstand the qualitative immediacy of workers' needs when these needs are organized into an offensive force.*[64]

The situation changes only slightly when relations of force prevent direct repression; then, containment operations by means of ideology become necessary and prominent. The antagonistic content of the emergence of processes of valorization must by all means be denied—so let us turn it into an organic and gradualist hypothesis of the transformation of reality instead, so that the question of the revolution is opposed to that of *transition*! This is a bloodless debate, unworthy both of the revolutionary tradition that has developed around the issue of transition, and more importantly of the Marxian treatment of this question.[65] But it is a dangerous debate too, because, like all other Proudhonian ideologies in the workers' movement, it works by systematically flattening antagonisms and by furnishing a framework that homogenizes the question of workers' needs and behaviors into organic continuity.

Let us now return to the issue of *repression in reformism*. Paradoxically, this question can *highlight* the processes of workers' self-valorization that would otherwise be subjected to and mystified by the mechanisms of state administration. At a given level of capitalist development, the large mechanisms of class self-valorization develop and perceive their own ongoing self-development when the level of antagonism is at its highest. *The mechanisms of valorization are emigration, the struggle for a social wage and for the autonomy of social reproduction, and the struggle in all total institutions, first of all in the prisons.*[66] The struggles against administration, instead of abolishing it, highlight the fact that the processes of self-valorization occur within the mechanisms of administration. As we shall see, they always enhance its contradictions and make it more difficult for administrative and political leadership to reach a unified conclusion.[67] The index of repression, instead of abolishing it, enhances the effectiveness of the processes of self-valorization, i.e. of the reproduction of class antagonism in the reproduction of capital.

This results in the capitalist urge to readjust totally the entire set of relations, proportions, and functions of command. *The transformation of the material constitution, i.e. of the regime, is the capitalist recognition of the development and historical solidification of new antagonistic relations in the system of reproduction.* Perhaps, at this point, it would be appropriate to introduce a concept that is rather common in current revisionist journalism: the concept of *hegemony*. We could add that the operations of the regime of power are the repressive correlatives to the level of hegemony achieved by the movement. But why use such a term today, when the concept of hegemony, like that of transition, is thoroughly tied to a gradualist and organic conception of the development of class struggle?

In a letter dated 28 December 1862, Marx writes to Kugelmann about his current work on "capital in general": "What Englishmen call 'THE

PRINCIPLES OF POLITICAL ECONOMY' is contained in this volume. It is the quintessence (together with the first part), and the development of the sequel (with the exception, perhaps, of the relationship between the various forms of state and the various economic structures of society) could easily be pursued by others on the basis thus provided."[68] These assertions need further analysis. Most of the available interpretations conclude that the mechanisms of reproduction unfold in equilibrium (Bernstein) and that they can only be destabilized exogenously (Luxemburg). On the contrary, it seems to me that in this letter to Kugelmann we find strong and explicit evidence of the dialectical, innovative, and antagonistic character of reproductive relations as such, in the "differential" relation Marx establishes between reproduction and the state and between different economic structures and institutional forms, with respect to the linear development of the exposition of the theory of value. *In fact, the antagonism of development finds its pre-eminent expression on the historical terrain of the relation between economic and institutional forms.* Here, on the plane of the historicity of the passages of reproduction, any inertia and entropy of the schemas of transformation is negated. Capitalist reproduction is antagonistic reproduction, the state–form develops by fits and starts, by renewing its ability to comprehend and mystify the novelty of class relations.[69] This becomes clearer, if not more explicit, in the chapter on reproduction in Volume 2 of *Capital*.[70] This chapter is famous because it supposedly presents the schemas of equilibrium.[71] It is true that in this chapter Marx rationalizes the equilibrium of the various sectors of reproduction, but what does equilibrium consist of? It is the formal possibility of equilibrium in circulation.

It is nothing more than the translation of Quesnay[72] and, contrary to any hypostasis, the latter conceals and mystifies the lack of class equilibrium that is supposed to be dominated in the equilibrium of circulation. The mystification does not even work. In fact, the mere formal possibility of equilibrium in circulation determines a new element of crisis. The reproduction of capital entails a capitalist tendency to affirm social capital: the equilibrium must be socialized in order to become real both historically and as a tendency. But the socialization of capitalist equilibrium is also the socialization of class antagonism, with a surplus of contradiction. At this point the commodification of capitalist production turns against capital, the univocity of the tendency is revealed as the production of antagonism and antagonism is revealed in its non–mystified and natural form.

> The product of an individual capital, i.e. each independently functioning fraction of the social capital endowed with its own life, may have any natural form whatsoever. The only condition is that it really should have a use form

... capable of circulation. It is completely immaterial and accidental whether or not it can go back ... into the same production process ... It is different with the product of total social capital. All material elements of the repro-duction must be parts of this product in their natural form.[73]

This means that the concept and the tendency toward domination of social capital fasten their claws on the use value and exchange value of commodi-ties, small- and large-scale circulation, the reproduction of labor-power and the reproduction of capital. At this point, the history of class struggle and the mechanisms of workers' self-valorization in circulation lie entirely within capital and its reproduction—and they do so in the form of antagonism. *The schemas of reproduction—for the tendency they comprehend and the new mode of exposition they require—are schemas of the reproduction of antagonism.* The power [*potenza*] of capitalist mediation is forced to operate on the totality of circu-lation. The *faux frais* have disappeared. In the totality, capitalist mediation is complementary to workers' valorization. Average capital and the working class determine this valorization: at this level, capitalist mediation can be nothing but command and the theft of the quality of workers' valorization—and its overturning against the working class into the antagonistic form that defines the entire process.

Therefore, at the level of the formation of social capital as we know it, the entire framework is dominated by the emergence of capital's capacity for command and the parallel emergence of the workers' strength that consol-idates its autonomous valorization through a continuous and formidable penetration of the adversary, both qualitatively and quantitatively. All stages of class struggle and of the transformation of the state-form are now dom-inated by this kind of relation. The formal possibility for antagonism in reproduction no longer exists. In its place, we find the real reproduction, in every passage, of the totality of the most radical antagonism.

We have nevertheless discovered that at the current level of capitalist devel-opment (and crisis), restructuring does not require the implementation of unfettered capitalist domination, and that in fact each restructuring and mod-ification of reproduction intensifies and expands the mechanisms of antagonism. Nonetheless, this is not enough. We have understood that Marx's analysis, far from enchanting itself in the dichotomy between a univocal cap-italist development and a marginal insurgency of the worker subject, actually provides the tools for a truly dialectical and unified investigation; but this is still not enough. Our research is in danger of being blocked again, exactly as the processes of workers' self-valorization risk an *impasse* at the level of their effectiveness, unless we *introduce a subjective variant that can allow us to perform an inversion in practice of the formal and real conditions of antagonism.*

Capital, for its part, already does it. As the processes of reproduction become the site and channel for the proliferation of class antagonism, they must be brought back ever more strictly into the mechanisms of *administration*. The state is the party, the party dictatorship of capital. Administration is the exercise of will of the bosses' state. From the standpoint of capital, subjectivity is narrowly grafted onto the question of development and thus into the structure of capital. Command is not a fungal growth, but rather a graft, a transplant that has passed the stage of rejection. The continuity of the objective and subjective elements in capital is such that only a Spinozian would be capable of providing an adequate reading of the process of capital. As the process of subsumption of labor under capital comes to its full realization, in its real form and its social dimension, the state administration becomes directly and subjectively capitalist. As Engels wrote, "the more productive forces [the state] takes over as its property, the more it becomes the real collective body of all the capitalists, the more citizens it exploits." This process unfolds in the face of the workers' offensive with the aim of pushing the capitalist relation to its highest point in the state-form.[74] Now we must analyze this will to continuity of administration with regard to capitalist development and its mechanisms of reproduction against class antagonism.

Parallel to this, we need to return in our analysis to the workers' point of view. *The passage from a structural analysis to a political analysis of administration, from an investigation of functions to a definition of antagonism, is only possible if the workers' standpoint is subjectively present.* From the workers' point of view, the growth of subjectivity (in the body of the great movements of self-valorization) constitutes a direct mechanism, an inversion of practice that is subjectively necessary. When, due to the strength of the capitalist or revisionist obstacle, this passage fails to take place, there is always a verifiable laceration on the body of the class. Since Lenin's time, the working class has engaged in a permanent revolution and learned the art of overcoming the power [*potenza*] of these blockages and lacerations, of subjectively overturning the practice imposed by means of constant political guerrilla warfare. Therefore, even though the party viewpoint is lacking on the workers' side, the infinite demands for the subjective inversion of existing practice can still help us face the question of the offensive against state administration. This will surely happen out of necessity and from a position that is disproportionate in relation to capital's capacity for management. At the present stage of revolutionary development, in the absence of a party and of the theoretical unity of the class standpoint, the proletariat establishes its massified power only through a series of approximations. But this does not prevent it from being able to attack the question of administration as if it were a party. Having said this, we can now move on to an analysis of antagonism in reproduction at the level of institutions, and to consider the current class relation as a clash of two subjectivities in the phase of real collective capitalist domination, i.e. the capitalists' state. This analysis calls for a party hypothesis.

## 4. TOWARD A CRITIQUE OF THE ANTAGONISMS IN ADMINISTRATION

The irreducibility of the development of antagonisms to the level of social capital, in the process of social reproduction, is fully evident when we examine institutions. A phenomenology of public administration shows to anyone with eyes—and many have them by now—how badly riddled with logical aporiae and practical contradictions it is. The asymmetries and mal-functions of administrative processes result in all kinds of blockages and jams,[75] and this happens under the best of circumstances! *In fact, administration is not superficially in crisis: the crisis involves above all the criteria and forms of its legitimation.* The old Constitution was founded on the hypothesis of reg-ulating civil society and its conflicts. As the Constitution confronts the intrusiveness of social capital and the virtual withering of civil society (in the real subsumption of social labor under capital), its obsolescence is the qualitative outcome of an accumulation of contradictions that completely unsettles the terrain of constitutional expectations. The critique of political economy and the complexity of its analytical power [*potenza*] find a new field of application in administration because the latter is itself a terrain of class antagonism.[76]

Having said this, as a result of our previous investigation, we have to take our analysis further. This is to say, given that administration—and with it the old Constitution—presents a surface full of malfunctions and asymmetries, the analysis ought to move on to the deeper contradictions that underlie these superficial aspects. At the level of social capital, the Constitution and administration are traversed by a fundamental antagonistic contradiction: the contradiction between organization and command, between labor process and valorization process. Thus, the persistence of capitalist dictatorship, its intensification and extension into and through administration, do not conceal the antagonism of these contradictory tensions. In this situation, for the first time, "no longer can the economist afford to confine his attention to the quantitative relations arising from commodity production; he must also direct his attention to the character of the social relations which underlie the com-modity form."[77] In other words, with regard to administration in (of) social capital, the latter is forced to continuously subsume the antagonistic process of workers' self-valorization and the quality (and not only the quantity) of struggles. The overall relation which leaps beyond the terrain of reproduction disturbs the surface as well as the core of administration. From this point of view, *the old Constitution is a mere mystification of the dictatorship exercised on the now-uncontainable processes of workers' self-valorization.*

If this is the old, lifeless, and dying Constitution, what is the new one? First of all, it is an act of political will that consists in the explicit subsumption of civil society within the form of the organization of production. "We saw ... that the exchange of commodities implies contradictory and mutually exclusive conditions. The further development of the commodity does not abolish these contradictions, but rather provides the form within which they have room to move. This is, in general, the way in which real contradictions are resolved."[78] But this *new form* is powerful: as powerful as the impact of workers' self-valorization, resistance to exploitation, and the ability to block it and produce alternatives. This new form, insofar as it must contain the enemy to defeat and subsume, has both attractive and contorted characteristics: ultimately it is *a social productive form itself.* Any "autonomy of the political" disappears the moment the political and the social, the state and the economy are superimposed and become interchangeable terms. Yet superimposition and mirroring are not enough. These processes are realized on an unremitting and irreducible basis. Only crisis can arise out of these relations of force.[79] How is the crisis mirrored in the state-form that—as social capital—was forced to swallow up civil society? To put it in Marx's words, this happens in a "Shylock-like" way.[80] In this situation, capital can only produce—in the state-form—the dissolution of the form of equality. *The state founded on the crisis of the law of value assumes the rule of inequality as the explicit content of its political will.*[81] Finally, the development of class struggle and the material relations of production impose a complete overturning "from the standpoint ... of juridical illusion": "the law [is] the product of the material relations of production", or rather the law is—on this terrain— the production of inequality![82] Finally, not "all Catholics can be popes" and "the form of direct and universal exchangeability" appears to be "an antagonistic form ... inseparable from its opposite, the form of non-direct exchangeability"![83] *Large-scale industry,* having reached a certain level of social expansion, destroys "the appearance of a contract between free persons," exchangeability and equality,[84] and *imposes its own form on the state.*

*Administration is the political will to continue this transformation and the new material constitution is its legitimation.* But the sequence is neither simple nor linear: the destruction of the appearance of equality in exchange is immediately dialectical and all the more antagonistic the more fully the processes of workers' self-valorization are developed. When "private production unchecked by private ownership" gets the upper hand, when all capital relations are based on the objective necessity for development—and on nothing else[85]—in other words, when social capital is immediately the legislator, administration becomes the unmediated fabric of antagonism. Well, this new and advancing Constitution is the crucible of the worst contradictions. Let us look into them.

> If capitalist leadership is thus twofold in content, owing to the twofold nature of the process of production which has to be directed—on the one hand a social labour process for the creation of a product, and on the other hand capital's process of valorization—in form it is purely despotic. As cooperation extends its scale, this despotism develops the forms that are peculiar to it.[86]

*The critique of the political economy of administration must*, in my opinion, reveal: *(a) the despotic norm of administration; (b) the twofold nature of its contents; (c) the rigidity of class in administration; (d) the rules governing the increasing rigidity and/or discontinuity of administration; (e) the totalizing form of the administrative process and (f) the density of antagonism.*

Points *a*, *c*, and *e* refer to the despotic form of capitalist leadership, which tends to become stronger as the scale of cooperation increases, and is thus particularly strong at the level of social capital ("private production unchecked by private ownership"). Points *b*, *d*, and *f* underline the twofold nature of the workings of administration and the deepening of the contradictions in antagonism as the scale of cooperation gradually increases, more fully subjectivizing them on the fronts of struggle that social capital's relation intends to mediate. Our analysis cannot be exhaustive but will develop around these points and consider them two at a time, given the importance of the dialectical links that connect them in pairs.

The passage cited from Marx provides us with the first form of dialectical relation: the twofold nature of the contents and the unity of the despotic form of capitalist leadership. *In social capital, capitalist leadership is entirely transformed into administration;*[87] in other words, due to the relative (and/or tendentially absolute) withering of "civil society," the "productive social force of labor" appears as the "social productive force of capital, as its immanent productive force" at the level of the organization of society as a whole. Under these circumstances, the despotic nature of administration and of the processes of social production is given. The form of administration, whatever its prior connotations, is at this point "transformed by the intervention of capital and the capitalist mode of production."[88] Any old political, social or traditional residue either disappears or, when it remains, is gradually transfigured and rendered functional.[89] Administration becomes necessary and comes to supplant the "heroic capitalists," the "heroes of accumulation," their "competitive cunning," and "fratricidal struggle."[90] *Administrative labor becomes productive.* It follows from this that the material constitution, the basis of power relations, is modified within a relation that is articulated with transformations in administration. This is in regard to the despotic form of the process.

In the close relation here determined, we immediately need to grasp another aspect: the twofold nature that characterizes the administrative process. Unless we do so, we end up capitulating to the numerous and repetitive definitions of the state in mature capitalism as a cruel and all-powerful Moloch. Marx's dialectic points in the opposite direction, namely that all capitalist reproductive capacities result in the reproduction of a class relation.[91] Moreover, the reproduction of the class relation through the reproduction of capital is articulated with and spreads to the transformations of the entire productive machine. Reproduction becomes increasingly adapted to the changing forms of the social extraction of surplus-value and to their transformations. The processes of reproduction (the always-changing relations between the labor process and the valorization processes) intensify by passing from reality to latency and back, thus assuming greater generality and incisiveness.[92] Therefore, administration becomes the form of exploitation at the level of social capital, while paying the necessary cost of the social reproduction of productive antagonism. Consequently, and by necessity, at the level of social capital administration is forced to assume, in the despotic form proper to it, the new identity of the collective subjects of production. The authoritarian co-management of capital's state must explicitly organize social *partners*, while naturally mystifying the potential for antagonism.

When the contradictions of administration at the level of social capital are seen from the point of view of functionality, the reverberations of the fundamental antagonism are perceptible even in this aspect of the process. Administrative functionality gives rise to aporiae, interruptions, accumulations, and jams. These are recognized and described by all analysts of administration, but are given the appropriate relevance only by Marxist analysts.[93] These malfunctions derive from the clash between the logic of power and the contradictions between labor processes and processes of valorization, where the latter are clearly traversed by a radical antagonism that is multiplied in each confrontation with power.

Let us now examine points *c* and *d* of the initial schema: the class rigidity of administration, dysfunctionality and the accelerating alternation of rigidity and rupture on the administrative plane. The class rigidity of administration is evident when the despotic nature of its foundation and legitimation is taken into consideration. This rigidity remains even in the absence of an explicit material foundation: *it is* a priori, *like the latency of capitalist command over the ordering of the whole.* When the constitutional system is slow to adapt itself to this rigidity of the administrative framework, the latter takes over. A series of centripetal motions starts to proliferate. What is represented here is the life of what is dead, which is no less real, nor is its logic less pressing. "The greater this antagonism, the greater the role that this work of supervision plays"; "this is productive labor that has to be performed in any combined mode of production."[94] The more capitalist production spreads, the more important the latency of the functions of internal mediation in the process of reproduction becomes: capital advances from production to the subsumption of circulation under command over reproduction; its laws of development and its "title, both by right and by might, to the labour and surplus labour of others" move from competition to planning, from the mediation of money to that of administration.[95] The passage from absolute surplus labor to the social organization of the extraction of relative surplus labor and from the formal to the real subsumption of labor sets into motion the centripetal power [*potenza*] of administration.[96] In this process, as Marx points out,[97] *centralization* occurs faster than *concentration* and command precedes and articulates accumulation. We now touch upon the other aspect of the problem: *administrative centralization functions according to its own specific dynamic,* as we have seen. It faces obstacles that it demolishes and, in the current situation, constantly tries to *anticipate.*[98] Nonetheless, this functional and centripetal force of administration constantly finds itself faced with internal dysfunctional elements. This means that the rigidity of class relations, sanctioned by the administrative command of capital, can only be sustained under a certain set of conditions. Undoubtedly, capital tries to bring about these conditions: administration's laws of motion and its capacity to absorb and/or exclude are established in the context of the material constitution. But these laws might well not work. In fact, as administration increasingly becomes the form of social capital, the fluidity and circulation of conflicts are given within this unified dimension. The decision to contain or endure conflicts, first of all on the formal plane of administration, is already an important one for capital! More importantly, regarding the reduction of the working day,[99] it is possible to raise these aporiae to a more useful level by exploiting their internal dynamism. In purely theoretical terms, this is possible: it is actually the rule of capitalist development.[100] However, in historical terms, as we will show in the next section, the issue is more complicated. Here, we want to emphasize that *this mechanism is the cause of the malfunctions of the administrative process in the specificity of its development.* This is the dialectical moment which, on the functional terrain, corresponds to the centripetal force of the administrative system, precisely because it is given as a fluid expanse of conflicts—which we can verify in the form of malfunctions—at the level of administration.

In points *a* and *b* we have seen how administration must (in a contradictory fashion) be inherent in the terrain of direct production and reproduction of capital; in points *c* and *d* we analyzed how this inherence determines both a formidable centripetal coherence of administration and its functional aporiae.

Points *e* and *f demonstrate a further consequence concerning the power [potenza] and quality of the contradictions present in administration and the force of its antagonistic transformation.*

First of all, from the standpoint of capital: when Marx analyzes circulation time,[101] he insists that in its struggle against the non-valorization of circulation, capital continually strains its process toward the goal of presence throughout production. In circulation, capital is latent: its impatience in "latency" relentlessly aggravates the process aimed at "presence." If "the production time is greater than the working time," if "during its circulation time capital does not function as productive capital, and therefore produces neither commodities nor surplus-value," then "the tendency of capitalist production is therefore to shorten as much as possible the excess of production time over working time," to abolish the limits to its process of valorization, to turn its "latency" into a "presence" and to totalize valorization.[102] This tendency in the administration of social capitalism is (immediately) a law. *Administration must rule society by totalizing the centrality of productive command.* The superstructure is latency that must be reduced to the presence of valorization at the base [*valorizzazione strutturale*]. In the first and last instance, the capitalist need to render administrative domination total stems from the first generic reduction to the terrain of capital and the subsequent functional dialecticization of the administrative process. This powerful tendency toward totalization definitively illustrates the logic behind the principle of proliferation of these centripetal tensions. Administration becomes the actual command of capital, the presence of command, the reduction of the latent circulation of command to actual valorization.

This passage in capitalist command over administration would be unthinkable unless the administrative process was structurally traversed by such weighty and effective *centrifugal forces* [*spinte*] that the unity of the process itself could only result if a reimposition of capitalist direct command, beyond all mediations, took place. "[T]he gradual upsurge of working-class revolt" *compels* the state "compulsorily to shorten the hours of labour,"[103] the revolt of the "mass of exploitation" determines-forces capital to entirely change its exploitative machine;[104] *finally, the quality of the organized workers' needs forces the productive structure of capital to alter itself adaptively so as to reabsorb "small-*

*scale articulation" into the process of reproduction and to reshape itself in relation to the strength of the organized workers' needs.* Administrative totalization is necessarily related to the *power [potenza]* and *quality* of these movements. The centripetal force of administration (the consequent tendency to overcome its malfunctions) is the correlative of the structural force of rupture (and the class's ability to bring about ruptures on the surface of the administrative mechanism): the totalizing thrust of administration corresponds here and now to the force and quality of the workers' ruptures of and in administration.

We have already discussed the mechanisms of class self-valorization: now their formal and real possibility will be considered directly within the structural dialectic of administration that we have analyzed both from the viewpoint of the theory of *Capital* and from that of the analysis of administration. All the pressures that can be reabsorbed by the administrative process (as they determine its growing number of malfunctions) are found intermingled in administration only so long as the latter is accountable to and rests on the ability to totalize definitively.

*The administrative process thus calls for a material constitution.* Qualitative contradictions and the malfunctions of the administrative process at this point impose a modification of the material constitution. Administration can only base itself on command and only the transformations of command guarantee its new functions, especially once it has been radically and internally corroded, upset and marked by the class movement.

(We say this, while bearing in mind that this administrative process—and the rules of exploitation that the critique of political economy rightly ascribes to it—is not only a process that competes to organize the state internally. The class movement has brought about analogous situations and motions on the international terrain. It is therefore difficult, if not impossible, to consider the movement of imperialism and the rules of its "right" or "law" ["*diritto*"] and its "politics," i.e. of administration at the international level, outside of these analytical parameters and orientations.)[105]

Let us return to the issues raised at the beginning of this section. The capitalist will to constitutional innovation, as we stated, must follow, overturn, and coercively (willingly) corroborate the new structure of class conflict, which witnesses the *social* confrontation between capital and the proletariat, in both general and particular dimensions. The material constitution must adapt itself to the functions of the control of antagonism by starting from this basic antagonism and calibrating its innovative movement through the various layers of contradictions as they are revealed on the terrain of administration. However, as we have said, this control must destroy the old form of exchange, equivalence, and equality and the old form of "right" or "law" ["*diritto*"], because any presumption of overcoming the crisis or at least controlling it today can only be predicated on the open affirmation of inequality. Civil society is the world of bourgeois right, freedom, and equality; the social state subsumes civil society and eliminates its distinctive characteristics while, pushed to this limit, it posits the relation between state and working class outside of any other intermediation.[106] *At this point the working class is no longer part of civil society* and does not confront the state through it. Civil society—the bourgeois part of society that is properly "civil society" in classical terms—lies within the state, while *the "other workers' movement" irreducibly* constructs *its own sociality within itself.*[107]

Well, if this is the reality, the material constitution must be renovated following the recognition that there is no exchange between capitalist power and working-class power, that exchange can only be posited as command, that the long shadow that class self-valorization casts over the processes of capitalist reproduction must be eliminated. Therefore, the dialectic of repression and conflict must be comprehensively scaled down. If the ultimate axis of legitimacy of the Planner-State was found in the law of value and the dialectic of labor, it can now only be explained as pure command. Command means neither totalitarianism—the dimensions of workers' and proletarian power would not permit it—nor destruction for the qualitative impact of organized workers' and proletarian needs—the reproduction of the system requires this confrontation. Command is therefore, here and now, the reproposition of the law of exchange, in any case and at all times. However, from outside the mediations of civil society, this imperative reproposition of command can only be traced directly onto the rules of production and reproduction, i.e. onto the imposition of the rule of capitalist reproduction that is the rule of inequality. The moment the functional dynamics that—whether successfully or not—connected repression and conflict break down, they are reunited in the "humanism" of co-management. The dictatorship of the law of value in co-management is not articulated; it could only be so if there were parts to it, but there are no parts: there is only opposition and externality at the level of society. The law of value is imperatively imposed in "co-management" style in the absence of its historical enforcement.

At this point, *administration is the rule of inequality.* Its centripetal and totalizing ability is exalted to an extreme. Leaving no margin for negotiation, it is boastful and overpowering. The new material constitution emerges to legitimate this unfolding of the commodity. But do not the movements of workers' self-valorization intervene on and against the administrative machine? Do they not project their independence along the lines of and against the articulations and/or the disarticulations, the asymmetries and logical aporiae of administration? The quantity and quality of overall social wage relations, the costs, services and in short all the tertiary dimensions of reproduction and "small-scale circulation" directly subsumed by reproduction *en général,* do they not "hegemonically" express workers' needs within and against administration? *The unfolding of the commodity is thus faced with the irreducibly antagonistic unfolding of workers' power.* The problematic that opens up at this point is completely subjective—the more extreme the antagonism is, the more the new material constitution subjectively constrains it.

### 5.  THE PROCESS OF CLASS SELF-VALORIZATION AND THE PARTY PROCESS

What we have said so far leads to the question of the state and the party: the *state* as the *party of capital* and the *party* as the *state of the working class,* or, rather, the anti-state of workers' power. Power is always exclusive and total. We have outlined the dialectic produced by workers' self-valorization within the structure of the administration of capitalist reproduction; we have understood its impact with regard to the restructuring of the material constitution and the leaps of its political process. Now, we must return to the fundamental issue: subjectivity, the accumulation of forms of behavior that leads to a qualitative leap over the *question of power.*

In Marx and Lenin we recognize the following dialectic. In Marx's *Eighteenth Brumaire,* the working class is perceived to be pushing forward the rationality of the capitalist government of society until, at their highest level, the internal contradictions of the bourgeoisie are exhausted and workers' antagonism is revealed;[108] in Lenin, from *Imperialism* to *The State and Revolution,* the question is articulated according to the same rhythm: closure of the contradiction, imperialist exhaustion of the law of value, definition of the weak point and explosion of antagonism.[109] But in the classics, this passage from the objective to the subjective never had any force other than the impulse of theory. Today, theory is superimposed on, added to and merged with a practice of colossal dimensions. The Leninist subjective inversion of existing practice needs a number of infinitely smaller passages than those required in 1848 or 1917. Self-valorization, autonomous working-class valorization, has assembled a platform from which it is necessary to leap forward. *If capital is transformed into administration, the working class becomes the normalization of the passage to the party.* The working class turns counterpower, in necessarily ephemeral ways, into the extension of subversive episodes and the irreducible intensification of revolutionary forms of behavior: such is the basis of this transformation. The continuity of such behavior is the source of conscious subjectivity and the greatest subjective rupture is normal and project-oriented [*progettuale*].

What is the concept of the party, then, if not the ability to pursue this constantly repeated abstraction of the vanguard's subjective behavior? And woe to those who take up old stereotypes and lament economistic reductionism in this conception! Economism is to be found wherever political economy is. Who would praise political economy and its effective mystifications when—from the standpoint of capital—everything is now a projection of command and a hypostasis of subjectivity?

The concept of the party and its reality emerged from a specific temporal period that necessarily influenced the way they were conceived. Obviously we will be accused of voluntarism—as a complement to economism—because we do not predetermine the number of months or years. What is to be done? Externality, ideology, and dilapidated orthodoxy can only be recalled to the revolutionary order of things by demonstrating the forward movement of the revolutionary order of the will. This is what we are doing.

And we are doing so with pleasure. Because at this degree of antagonism of administration and capitalist development, the processes of class self-valorization are forcefully marching forward. Class independence, regarded by Marx and Lenin as the prior condition for the existence of a party, is a process. It is a great encumbrance on administration; it is the scandal that the innovation of the material constitution and of the material basis of state legitimacy must constantly cover up. It is a process of counterpower whose force of proliferation must be seen through the same analysis that keeps revealing the practical malfunctions and logical aporiae of administration. *Proletarian independence, self-valorization, counterpower: these are successive and highly integrated levels—they are faculties that a new composition of the working and proletarian class shows to be different yet complementary moments of its own subjectivity.* The articulated framework of Marxian theory is unified into a point of attack. Let us not lament this unification: it is given in practice.[110] Let us not demand of it more than is possible: it can give us everything on the terrain of the party, but very little when it comes to transition and extinction, because the whole question is opened up again in all its violence. But more on this later.

Marx himself sketches the passage from proletarian self-valorization to the party process, albeit in summary and (photographically) negative terms, because his critique is constrained by the force of capitalist political economy. But if critique is the allusion to the alternative, this is the direction in which it needs to develop. Now, let us again examine the way Marx deploys the dialectical category of the qualitative passage within capital in relation to the social movements of capital. This is, as we have stated elsewhere, the dialectic of latency and presence. Thus latency is not absence but accumulation. Presence is the circuit of the potential arising from the accumulated elements that have been constructed during latency. The capitalist tendency is entirely geared toward the preparation for this passage and the creation of the conditions in which it can operate as rapidly and violently as possible.

> Besides real accumulation, or the transformation of surplus-value into productive capital (and, correspondingly, reproduction on an expanded scale), there is thus accumulation of money, scraping together a part of the surplus-value as latent money capital, which is only to function as additional active capital later on, when it has attained a certain volume ... The simplest form which this extra latent money capital can assume is that of a hoard.[111]

But this is exactly the reverse of the condition created by the process of working-class and proletarian self-valorization. There is a workers' "hoarding" that is as relevant as the capitalist one, there is an accumulation of elements of struggle that are transformed into needs and that enrich the composition. *The unfolding of the commodity toward capitalist totality comes to a halt when the accumulation of workers' self-valorization sets an alternative unfolding into motion.* The latter, latent but no less powerful, feeds the explosion of subjectivity and the modifications of class composition. *The Marxian negative becomes positive.* The accumulation is directed toward innovation in class composition, and under the present conditions of class struggle, innovation in class composition leads toward the emergence of subjectivity.

Marx's attention to this development is necessarily fleeting. But what are the conditions Marx registers? They are characterized by an extreme division in the processes of reproduction and the corresponding class relations.

> The continuous supply of labour-power on the part of the working class in department I, the transformation of one part of department I's commodity capital back into the money form of variable capital, the replacement of a part of department II's commodity capital by natural elements of constant capital $II_c$[112]—these necessary preconditions [of reproduction] all mutually require one another, but they are mediated by a very complicated process which involves three processes of circulation that proceed independently, even if they are intertwined with one another. The very complexity of the process provides many occasions for it to take an abnormal course.[113]

While rightly recognizing the image of the current unfolding, here we also perceive that the "great complication" is only an epiphenomenon of administration, whereas the reciprocity of cycles is brought to a close in the form of identity. Then it is precisely the negative element in Marx that comes closest to the possibility of overthrow by the workers, because the workers' determination of development provokes articulations and disarticulations in the reproductive cycle. Therefore, the "abnormal course" is no longer ascribed to the disproportions of the cycle, but brought back to bear on the disproportionate and unsettling force of the working class.[114]

*Innovation is the workers' overturning of the totality of the reproductive conditions of capital,* grounded in the accumulation of moments of incidence which are obtained gradually yet always totalizing. Of course, the tiresome possibility of an overall restructuring of the conditions of reproduction is conceded to capital, in the face of workers' innovation. But for how long? Neither the infinite nor the indefinite are suitable categories for materialism, especially at this level of class contestation.

From the workers' standpoint, the concept of innovation means *both* the enlargement and intensification of the productive force of labor *and* the refusal of work. Unless we acknowledge this dialectic of development of the productive forces, *this* dialectic of the *refusal of work,* we cannot comprehend the workers' view of the party. The latter is the chance to push forward workers' self-valorization to the point of its negation, to increase its own material independence to the point of totally overturning it. The very concept of class composition fully comprehends this dialectical doubleness. At the level of the social organization of exploitation, capital ceases to put individual labor-power to work. It puts to work labor-power that is recomposed as the working class, as massified determinations of class. *Any determinate class composition is thus twofold:* both object of exploitation and subject of self-valorization. *However, its self-negation as object of exploitation is not simply self-affirmation as subject of self-valorization: it is rather the negation of the relation itself.* All the preceding transformations (from the functioning of the law of value to its exhaustion, from the Planner-State to its crisis) have reproduced this relation. In this, the relation of force has often been advantageous to the working class. As a whole, the ability of the working class to grow as a productive force has been enormous. But this is not sufficient. *The refusal of work is refusal of the relation.* Marx outlines the passage from the "law of value" to the "law of planning," when all the conditions of capitalist development are mature (and, in particular, when we come to the period of "private production unchecked by private ownership").[115] This passage can be defined as the radical overthrow and negation of capital.

There is a paradox here, but it is entirely dialectical. Only the refusal of this dialectic can create the opposing positions of *reformism* (as the uninterrupted continuity of processes of self-valorization) and *extremism* (as the unbreakable perseverance in the refusal of work): the price of these positions is illusions and appearances. On the other hand, only a materialist intensification of this dialectical paradox can be the foundation of a theory of the party, because this paradox explains and grounds the connection between *the objective and the subjective dimension of this process:* it does so by demonstrating that *between the two there is no difference in essence* (materiality of conditions against subjectivity of the proposal) *but merely difference in functions. Subjectivity is a catalyst that can only function in relation to a materially determined structure; its creativity is given insofar as it is organic to the system.* On the issue of organization, Marxism always follows this line. In Marx we find the definition of "permanent revolution" that determines the conditions for an increasingly advanced unity of class and with them the basis for the revolutionary leap.[116] In Lenin, the subjective inversion of existing practice is founded on the awareness and motivated by the recognition of a materially cogent relationship between the exhaustion of capitalist development and the grounds for the revolutionary passage.[117] In Mao, organization in the period of proletarian dictatorship must continually propose the reconstruction of practice for transition while precisely articulating its different conditions.[118] The moment of the *refusal of work* is closely linked to a consideration of the increase of the *productive forces*, albeit in a dialectical manner, with the constant ability to overturn existing practice. "Communism [is] the *real* movement which abolishes [*distrugge*] the present state of things."[119]

*The process of class self-valorization,* which is the current form of class existence, is thus present in the party process as the basis of a reconstructive dialectic that *in no way prefigures*, but rather demands an alternative and destructive totalization. In the society of capital, workers' self-valorization means the possibility of not working hard, of living better, of enjoying a guaranteed wage: the higher the level of workers' reappropriation of the productive forces, the greater this possibility. Yet this is not enough. The *breakdown*[120] of the system is not automatic. On the other hand, these processes of self-valorization play a double role in being both inside and outside of capital. It is hard to see what, other than politically organized class force, could possibly accelerate and lead toward a definite rupture of the capital relation inherent in things. Theory can define all the conditions of possibility, but only the concrete labor of organization can really bring them about. *The labor of the party is thus the exact opposite of that which constitutes the modification of the material constitution on behalf of capital.* The party is the anti-state, through and through. To the two-fold character of this class composition correspond, from opposite standpoints, the capitalist will to legitimate anew the processes of the administration of exploitation and the workers' will to administer proletarian independence to the point of the offensive against the state and the destruction of the wage system. Parallel and opposed, equal and contrary, these two forces act upon class composition. We should also point out that the tendency of class struggle to develop around these great aggregates is exactly the same one that makes the revolutionary passage necessary.[121]

In general, the *history of bourgeois constitutionalism* can only be the history of the attempts to grasp, time and time again, the fundamental characteristics of the political class composition and to subjugate its existence to the necessity of capitalist development. The subjugation of existence means on the one hand the identification and organization of the elements of class reproduction and their mystification and ownership on behalf of capital; on the other hand, it means the identification and (coercive) exclusion of all the moments in class composition that allow for the organization of the revolutionary party.

The old Constitution of 1948 has been able to bend and to concede remarkable ground to the political class composition as it emerged out of the second great imperialist war. This was marked by a medium level of conflict, understood within the triumphant ideology of work, and a possibility of mediation based on the backwardness of the relationship between working class and peasantry as well as the condition of poverty of the lower classes (including the petty bourgeoisie) to be played out in the project of development: *the Constitution of 1948 is in reality a "work plan [piano di lavoro]."* On such a basis, capital successfully presented its project to pass to a more advanced stage of development in all its dimensions, to (increasingly socialized) production and (democratic) reproduction. From the point of view of the ideology of the old workers' left, this project was flexible enough to include the tradition of workplace democracy and to allow an integrative dialectic of the new needs for struggle to unfold.[122] The organic relation of the Italian Constitution to capitalist development is no longer a mystery or blasphemy: measured analysis, beyond the raving over its "alternative uses," suffices to prove this.[123] The material political relation that underscored the Constitution was included in it: that is to say, the Constitution of 1948 comprehended both the initial limits and the progressive dimensions of the capital relation. In fact, the Constitution of 1948 found its true actualization in the organic project of capital that subsumed it. The actualization of the Constitution was more than a matter of words: it was the development of premises that were actually foreseen in the relations of force that made up the material constitution of the state.[124]

Today, the Constitution of 1948 and the material constitution that characterized it as a project are dead. The relations of force that presided over every possible model of development have been shattered. The so-called "Historic Compromise" will not revitalize this constitutional shell of class relations. The new is too powerful and cannot be contained by a progressive constitutionalism. The flexibility of the terms foreseen in 1948 has already been stretched too far: any small strain could snap it. Thus we are witnessing a familiar spectacle in the history of the modern state, that of a *new "constituent group,"* not formally organized, that is working to found a new constitution. The new material constitution that is taking shape considerably anticipates the new formal constitution. This group needs to grasp this new class composition in its general dimensions, and to operate inside it in order to predict and control it. What is now at stake is a new overall legitimacy of development.

However, as we have seen, the present conditions are sufficiently damning for the bourgeois constitutionalist and the reformist. All the contradictions point *directly* to the fundamental antagonisms of capitalist development. The processes of class self-valorization are of such massive scope that it is almost impossible to affect the body of class composition. The rigidity, complexity, and quality of class behavior refuse to be mystified. So long as there is an appearance of democracy, the co-management necessary for the capitalist plan to overcome the crisis and recover development encounters enormous obstacles. This affirmation is not a prediction of a totalitarian reassertion of power: it is simply the affirmation that *the new material constitution must form a constitutional system in which the fullest participation is imposed by the greatest violence.* The latter is basal [*strutturale*], internal and aimed at the determinate passages for overcoming the crisis, before being superstructural and instrumental. The new material constitution is thus first and foremost the disarticulation of class, and violence pre-arranged for this function. In the new constituent group, the commissions for "Internal Affairs" and "Justice" are marginally the most important ones. This is neither "social fascism" nor a new kind of totalitarianism: what is sought is a more refined form of bourgeois dictatorship.

But be careful! This is a slippery slope, more so than it has ever been. The terms have changed and not only the material ones. The very form of constitutionalism has changed. Decisions are not left to the professor of the Constitutional Court (poor derelict and functionary of the new government). Instead, they will be in the hands of the financial economist, the corporative politician, the expert on multinationals, the agents of the mass media, etc.

On the other hand, another "constitutional group" is at work. Again, as in all the fundamental moments of class struggle, the *Charter* [Statuto] *of the party is on the agenda.* Today, to pose the question of the Charter [*Statuto*] of the party is to grasp the level of maturity of a new class composition and to begin to measure its subjective continuity, programmatic aims, and subversive effectiveness. Above all, it requires us to follow the processes of class self-valorization and set them in contradiction to the capitalist project of recuperation and the new material constitution in all the complexity of motives that contribute to its construction.

Let us take an example. Today a new productive base is being constituted (and it has already exceeded the elementary limits of meaningfulness). It is socially extended—and it is being integrated by a stricter and higher level of the (multinational and automated) capitalist relation—but it is also extended at the level of society, tertiarized, pressed into an arch of productivity that is all the more efficient the wider its social basis.[125] The political problem is to grasp this extension of the initiative of the mass worker over the social terrain, its project for a social wage, its drive toward alternative self-valorization on the whole terrain of reproduction. But the adversary keeps moving: for instance, he constantly attempts to set in opposition different moments of workers' self-valorization, thus reintroducing into the class elements of competition and contrast as well as scabs. In the current growing proletarianization, the rigidity of the working class in the large factories is shaken by the self-defensive practice of clusters of labor dispersed across the territory. It is fundamental to break this and other contradictions that are reproposed by the divisive capitalist activity. The task of the party is to centralize the specificity of various proletarian sectors into a project of wage demands that lays out the basis for the struggle for a full reappropriation of expanding social productivity.

*There can be no class recomposition without centralization.* The passages of recomposition attack all the moments and passages of capitalist command over society and against the workers that aim to divide them. Recomposition entails the continuous rupture of the capitalist articulation of the periods of alternation of capital and of the phases of subsumption of circulation under reproduction; it entails the subjective expression of the limits and obstacles that capitalist production necessarily determines for and by itself. This work of recomposition by means of destruction must be completely under the control of the collective brain of the workers' struggle. So long as there is a state, the political centralization of the proletariat will be absolutely necessary. It is an element of proletarian strength and dignity.

There can be no centralization in recomposition without an appreciation of the *specificity of proletarian power.* This specificity consists first of all in the quality of the processes of self-valorization and the organization of essential needs. Therefore, it is also the rigidity and struggle imposed on the mechanisms of capitalist reproduction. Secondly, but not secondarily, it is a matter of power, self-subsistent, self-valorizing, and politically autonomous power. The proletarian *refusal of delegation* and the refusal to be expropriated of organization at any time are based on the specificity of needs and struggle. The mass dimension of this proletarian specificity must be guaranteed in struggle, just as it can be reinforced and corroborated by centralization.

The campaign for the Charter [*Statuto*] of the party will be launched very soon, of this we are certain. It is in the interest of workers and the proletariat to enhance its intensity and shorten the wait. As usual, capital plays the game of anticipating the success of its project of command after having endured in its turn the anticipation of struggle. We have already seen in the course of this essay that the match is far from over: moments of workers' self-valorization irreducibly infiltrate every moment of the nervous system of reproduction. Far from enclosing struggle within production, capital is forced to endure it at all levels of reproduction. Here, therefore, the material constitution can find only a climate of permanent instability. On the contrary, this situation can provide ample space for the constituent group of workers. *The party hypothesis is mature.*

And no tears will be shed for the dilapidated old Constitution and its parties!

### Notes

1. TN: As Negri and Michael Hardt note, the term "material constitution" refers to "the continuous formation and re-formation of the composition of social forces" in a state, which is distinct from—though prefigured and regulated by—that state's "*formal constitution*, the written document along with its various amendments and legal apparatuses" (*Empire*, Cambridge: Harvard University Press, 2000, pp. xiv, 9).

2. G.W.F. Hegel, "The German Constitution (1798–1802)," in Hegel, *Political Writings*, Laurence Dickey and H.B. Nisbet, editors, Cambridge: Cambridge University Press, 1999, p. 6. Translated by H.B. Nisbet.

3. I use the expression "material constitution" in Carl Schmitt's and C. Mortati's terms [TN: For Schmitt's conception of constitution, see George Schwab, *The Challenge of the Exception: An Introduction to the Political Ideas of Carl Schmitt Between 1921 and 1936*, 2nd edition, Westport: Greenwood Press, 1989, and Gopal Balakrishnan, *The Enemy: An Intellectual Portrait of Carl Schmitt*, New York: Verso, 2000. For Mortati's definition, see his *La Costituzione in senso materiale*, Milan, 1940, and "Il lavoro nella Costituzione" in *Il diritto del lavoro*, Milan, 1954, pp. 149–212; see also Negri's essay "Labor in the Constitution" in Michael Hardt and Antonio Negri, *Labor of Dionysus: A Critique of the State-Form*, Minneapolis: University of Minnesota Press, 1994, pp. 53–136, especially pp. 63–66.].

4. E. Cheli, "Il problema storico della Costituente," in *Politica del diritto*, no. 4–5, October 1973, p. 523. [TN: Sessions of the Italian Parliament are numbered from the first postwar election of 1948; thus the fifth Legislature was the Parliament

elected in 1968 and serving until 1972. When Negri was elected in 1983 to the Chamber of Deputies, the lower house of Parliament, he served in the ninth Legislature.]

5. N. Bobbio, "Sulla funzione promozionale del diritto," in *Rivista trimestrale di diritto e procedura civile*, 1969, p. 1323.

6. U. Romagnoli, "Il principio d'uguaglianza sostanziale," in *Rivista trimestrale di diritto e procedura civile*, 1973, p. 1289ff.

7. TN: In English in the original.

8. S. Rodotà, "Funzione politica del diritto dell'economia," in *L'uso alternativo del diritto*, Barcellona, editor, vol. 1, Bari: Laterza, 1973, p. 233.

9. C. Napoleoni, in *La Repubblica*, 11 settembre 1976.

10. Joan Robinson, "What Has Become of the Keynesian Revolution?" in Robinson, editor, *After Keynes*, Oxford: Blackwell, 1973, p. 10.

11. TN: Latin for "praise for times past".

12. Marx to Engels, 30 April 1868, in *Marx–Engels Werke*, Band 32, pp. 74–75; English translation: Marx and Engels, *Selected Correspondence*, third revised edition, Moscow: Progress Publishers, 1975, p. 195, slightly revised.

13. On this issue, see my analysis in *Crisis of the Planner-State* in this volume.

14. Marx, *Capital* Volume 2, New York: Penguin, 1978, chapter 1, p. 120. Translated by David Fernbach.

15. Cf. G. Ruffolo, *Rapporto sulla programmazione*, and G. Amato, *Il governo dell'industria in Italia*.

16. Allow me to refer you to my *Proletarians and the State* in this volume.

17. On all of this, see James O'Connor, *The Fiscal Crisis of State*, New York: St. Martin's Press, 1973.

18. On this issue, see my *Workers' Party Against Work* in this volume.

19. Obviously, the crucial text on this issue is the 1976 CeSPE [TN: Centro Studi di Politiche Economiche] report. See also A. Graziani's review of this text and its reactionary aspects in *Rinascita*, 15 October 1976, pp. 14ff.

20. See for instance many articles in the corporate journal *Mondo Economico*. On all of this, see C. M. Guerci, "Difendere l'economia," in *Mondo Economico* XXXI, 30 October 1976, pp. 13ff.

21. The level of awareness of this change in the German constitutionalist class in Bonn is well researched and acutely analysed by the authors of *CDU-Staat: Analysen zur Verfassungswirklichkeit der BRD*, G. Schafer and C. Nedelmann, editors, Frankfurt am Main: Suhrkamp, 1972, and by Johannes Agnoli, *Überlegungen zum bürgerlichen Staat*, Berlin: Wagenbach, 1975.

22. TN: Negri's phrase here is *"modalità garantiste,"* which refers to the Italian debate over *"garantismo,"* the political struggle for the formal respect and recognition of those individual civil rights that were supposedly guaranteed by the Constitution. This debate arose as a result of the conflict between the normative

system of legal guarantees (to due process, access to counsel, etc.) and the effective functioning of punitive institutions, a conflict that intensified during the seventies because of the "state of emergency" produced by the clash between the Italian state and clandestine terrorist groups.

23. See section 4 of this essay.

24. Marx, *Capital* Volume 2, chapter 19, p. 462.

25. TN: Negri draws this term from medieval Scholastic philosophers such as Duns Scotus, who used it to express the concept of a singular predication of Being common to God the creator and creatures alike, as opposed to "equivocity," the predication of distinct modes of Being to God the creator on the one hand and creatures on the other. See *Domination and Sabotage* below, p. 235: "In fact, for these comrades power can be—in the words of the old philosophers—predicated only univocally, that is, defined and qualified solely as an attribute of capital or as its reflection." The corresponding German term is translated into English as "one-sidedness" in the standard Marx translations, but we have opted to follow Negri's usage in this regard.

26. Marx, *Capital* Volume 2, chapter 19, p. 449.

27. See the Panzieri-Tronti theses (1962), in *Aut Aut* 149–150, settembre–dicembre 1975, p. 6.

28. TN: "Luxemburg's lesson is again demonstrated."

29. A useful approach to the issue is found in B. Rowthorn's review of Mandel's *Late Capitalism* in *New Left Review*, 98, July–August 1976, p. 60ff.

30. In this problem I see one of the fundamental elements at the basis of 'conventionalist' analyses of the history of the ideology of capital—to which correspond political hypotheses that smack of traditionalism ("revolution from above," "autonomy of the political," etc.).

31. Marx, *Capital* Volume 2, chapter 1, p. 132.

32. Marx, *Capital* Volume 2, chapter 2, p. 162.

33. See once again Rowthorn's review, cited in note 29 above, pp. 61ff.

34. See Marx, *Capital* Volume 2, chapter 2, in particular pp. 150–56, 160–62.

35. Marx, *Capital* Volume 2, chapter 3, p. 172.

36. Marx, *Capital* Volume 2, chapter 3, p. 175.

37. Marx, *Capital* Volume 2, chapter 20, p. 470.

38. Marx, *Capital* Volume 2, chapter 3, pp. 175–78.

39. Marx, *Capital* Volume 2, chapter 3, p. 176.

40. Cf. also p. 175 and the following deductions regarding this "presupposition" of extracted social labor, on pp. 244ff.

41. Marx, *Capital* Volume 2, chapter 6, p. 229, but see in general pp. 206, 219–20, 225–29, 357–58, 365–66.

42. Marx, *Capital* Volume 2, chapter 1, p. 135.

43. Marx, *Capital* Volume 2, chapter 8, p. 237–38.

44. Cf. the theory of *faux frais*, above all in *Capital* Volume 2, chapter 6, pp. 207–29.

45. Cf. A. Negri, *Proletarians and the State,* cited above; and G. Formenti, contribution to the seminar on the "tertiary sector" at the Political Science Collective, Padua.

46. Marx, *Capital* Volume 2, chapter 2, p. 144.

47. Marx, *Capital* Volume 2, chapter 3, pp. 176–78.

48. Marx, *Capital* Volume 2, chapter 4, p. 194.

49. Marx, *Capital* Volume 2, chapter 4, p. 194.

50. Marx, *Capital* Volume 2, chapter 6, pp. 207–29.

51. Marx, *Capital* Volume 2, pp. 331–32, 360, 364.

52. Marx, *Capital* Volume 2, chapter 13, pp. 317–20. On this and other issues discussed here, see Geoffrey Kay, *Development and Underdevelopment: A Marxist Analysis,* London: Macmillan, 1975.

53. Marx, *Capital* Volume 2, chapter 15, pp. 334–42.

54. Marx, *Capital* Volume 2, chapter 5, pp. 202–03.

55. Marx, *Capital* Volume 2, chapter 5, p. 203.

56. Marx, *Capital* Volume 2, chapter 5, p. 204.

57. Marx, *Capital* Volume 2, chapter 4, p. 190, but also pp. 362–67.

58. Marx, *Capital* Volume 2, chapter 5, p. 204.

59. Marx, *Capital* Volume 2, chapter 4, pp. 183–85.

60. See also my comments on these passages, cf. *Crisis of the Planner-State,* op. cit.

61. Cf. *Crisis of the Planner-State,* op. cit.

62. The full passage: "The recognition [*Erkennung*] of the products as its own, and the judgment that its separation from the conditions of its realization is improper—forcibly imposed—is an enormous [advance in] awareness [*Bewußtsein*], itself the product of the mode of production resting on capital, and as much the knell to its doom as, with the slave's awareness that he *cannot be the property of another,* with his consciousness of himself as a person, the existence of slavery becomes a merely artificial, vegetative existence, and ceases to be able to prevail as the basis of production" (463).

63. Cf. in particular Karl-Heinz Roth, *L'altro movimento operaio,* Milan: Feltrinelli, 1976, and Gisela Bock, Bruno Ramirez, and Paolo Carpignano, *La formazione dell'operaio massa negli USA,* Milan: Feltrinelli, 1976. But from the methodological standpoint, very important contributions can be found in George P. Rawick, editor, *The American Slave: Unwritten History of Slavery,* Westport, CT: Greenwood Press, 1974, and especially in E.P. Thompson, *The Making of the English Working Class,* London: Penguin Books, 1963.

64. Massimo Cacciari's review "C'é un altro 'movimento operaio'?" in *Rinascita* no. 41, 15 ottobre 1976, p. 28, does a great disservice to the understanding of the thought of others by combining a base operation of cultural defamation with the radical lack of intelligence of a bureaucratic approach to these problems.

65. Allow me to refer you to my *La fabbrica della strategia: 33 Lezioni su Lenin,* Padua–Milan: CLEUP, 1977.

66. Cf. in particular the research of Luciano Ferrari Bravo and Alessandro Serafini, *Stato e sottosviluppo,* Milan: Feltrinelli, 1972; and the collective volume *L'operaio multinazionale in Europa,* Milan: Feltrinelli, 1974, in particular the essays by Alessandro Serafini and Mariarosa Dalla Costa.

67. See paragraph 4 of this section, above.

68. Marx, letter to Ludwig Kugelmann, 28 December 1862, in Marx and Engels, *Collected Works,* vol. 41: *Letters 1860–1864,* New York: International Publishers, 1985, p. 435.

69. Cf. my "Marx on Cycle and Crisis," in Negri, *Revolution Retrieved: Selected Writings on Marx, Keynes, Capitalist Crisis and New Social Subjects 1967–1983,* London: Red Notes, 1988, and *Rassegna Stato.*

70. Marx, *Capital* Volume 2, chapter 20, pp. 468–564.

71. Cf. Paul M. Sweezy's comment in the "Introduzione" to the Italian translation of Luxemburg's *Accumulazione del capitale,* Turin: Einaudi, 1960.

72. TN: François Quesnay (1694–1774) was a French physician who founded the Physiocratic school of political economy.

73. Marx, *Capital* Volume 2, chapter 20, p. 508.

74. Frederick Engels, *Herr Eugen Dühring's Revolution in Science [Anti-Dühring],* New York: International Publishers, 1934, p. 306, translated by E.P. Burns. But this is already in Marx, *Capital* Volume 3, New York: Penguin, 1981, p. 567. Translated by David Fernbach.

75. Offe, Hirsch, O'Connor, and others have insisted persistently and with clarity on these issues. See chapters 6 and 7 of my *La forma stato,* Milan: Feltrinelli, 1977.

76. *Ibidem.*

77. Paul M. Sweezy, *The Theory of Capitalist Development,* New York: Oxford University Press, 1942, p. 25.

78. Marx, *Capital* Volume 1, New York: Penguin, 1976, chapter 3, p. 198, translated by Ben Fowkes.

79. Cf. *Crisis of the Planner-State* and *Workers' Party Against Work.*

80. Marx, *Capital* Volume 1, chapter 10, p. 400.

81. Marx, *Capital* Volume 1, chapter 1, pp. 163–77, and Sweezy's comment, op. cit., pp. 52–54.

82. Marx, *Capital* Volume 1, chapter 25, p. 766, n. 4.

83. Marx, *Capital* Volume 1, chapter 1, p. 161, n. 26.

84. Marx, *Capital* Volume 1, chapter 15, p. 517–20.

85. Marx, *Capital* Volume 1, pp. 723–24, 920 and Volume 3, chapter 27, p. 567–69.

86. Marx, *Capital* Volume 1, chapter 13, p. 450. Translation slightly modified.

87. Cf. "Keynes and the Capitalist Theory of the State Post-1929" and "Marx on Cycle and Crisis," in *Revolution Retrieved*, op. cit.

88. From here on we will refer to some of Marx's notes on the change in the form of landed property: cf. *Capital* Volume 3, chapter 37, pp. 751–55, 763, 775, etc.

89. On this issue, see Marx's analysis of the function of the elements of mediation (e.g. "custom" and "legal tradition") and their "transformation" in *Capital* Volume 3, chapters 22 and 23, pp. 485–86, 496–97.

90. Marx, *Capital* Volume 3, chapter 14.

91. Marx, *Capital* Volume 1, chapter 23, pp. 717–18; *Capital* Volume 2, New York: Penguin, 1978, chapter 1, pp. 117–18.

92. Marx, *Capital* Volume 3, chapter 21, pp. 477ff.

93. Cf. the positions of German authors, in particular Claus Offe and some of his comrades, who refer to the positions of the review called *Leviathan*. For references see chapters 6 and 7 of *La forma stato*.

94. Marx, *Capital* Volume 3, chapter 23, p. 507.

95. Marx, *Capital* Volume 1, chapter 11, p. 425.

96. Marx, *Capital* Volume 1, chapter 16, pp. 645–46.

97. Marx, *Capital* Volume 1, chapter 25, pp. 777–80.

98. Johannes Agnoli, *Le trasformazioni della democrazia*, op. cit.

99. Marx, *Capital* Volume 1, chapters 8 & 13.

100. Mario Tronti, *Operai e capitale*, Turin: Einaudi, 1966.

101. Marx, *Capital* Volume 2, especially pp. 200–06.

102. Marx, *Capital* Volume 2, chapter 5, pp. 201–03.

103. Marx, *Capital* Volume 1, chapter 15, p. 533.

104. Marx, *Capital* Volume 2, chapter 10, pp. 275ff; Antonio Negri, *Workers' Party Against Work*, op. cit.

105. The issue of imperialism has been treated from this perspective by Ferrucio Gambino in his contribution to Luciano Ferrari Bravo, editor, *Imperialismo e classe operaia multinazionale,* Milan: Feltrinelli, 1975, p. 318 ff.

106. Marx, *The Eighteenth Brumaire of Louis Bonaparte,* in *Surveys from Exile: Political Writings* Volume 2, edited by David Fernbach.

107. On the notion of the "other workers' movement," see Karl-Heinz Roth, *L'altro movimento operaio*, op. cit. and Gisela Bock, Paolo Carpignano and Bruno Ramirez, *La formazione dell'operaio massa negli USA, 1898–1922.*, op. cit.

108. Here we are referring once again to Marx's analysis of the revolutions of 1848 and the following years.

109. Antonio Negri, *La fabbrica della strategia: 33 Lezioni su Lenin*, op. cit.

110. This is the attitude of some of the reviews of my *Proletarians and the State*, in particular Sergio Bologna's in *Primo Maggio* [TN: English translation: "Negri's *Proletarians and the State*: A Critique," translated by Ed Emery, in Timothy S.

Murphy and Abdul-Karim Mustapha, editors, *The Philosophy of Antonio Negri: Resistance in Practice,* London: Pluto Press, 2005] and P. Petta's in *Praxis.*

111.  Marx, *Capital* Volume 2, chapter 17, p. 396.

112.  This is a summary of the development of the broader schemas of reproduction. For a good commentary see Paul Sweezy, op. cit.

113.  Marx, *Capital* Volume 2, chapter 21, p. 571.

114.  Antonio Negri, "Marx on Cycle and Crisis," op. cit.

115.  Much work still needs to be done on the issue of Marx and socialism and how to realize the law of planning against the law of value (cf. Paul Sweezy, op. cit., pp. 52–54), and on the issue of Marx and communism as the actualization and overcoming of the law of planning (see Rosdolsky's comments on the *Grundrisse*). But much work is needed in terms of the critique of political economy and of workers' science, rather than in terms of the philology of "transition"!

116.  See especially the "Address of the Central Committee to the Communist League" in Marx, *The Revolutions of 1848: Political Writings* Volume 1, New York: Penguin, 1973, pp. 323, 330.

117.  For documentation of this, I refer you to my *La fabbrica della strategia,* op. cit.

118.  For Mao Tse-Tung on this issue, see the collected writings in *Per la rivoluzione culturale,* Turin: Einaudi, 1975.

119.  TN: Marx and Engels, *The German Ideology,* Amherst: Prometheus Books, 1998, p. 57. Recall that "abolishes [*distrugge*]" = *aufhebt* (from *aufheben* = eliminate, suppress, overcome).

120.  TN: In English in the original.

121.  The fundamental reference is to the so-called "Fragment on Machines," already cited from the *Grundrisse*.

122.  Cf. P. Petta, *Ideologie costituzionali della sinistra italiana, 1892–1974,* Rome: Savelli, 1975.

123.  V. Rescigno, *Costituzione italiana e stato borghese,* Rome: Savelli, 1975.

124.  Cf. chapter 2 of my *Forma stato,* and especially the exposition and analysis of C. Mortati's take on the "material constitution". [TN: Negri is referring to his article "Il lavoro nella Costituzione", pp. 27–110 in *La forma stato,* translated into English as "Labor in the Constitution" in Michael Hardt and Antonio Negri, *Labor of Dionysus: A Critique of the State-Form,* pp. 53–136; his exposition of Mortati is found on pp. 63–66.]

125.  Antonio Negri, *Proletarians and the State,* op. cit., in particular the "Preface to the Second Edition" against the positions recently defended by Sylos Labini and Fuà. [TN: Paolo Sylos Labini (b.1920) was a left-leaning economist and sociologist at the University of Rome, whose major work is *Saggio sulle classi sociali,* Bari: Laterza, 1974. Giorgio Fuà (1919–2000) was a statistical economist and policy researcher at the University of Ancona. In the preface to the second

edition of *Proletarians and the State* (pp. 119–21 above), Negri ridicules their defensive critiques of the excessive "aspirations to consume" of the Italian workers' movement of the seventies.]

# V

# Domination and Sabotage: On the Marxist Method of Social Transformation (1977)

*Translation by Ed Emery revised by Timothy S. Murphy*

## PART ONE: CAPITAL'S DOMINATION

### 1. LENIN IS SUPPOSED TO HAVE SAID ...

Lenin is supposed to have said (according to a claim made by Keynes) that inflation is the weapon best guaranteed to bring about a crisis of the capitalist regimes. The attribution of this statement—a statement so much beloved by bourgeois economic culture and not just by Keynes, as evidenced by their continual repetition of it—to Lenin is undoubtedly apocryphal.[1] The offending phrase is nowhere to be found in Lenin's works. In fact, insofar as Lenin expressly deals with the problem of inflation, his emphasis is along the lines of a moralistic denunciation of its effects on the poorer classes—a denunciation well within the socialist tradition. This does not mean, however, that other Bolsheviks did not, at various points, stress the destabilizing function of inflation in relation to capitalist power. Preobrazhensky speaks for them all with his description of "paper money as a machine gun for the Finance Commissariat to fire at the bourgeoisie, enabling the monetary laws of that regime to be used in order to destroy it." However, I am not implying that such a statement would have been uncharacteristic of Lenin; he was, after all, intent on grasping the conjuncture between the revolutionary insurgence of the proletariat and the crisis of imperialism.

However, I am convinced that the sense of any such assertion by Lenin would have been a complex thing. In fact, in Lenin's teaching, any action that *destabilizes the capitalist regime* is immediately accompanied by action that *destructures* capital's *system*.

Insurrectionary action against the state is articulated in relation to the work of destroying the state. I am not giving an anarchist interpretation of Lenin's thought. I am simply insisting upon the "destabilization–destructuring" nexus which is present in a precise and continuous manner in Lenin's thinking, as in all revolutionary Marxist thinking (with the exception, realistically speaking, of anarchist immediatism). Thus, in this sense, F.W. Fetter is right when he says that the assertion regarding the positive effect of inflation for the revolutionary process cannot be unreservedly attributed to Lenin: the destabilization effect cannot be an exclusive one. Capitalist crisis has to have a direction [senso] which is imposed and dominated by proletarian power. Destabilization of the regime cannot be seen as distinct from the project of destructuring the system. Insurrection cannot be separated from the project of extinguishing the state.

With this we arrive at the heart of today's political debate. Two different positions are present within workers' and proletarian autonomy. Destabilization of the regime and destructuring of the system sometimes appear as divergent objectives, and as such they are invested in differing tactical and strategic projects.[2] Is there a reason that *this divergence* should exist?

Let us start by considering the problem from the viewpoint of capitalist practice. For capital there is no problem: *restructuring of the system is a condition for the stabilization of the regime,* and vice-versa. The tactical problems arise within the relative rigidity of this relationship, and not outside it—at least, ever since capitalist development has rendered undesirable the option of using force (in the sense of mere physical force) against the working class and the proletariat.

For capital, the solution of the crisis consists in a restructuring of the system that will combat and reintegrate the antagonistic components of the proletariat within the project of political stabilization. In this sense, capital is well aware of the importance of proletarian antagonism, and is also—often, in fact—aware of the unique quality of that antagonism. Capital has often accepted that the workers' struggle is the motive force of development—and has even accepted that proletarian self-valorization should dictate the rationale for development: what it needs to eliminate is not the reality, but the antagonistic direction [senso] of the workers' movement. At the limit, and paradoxically, we could say that for capital there is no possibility of effective political stabilization (that is, no possibility of command and exploitation within a dimension of an enlarged reproduction of profit) except to the extent that it proves possible to take the proletarian movement as the starting point for restructuring.

The interests of the proletariat, however, are quite the opposite. The proletariat aims at a critical seizure of the nexus between stabilization and restructuring, in order then to attack it. To overturn this relationship and transform it into a project of destabilization as well as destructuring: this is the interest of the working class, in general terms.

Now, to be particular: the antagonistic divergence in the direction of the movement of the two opposing fronts—that of capital and that of the pro-letariat—is absolutely clear. This is due to the singularity of the relation of force between the two classes in struggle. Both classes have the ability to take action both on the level of the system and on the level of the regime; the actions of both are capable of directly investing the nexus of the overall relationship. Thus, if we do not focus our discussion on this nexus, on the way in which it is invested in an antagonistic manner by the two classes in struggle, we risk dangerously oversimplifying the debate.

For capital, as we have said, the problem exists only in a relative form. We could cite one or two examples. During the past ten years, we have wit-nessed such a continuous and active interpenetration of these two moments as to eliminate all "catastrophist" conceptions, whatever their motivations. The Crisis-State has not for one moment ceased to be a Planner-State as well. All the elements of destabilization that the workers' and proletarian struggle have brought into action against the state have, one by one, been taken up by capital and transformed into weapons of restructuring. Inflation in particular, far from being a moment of destabilization, has been trans-formed into its opposite—into a decisive weapon of restructuring. At a very high cost, admittedly: albeit in a situation defined by an increasing tendency of the rate of profit to fall, capital has been constrained to take planned action which included the maintenance of (high) levels of worker valorization—and thus the unsuccessful devaluation of (overall) labor-power. This notwithstanding, the "catastrophe" has been avoided! Obviously, this process has not been free of situations of subjective crisis for the capitalist elite. But the continuing work of *reinforcing the state-form*—that is, of the *imposition of the law of value* (albeit in continuously modified form) as a measure and a synthesis of stabilization and restructuring—has never faltered. When we speak of a crisis of the law of value, we must be careful: *the crisis of this law does not at all mean that the law does not operate;* rather, its *form is modified,* trans-forming it from a law of political economy into a form of state command. But for capital there is no such thing as command without a content, and a quite specific content at that—a content of exploitation. Thus the rhythm according to which exploitation must dance, according to which the social mechanism of the reproduction of exploitation must be stabilized, must be dictated by the law of value. When the proletariat respectfully declines this invitation to dinner, when all the economic parameters of the relationship explode, then it is enterprise-command [*commando d'impresa*], it is the polit-ical transformation of enterprise-command into the form of the state which takes the upper hand in order to again determine the functional relationship of value, the law of exploitation. Recent studies[3] have largely confirmed and documented this trend, with particular regard to monetary questions—questions which today are undeniably fundamental to any consideration of the transformation of the law of value. This has led to a justified insistence on the theory of the capitalist state (and its development) as the authoritative *form* of the capital relation.[4] Thus, in the critique of political economy, the structural relation of capitalist development (and capitalist crisis) has become clear, in opposition to existing, purely objectivist conceptions.

But all this is not enough. The workers' consciousness of the critique of political economy must transform itself into a consciousness of the revolutionary project. The proletarian opposition has no choice but to consolidate itself in practical overturning, in subversion. But it is the whole relationship, in both its political aspects and its structural foundations, that is to be subverted. It is not possible simply to eliminate the complexity of the relation imposed by the state form of the organization of exploitation; we cannot escape—either via subjectivist voluntarism or via collective spontaneism—the difficulties, the problems, the determinations that arise from this form. We have come perilously close to this during the last phase of the struggle. The divergence has, as I stated earlier, invested strategic and tactical projects that tend to diverge. Is there a reason that this divergence should exist?

In my opinion, it risks proving fatal for the entire movement. And in this situation, I am really not sure which is preferable—a rapid demise brought about by the plague of subjectivity, or the long, slow agony and delirium of the syphilis of spontaneism. However, counter-poisons do exist; a constructive project is possible. It is to be found and is being developed through the articulations of the *mass line,* in the dialectic that the proletariat continually sets in motion, the dialectic between its activity of structural consolidation (the strengthening of that mass counterpower which, as such, tends to disorient and throw out of balance capital's activity of restructuring) and its action of destabilizing political attack (which shatters the nexuses of the enemy's power, which heightens and empties out its spectacular character and exhausts its force). This dialectic is internal to the mass movement, and we need to deepen it further. The project of destructuring capital's system cannot be separated from the project of destabilizing capital's regime. The necessity of this interrelationship is revealed at the level of the relation of force between the two classes today, inasmuch as the mass line has been completely developed into a *project of proletarian self-valorization.*

I should explain: *the concept "proletarian self-valorization" is the opposite of the concept "state-form"*—it is the form that power assumes within a developed workers' standpoint. Proletarian self-valorization is immediately the destructuring of the enemy power; it is the process through which workers' struggle today directly invests the system of exploitation and its political regime. The socialization of capitalist development has permitted the working class to transform the diverse moments of communist strategy (insurrection and the extinction of the state) into a process and unify them into a project. Proletarian self-valorization is the comprehensive, mass, productive figure of this project. Its dialectic is powerful insofar as it is comprehensive, and comprehensive insofar as it is powerful. Elsewhere, I have tried to demonstrate the *formal conditions* whereby the Marxist critique of political economy reveals the independence of the working class as a project of self-valorization.[5] Now we are forced by the constructive polemic that is going on in the movement to think out the real and immediate *political conditions* of this proletarian independence. And within the movement we shall have a battle, on two fronts: against the plagues of insurrectionism and subjectivism on the one hand, and on the other—most importantly—against the opportunism, streaked with pacifist utopianism, which mythologizes the gentle growth of an impotent "movement" of desires.

It is clear that the polemic within the movement can only develop if it takes as its practical and theoretical starting point the *intensification of both the concept and the experiences of proletarian self-valorization*. This is something I shall attempt to do in the course of this work. But it may be useful to anticipate one particular polemical point of departure, in relation to two recent proposals: that of Lea Melandri[6] and that of Furio di Paola.[7] In both these cases, the discussion is built around a radical initial mystification, from which we must free ourselves right from the start. It is a mystification that arises from a radicalization of the polemic against "power," in which the specificity and determinacy of power is denied. In fact, for these comrades power can be—in the words of the old philosophers—predicated only univocally, that is, defined and qualified solely as an attribute of capital or as its reflection. This assertion is false, even if it does correctly pose the problem of the impossibility of establishing a homology in the concept of power between its capitalist usage and its proletarian usage (that is, the untranslatability of the term). But this is precisely a problem of method that cannot be answered with a reply that is radically negative in substance. From this point of view, you end up playing into the enemy's hands—that is, you maintain that the only meaningful linguistic horizon is that pertaining to the structure of capitalist power (a position which, apart from anything else, contradicts the spirit and the fundamental axis of the analysis of self-valorization within women's autonomy and youth autonomy, which preoccupies these two essays).

And it is this that is false. Power, party: Panzieri used to say that "In such conditions the party will become something wholly new, and it even becomes difficult to use that term."[8] Very true. But elsewhere, and in the same sense, he adds: "No revolution without a party." And we might further add:

"Without power, no proletarian self-valorization." And then we could even change the terminology, if you like! But first let us regain the dialectical unity of the process of proletarian self-valorization, its tendency toward the destructuring of the enemy power as a project for its own liberation, as a powerful and effective struggle for proletarian independence.

One final note, as a prelude. It is not difficult to understand how important it is *on the plane of militancy* to stress the necessary relationship between action that materially destructures and action that politically destabilizes the enemy power. Here, in fact, that slender but strong thread that nourishes subjectivity with a mass content, that transforms proletarian love into struggle against the enemy, that founds and joins together class hatred and the passion for freedom, finds once again its unifying wellspring. The personal is political through this collective mediation. The collective practice of proletarian self-valorization determines the unity of subjective consciousness. This dynamic and productive being constitutes our dignity as revolutionaries. Thus, both objectively and subjectively, we have no choice but to fight to re-establish the complexity of the revolutionary hypothesis from the point of view of the independence of proletarian self-valorization.

## 2. A FIRST PARENTHESIS, REGARDING METHOD

When I assume the viewpoint of an independence of the process of proletarian self-valorization, and when I examine the possibility of its having an internal dialectic of continuous recomposition between structural functions and offensive functions, I am bound to draw certain methodological conclusions. First, it seems to me fundamental to consider the totality of the process of proletarian self-valorization as alternative to, and radically different from, the totality of the process of capitalist production and reproduction. I realize that I am exaggerating the position and oversimplifying the complexity of the problems. But I also know that this "intensive path [*via intensiva*]," this radical rupture with the totality of capitalist development, is a fundamental experience of the movement today.

*Today, the process of the constitution of class independence is first and foremost a process of separation.*

It is a "downward path [*via in giù*]," a forced separation that serves to clarify the overall meaninglessness of a capitalist world within which I find myself constituted in non-independent form, in the form of exploitation. I thus refuse to accept the recompositional dialectic of capital; I affirm in a sectarian manner my own separateness, my own independence, the difference [*diversità*] of my constitution. As Hans-Jürgen Krahl has intuited,[9] the totality of class consciousness is first and foremost an intensive condition, a folding back on the totality of productive being, which elides the relationship with the totality of the capitalist system.

Class self-valorization is above all *de*-structuring of the enemy totality, taken to the point of exclusivity in the self-recognition of the class's own collective independence. I am not depicting the history of class consciousness in a Lukácsian sense, as some predestined, all-embracing recomposition; on the contrary, I see it as a moment of intensive rooting within my own separateness. I am *other*—as is the movement of that collective practice within which I am included. I belong to the *other workers' movement.* Of course, I am aware of all the criticisms that could be leveled at this position from a traditional Marxist viewpoint. For my own part, I have the sense of having situated myself at the extreme limit of meaning in a political class debate. But anyone who comes with accusations, pressing me with criticism and telling me that I am wrong, must in turn accept the responsibility for being a participant in the monstrosity of the development of "socialism" and in its illicit dealings with the most disgusting results of the capitalist mode of production. It is only by recognizing myself as other, only by insisting on the radical totality of my difference, that I have the possibility and the hope of renewal.

Furthermore, in my assertion of this radical methodological break [*cesura*], I am in good company. The continuity of the *history of the revolutionary workers' movement* is the *history of the discontinuity of that movement,* the history of the radical breaks that have characterized it. The revolutionary workers' movement is continually reborn from a virgin mother. The whores of continuity are still alive and well in the Official Labor Movement's institutes of history. But, luckily, militant historiography is undergoing a renaissance too, according to the rhythm of the movement's breaks—and on the plane of historiography we are not afraid to present ourselves as the "other workers' movement." Thus the methodological condition of an initial radical break (which we consider fundamental for any renewal of the social practice of the proletariat) is corroborated by an extensive documentation (limited, perhaps, in scale, but remarkable in its intensity). When Karl-Heinz Roth[10] or Gisela Bock[11] tells the formidable story of how the working class in struggle has continually destroyed its own traditional organizations, they are certainly not animated by a spirit of iconoclasm; rather, they are highlighting the radical, irreducible difference of the revolutionary movement. This is a perspective that could also give us a taste of other revolutionary experiences of the proletariat—experiences that have proved victorious and have therefore been betrayed.

So, I must assume this radical difference as a methodological condition of the subversive case we are arguing—namely, the project of proletarian self-valorization. But what about the relationship with the historical totality, the relationship with the totality of the system? I must now face up to the second methodological consequence of my assumption: *my relationship with the totality* of capitalist development, with the totality of historical development, is guaranteed solely by the *force of destructuring* that the movement determines, by the overall *sabotage* of the history of capital that the movement enacts. There is only one way that I can read the history of capital—as the history of a continuity of operations of reordering that capital and its state have set in motion in order to counter a continuous rupture, a permanent provocation toward separation that the real movement of the proletariat brings about. *The present state of things is built upon a continuity of destruction, of abolition, of overcoming that the real movement brings about.* I define myself by separating myself from the totality; I define the totality as other than me— as a net that is cast over the continuity of the historical sabotage that the class carries out.

And thus—here is the third methodological implication—there is *no homology*, no possible immediate translatability of languages, of logics, of signs, between the movement's reality for me and the overall framework of capitalist development, with its contents and its goals.

Let us now pause and take up the debate from another angle. The fundamental point, however you look at the argument, is obviously still the nexus between the process of self-valorization and the effects of destructuring. I have pushed this nexus to an extreme, and I have recognized it in separation. Basing myself on the experience of the movement, I have insisted first and foremost on the subjective element. If I now approach the argument from the objective point of view—*the viewpoint of the Crisis-State*—the result is no different. When the state, faced with the crisis in the functioning of the law of value, attempts to reimpose that law by force, mediating its own form of the capital relation and the commodity form in general, the state itself registers, in effect, the crisis of all homologous functions. Force does not substitute for value, but provides a surrogate for its form. The law of value may be forcibly reintroduced, in spite of the crisis of that law, and its operations may be imposed in modified form—but this does not fill the void of meanings that power is constrained to register. The Crisis-State is a power that lives in a void of meanings, a logic of logic-power [*forza-logica*] which is itself destructured. This logic, this critical form, is a "dark night in which all cows are white":[12] in other words, the meaning of the whole does not in any way arise from the perfect connection of the parts. The state's investment in the totality is purely negative, in terms of meaning. The reign of total alienation is the only possible content of this project. The totality is a void, is structured as destructuring, as a radical lack of value. Thus it becomes clear what a lack of homology means in this framework. All the elements of the whole are unified in a technical sense; they hang together only in their mutual untranslatability, only in the form of a forced relationship. Neither a historicist approximation nor an Enlightenment-rationalist projection are thinkable at this level. So, from an objective viewpoint too, the system can be seen—*must* be seen—as destructured.

However, while our consideration of the objective aspect of the situation confirms our analysis of the subjective aspect, the objective aspect has neither the same logical extension nor the capacity to substitute itself for the subjective. One cannot move from the understanding of destructuring as an effect to the identification of the process of self-valorization as the cause. This is particularly obvious in the analytic principles of Michel Foucault,[13] which have caught my attention because of the way they strain for the productivity, the creativity of an *unknown quantity* situated beyond the cognitive horizon. This is also obvious—and furthermore scandalous—in the various surreptitious attempts that are being made to reimpose a conclusive meaning [*senso*] on this destructured horizon. These attempts, be they humanistic in inspiration or conceived in terms of *Wille zur Macht*, do nonetheless start from a correct perception of the blind objectivity of the development of capital's system.[14] But this surreptitiously restated homology, this "revolution from above" in the absence of radical meaning, can be seen clearly, in the light of what we have said, for what it is—a fraud.

The above considerations lead me now to confirm my original hypothesis of the *prevalence of the subjective* in the explanation of the current dialectic of capital. Taking the subjective viewpoint to extremes does not negate its methodological validity. Rather, it confirms and extends it. It allows me, in the articulation between self-valorization and destructuring, to avoid both reductive foreclosures of the problem (because in fact it is the productivity of the proletarian subject that structures the destructuring, that is, negatively determines its own opposite) and, on the other hand, totalitarian dialectical extensions of the discourse, because, in this case, there are no longer homologous functions of any kind.

It is clear that methodology does not in any way resolve the problems that face us (although it does facilitate a correct framing of the solution). We know that the methodological hypothesis requires confirmation from class analysis. It is only the theoretical-political determination of the composition of the working class that can offer a sound basis for a methodological hypothesis such as ours. And, in fact, the following methodological approximations, without pretending to be exhaustive, confirm our initial methodological assumption that, today, the constitution of class independence unfolds first and foremost in its separation. But *separation* in this case means *the rupture of the capital relation*. Separation also means that, having reached the point of maximum socialization, the working class breaks the *laws of the social mediation* of capital. Marx, in *Capital* Volume 2, chapter 1, calls for another mode of investigation in the analysis of the metamorphoses of total social capital. Is this to be a logic of separation? Is it to be a *Darstellung* built on the extremity and radicality of this independent proletarian subjectivity, built on the movements of proletarian self-valorization as such?

I think that these questions are important for the further development of this work. However, before we go on, they can be further articulated on a formal and methodological plane, in order to constitute a framework for the ensuing debate. Let us look more closely. As I have said, the separateness of the proletarian subject is organized in the dialectic between self-valorizing productivity and functions of destructuring. I know, however, that this dialectic does not produce effects of homology and totalization because it is a dialectic of separation. But, equally necessarily, it is inherent in the complexity of the events that are being determined. How? In particular, how does this special articulation of a separate subject relate to the constitution of capitalist domination? Secondly and conversely, how precisely does the constitutive process of collective subjectivity proceed, in all its radicality and intensity? In short, *what are the laws that preside* (albeit in a situation of separateness, of the lack of any homology) *over the parallel and opposed processes of the state-form and of proletarian self-valorization?*

The further development of this work will be dedicated to answering these questions. But in defining the problems, we can now add several further notes—first in relation to the *self-valorization/destructuring nexus*. In the history of socialist thought and practice, the sense of proletarian self-valorization has often been expressed with original intensity (if Gramsci's teachings can be retained in any useful sense today, it is certainly in this regard). But it is never expressed in terms of separateness—rather, it is always expressed in a dialectical sense in relation to the totality. Reciprocation [*Corrispondenza*] takes the place of opposition. In the social-anarchist tradition this reciprocity, this correspondence, has been played out in terms of the dialectic between centralization and decentralization. Thus it is not difficult, in a critique that starts with Marx and stretches through to Foucault's edition of the *Panopticon*, to demonstrate the perfect compatibility of Proudhon and Bentham. But this compatibility also exists in the tradition of "scientific socialism"—this time not in extensive (between centralization and decentralization), but in intensive form (between the workers' particular interests and the general interests of society, between socialism and democracy). This compatibility of the process of self-valorization with the productive structuring of society is a myth. It is not Proudhon and Bentham, but Rousseau and Stalin who are the fathers of this much-loved synthesis. Personally, I have nothing to do with the so-called "New Philosophers,"[15] but I must say I am rather disconcerted when I see representatives of the historical parties of the working class, who have always been enamored of the link between Enlightenment rationalism and productive Stalinism, insulting these young philosophers for having drawn attention to this mystifying connection. In short, they are addressing themselves to a problem that no longer exists. Class self-valorization has nothing to do with the structuring of capital, but it has a lot to do with its destructuring. The whole of capitalist development, ever since the working class established itself at a high level of composition, has been nothing other than the obverse of, a reaction to, a pursuit of proletarian self-valorization—an operation of self-protection, of recuperation, of adjustment in relation to the effects of self-valorization, which are effects of sabotage of the capitalist machine. Tronti says it well in his latest work: the modern state is the political form of the autonomy of the working class.[16] But in what sense is he correct? In the sense—for him too, with his revived "socialism"— of compatibility and convergence? Not at all, my dear comrade: here the methodology of the *critique of political economy* has to be modified, taking as its starting point proletarian self-valorization, its separateness, and the effects of sabotage that it determines. It is within *this* perspective in particular that we must frame our analysis of the state-form.

If our analysis of the nexus between self-valorization and state structure leads us along a path of causality that is negative and destructuring, the situation is different when we come to consider our methodological approach to the *nexus of self-valorization with itself*, in its separateness. Here we shall have to stress and adequately analyze the synchronic dimensions of the process. But here, too, there can be no recourse to models of continuity, to functional determinations! What can be said straight away—because it constitutes the substantial core of the methodological proposition itself—is that the separateness of proletarian *self-valorization* presents itself *as discontinuity*, as a set of leaps and innovations. The method of social transformation that derives from the self-valorizing separation of the proletariat has nothing in common with the progressive capacity for homology of Enlightenment rationalism and historicism. Proletarian self-valorization is the strength [*forza*] to withdraw from exchange value and the capacity to base itself on use values. Every progressive capacity for homology relates to exchange value. The rupture of an anchorage in use-value and the recognition of the class's own independent productive force remove any possibility of dialectical resolution. From the radically separate viewpoint of proletarian self-valorization, the dialectical positivity of method is wholly and solely innovative.

## 3.  THE FORM OF DOMINATION

Having outlined our polemical methodological premises, we can now enter into the substance of the matter. Facing us stands the state; between us—and sometimes within us—stands the form of domination. To struggle means to recognize the monstrosity of the power that stands facing us, recognize it with the same immediate clarity and on the same level as we have viewed the relationship between self-valorization and destructuring. Now, *this monstrosity of power is the effect of our sabotage;* it is the negative result of our actions: "Crime," says Marx, "through its constantly new methods of attack on property, constantly calls into being new methods of defense, and so is as productive as strikes for the invention of machinery."[17] This is no paradox—Marx does not like the paradox label, not even in the case of Mandeville's *Fable of the Bees;* this pleasure he leaves to the "philistine apologists of bourgeois society." It is, rather, a key to understanding. In point of fact, the more we sabotage the state and the more we give expression to the self-valorization/destructuring nexus, the more the rules governing the development of capital's state–system become ferocious, monstrous, and irrational. So let us now look at how the state and the system of social domination respond to the social sabotage which results from self-valorization, and let us look at the logic that they express—a logic which is internally coherent, but which is nonetheless negative; a logic of destructuring which can never be sublimated, but only precipitated further.

Capital's continual restructuring is its response to the workers' sabotage. *Restructuring is the empty, but efficacious, content of the state-form*—empty, because it lacks any rationality save that accredited by the workers' sabotage; efficacious, because the form of the restructuring is command. But bourgeois political economy's critical consciousness is obliged to fill the vacuum of its own process by spreading a wafer-thin (recuperated and mystified) formal rationality over the rhythm of workers' and proletarian struggles. Let us see how it proceeds. Within the critical consciousness of bourgeois political economy, the evolution of the logic of command has taken place in at least *three distinct phases*, following the great crisis of the thirties. Each one of these phases corresponds to a particular quality and intensity of workers' and proletarian struggle. Elsewhere I have indicated the fundamental characteristics of the *Keynesian epoch.*[18] In that epoch, control of the workers' struggle was to be achieved in global terms. Keynes replied to the formation and struggles of the mass worker with an overall adjustment—in progressive terms—of supply and demand. But Keynes based himself on a political proposition that was pure and general—he had stressed the overall *trend.*[19] But when the trend comes into contradiction with the actual progress of the cycle (because the workers' conflictuality does not respect conclusive equilibria), the Keynesian State goes into crisis. Who commands in the crisis? The Keynesian political elite tries to invent a "political trade cycle,"[20] tries to form "intermediate regimes"[21] etc.: in practice, control is little by little slipping out of their hands—the control dimension no longer matches the dimensions of proletarian and workers' conflictuality. A *second phase* opens. Alongside the theoretical "progress" that leads Sraffa and his ilk to a dissolution of the aggregate categories of capital, more concretely we can observe that the workers' struggle has a discontinuous continuity, and that the apparent continuity of the struggle is the result of an infinite series of individual points of emergence. The economic and political sciences of restructuring must take account of this. It is no longer possible to dream up indeterminate macro-economic equilibria that are independent of short-run[22] variations and independent of the micro-economic components that are variable within the unforeseeable pacing [*tempi*] determined by the struggles of the collective worker. Based on this necessity, we now see the formation of the theory of the *Crisis-State*, along the following lines: divide up the overall thrust of the working class; control it within the mechanisms of its own accumulation; and forestall it by attacking it in its class composition. Keynes's broad equilibria are replaced by an internal rupture of the class, a tactic that is precisely oriented toward dealing with individual points of class emergence—a microphysics of political economy. The "long-run trend is but a slowly changing component of a chain of short-period situations ... it has no independent entity."[23] Thus, it becomes impossible to produce a model of development unless it takes explicit account of the interruptions that occur in the process of production and reproduction, and thus a fresh foundation is laid for a theory of development based on the theory of cyclical fluctuations, incorporating the dynamics that occur at the micro-economic level. A long phase of bourgeois economic theory now develops around these premises. Michal Kalecki is the leading light in this movement.[24] But this theory also falls short. Crisis-State theory is, after all, a *reformist* theory. It faces up to the emergence of the mass workers' productivity, and tries to lay out an economy of oligopolies—on two sides: on the one hand the capitalist entrepreneurial oligopoly, and on the other hand the worker/union oligopoly in the factory.[25] But in the meantime, the struggle has advanced; the action of the mass worker has gradually invested the whole of society. The worker presents himself as a "socialized worker [*operaio sociale*]"—even (and particularly) if still a "factory worker." The worker responds to the Crisis-State even more violently than previously to the Planner-State. If the latter went into crisis because of its inability to control the quantity of the workers' demands, the Crisis-State is forced into an internal self-criticism of what is now a socially inescapable (and immediately efficacious) extension of the workers' action. The Crisis-State is not only a state-form that is reformist to its roots—it is also, and above all, a state-form that is still linked to the dimensions of direct production, to enterprise-command. But when the workers' sabotage expands to invest the whole of society, the entire mechanism of circulation, forcing total capital into a confrontation over the rules governing the reproduction of the system, at that same moment the consciousness of bourgeois political economy—which had actually been consolidating itself up to that point—reaches a further degree of crisis and dissociation.

It is interesting to note the formation of a *third phase* of theoretical development in the political economy of the Keynesian epoch. This is in the process of formation today, and draws on the elements of crisis in the previous proposals. In particular it tries to operate in a more comprehensive way on the social movements of the working class. Its interest centers on *circulation*. The simple transition from (Keynesian) global control of production to (Kaleckian) dynamic control of production is insufficient. The problem is that of the functional control of circulation, the dynamic nexus linking production and reproduction. And here the problem of *time* becomes fundamental. Keynes never concerned himself with the temporal determination of equilibria and secondary equilibria. Kalecki, on the other hand, insisted upon the necessity of determining Keynesianism via the redefinition of phenomena within individual "time units."[26] And now, today, the temporal dimension is being extended to the whole of the process. In analytic terms, this is a sort of Einsteinian theory of relativity: it involves the insertion of another dimension of analysis, in order to relativize its contents. But this is a strange kind of relativity indeed: it is above all a relativity of time, the reduction of time to an *indifference of command*. In practical and political terms, we have an analytic mechanism that assumes circulation time as a terrain of both theory and control. The totality of circulation time is drawn into the economic analysis; the totality of circulation time is to be dominated by economic policy: the hypothesis of the simultaneity of functions and operations within the cycle is not assumed in advance and abstract (*à la* the neo-classicists), but operational and political (*à la* Milton Friedman and his monetarist bedfellows). The Kaleckian interruptions of the short cycle are still mediations between the trend[27] and the overall cycle: here, science does not become separated in its application, does not waste its efforts in forecasting, but intensifies its attentiveness to every passage. It is a physics of elementary particles—and science stands watchful, like a policeman, over everything.

It is not the Marxists' job to observe that the temporal dimension is decisive in the nexus between circulation and reproduction, and in general within

the relationship as it impinges on the class struggle in the sphere of reproduction.[28] It is not surprising that the problem is arising again. Rather, what
is surprising is the fact that the proposition arouses so much passion. The
philosophers are well aware that the dimension of time is problematic: indefinitely subdivisible and indefinitely extendable. The idea of the bad infinity
is embodied in the idea of time. So how should we grasp the analytic proposition in operational terms; how are we to concretize the political project?
It is not our job to answer this: it suffices to draw attention to the indeter-
minateness of the project. Rather, our task is to note how *the process of
destructuring that is internal to the logic of political economy* is taking a further step
forward in this case.[29] In its anxiety to keep up with the process of the
workers' offensive against the general dimensions of exploitation, bourgeois
political economy strips even the appearance of coherence from its logic,
and forces itself into the role of a technical instrument against the emergence
of the destructuring power of the class; it spreads itself over the indefinite
discontinuity of the movement of self-valorization. State restructuring
increasingly becomes an indiscriminate succession of acts of control, a precise
technical apparatus which has lost all measure, all internal reference points,
all coherent internal logic.

The happy theoretical consciousness of the worker rejoices at this. But,
being responsible people, we must recognize the enormous weight of suffering, inhumanity, and barbarism that all this brings with it. This
manifestation of the internal void of capitalist restructuring, this successive
self-destruction of the moments of capitalist control, and this *dissolution of
theory into a technique of power*, bring closer the deadlines [*scadenze*] of revolutionary struggle. But, at the same time, it renders the everyday struggle
painful and capital's continued existence cruel.[30] And yet it is still the workers'
action that brings about these effects—to the extent that *the destructuring
tension of these struggles has a direct effect on the very rationality of capitalist restructuring*, and *eliminates this rationality*, even in its formal aspect, leaving us with
a whole that is destructured, technical, and repressive. The varied and
combined modality of the workers' action is respected in every moment of
the restructuring of capital: from the actions of the mass worker, and from
those of the socialized worker, follow effects that are well adapted for a subsequent radical destructuring of the enemy power.

Thus it is not by chance that today, grand capitalist reformism has adopted
—at a world level—*a terroristic strategy of savage deflation* (or "dis-
inflation," if you prefer). On the basis of the experience of the *fiscal crisis of
the American cities*, this political line has been correctly described as a "regressive redistribution of income, wealth, and power."[31] The destructured logic
of economic compatibility must in fact be extended downward, to reach

individual social groups, in such a way as to destroy every consolidation of proletarian self-valorization at every level. Generalized control must be intensified so as to act on every nodal point in the process of reproduction; it must allow the destruction of all rigidity; it must make fluid, in a new manner, the cycle of capitalist reproduction. But this has always happened! This is one of the laws of capital! Certainly. But what makes the current situation specific is the depth, the intensity, the extent of the control. Capital has been subjected to class pressure on the social terrain, which has definitively destructured its terms of reference. Enterprise-command itself is in crisis at this level. Restructuring, at this point, is domination in its pure form. It aims to adapt itself to the level of the individual unit of production, the individual social group, the individual person. Thus it is not by chance that, acting at such a depth and within such micro-economic dimensions, power is once again, for the first time in several decades, resurrecting the ideology of freedom!

Here, capitalist determination (whose articulations follow the social emergence of the processes of proletarian self-valorization, and which has to face up to the effects of destructuring that these engender) reaches a maximum of logical vacuity: here, *the reimposition of the law of value within restructuring is violence, to the extent that it hinges logically on criteria of indifference.* However, this in no sense reduces the efficacy of the project of restructuring. Command lays out the specifics of this indifference. If the social struggle of the working class has driven the capitalist mind to the point of formal indifference, then capitalist command tries to specify and materialize this possibility. It is important to emphasize this passage, because with it comes a fundamental shift in the development of the contemporary form of the state. That very *social-democratic project,* which since the time of Keynes has been at the center of capital's interest in restructuring, is now *subsumed into the indifferent possibilities* of capital. This is perhaps a splendid example of how workers' and proletarian self-valorization has destroyed an instance of the enemy. The social-democratic project is beginning to disintegrate, and from this point of view, the euphoria that accompanies the present development of the various Eurocommunisms is slightly macabre.[32]

So, concretely speaking, what is the center of the capitalist restructuring project today? How is the form of domination taking shape? The extreme volatility of command faced with the law of value is not something new: but *what is specific to restructuring is the conjuncture of command and the indifference of the contents of command,* of its articulations. This capitalist conclusion derives from the powerful socialization of the revolutionary movement of the proletarian class; it is the obverse of this. In this situation, capital's initiative becomes regressive—in other words, it has to base itself on a logic that is as empty as it is separate. Once again a methodological premise that, to us, is fundamental—that is, the *separateness* of the cycles of capital and its state-form from the cycle of working-class self-valorization—is verified. But at this point a whole series of problems re-emerges, particularly if we want to identify not so much the center, as the specific content of capitalist restructuring. How is this terribly empty and indifferent, this terribly weak and at the same time ferocious freedom of capital determined today?

For the moment I know only one thing: that from the workers' point of view—having arrived at this level of awareness—the effects of the destructuring action that I have set in motion force me to confront—in a destructive manner—capital's force of stabilization. And this means, first of all, confronting that force which promotes the multiple indifferent possibilities of domination. Destructuring the enemy system involves the immediate necessity of attacking and destabilizing its political regime.

## 4. A SECOND PARENTHESIS, ON THE WAGE

I find myself in a complex theoretical position. I must, at one and the same time, show how the form of capitalist domination is subordinated to the process of workers' and proletarian self-valorization—and also show the resulting determinations in the destructured separateness of command. This, in fact, is the sense of the question that I posed earlier: how does one specify and determine the *indifference of command?*

As regards the first point, I think I have already gone some way toward proving it. In short, at the very moment when capital is living through the complete socialization of the productive force of the working class, the (Keynesian and/or Kaleckian) instruments that it had at its disposal for controlling the interrelationship between production and reproduction (based on a balancing of supply and demand, on the twin basis of an expanding employment base and an expanding production base) fail. Why do they fail? Because *the mechanisms of capital's reproduction and the mechanisms of reproduction of the working class are no longer operating synchronously.* The social self-valorization of the working class accentuates, in an antagonistic manner, both the quality and the quantity of the workers' needs. It radicalizes the aspect of simple circulation, over and against the overall reproduction of all the dimensions of capital. At this point, as we have seen, "the needs of social expenditure have to be met, inasmuch as they *must* guarantee a continuity of production and reproduction of overall labor-power. This therefore sets in motion a state monetary phenomenon which, unlike Keynesian *deficit spending*,[33] must allow for a *simultaneity* of both capitalist and working-class reproduction."[34] Thus all the channels of administration—and not merely the monetary aspect—must provide possibilities of reducing to zero the relation between supply and demand. Given the actual strength of the working class, the problem is thus to reduce its autonomous reproduction time and strength. Thus the separateness of capitalist command could not be clearer. Its destructuring springs from capital's realization that every attempt to adapt to the determinate articulation of the working class and the proletariat fails, for this very reason. Only command conceived as indifference, conceived as a separate capacity for self-reproduction, can be enforced at this point. Capital is driven to daydreams of self-sufficiency. It is not by chance that, at this limit, we see the re-emergence of economic theories that we thought long dead and buried—theories of the self-sufficiency of capital and its money, mementoes of neo-classicism and quantitative monetarist practices.

But dreams are only dreams for all that: that noisy alarm clock of the class struggle is still there to wake you up. So the capitalist state now has to rearticulate in positive terms the separate essence of its command. From a practical and theoretical point of view, there has certainly been a profound and significant advance: here, *the destruction of the value-terms of the capitalist relation is no longer a result, but a starting point;* it is no longer a painful injury suffered, but a proud and arrogant act of will. Indeed, never before has the capitalist state been so politically autonomous! It still remains necessary for capitalist command to be articulated, but henceforth its parameters will be based on this separateness. The source and legitimation of power are no longer the law of value and its dialectic, but the law of command and its hierarchy. Having been forced into the most radical *material* destructuring, capital's state must now restructure itself *ideally*. The free productive state of the capitalist revolution is now reduced to a *corporative, hierarchical* form—to the organization of appearances. This is the only logic of the "autonomy of the political." Henceforth neither political economy and the critique of political economy nor the analysis of class and class composition can adequately explain this destructured reality; only descriptive sociology can follow this phenomenon!

This is the *State-based-on-Income-as-Revenue*, the Income-State [*Stato-rendita*]—a state of political income. The one absolute value against which all other hierarchical values must measure themselves is political power. And this one absolute value is the foundation for the construction of a scale of *differential incomes*, whose value is calculated on the basis of one's greater or lesser distance from the center, from the site of production of power.[35] Power is the simultaneity, the site of perfect compatibility of the mechanisms of production and reproduction, and it is from this that circulation must proceed, accepting its authority. One's location in the hierarchy, the corporative structure, and the respective positions of the various separate bodies—all these are articulated according to this logic. These differential incomes are signs of the variability of one's insertion into the hierarchy, into the articulation of command. This, then, is the only form within which the indifference can be determined. The "Party-State" [*Stato dei Partiti*] and the system of public administration tend to guarantee this specification of differential income as the form and the content of political power.[36]

Now, all of this touches directly on *productive labor*. What, in short, is the nature of productive labor within the Income-State? From capital's point of view, it is that *part* of social labor that has been unionized, corporatized, situated within the separation of the state hierarchy. From this point of view, the indifference to the value you produce is equaled by the attention paid to the extent of your faithfulness to the system. The *labor market*—that is, overall labor-power in its relative independence—is sectioned off according to the hierarchical values advanced by the system.[37] Of course, every time the state mechanism intervenes in the reality of the class struggle in a direct manner, the game becomes harder, particularly when the intensity of the approach cannot be mystified, when the intervention takes place at the point of greatest contradiction. To impose upon the labor market in order to divide it, to section it up, to hierarchize it *(when it is precisely at this level that productive labor has made itself general,* where "small-scale circulation" has made itself independent, and where reproduction seeks to be self-valorization[38])—to impose upon this reality guarantees a maximum of violence and mystification. Because here the two extremes of the process that we are describing meet: on the one hand, the unified material base of the processes of proletarian self-valorization, and on the other, the active, repressive figure of power that has been destructured by the struggles.

It is worth pausing briefly to consider this central moment, and to emphasize some of the consequences of what we have been saying, from a theoretical point of view, about proletarian self-valorization. Now, two elements are immediately clear. The first is that, at this point, *the wage is no longer*, in its economic identity, *an independent variable.* It is completely subordinated to the entire dynamic of power, to the entire framework of the political autonomy of the state. The wage is reduced to the hierarchy of command, in a process that is the counterpart, the obverse of the repression of proletarian unity at the social level. This leads us to the second consequence: the center of the workers' and proletarian struggle consists in *the recognition of the general aspect of the wage as a cost of reproduction of the unity of the proletariat*, of its self-valorization. *The problem is political, on both sides*—even if, as in this case, it is obvious that the meanings of the term "political" are not homologous—because we are dealing with meanings that are mutually opposed, completely and precisely antagonistic. For capital, politics is division and hierarchy, for the proletariat it is unity and equality; for capital it is the subsumption of labor, for the proletariat it is the process of self-valorization; for the state it is the simultaneity of the processes of production and reproduction, for the proletariat it is the development of the independence of its own processes of reproduction, dissymmetry, and discontinuity.

At this point, therefore, the problem of the wage (as the pivot-point on which the antagonistic capital relation turns) takes on a new figure. The logic of separation—which flows from the process of self-valorization, and which capital undergoes in a destructured and idealized form—leaves no margins of compromise in this respect. So it is not by chance that the capitalist reaction to the development of the class struggle has been unleashed above all around the problem of *public spending*—understood as the terrain on which the thrust of the workers' struggle was effectively and offensively reshaping the issue of the wage, adapting it to the fundamental instances of the project of self-valorization. In the struggle over public spending, capitalist hierarchization, the differential incomes of power, the corporative mystifications of the unions, were coming under heavy attack, while the unity of social productive labor as the basis of the process of self-valorization was increasing. This was, indeed, a "battle for production"! It gave the working class the possibility of regaining its own productive dignity, its unity, outside and against the mechanisms of political income, of state parasitism, which the unions and power sought to impose on it. It gave the working class the possibility of materially grounding its own productive unity—of opposing exploitation by means of self-valorization.

*Public spending and the wage constitute issues to which the analysis, the theory and the practice of revolutionaries will continually have to return*, because in a situation of discontinuity in the cycle of the class struggle, the problem of public spending will, in the coming years, assume the same importance that the wage, narrowly defined, has had in years past. But we must be clear here: in the discontinuity of the movement, once again, no homology is permissible. In other words, the issue of public spending is not simply an extension, a completion of the wage issue. *The problem of public spending is not that of the social wage.* It is, rather, the recognition, the imposition of the recognition that *the unity of social labor, of the whole of social labor, today constitutes the only possible definition of the productivity of labor*: this is the base for which capital *must* pay. It must pay for it with respect to its quality, its articulations, its determination. It must recognize the independence of workers' self-valorization.

But as we have seen, this does not happen. Instead, the contrary happens—the whole of capital's attention turns to the functioning of differential income (restructuring) and to the consolidation, in absolute terms, of its political resources (stabilization). Now, *the mechanism of political income must be destroyed*:

DOMINATION AND SABOTAGE   **251**

the struggle over public spending is a struggle that directly attacks the mechanisms of command and the determination of political income and destroys them. It destroys them by *quantitatively raising public spending* to the point of making it incompatible with the proportions of command over reproduction, and by *qualitatively blocking* the relative choice of options. But this is not enough. There is also direct action to be taken. Some groups of workers, some strata of the working class, remain tied to the dimension of the wage, to its mystified terms. In other words, they live off this political income. Inasmuch as they are living off this political income (even some who work in the large factories), they are stealing and expropriating proletarian surplus-value—they are participating in the social-labor racket on the same terms as their bosses. These positions—and particularly the union practice that fosters them—are to be fought, with violence if necessary. It will not be the first time that a procession of the unemployed has entered a large factory so that it can destroy the corruption of the labor aristocracy along with the arrogance of political income! This was what the unemployed were doing in Britain in the 1920s, for example[39]—and quite rightly so. Here, however, it is no longer simply a matter of the unemployed. Here we are dealing with all the protagonists in the social production of value who are rejecting the operation that capital has set in motion in order to destroy their unity: *the workers of the large factories need to be brought back again to this front of the struggle.* This is fundamental. The *social majority of the proletariat,* of socially productive labor-power, must impose the issue and practice of unity, bringing it once again to the attention of the workers in the large factories. The *mass vanguards* of the large factories must struggle, in conjunction with the proletarian movement, to destroy the parasitic filth celebrated and guaranteed by the unions in the large factories. This is fundamental. Here, in fact, we are dealing with the project—the living, effective project—of workers' self-valorization, which refuses, and must destroy, the vacuity of the *rentier* logic of capital and all its apparatuses. Now, at this point I should answer those jackals that I already hear howling: I am not saying that the Mirafiori worker is not an exploited worker (this is how far you have to go in order to polemicize with jackals!). I am saying that the "Party of Mirafiori" must today live the politics of the proletarian majority, and that any position which is restricted purely to the necessary struggle in the factory, and which is not connected to the proletarian majority, is a position that is bound to lose. *The factory struggle must live within the proletarian majority.*

*The privileged place of the wage in the continuity of proletarian struggles must today be extended to the struggle over public spending.* Only this struggle can enable the full self-recognition of the proletariat; can establish the bases of self-valorization; can attack directly the theory and practice of political income. On the other hand, the capitalist practice of political income is utterly fragile—fragile because it is completely ideal. Here the problem is no longer that of differential income, but that of its political foundation. Now, this "absolute" foundation is itself ideal—it is an indictment of the whole machinery of capitalist development, to the extent that it has registered the crisis of the law of value. It is, therefore, a limit. And thus it is a will to the overall mystification of the system of exploitation. When Marx criticizes Ricardo's "underestimation" of absolute rent [*rendita*], he admits nonetheless that its tendency must be to disappear: Ricardo's "overestimation" of differential rent would, in these conditions, become plausible. But here, we are already in the situation where the survival of moments of absolute rent has already given way to the development of capitalist socialization and the global predominance of the capitalist mode of production. Here the reappearance of political income no longer has any criterion of verisimilitude or any material foundation. It is a phantasm. And then? The Income-State develops *two mystifications*. The first is the one which joins differential political income and its mechanisms to a generic emergence of the law of value (which, as we already know, has been transformed into the form of command); the second is that which seeks to consider the absolute nature of political income at the level of the origination of power, as its fundamental condition. But this too is pure and simple mystification: here we are not seeing the expression of a historical necessity tied to the period of development of the law of value—we are merely seeing the expression of the extreme limit of mystification, of the forcible reimposition of a law on a proletarian world which otherwise would be impossible to dominate. Nevertheless, this proletarian movement brings about the *extreme dissolution of the very concept of power*. And now, enough bluster about the nexus between Lenin and Max Weber! Here, as in the thought of Lenin, thought and practice go in two opposite directions: worker freedom and bureaucratic indifference are polar opposites—with the first being rationality, the second irrationality; the first being struggle, the second mere formalization of political income (unless the "autonomists of the political" do not have the same one-dimensional conception of power, so to speak, that the New Philosophers have!).

The indifference of command, therefore, is specified in a sort of political practice of income, whose absolute foundations lie in political authority, and whose differential lies within the hierarchical system. This situation brings about a conception (and a reality) of the wage system that differs radically from the experience of wage struggles conducted by the "other" workers' movement in other historical eras. Today, in fact, the *wage struggle* cannot be other than immediately *political, general*, and *egalitarian*. The privileged terrain on which it moves is that of *public spending*, of the self-valorizing overall reproduction of the proletariat. This terrain has to be rebuilt, together with the workers in the factories; this struggle must reunify the proletarian terrain. And it can be done. And anyway, there is no alternative: or rather, the only alternative is to accept subordination, to plunge into the maelstrom of destructuring, to abandon ourselves to destruction.

## 5. ... AND NIETZSCHE WENT TO PARLIAMENT

Once upon a time there was the "salami theory": the reformists intended to take power just like slicing a salami.[40] When this culinary witticism fell into disrepute and the conception of power as totality was restored, some thought that power could be conquered by putting salt on its tail.[41] They had good structural motives for thinking that way: a peaceful strategy that would have taken into account the class's socialization, however cautiously managed, could only have brought about a relation of force that would have tended to be more and more favorable to the class. In this fable, there seems to be no recollection that the power of the bourgeoisie was quite a nasty hawk, far from willing to do business with the industrious little sparrows. There was also no recollection that peace could not, therefore, be considered a precondition but would have to be imposed, and that, in the dialectic of its determination, the worst could continually blackmail the best. The fable doesn't record any of this, even though the concept is one of the Aesopian archetypes of fabulation. Finally, there was no recollection that workers' self-valorization in itself was destructuring and destabilizing to capitalist power. There is really no more to be said about this, because in this case we cannot play at fables.

Now, once again, the only point that we are interested in pursuing is *the relationship between self-valorization and destructuring. Reformism fundamentally denies this sense of the relationship; instead, it asserts that self-valorization is consistent with structuring,* not destructuring. Valorization, for reformism, is univocal: there is only capitalist valorization. The problem is how to gain command over it. Everything else is utopianism. *Eurocommunism* sets itself up as a candidate to represent the developed working class, as a party that mediates between the process of proletarian self-valorization and the restructuring of capital. Eurocommunism is the party of restructuring—it is the party of the synthesis between proletarian self-valorization and capitalist valorization. Having picked up out of the mud the banners of democracy that the bourgeoisie had let drop, Eurocommunism now sets about gathering up the banners of economic development which capital had destructured. Thus, there is no discourse on power that is not organized exclusively within the virtuous circle of restructuring. As for Eurocommunism's goals, they are more than clear: the conscious extension of the capitalist mode of production to the whole of society and its ("socialist") state management.

Our intention here is not to demonstrate that this project is bad and ugly. Rather, we believe we can show it to be impossible—undesirable, in fact, because it is not realistic but mystified. We believe it can be shown that the working class is proceeding—increasingly so, as it becomes more socialized—in terms that are antagonistic to this project. The battle is between the true and the false, and initially it can take place on no other horizon—but thereafter it will occupy every other horizon. And to conclude, we believe it can be shown that Eurocommunism, inasmuch as it proceeds along these lines, presents no alternative whatsoever to capitalist development, but rather is the representative of a catastrophic subordination of the class to capital, a fragile and transitory element of capital's state-form.

Thus self-valorization and restructuring. In reality, the decision as to whether these two terms are compatible or antagonistic is not merely a question of fact. Eurocommunism is innovative in relation to Marxism, not because it denies the empirical conditions of the process of *self-valorization,* but because it denies the *worker and proletarian character,* the *radically antagonistic potential,* and the *political relevance* of that self-valorization.

First, the worker and proletarian character. Eurocommunism does not use the term "self-valorization," but rather the term "hegemony." This term allows the processes of working-class socialization to be interpreted as tending toward the dissolution of the class into society. It substitutes a Hegelian and populist terminology for a Marxist class one. Operating in this framework, Eurocommunism displaces the debate from the terrain of class struggle over reproduction, over productive labor, that is to say, the terrain of class composition, to "society" understood generically, and politics as the complex of institutions. By this means the term "self-valorization" is robbed of its meaning as part of a class vocabulary. For Eurocommunism, the terrain of proletarian self-valorization becomes a liminal zone, meaningful only in terms of the reconstruction of a social totality.

Second: the negation of the radically antagonistic potential of the processes of workers' self-valorization is the dynamic consequence of the first negation. Once workers' and proletarian self-valorization is seen at the limit of a merely phenomenal manifestation, it can only be expressed dynamically through the social synthesis. This synthesis is determined by the society of capital. So we are not dealing with an antagonism, according to Eurocommunism, but with an organic and functional dialectic between the classes, the terms of whose solution are provided by the relation of force and by its compatibility with the general interest. And the general interest is the development of capital.

Finally, the political relevance of workers' self-valorization can only be restored by a general, external function, one that can differentiate the functions within the global project of development. No unmediated political relevance can be granted to workers' and proletarian self-valorization, all the more so since it is interpreted as being at the furthest limits of the phenomenology of production. Its movements do not contain a generality; its separateness is to be politically mediated through society, with society, in society; and the particularity of its interest is to be articulated with the generality of capital's development.

Now, from negation to affirmation. Only restructuring—say the Eurocommunists in addition and in conclusion—will provide the possibility of restoring the formal conditions for proletarian self-valorization within the capitalist mechanism of development. Restructuring reorganizes the rationale of capitalist development and structures it in relation to the needs of the proletariat: it goes, therefore, from the general to the particular, and only by proceeding in this direction can it give meaning to the liminal manifestations of the proletariat. The only way that the particular interests of the proletariat can be repaid in economic terms (but in a different manner, a manner which is organic and compatible with development) is by destroying the antagonistic harshness of particular interests that arise along the road that leads to the centrality of the function of restructuring. The socialized worker's brain—the reformists continue—is the center of the process of restructuring: it negates the economism of its stimuli by transforming them into political starting points; it negates the political starting points by molding them into a force to manage capital. In the more refined versions,[42] Eurocommunism's insistence on the centrality of the political functions of restructuring vis-à-vis the class mechanism of self-valorization reaches the point of extreme essentialism: the Weberian/Nietzschean functional formalism of the bourgeois tradition is recuperated and inverted into an instance of proletarian command, a pure autonomy of workers' politics.

I think I have done justice to Eurocommunism in expounding its theory in these terms. In reality, the opposition is so clear-cut that there is little point in resorting to polemic. In fact, as has quite often been emphasized, beyond the debasement of Marxism that this conception entails, it is shown to be false by the reality of the movement. *When we say self-valorization, we mean the alternative that the working class sets in motion on the terrain of production and reproduction, by appropriating power and reappropriating wealth, in opposition to the capitalist mechanisms of accumulation and development.* We have reached a point where the process of proletarian self-valorization has begun to invest the entire terrain of the socialization of production and the circulation of commodities (increasingly subsumed within the mechanism of capitalist reproduction). Therefore, when this extension of the processes of valorization (including essential modifications that are inherent in the concept of productive labor) is accomplished, every possibility of considering an antagonistic or generalizing valence (the party, the worker's brain, the "autonomy of the political") outside the process of self-valorization itself becomes less and less viable. Certainly, it is true that, *according to the rhythm of the workers' socialization, capitalist society has been permanently restructured*: infrastructures, services, education, housing policies, welfare policies, etc. multiply and determine an ever-wider context for the processes of self-valorization. But *precisely this process reveals the characteristics of self-valorization*: in fact it reproduces within itself—the more so the further it extends—the antagonistic characteristics of workers' power. The workers' struggle imposes a reorganization of society, a capitalist restructuring. This restructuring must be adapted to a series of needs that are imposed by the struggles themselves. The quantity and quality of the struggles determine the reforms. But nevertheless, these still remain capitalist reforms, and the effect of the workers' struggle on them is immediately double: it reopens the struggle within this restructured fabric; and through the subsequent extension and generalization of the struggle, it destructures capitalist command at this level too, at this degree of extension. Workers' self-valorization does not find its continuity within restructuring; in restructuring it sees only an effect of its own strength, an increase of its own offensive possibilities, an extension of its own power to comprehensively destructure capital. Thus *there is no political mediation possible at this level, either in institutional terms or in terms of economic restructuring*. Eurocommunism, seen from this perspective, is living a lie: it claims a continuity with the processes of self-valorization which is not given, and consequently it is constrained to mystify and fight the effective movement of self-valorization on that movement's own terms, the terms in which that movement actually expresses itself—as power [*potenza*] of destructuring.

So it is not by chance that the positions within Eurocommunism that have laid claim to a correct institutional mediation of the processes of self-valorization have also ended up overwhelmed by the illusion of mediation. From the factory struggles to the struggles for reforms, they said; then, from the struggles for reforms to a campaign to restructure the capitalist undertaking, to restructure the state. Was this a necessary continuity? Only as a step along the road of mystification! In fact, after a short while, we then saw this naïve spirit coming back into the factory: of necessity, the continuity that had led "from the struggles to the state" had now been thrown into reverse. Now they were speaking from the point of view of the state, and the antagonistic content of the workers' factory struggles and the struggles for reforms was totally subordinated to the state. The processes of self-valorization were now to be seen as "functions" of the capitalist state.

Let us now look at the workers' viewpoint. It extends from the factory to the society; it imposes upon capital the organization of social productive labor; it reopens on this terrain a struggle that is continuous and increasingly efficacious. In valorizing itself socially, the working class increasingly destructures capital as capital is increasingly constrained to extend its direct command over society. Within this framework, the activity of reformism and of *Eurocommunism* is an *element of the state-form* of capitalism—but, we should note, *in a subordinate and threadbare form*. It does not succeed—indeed, it cannot succeed—in ensuring that the rationale of self-valorization prevails within capitalist restructuring. It remains prisoner of a destructured rationality that cannot be translated; it is overwhelmed by the indifference of power, the transcendence of its unity. The rhythm of collective bargaining which is proper to reformism has dissolved into the trajectory of political income. Only in the form of corporativism does reformism win back some credibility. To make up for this subordination, reformism refuses to accept the fact that it has been transformed into mystification, the mystification into bad conscience and mystified will, and the mystified will into repression of the struggle, into terrorism against the processes of workers' and proletarian valorization. At this point, reformism and Eurocommunism have earned the right to call themselves, and to feel themselves, participants in the state-form of capitalism. But at what a price! *Germania docet.*[43]

So this Nietzschean presence in Parliament is cause for rejoicing. The situation is such that *every failure of mystification is a victory for the workers*. Faced with the impetuousness and force of the processes of workers' self-valorization, *the coalitions that have determined the state-form of late capitalism are necessarily surrendering to the workers' antagonism*. Oligopolies, unions, the "middle classes" have for half a century—and certainly since the Roosevelt revolution—dominated the framework of the state-form and have determined its constitutional foundations throughout the whole of the Western world. The working class is now emancipating itself from the institutions, imposing a continuous investment in public spending that is now purely and simply appropriation, a fact of power, destructuring of the enemy. The capitalist response is divestment, the flight from confrontation with the class. There is no alternative to the fall of the rate of profit in this situation: whatever road is followed—that of the defense and maintenance of employment, or that of public spending—come what may, the rate of profit is decreasing.[44] But if there is no alternative to the fall of the rate of profit, then this space will be occupied by workers' initiatives that constantly destructure, and in this case also destabilize, the political balances of power.

The proletarians do not lack destructive cynicism, even if they only know a little Nietzsche.

The relation of self-valorization to restructuring—which is the basis for any remaining dignity of reformism and Eurocommunism—thus has no standing whatsoever, from any point of view, neither that of the working class, nor that of capitalism. From both standpoints, the relation appears antagonistic. And yet, in the name of that efficacy that power concedes to mystification, it can *still* be part of the state-form. Up to what point? From the moment when its function has been totally subordinated, the point will be established by the struggle between the two classes over the question of power. For the moment, reformism and Eurocommunism are living an opaque, subordinate life within the framework of capital's state-form. Corporativism and parasitism are the qualities of their existence.

## PART TWO: WORKERS' SABOTAGE

### 6. WE NO LONGER HAVE ANY CHOICE ...[45]

*Self-valorization is sabotage.* That sentence is probably prosecutable by some state prosecutor in this Republic of Italy, with its Constitution "founded on labor." But the more interesting problem is the sentence's reversibility, the complete inter-translatability of self-valorization and destructuring. Sabotage is the *negative power* [potenza] *of the positive*, its inverse, which is now at stake.[46]

Nevertheless, before elaborating on this stake, a stake that is completely subjective, I am pleased to conclude the objective part of the discussion on the form of domination by simply adding an adjective to what has already been said about Eurocommunism: *reformism is disgraceful* [*infame*]. Its disgrace [*infamia*] resides in the structural position that the state-form assigns to it as the center of mystification, the center and motive force for the organization of consensus and thus of *repression* against both real and merely possible opposition. This disgrace is a superfluity, a mathematical point, a mannerism of structural function, though it is no less serious for all that because its effective projection takes on, within the spectacular character that the regime grants it, an original and general significance. It is brutality that is open to the temptation to be arrogant; it is arrogance that is open to the temptation to be terror; it is terror that is open to the possibility of being comical. A paradox arises here: the *negative power* [potenza] *of the negative* does not manage to be credible. Repression is not credible. Its spectacular form is paradoxical and ridiculous. Indeed, why not "swap Brezhnev for Pinochet"?[47] To laugh at repression is not to defend oneself but to define it, facing it as it presents itself. "At the same time, we must laugh and philosophize."[48] But when you begin to philosophize, you notice that this detachment is actually contempt. The negation of self-valorization is disgraceful. An incommensurable, irresolvable, unsurveyable space separates you from this disgrace. The disgrace of reformism is the measure of this detachment, and thus the proletarian refusal of repression, its organs and institutions can only be total and radical.

Yet we must laugh at the disgrace and philosophize, not over this disgrace that is detachment, but rather by amicably deepening the discussion of central issues such as this sensation that is knowledge, that is the negative power [*potenza*] of the positive, and sabotage as a function of self-valorization. I am therefore within this separation that connects me to the world as a force of destruction. I am within it and I feel the intensity of the leap of change that is presupposed every time that I free myself through destruction. Leap, change, discontinuity—but doesn't that mean Sorel and anarcho-syndicalism?[49] Only fools could think so. At this point there is neither organicism nor myth, neither generality nor improvisation, but rather the intensity of a relationship between wealth and poverty that refuses to be resolved, and that is felt to be scandalous by virtue of the fact that all its terms are reversed from this point on: wealth before poverty, desire before need. Separation is what is sought, but it is expressed in a powerful will to conflict; rupture is what continually launches relays of destructive will against reality, and desire is what exerts itself to be desperation. In short, it is a positivity that commands the negative and imposes it. Yet you don't know how to transform this uncontrollable tension into hope except by living it. Hope is a projection, a continuum, an analogy to be postulated. At this point there is no homology of any kind, neither Ernst Bloch's utopia nor Georges Sorel's myth.[50] Here, wealth is tested and desperation wins. I look around myself in amazement. Is this really the spirit of the century? Is this really the creative Marxism in which we live? Nothing reveals the immense historical positivity of workers' self-valorization more completely than sabotage, this continual activity of the sniper, the saboteur, the absentee, the deviant, the criminal that I find myself living. I immediately feel the warmth of the workers' and proletarian community again every time I don the ski mask. This solitude of mine is creative, and this separateness of mine is the only real collectivity that I know. Nor does the happiness of the result escape me: every act of destruction and sabotage redounds upon me as a sign of class fellowship. Nor does the probable risk disturb me: on the contrary, it fills me with feverish emotion, like waiting for a lover. Nor does the suffering of the adversary affect me: proletarian justice has the very same productive force of self-valorization and the very same faculty of logical conviction. All this happens because *we are in the majority*—not the sad one that is measured at some time in every decade among adults who put on the regulation student uniform and return to school, but a qualitative and quantitative majority of social productive labor.

Yet all this is not enough. The dawning violence, the emotional intensity that the consciousness of class composition immediately reveals, must rearticulate itself, it must bring to life its system of rearticulations. It is real, but insufficient in the face of the desire that suffuses it. The passage, the leap forward, and the rupture are the fruits not of external activity, but rather of the tension that my separateness inspires and unleashes.

No, I am not looking for a program or a menu—a fancy menu with easy recipes that make it simple for the cook to govern. A menu is still a menu, and until proofs to the contrary appear, the ones who end up eating best are still the bosses. What is required by the tension of class separation is an indication, a path, a *method*. I do not want the other [*l'altro*], I want instead to destroy it. The fact of my existence implies the destructuring of the other. Above all else, I want to acquire a method by which to increase my separation, to conquer the world by appropriating the network of class self-valorization. Every time I leap forward, I enlarge my existence as part of the collectivity. Every time I break capital's margins of valorization, I appropriate yet another space for workers' valorization. For the proletariat there are no vacuums. Every space left empty by the enemy is filled, occupied, appropriated, attacked by an expansive force that has no limits. The relation with capital has no points of homology: capital is defeated in order to replace it. Nothing that I am saying means anything other than what I am saying, in terms of capitalist valorization overturned, of violence, of mass action. The pins and needles of the humanist dispersal of desires and needs are not really it. My way of moving, on the other hand, is constructive, material. Imagination now wears a good pair of boots; desire carries violence; innovation is accompanied by organization. Our *method of social transformation* can only be the method of *proletarian dictatorship*. Understood in its own terms: as a struggle for the extinction of the state, and for the total replacement of the capitalist mode of production by proletarian self-valorization and its collective process. How should we answer those history professors who will (and do) accuse our (future) will of being (past) unreality? It is obvious that we are talking about different things—it is as if we were both speaking of a great bear, but for them it means some distant constellation of stars, while for us it means the present reality of a ferocious animal. We are this developing, animal reality; we have the same strength, the same necessity and the same fierce irreducibility. Our existence is collective. Our method of social transformation is the method of democracy and freedom within the collective growth of proletarian self-valorization. This method of social transformation is based on the method of dictatorship, in the sense of exclusion of the enemy. But our wretched star-gazers ask how we are going to use this method of dictatorship among ourselves, and whether it is possible that we may commit errors. It certainly is possible, but it is sickening to hear such counsel from the accomplices of capital. We can only reply that the class dictatorship does—and must—exist, and we shall do everything—including staking our lives on this dictatorship as we are now staking them in the revolution—in order to make it a collective process, informed through and through by freedom and by workers' self-valorization. And there will be no pity for the enemy![51] In any event, *sabotage* as self-valorization is certainly not a law that would cease with the communist dictatorship that we are going to set up. No. It is instead *a law of freedom that, now and in the future, we conjugate with that of communism.*

Let us return to the fundamental problem. Proletarian self-valorization is sabotage. How does this project become concrete? The leap from the phenomenological revelation of our separate existence to the expansion of the force of the process of self-valorization is organized around a method of social transformation which is immediately a method of new knowledge [*conoscenza*]. The determinate objective of the process is to increase the use value of labor, against its capitalist subsumption, against its commodification, against its reduction to a use value of capital. But how does this capitalist subsumption of labor come about today? It comes about through command, through hierarchy, and through income-as-revenue. Capital tries to dominate and control, via divisions, that unity of social labor that the working class, with its struggles, has tended to bring about. The fundamental issue of the communist project has always been that of the unity, the recomposition, of the working class. *Today the issue of unity must be tested entirely in relation to the problem of the recomposition of social productive labor.* From this point of view, it is a fundamental necessity to destroy the mechanisms of political income. In the coming years and months, we must not be afraid to go into the factories, as commandos [*reparti*] of social productive labor, in order to impose on those factory workers who have been bought off and mystified by the practice of the reformists—to impose on them the recognition of the centrality of social productive labor. They are part of it. They are neither above nor below nor to the side of it. They are themselves inside it, and they must recognize it. They must rejoin that vanguard of the proletariat from which reformism and Eurocommunism have excluded them!

In this instance, workers' self-valorization becomes specific sabotage of the mechanisms of workers' separation that the state-form has assumed in its material constitution. On the other hand, as we have seen, capitalist development itself, trapped in the vise of destructuring, is now removing the structural reasons for the separation between workers, in order to replace them with a justification that is purely political—take, for example, the destruction of Roosevelt's coalition in the USA. In this case too, however, the problem of the use value of the working class's antagonistic independence must be addressed. Perhaps the key to the *assault on the corporative organization* of factory workers is the imposition of a *drastic reduction of the working week,* as a possible means of bringing the moments of innovation and revolutionary force back into the unity of the process of self-valorization. But more of this later on. What we are discussing now is the general objective and not its concrete determinations.

However, once again this is not enough. I have proceeded along the road of self-valorization; I have recognized both the strength and the limits inherent in the immediacy of its process; I have made an initial determination of a method which sees in its separateness an adequate synthesis of freedom and dictatorship; I have recognized the way that the process currently takes place at the level of sabotage of the mechanisms of division that leads me to a higher level of social recomposition of productive labor. This is still not enough. This method must be substantiated in more specific and at the same time more general terms, but also in more determinate as well as more focused terms.

Now, what does it mean to destructure capital? It means reducing it to the indifference of command, and thus to a lack of "measure," a lack of any relation with itself, however fragile, other than an indeterminate will to exploitation.

And what does the process of valorization start to mean, once we have rigorously understood it as the class's capacity to bring about a development that is completely alternative to capitalist valorization? It means *a tension toward the rational organization of this process.* The profound rationality of this process is undoubtedly inherent in its freedom, but this freedom is material, the organization of a collective process. *What is the law governing this collective process? What is the "measure" of its materiality?* There is no method that does not include some form of measure, whatever the nature of that measure may be. The problem of "measure" in the process of self-valorization is part and parcel of the problem of the method of social transformation. On the other hand, a measure has already in part emerged. As regards destructuring, we already possess a (negative) measure: namely, the fall in the rate of value, and capital's failure to control development. On the other hand, when we concretely analyze the processes of proletarian self-valorization, we also have a measure—this time a positive one: it is the measure corresponding to the spaces which have been conquered and taken back from exchange value in the processes of proletarian reproduction. But we are very much behind when we start to pose the problem of measure within the method of social transformation. It is not a new problem in a formal sense: it is the problem of *specifying the issue of the transition*—so that it does not remain a jumble of worn-out phrases. It becomes a completely new problem if it is resituated in the communist potentiality of the movement today.[52] We must be careful: here again, capital completely manifests its crisis, since it is no longer able to structure the relation between quantity of profit and quantity of socially useful value (nor should it, unless the workers' struggle forces it to do so). For this reason, we must make a leap forward: it is up to us and us alone to determine the *measure of collective value within the processes of self-valorization*. We shall return to this problem shortly.

For the moment, it is worthwhile to conclude this section by stressing the main point that runs through the whole of it, namely that the link between self-valorization and sabotage, and its inverse, does not allow us to have any truck whatsoever with "socialism" and its tradition, and even less to do with reformism and Eurocommunism. In jest, one might say that we are a race apart. We no longer have anything to do with that paper project of reformism, with its traditions and its disgraceful illusions that have so much to answer for. We exist within a materiality that has its own laws—either revealed, or yet to be discovered within the struggle, but in any event "other". Marx's *new mode of exposition*[53] has become the class's new mode of existence. We are here; we are indestructible; and we are in the majority. We have a method for the destruction of work. We are in search of a *positive measure of non-work*, a measure of our liberation from that disgusting slavery from which the bosses have always profited, and which the official socialist movement has always imposed on us like some sort of title of nobility. No, we really cannot call ourselves "socialists," for we can no longer accept your disgrace.

> At long last,
> > We are all bastards.
> And that most venerable man which I
> Did call my father, was I know not where
> When I was stamp'd.[54]

## 7. A THIRD PARENTHESIS, ON THE PRODUCTIVE FORCES

Ten years ago, we foresaw very clearly that the capitalist counteroffensive against the workers' struggles was to concentrate on the problems of *automation* and *energy*. But few realized what this passage of restructuring was to mean. It was to mean—as we are beginning to see today—a *fundamental leap in the relation between state-form and class composition*. Through advanced automation and the control systems that it made available, capital put itself in a position where it was able to organize social labor-power, to put into effect its project of command via its capacity to articulate, hierarchize, and eliminate or obstruct by whatever means the possibility of a recomposition of the class as a basis for revolutionary organization. *With automation, the capitalist state puts itself in a position to operate the mechanisms of what we have called differential political income as a means of command over the whole social field of labor.* But it is energy policy above all which enables capital to play its trump card— the monstrous attempt to make its power absolute, to consolidate capital's command and the regime of profit irreversibly and in the long term. It is through energy policy that the state tries to re-establish the absolute income of command.

This is not the place to take up the various current analyses relating to the effects arising from the generalized use of nuclear energy in industry and elsewhere. These range from the ever-pressing threat of nuclear deaths to the effects related to the state-form: *the "Nuclear-State"* [Stato nucleare] *uses nuclear energy as a fundamental source of blackmail, as the basis on which it can legitimate the power of a more destructured command.* Anyway, here we are not interested in examining this phenomenology. Rather, we are interested in the theoretical problem that this monstrous development raises for revolutionary Marxists.[55] For socialism, the fundamental goal has always been the *development of the productive forces.* The liberation of the productive forces from the relations of production and exploitation within which they are organized is a process that is internal to the development of the productive forces. But socialism has always interpreted this as a closed connection, a necessary and unbreakable nexus. But now that we are faced with the Nuclear-State and the irreversibility of the effects arising from the nuclearization of economic development, how is it possible to make inherent—or even merely compatible—the nexus between this potential of anti-worker destruction and our yearning for liberation? Oh, for those fine old days when Lenin could unite in a single conception "soviets plus locomotives," "soviets plus electrification"! But now this convergence, this compatibility is no longer possible. Today, capital drives the locomotive against us. *And here, the unitary concept of capitalist development breaks down.* On the one hand, the development of constant capital becomes a destructive development; on the other, the productive forces must liberate themselves radically from the capital relation. Capital's subsumption of living labor thus reveals an impassable inner limit. Subsumption becomes a terroristic function: the synthesis of dead labor and living labor, instead of determining new value, produces a possibility of destruction that is inevitable, general, and close at hand. We are now once and for all *on the terrain* indicated by Marx: in fact, Marx's whole analysis is designed to indicate the points where, in the course of development, capital's elements of synthesis must necessarily split and separate. On the one hand we have the capitalist system, prey to its own destructuring: this means an indifferent power, absolutely separated from value, and thus the possibility (or rather necessity) of destruction. And on the other, we have the conditions whereby living labor can liberate itself in a collective form. Thus we are on Marx's terrain: but as this tendency becomes actual, it inspires strong emotions in us.

Now, we have seen that both our analysis of the state-form and the phenomenology of collective practice (proletarian subjectivity and the process of self-valorization) lead us to a *logic of separation*. But here, the interweaving of present-day history with the realization of Marx's tendency gives a completely new basis to the problem. The inner limit of the capitalist system is not just a prospective dimension—it is transparently immediate. The separation that I outlined as a methodological break [*cesura*] is here corroborated by the full intensity of history and by a definitive theoretical limit. *This is no longer tendency but actuality: we are no longer able to attribute any notion whatsoever of productive force to capitalist development;* it is only the composition of the proletariat that reveals, represents, and can be the development of the forces of production, and of productive force in general. The limit is historically substantial, and is bound to consolidate further. At this point of development, therefore, there is a material break in the dialectic between capital and the productive forces, the dialectic of variable and constant capital. *Productive force becomes divorced from capital.* Marxism itself, as a theory of the development of the productive forces, now applies only to class composition and to the process of proletarian self-valorization. *Marxism now becomes a logic of separation.*

But let us return to the matter at hand—to the emergence of the Nuclear-State. From this viewpoint, as I have said, our analysis of the processes of destructuring proper to the capitalist state (in the context of the law of value and its crisis) is confirmed. In what sense? In the sense that capital's "autonomy of the political" organizes itself in an *irreversible* manner. From constant capital it obtains a foundation from which it utters forth a blackmail threat of destruction. Atomic terror passes from the level of international relations to that of the internal organization of individual states; it insinuates itself into the mechanisms of administration and the management of consent. *The crisis of the law of value, its vigor as a form of command, now finds a material foundation*—a good, solid material foundation, both in substantial and in formal terms. In formal terms, indeed, the rule of terror has a positive efficacy as command that a simple appeal to the general interests of economic development—even when backed by physical force—can no longer have.

Furthermore, terror has another positive aspect for command: it is indifferent; it reveals the necessity of order without specifying its articulations, its motivations, its directions. In substantial terms, command based on the possession of the nuclear threat also has specific characteristics. That is, it introduces a rigidity, both of centralization of command and of society's hierarchical and repressive articulations, which is, so to speak, "in the nature of things." *Constant capital directly becomes command*—it becomes a central, command-absorbing function, as much as it is a function of the expansion and reproduction of command. Unlike what we hear from the accredited theoreticians of Eurocommunism, the highest level of the "autonomy of the political" is wholly structured by the terroristic movements of dead labor. As for the superstructural effects of this development, they can easily be deduced: it will not be long before *the ideological state apparatuses* serve them up in all their different flavors. We can well imagine how the horizon of consensus is going to be rolled back to the point of identifying law and order as the only alternative to terror. Only in such a situation can the destructured figure of power manage to reveal itself with such violence in the realm of ideology as well!

If some people allow themselves to slip into pessimism, at first glance one might sympathize with them! But doesn't this pessimism simply correspond to the destructured will of the capitalist state today? It would seem to be difficult to claim this when the "New Philosophers," for example, attack the gospel of "progress and enlightenment" preached by the socialist vulgate in its praise for the magnificent outcome of the development of the productive forces subsumed under capital. In their iconoclasm, in their refusal to accept pacification under the grand regimes of production, and in their destructive insights into the values of capitalist technology—in all this can be read a fundamental *pars destruens*.[56] The hatred for the despotic power that dead labor tries increasingly to exercise over living labor—this hatred, even if it is shot through with pessimism, exercises a function which, if not creative, plays a certain maieutic role. It is a basis, a fundamental "rip" in the "lining of History," in the "sediment of the Institution," or in the "artifice of the Law."[57] There is no doubt that this angelic pessimism is important. However, it is not the most important aspect of this polemic. This pessimism aborts into a philosophy that simply reflects the destructured power of capital, inasmuch as it uses the categories within an absoluteness that is neither dialectical nor revolutionary. It is not dialectical because it considers power in unqualified terms, "without adjectives"; it is not revolutionary because, consequently, it cannot develop a logic of separation. For these beautiful souls, constant capital can represent only suffering. For uglier souls too, constant capital is also suffering. Outside of collective practice, as Foucault stresses, our individual resistance (not "'the' plebs [but] rather … a certain plebeian quality or aspect [*'de la' plèbe*]" inside all of us)[58] can only be liminally dialectical—a residual product of the dialectic of capital, which acts as an effective mystification of its power. But now collective practice rises up, in its theoretical and practical aspects. Both lead to the logic of separation, of which self-valorization and sabotage represent the moment of innovation. In other words, they lead to that moment in which the monstrous autonomy of capitalist power clashes with (but is also explained by and originates from) the autonomous power of the proletariat.

*Productive force, the whole of productive force, is henceforth in the hands, in the brains of living labor.* If the separation and the destructuring of capital's state are given, if they have reached this high point of their ignoble perfection, then this cannot be explained except as an explosive result of the dialectic of development. The end point of development establishes the limit from whose realization the two opposed paths unfold in their mutual independence. At this point the mutual independence, the lack of continuity, analogy, homology, and specificity of the mechanisms and modality do not alter the fact that these divergent developments determine effects on the whole structure within which they are inscribed.[59] But this interweaving is not indeterminate: its determination resides in the resolution of the struggle between the subjects who regulate separateness. It is here that we can read the full power [*potenza*] of living labor, its present active emancipation, its creative quality. And then, certainly, it is not permissible to be a pessimist!

Because, from these interweavings and separations, as proletarian productive force becomes solidified in the face of the terrible but destructured rigidification of the enemy power [*potenza*], it registers a series of quite determinate subversive effects. Constant capital, in the terroristic and irreversible aspect attributed to it by the Nuclear-State, tends toward totalitarianism; to that same extent, the separate existence of the proletariat is socially compacted and tends to resolve within itself, within its own mechanisms of self-valorization, the whole of social labor. The more the Nuclear-State is destructured, condemned to an obstinate indifference of its own will, the more labor-power, socially unified within the process of its own self-valorization, is endowed with an extraordinary innovative vigor. It is neither a contradiction nor a balanced opposition: it is the antagonism of the century, and its resolution will be the fruit of the present struggle.

To examine the *socialization of the process of proletarian self-valorization* is to grasp a *qualitative leap.* All the categories that, subjectively or objectively, are linked to that of *productive labor* are becoming socialized. This is a change that is part of the transformation of productive force into an exclusive attribute of the proletariat. Henceforth productive force is always, and only, social.

Marx's new mode of exposition relates to this new mode of existence of the proletariat, unified in its independence and socialized in its productive force. A qualitative leap. Therefore, if this change of categories has taken place, then we find ourselves facing a reality that is quite new, new from the point of view of its social substance, and, what is more, new in its dynamic too. It is a social productive force, a force that emerges qualitatively from the field within which it was dynamically formed and recomposed. The result is an original, new tendency, a common and collective force. *The result of the synthesis that has been taking place is the trigger of a more advanced passage of social transformation.* Up to this moment, we have viewed the concept of the political composition of the class in a rather static manner. But the conditions of the movement that we have been defining now offer instead a perspective that is dynamic, allowing us to take a further step forward. The reappropriation of productive force transforms class composition from a passive result into a motive force, from an effect into a cause.

This passage is qualified in material terms: *from labor-power to invention-power* [*forza-invenzione*]. This is a second specification of the process that brings the working class and the proletariat to the conquest of their own independence. On the one hand, a dynamic essence, an internal tension, an active projection; on the other hand, the materiality of this expression, the capacity to respond to proletarian needs in an adequate manner, to insert them into the productive network of self-valorization. This moment is fundamental. *We define invention-power as a capacity of the class to nourish the process of proletarian self-valorization in the most complete antagonistic independence; the capacity to found this innovative independence on the basis of abstract intellectual energy as a specific productive force* (in an increasingly exclusive manner). Proletarians are fed up with the situation in which their struggles lead to the reinforcement of the bosses' machinery: in this new phase they produce for themselves, according to the measure of non-work, and via the method of social transformation. The materiality of proletarian invention-power refers to the needs that they satisfy, to the desires that they articulate, to the determinateness of the process of reproduction; their innovative specificity refers to the solution of the multiplicity of projects—to the socially relevant overall project of innovation (which is central for the proletariat) that it sets in motion. The bosses tremble. Their social scientists are hard at work trying to capture and imprison what they call the "quality of life," the "allocation of non-work time," and innovation in the strict sense.[60] Fine work! In fact, even when we hurl it in their teeth, they will never understand sabotage, the antagonistic, subversive force of the project of workers' self-valorization.

Nor should we forget the "superstructural" effects (if it is still permitted to use this most abused and erroneous term!) of this proletarian reappropriation of social productive force and its transmutation into independent invention-power. It is the sense of being a majority, of proud confidence, which runs through every action of the proletariat. It is above all the irreducible determination that accompanies the political life of the proletariat. Only in the reappropriation of invention-power do the personal and the political become effectively one single whole—positive, open, and victorious. But with this, let us not forget the weightiness of our task. The very fact that this separateness is the precondition for the liberation of the productive forces opens up a whole range of difficulties. But then, was any other way possible? And in fact, when all is said and done, is this not the most desirable of situations— the victorious increase in our own separateness; the intensification of our own independence; this (Promethean?) self-reliance. Indeed, we repeat after the poet:

> Poor dead flower? when did you forget you were a flower?
>    when did you look at your skin and decide you were an
>    impotent dirty old locomotive? the ghost of a locomotive?
>    the specter and shade of an once powerful mad American
>    locomotive?
> You were never no locomotive, Sunflower, you were a
>    sunflower![61]

## 8.  THE REFUSAL OF WORK

More than any other single watchword of the communist movement, the refusal of work has been continually and violently outlawed, suppressed and mystified by the traditions and ideology of socialism. If you want to provoke a socialist to rage, or deflate his flights of demagogy, provoke him on the question of the refusal of work! In the hundred years since Marx first spoke of work as "unhuman nature,"[62] no single point of the communist program has been so fiercely fought against—to the point where, nowadays, the excommunication of the refusal of work has become tacit, surreptitious and implicit, but no less powerful. The argument has been shunted out of sight. But now the shrewdness of proletarian reasoning has begun, on this indirect terrain, to reinstate the *centrality of the refusal of work in the communist program*. From ethnology to psychology, from aesthetics to sociology, from ecology to medicine, this centrality repeatedly reappears, sometimes disguised in strange ways, and sometimes almost invisible. Nonetheless, it is springing up everywhere, and soon they will be constrained to pursue it, just as in earlier times similar high priests had to deal with the omnipresent sorcerous truth of the Devil.

Our task is *the theoretical reinstatement of the refusal of work in the program, in the tactics, in the strategy of communists.* Today, as never before, at our given level of class composition, the refusal of work reveals its centrality as a point of synthesis of the communist program, in both its objective and its subjective aspects. The refusal of work is, in fact, the most specific, materially determinate foundation of the productive force reappropriated to serve the process of workers' self-valorization.

*The refusal of work is first and foremost sabotage, strikes, direct action.* Already, in this radical subjectivity, we can see the global nature of its antagonistic comprehension of the capitalist mode of production. The exploitation of labor is the foundation of the whole of capitalist society. Thus the refusal of work does not negate *one* nexus of capitalist society, *one* aspect of capital's process of production or reproduction. Rather, in all its radicality, it *negates the whole of capitalist society.* So it is not by chance, then, that the capitalist response does not try to deal with the refusal of work by partial means: it has to be a global response at the level of the mode of production, in terms of restructuring. Seen from this point of view, *the effects of the refusal of work exercise a direct productive action on the capitalist mode of production.* But the more fully the refusal of work is socialized and radicalized, according to the very rhythm of capitalist restructuring, the more its "productive action" intensifies the aspects of destructuring of the capitalist mode of production. The falling rate of profit, the crisis of the law of value, and the rearticulation of the law of value within the indifference of command are direct (albeit neither continuous nor homologous) effects of the refusal of work. The continuous effect, on the other hand, is to be found on the obverse side of capital's dialectic—where sabotage is revealed as class valorization, and *the refusal of work becomes the key to reading self-valorization.* It becomes the key to reading in two fundamental senses (from which other radical consequences then follow): in the sense that it is one of the contents, if not *the fundamental* content, of the process of proletarian valorization; and in the sense that it provides a criterion of *measure* for the method of social transformation. We should look first at these two fundamental senses, and then at the consequences that derive from them.

*(a) The refusal of work as the content of the process of self-valorization.* Please note: "content" here does not mean "objective." The objective, the aim of the process of self-valorization, is the complete liberation of living labor within production and reproduction; it is the total utilization of wealth in the service of collective freedom. It is therefore more than the refusal of work—although this covers the fundamental space of the transition, and characterizes its dialectic as well as establishing its norms. So, the refusal of work is again a moment of the process of self-valorization as it relates, in a destructive

manner, to the law of value, to the crisis of the law of value, and to *the obligation to productive labor of the whole society.* The fact that in the society based on self-valorization, in the transitional phase, everyone must work, is a norm that is pertinent to the refusal of work, exactly as is the campaign to reduce working hours and to reduce the labor involved in reproduction and transformation. To recognize this normativity of the refusal of work is to grasp it as a content of the process of transition, and not as a final objective of the process of self-valorization; not to mystify it, but to determine it within the class struggle, in the specificity of its constructive function. Thus, as well as being a *fundamental tactical function in the destructuring of the enemy,* we see the refusal of work as the content of communist strategy. The two aspects are deeply related. The struggle for the destructuring of capital, and particularly for the destructuring-destruction of constant capital in the form that it assumes in its most recent phase (of the maturity of the capitalist mode of production and its state), establishes particular relationships with the continuing existence of wealth in its capitalist form. The process of class separation runs up against the hard constancy of capital—against *constant capital.* In the short term, this relationship cannot be eliminated, but only dominated. Invention-power, as the transfiguration of labor-power in this first phase of transition, must apply itself to the destructuring of constant capital. The refusal of work is its first, fundamental weapon, and to this is added *invention* in its proper sense (the qualitative determination of a mode of production no longer dominated by the categories of capital). But the refusal of work is precisely fundamental because it continuously reposes class struggle *within the problem of transition,* because within its experience it carries the complexity of the destructuring-liberation dialectic. This can also be seen from a further point of view. When the critical consciousness of political economy realizes the actuality of the proletarian process of the refusal of work, it reacts either in utopian terms, or in purely ideological terms. The *technological utopia* is the negation of the concreteness of the refusal of work and the attempt to attribute the exigencies that arise from this concreteness to technological development, to the expansion of fixed capital, and to an increasing intensity of the organic composition of capital. The *ideology of quietism* is the attempt to reverse the collective terms of the experience of the refusal of work into a perspective of artisanal liberation—isolating the big collective event and confining it in the recesses of individual consciousness, or in communitarian intercourse between individuals. So all this can be ignored. The refusal of work is at one and the same time destructuring of capital and self-valorization of the class; the refusal of work is not an invention that puts its faith in the development of capital, nor is it an invention which feigns the nonexistence of the domination of capital. It is neither a (utopian) flight of fancy, nor a (quietist) retreat into isolated consciousness: it faces foursquare that collective relationship which alone permits us to introduce a logic of (collective) class separation. Liberation is unthinkable without a process that constructs the positivity of a new collective mode of production upon the negativity of the destruction of the capitalist mode of production. The exultant and demonstrative force of the concept of the refusal of work consists, in Marxian terms, in the twofold nature of the functions in question, in their complementarity. It is clear that in the process of transition the weight that each function gradually assumes will be different. But beware of dividing the fundamental core that produces them, and beware of making homologies between them in their alternating development: the history of the socialist perversions of the revolutionary process has always been based on the extolling of one of these moments to the detriment of the other—and in the end, both were destroyed and utopianism and individualism reappeared, because the collective practice, the unitary content of the revolutionary process, the synthesis of love and hate, the refusal of work in its materiality, were destroyed with them.

(b) The refusal of work as a measure of the process of self-valorization. So, the refusal of work is indeed a strange concept. It is the measure of itself, it is the measure of the process of self-valorization of which it is also the content! Yes indeed. This is possible because of its dialectical nature, because of the intensity of the synthesis of destructuring and innovation that invests it. In the first place, then, the progress of the process of self-valorization is measured, negatively, by the progressive reduction of individual and overall labor-time, that is, the quantity of proletarian life that is sold to capital. In the second place, the progress of the process of self-valorization is measured positively by the multiplication of socially useful labor dedicated to the free reproduction of proletarian society. *Hatred of work and hatred of exploitation are the productive content of invention-power, which is the prolongation of the refusal of work.* To grasp the refusal of work as a measure of the method of social transformation for us means a tremendous step forward. It means focusing on the *generalized reduction of working hours* and linking it simultaneously with a *process of revolutionary innovation,* theoretical and practical, scientific and empirical, political and administrative, subordinated to the continuity of the class struggle over this content. It means being able to start to *put forward material parameters for measuring the workers' progress in terms of communism.* The problem of how to measure productive force, in fact, is not only a problem for the capitalists; on the other hand, in any case, it does not appear that, given the continuing crisis of the law of value, capital is really very capable of self-measurement. Command is not a measure, but is simply efficacy, an act of force. Neither the criterion of the wage hierarchy nor the monetary system any longer has any logic other than that of command. The productive force of social labor is not so much organized by capital as undergone by it, turned back against it as destructuring. Measuring the productivity of labor in terms of the refusal of work allows a complete demystification of capital's command over productivity; it negates the possibility of a productivity of labor which is still exploitation and introduces a measure which at the same time unbalances the system—*a measure of the increasing revolutionary intensity of the process of self-valorization*. At this point, finally, we should come to consider the measure not as a function of exploitation (as it has always been so far, and as the economists—even those of the school of value— continue to think: true to themselves!), but rather as a measure of freedom. A measure adapted to living labor, and not to the results of exploitation and the death of labor consolidated into capital. A measure of the quantity of revolution produced, of the quality of our life and our liberation. And this measure will provide the basis for our continuous formation and transformation of the method of social transformation.

To see the refusal of work both as a content and as a measure of the processes of self-valorization implies, as we have said, a number of relevant consequences. Here we need only highlight one fundamental one, since it has an immediate impact on class composition. It is the dynamic *nexus* that, on the basis of the practice of the refusal of work and its theoretical/practical extensions, is posited *between the workers' vanguard in direct production and the proletarian vanguard in indirect production*. Now, even in the most revolutionary variants of theoretical Marxism, the nexus between direct and indirect productive labor has never been correctly posited; it has only been posited within a tendency of a merely objective character. Capital enlarges, integrates, develops, and socially recomposes productive labor in general: fine—and some have ventured to identify in this framework a movement of unification between directly and indirectly productive labor. But if we start from the standpoint of the refusal of work, then we can reinterpret these tensions deriving from the logic of capital; we can identify, in a complementary and/or antagonistic manner, a far deeper dialectical process running through the fabric of productive labor (and one which is desirable from the class point of view). The refusal of work is, first and foremost, the refusal of the most alienated—and therefore the most productive—labor. Secondly, it is the refusal of capitalist work as such—that is, of exploitation in general. And thirdly, it is a tension toward a renewal of the mode of production, toward an unleashing of the proletariat's invention-power. *In the interweaving of these three motifs, the dynamic intensity of the refusal of work invests the entirety of the capitalist mode of production.* If all this is true, the social interchange which capital imposes and the division that slowly disappears between directly and indirectly productive labor ought to be assumed as a fundamental issue for the refusal of work. In the refusal of work, there is a recognition of the interchange between directly and indirectly productive labor, because there is a destructive tension on the part of the most exploited labor and the entirety of its social reproduction which is quite unifying. It is in the interests of the workers to tear aside the veils which capital draws over the unity of social labor, and instead to strengthen and articulate this unity. The refusal of work, once it presents itself as invention-power, must move within the unity of all the aspects of social labor, of both directly and indirectly productive social labor. The radical method of social transformation can only be applied to this unity; it can only reassume and rearticulate it from the inside. The refusal of work, whether in terms of definition or in terms of prospects, thus invests the given composition of the class, bringing out its unitary characteristics, and insisting on the workers' rearticulation of productive labor in all its aspects.

As regards the consequences that derive from the dynamics of the refusal of work, we shall take these up in the following two sections. Here, it has been important to insist upon the *unity of social productive labor in terms of the refusal of work*. Now, in this case our operation has been not only scientific, but also—and above all—political, because in fact it is within this complex unity of the refusal of work, based on the breadth and density of this definition of the class, that the threads of the revolutionary workers' program thus far outlined all tie up. This class composition, then, seeks a communist program that will be adequate to its own social figure, which will strike effectively at the level of production and equally so at the level of reproduction. On the terrain of reproduction, the most immediate form taken by the refusal of work is that of the *direct appropriation of wealth*, either on the commercial level or on the institutional level. On the basis of this composition, the refusal of work launches an attack on the working week and proposes itself ultimately as the primary norm in relation to the development of proletarian invention-power. In short, this class composition which we see invested by the refusal of work and by invention-power begins to represent globally the process of self-valorization, in its independence and separateness. (Allow me to add once again that this separateness is not technological utopianism, nor is it individual solitude, nor is it a communitarian illusion. On the other hand, after the experiences of the past ten years, is there anyone who can still doubt the efficacy and the complementarity of the double action that has been set in motion by the refusal of work—the destructuring of capital's system and the destabilization of capital's regime?)

## 9. A FOURTH PARENTHESIS, ON THE PARTY

The party, its concept, the proposition of the party: *does it still make sense for us to pose this problem?* I am forced to put the question in such a radical way because the polemic itself is a radical one. Many people understand the process of self-valorization as excluding the party, and maintain that the issue of destructuring applies very precisely in regard to the concept of the party. All this is institutional, it is an attribute of the enemy's power. The proletariat can exist only as a movement, as an antagonistic project. The history of the socialist parties looms over us like a nightmare. There seems to exist a necessary relationship between institutionalization/reformism and the destruction of the independence of the proletariat, its betrayal. The party is dead labor, it is necessarily the negation of the refusal of work, the attempt to establish a laborist metric of the workers' action. In the classical party, the needs and desires of the proletariat are subordinated in a sadistic manner to the supposed, but always mystified, unity and generality of the program. The internalization of this necessity within the class becomes pure masochism. The delegation of needs to generality is personified in the cult of leadership: through the formalism of its structure, the party expropriates the class of its invention-power. The party, through the necessity imposed by the generality of its own project, appears either as a powerless agent of mediation, or as a vanguard, admittedly powerful but arrogant and tending to prevaricate when faced with the mass movement. The present structure of the state-form is such that the institutional emergence of the party allows the state to pose an effective alternative (blackmail) between the destruction of the insubordinate aspects and the ordering effects of the party's emergence.

Now, we do not have to be anarchists to admit that there is a lot of truth in this string of accusations—particularly in light of an almost uninterrupted history of socialist betrayal. But this does not alter the fact that in my consciousness and in my practice as a revolutionary, *I do not know how to jettison the problem of the party.* It may be that the problem actually poses itself under another name—for example, the problem of organization; the collective problem of matching means to ends, the matching of strategy and objectives, of mass participation and vanguard action, of organization and the circulation of information. However, the whole of my political existence is interwoven with these problems. These problems are the necessary and inevitable form in which the emerging subversive will finds meaning. In other words, I do not deny any of the contradictions that I have just listed— but I cannot accept that those contradictions cancel out the problem. The substance of the problem is revealed to me, therefore, as contradictory, but nevertheless it exists. *The problem of the party today is the present reality of a real contradiction.*

However, having said this, I have not said much. I could in fact demonstrate that similar contradictions also exist in other fields of experience. It is the same contradiction that you find between the personal and the political, between self-valorization and destructuring, between destructuring and destabilization. In all these cases, relative but determinate degrees of activity are opposed to relative but determinate degrees of exteriorization, of institutionalization, of alienation. Of course, in these fields I can also identify specific solutions to the contradictions. So *does there exist a "specific" terrain for the contradiction inherent in the "party experience"?*

I should say at once that I do not believe so. I think that the specificity of the "party" contradiction lies in its *non-resolvability*, and that the party consists precisely of the persistence of the contradiction. But why?

In order to consider the problem in overall terms, we need to distinguish a number of planes. On the first plane I have to consider the "party" concept in relation to a series of other fields of experience that the revolutionary struggle offers me. If I succeed in demonstrating a specific function for the party in these fields, I should then be able to go on to consider in more determinate terms the degree of historical contradictoriness that this specific function presents.

Now, the fundamental characteristic of the revolutionary development of the proletariat is the process of proletarian self-valorization. This is a material process, built on the direct appropriation of wealth and power, the development of radical needs and desires, and the accompanying—but ever more independent and autonomous—transformation of the class composition. Certainly, within this framework *the party* is not resolvable: *it is not an immediate element of the process of self-valorization*. But having said this, another order of problems enters the picture: the process of self-valorization is the opposite of the state-form; it is—albeit outside of any homologous criterion—a faculty of destructuring and continuous destabilization of the enemy power. This, however, describes only an extremely general form of the relationship. We have seen how this very general form is determined from the capitalist point of view: the indifference of capitalist command articulates itself in restructuring, in the hierarchical mechanisms of political income, in the increasingly terroristic function of command. How is this very general form of the relationship determined from the angle of workers' self-valorization? This can only be answered from within the logic of separation: *the party is a function of proletarian force, conceived as a guarantor of the process of self-valorization.* The party is the army that defends the frontiers of proletarian independence. And naturally it must not, cannot get mixed up in the internal management of self-valorization. The party is not a direct, radical counterpower anchored in the full materiality of self-valorization.

It is a function of power, but separate, sometimes contradictory with the process of self-valorization. If jesting were allowed, I might say that the party is a militant religious order, not the ecclesiastical totality of the process. The party is a function of the command that the proletariat exercises against its enemies. I see no contradiction in the fact that, within the dictatorship of the proletariat, there might be more functions for the party: in fact, I believe that these multiple functions may exist—but only from the starting point of the dictatorship of the proletariat (and also from the starting point, obviously, of that proletarian command that is unified in the course of the revolutionary process). Command resides in the mass counterpower of the proletariat, in the organization of the processes of self-valorization: the party is a function of this. *The politics of self-valorization hold command over the party.* The guiding force consists in the masses organized in the process of self-valorization, in the constitutive and constitutional process of proletarian self-valorization.

Having said this, however, *it appears that the contradiction as a specific element of the definition of the party has been eliminated.* We now have a clear-cut situation: on one side, the force of the proletariat organized within the process of self-valorization, and on the other, its subordinate function. This is an abstract situation, though.

*Concrete reality reinstates the element of contradiction in the party.* Today, the party exists as an ensemble of inextricable functions—defense and attack, *counterpower.* In the term "counterpower" we have the most precise representation of the contradictory situation that we are experiencing. For this term, while it extols the process of self-valorization in terms of victorious efficacy, at the same time confuses all its functions in the transitoriness and precariousness of the process. For this reason, today's militant is a double figure—rooted on the one hand in the practice of self-valorization, and tied, on the other, to the functions of offense. From this situation arises a (sometimes tragic) superimposition of planes, the explosion of violent contradictions. And yet this contradiction is vital, and it is only by carefully following it through, with all the clarity of which we are capable, that we can think of resolving it. Following this contradiction through with clarity, we can impose, through criticism and self-criticism, the distinct determinations that mark on the one hand the emergence of the self-valorizing power of the proletariat, and on the other hand its "party-type" functions.

All this is inscribed in the materiality of the revolutionary process. There is not one of its aspects that does not reveal the double nature of the functions in question. (But take note: from everything that has been said so far, it should be clear that when we refer to the "double nature" of the necessary functions, we mean, in absolute and inalienable terms, that the *self-governance of the masses*, in self-valorization, *must prevail* over any other subordinate functions, however important these may be.) In relation to the determinacy of the class composition, we find ourselves, in fact, within the division between directly productive labor and indirectly productive labor: were it not for the fact that capitalist power insists on this division, would there in fact be the need for a special (party) function in order to assist the processes of recomposition? But on the other hand, is it possible to negate the relative contradictoriness of this function, in relation to the processes of self-valorization in their immediacy? Those who fill their mouths—and hearts—with myths of the past call this function "central." We know that it is transitory, and we accept with materialist determination its contradictoriness, just as we agree to live this contradictoriness within the revolutionary process. We know that this contradictoriness is complex. We shall conquer it, certainly. We shall overcome it, and it will not be long. Henceforth, indeed, this becomes a central problem for revolutionaries, and its material solution is to be found within class composition. To conceive of the revolutionary process as being dense with these contradictions is to be allowed to envision a solution that, even in extremely determinate terms, is imminent—*a proposal for the constitution of the dictatorship of the proletariat.* But we shall return to this in the next few pages.

For the moment, let us deepen our perceptions of this necessary contradiction. It appears when we analyze the processes of proletarian recomposition. It appears with even greater force when we go further into the issue of the program. Consider the nexus between proletarian recomposition and attack on the terrain of public spending, the smashing of the practice of the wage as differential political income which capital seeks to impose on the social terrain—how is this passage thinkable, how is it possible, except through a *practice of offensive anticipation of capital, of a general timetable* [*scadenza*], and therefore of defense of the levels of *counterpower* that have been achieved? Even here we notice a gap between the political functions of the proletariat, which often becomes a contradiction. But it is a necessary contradiction—like that posed between the need for a drastic reduction of the length of the working day and the obligation of all to work; like that which arises between the measurement of social transformation and the unleashing of the proletariat's invention-power; like that which is posed between a long and steady process of destructuring of the enemy, and action that destabilizes his initiative. *A contradiction which we must live and control within the overall development of the process of proletarian self-valorization.*

Furthermore, we cannot imagine that the conquest of power, the installation of proletarian power, will resolve these contradictions in one fell swoop. All the first decrees must be aimed at making the conquest of power irreversible, but at the same time, in unison, they must aim to *destroy the reality of power as the obverse of the capitalist state-form*. In other words, overthrow it truly—not nominally, but substantially. In other words, *power is to be dissolved into a network of powers, and the independence of the class is to be constructed via the autonomy of individual revolutionary movements.* Only a diffuse network of powers can organize revolutionary democracy; only a diffuse network of powers can enable the opening of a dialectic of recomposition which reduces the party to a revolutionary army, to an unwavering executor of the proletarian will.

The revolutionary process of self-valorization has one main quality that it methodically asserts: it does not simply expand abstractly, but concretely draws into itself all the diversity of contents and functions of the proletariat. We cannot think of communist society as anything other than a society which will destroy every separation of functions and contents, every transcendental projection of the process of its own unity, and which therefore lives wholly compact within this process. This unity is a production of moments of power that are pluralistic (if social democratic usage has not sullied this word beyond repair); it is proletarian command over the synthesis of the autonomous contents and the different functions of the movement. It is a living animal body in which the various different functions and contents are unified. Let us reappropriate this image, so worthy of the working class; let us seize it back from the iconography of the bourgeois state—for these are the terms in which the theorists of the bourgeois state have always expressed themselves in destructuring the proletariat.

A living animal which is fierce with its enemies, and savage in the protection of itself and its passions—this is how I foresee the constitution of the communist dictatorship. The ordering of functions and contents can only be established on the basis of the vitality of the proletarian beast, on the unity of its diversity. But today we are still within an open contradiction, and this we must never forget, especially when the question reposes itself at the personal level, on the terrain of genuine subjectivity. Here the contradictions reveal themselves with a tension that only immediate participation in the process of proletarian self-valorization can resolve. It is not the party that has to encounter or confront the subjective and the personal: it is the movement at its most intense. Now, at this point I must put myself within the contradiction. To say that living this contradiction brings a lot of suffering is merely to speak the truth. Well and good—but can the suffering be borne? Yes it can—if over and above (and occasionally against) the party you set the autonomy of the proletarian movement. Yes, if at all times you have the strength to identify the process of proletarian self-valorization in its always victorious depth and intensity. As Rimbaud wrote in May 1871:

*Quand tes pieds ont dansé si fort dans les colères*
*Paris! quand tu reçus tant de coups de couteau,*
*Quand tu gis, retenant dans tes prunelles claires*
*Un peu de la bonté du fauve renouveau.*

[When your feet danced so strongly in anger,
Paris! when you took so many cuts of the knife,
When you lay, keeping in your bright eyes
A little of the bounty of savage renewal.][63]

Here is the path that permits us to master the contradiction and its knife-cuts: it lies wholly in tying ourselves directly to that experience of savage renewal. This is the proletarian foundation that turns the contradiction into the basis for a further leap forward, that turns *organization* into a powerful weapon, built by our strength and collectivity, that is aware at one and the same time of its instrumental character and its fundamental role.

## 10.   ... AND THE PROLETARIANS STORM HEAVEN[64]

If it is true that all revolutions hitherto have only tended to perfect the state machine, this does not mean that the same fate necessarily awaits the actions taken by the working class in the future. If it is in fact true that the destructuring power of the proletarian class is already weighing heavily on the state machine, then it follows that this perfecting of the state machine is gradually pushing it to the point of senselessness. But this is not just a generic diagnosis: the tendency is developing into an actuality that shows *very solid signs of capitalist crisis.* Is this a definitive crisis? The question is merely rhetorical. Our whole position, in fact, is that, if there is a crisis, it is solely a crisis of the relations and form of capital's domination. We shall leave it to historical determinism and the ideology of socialism to make forecasts based on "objectivity," on the determinacy necessitated by the "objective contradictions." Here, the crisis is a crisis *of* the relationship, but above all a crisis *in* the relationship. It will be definitive when workers' subjectivity has defined it as such. The crisis is a risk, a gamble by the working class and the proletariat. *Communism is not inevitable.* It is for this reason that we are so optimistic today: the contradiction between the state-form and the processes of proletarian self-valorization shows us, quantitatively and qualitatively, a schism in the capital relation that is antagonistic. This contradiction is irreversible. It is cumulative. It is general. Capital runs the risk of getting used to its own state of crisis. In very bad conscience, it considers the crisis to be one of its modes of existence. The working class does not see it that way. The direct and immediate overturning of the passages of restructuring into opportunities for struggle shows that the working class is tending to force a political simultaneity between the workers' cycle of struggle and the cycle of capital—and occasionally even to anticipate capital's cycle. This "simultaneity" is very different from the one that capital and its science would like to see. The crisis, in fact, establishes itself on the *failure of capital's cycle to anticipate the cycle of workers' struggles.* The workers' understanding of the cycle precedes, and destroys, capitalist planning; it destructures capital's state-form and its system. This is the crisis of capitalism as Marx defined it. It is a Marxian crisis in the most orthodox of terms: in the sense that the consciousness and reality of an alternative mode of production are foreseen by Marx as coming together, expressed through the productive forces—a process in which subjectivity is the key. The opportunity to grasp this antagonistic potentiality of the process could only have been presented to today's working class, in the sense that the opportunity is constructed from the intersection of struggles with the liminal development of capital.

Capital responds to the presence of this crisis by increasing the rigidity of its own movements. The pure indifference of command transforms itself into ferocity, organizes itself into the blackmail threat of nuclear destruction.

So here we stand, on the eve of [*alla scadenza del*] storming heaven. On one side, a workers' power which is fully aware that it has emerged from its prehistory; that it has reappropriated the mechanisms of its own reproduction; that it has won autonomy and independence from valorization; that it has brought about a very profound crisis of capital. And on the other, a capital which, at the very moment that it acknowledges this tendency, rigidifies its own forms of expression, tragically, both as regards the political form in which it makes itself manifest, and as regards the mode of production that it organizes.

Marx said that between two equal rights, force decides. And in fact, as the crisis increasingly takes root, *violence takes on a fundamental valence.* On the one hand, it is the state counterpart of the indifference and rigidity of command. On the other hand, it is an ardent projection of the process of workers' self-valorization. We cannot imagine anything more completely determinate and laden with content than the workers' violence. Historical materialism defines the necessity of violence in history: we, for our part, charge it with an everyday quality arising out of the class struggle. We consider violence to be a function legitimated by the escalation of the relation of force within the crisis and by the richness of the contents of proletarian self-valorization.

In the socialist tradition, violence and the use of violence are attributes of the party. The socialist party is the institutionalization of violence. But we are against this image of the party, and against all of the various attempts to revive it today, be they overt, conscious, or implicit. It is the party's monopoly on violence, the fact of its being the inverse rather than the determinate antithesis of the state-form, that has brought about the functional possibility of repression of proletarian violence—the Gulag is born here. We are opposed to the conception of violence that this type of party has built for itself. For us, *violence* always presents itself *as a synthesis* of form and content. First of all as an expression of proletarian counterpower, as a manifestation of the process of self-valorization; then, directed toward the outside, as a destructuring and destabilizing force. Thus as a *productive force* and an *anti-institutional force*. So it is obvious that proletarian violence has no need to exhibit itself in an exemplary manner, nor to choose for itself exemplary objectives. But this is not all. In the tension that class composition reveals toward the transition to communism and the dictatorship of the proletariat, violence presents itself not only as central, but increasingly as a synthesis of form and content: a form which is exclusive, excluding the enemy, and a rational content which is measured and defined by the refusal of work. Violence is the *rational thread* which links proletarian valorization to the destructuring of the system, and this latter to the destabilization of the regime. Violence is the revolutionary project at the point where it becomes efficacious because the desirability of the content has been transformed into a program, and because the program is tending toward the dictatorship of the proletariat.

Enough of the bourgeois and reformist hypocrisy against violence! Even children know that the capitalist system is based on violence, and that this violence is certainly not clean in relation to the violence of the proletariat. *It is not by chance, then, that all the bourgeois and revisionist excommunications of violence are based on the threat of an even greater violence in return.* Whereas the Marxists' credo in this regard is precisely the overcoming of the violence of history, in the only way that is given to people and to classes to overcome it: by recognizing it—recognizing violence and dominating it within the fabric of social relations; relating it back to its real content, to the mode of collective production, in both the phase and the method of transformation of society, but also, above all, in the phase of communist dictatorship; making it immanent. But hypocrisy does not pay. So now let us speak of our proletarian violence with clarity as a *necessary and central ingredient of the communist program.*

Let us speak clearly, because if the exercise of violence by the proletariat is the efficacy of proletarian self-valorization, we must produce and reproduce the effort to legitimate it. For the bourgeoisie, the legitimation of violence means the construction of ordered systems [*ordinamenti*], whether juridical, economic or administrative. Every bourgeois social order is a sure legitimation of violence. Capitalist development was the "rational" well-spring of the legitimation of violence in those ordered systems. With the law of value entering into crisis, capitalist violence and the ordered systems that allow it to function find that they no longer have a sphere of exercise and credibility. Violence is no longer mediated, is no longer rationally legit-imated: the destructured orders live on as pure violence. We, the working class and the proletariat, have produced this destructured senselessness of power! And on the other hand, acting for the destructuring of its enemy, self-valorization develops in the absence of any homology, however small, with its adversary and in the discovery of the *rationality of the development of living labor* against capital's deadness in the revelation of the richness of the possibilities and qualities of collective life. This rationality of living labor, this qualitative intention, is the foundation for the collective and its practice; therefore *it is this rationality of fundamental needs that determines the legitimacy of our violence.* This violence is *not capable of homology* with capitalist violence, because the rationality that rules it is other, proletarian, absolutely different. (However, in saying this, we should once again try to avoid confusing the proletarian determination of a new rationality by erasing its functional char-acteristics and plunging into a new irrationalism or—the correlative of the previous mistake—by denying the specificity of the function of violence.) This violence is *contrary* to capitalist violence; it aims at the destruction of capital's system and regime; it is founded on class self-valorization; it is *not equal* in intensity to capitalist violence—it is *stronger,* more efficacious than capitalist violence. This is an essential precondition if we are to win. An obvious condition. The whole of the process of self-valorization determines (and lies within) this violence, both in its qualitatively different aspect and in its quantitatively greater intensity. So we are not speaking of meeting terror with terror, and those who amuse themselves picturing the proletariat as intent on building its own pocket atomic bomb are mere provocateurs. Instead, we are speaking of opposing terror with an operation of sabotage and the reappropriation of knowledge [*conoscenza*] and power over the whole circuit of social reproduction, in such a way as to make the capitalist's recourse to terror into a suicidal prospect.

But how can we avoid the re-emergence of violence under the commu-nist dictatorship, as an attribute of episodes of betrayal and restoration? Precisely by denying it a separate existence. *Violence is one element of the ration-ality of the processes of self-valorization.* Nothing else. The party, with the vanguard functions of violence that must be assigned to it, and the contra-diction that this embodies—all this is to be subordinated *not dialectically, but violently,* to workers' and proletarian power, to the direct organization of the processes of self-valorization. In the history of proletarian revolutions, every time the party's management of power takes precedence over the powers of proletarian organization, at that moment the revolution is finished. It happened in the Soviet Union and it happened in China. In our case it will not happen because the history of the revolutionary process already reveals to us a class composition that, when faced with any separated function what-soever, increasingly exercises its powers of critique and destruction. Ultimately, only the process of workers' valorization can exercise the logic of separation—and to the extent that it exercises that logic, it becomes the exclusive source of proletarian power.

From this point of view we can—and must—*begin our discussion of the constitution of the communist dictatorship.* It is time that we stopped laying out programs that are at best hazy. Of course, it is not on the terrain of the program that the project will find its greatest difficulties. On the other hand, on the terrain of the program, we have a number of powerful guiding ideas, such as the practice of the refusal of work and its projection in rational terms as a law and a measure of the transition; such as the development of inno-vative hypotheses, etc. The task of the proletariat is to unfold these propositions directly through the struggle. It is, rather, on the terrain of struc-ture and constitution that we shall have to exert our greatest efforts now, operating, as ever, on the terrain of the mass movement, confronting the practice and institutions of the struggle with the overall project. Let us begin: many discoveries—we shall soon see—have already been made. Why have they not been theorized? Often because the practice has been too transitory and the experience too precarious. But in the struggles of the first years of this century, when the soviets were born—was not that experience of workers' government also something precarious and transitory? The real reason why we have not started on a mass attempt at intensifying the debate on the constitution of communist dictatorship is because this has been impeded by a repetition of the old expostulations of dogmatism, or by the ideological strength of revisionism. Both of these destroyed the credibility of the developing project on the terrain of communism. Enough; it is time to start. The richness of our revolutionary imagination must be put to the test in mass debate, in a practical testing among the masses. The answers are to be found within the independence of the proletarian struggle.

This too is a target date [*scadenza*] for the storming of heaven. A funda-mental target date. And let them now accuse us of "rationalism"—those who have for so long cursed our "irrationalism"! Or vice versa—what does it matter to us? What matters is something else. What matters is to be within this fine thing that is the independent struggle of the proletariat, to discover the density of the project. What matters is the rational, desirable foundation that joins together our theoretical and our practical experience.

Domination and sabotage. *Sabotage* is, therefore, the *fundamental key to rationality* that we possess at this level of class composition. It is a key that permits us to unveil the processes through which the crisis of the law of value has gradually come to invest the entire structure of capitalist power, stripping it of any internal rationality and compelling it to be an efficacious spectacle of domination and destruction. Conversely, it is a key that allows us to identify the ability of the proletarian struggle to gain its independence (according to the very rhythms of capitalist destructuring, but not in a homologous manner), to make progress in the process of its own self-valorization, and to transform the refusal of work into a measure of the process of liberation. The form of capitalist domination is disintegrating before our eyes. The machinery of power is breaking down. *Sabotage follows on the heels of the irrationality of capital, and dictates the forms and rhythms of its further disorganization.* The capitalist world reveals itself to us for what it is: once a machine for grinding out surplus-value, it has now become a net thrown down to block the workers' sabotage. But it is a net that is already too frayed. *The relation of force has been overturned:* the working class, its sabotage, is the highest force—and above all, the only source of rationality and value. From now on it becomes impossible, even in theory, to forget this paradox produced by the struggles: the more the form of domination perfects itself, the emptier it becomes; the more the workers' refusal grows, the more full it is of rationality and value. Force, violence, power: they can measure themselves only against this law. And it is on this law, on the series of corollaries that derive from it, that the organization, the program, the forecasts of communists must be based. Our sabotage organizes the proletarian storming of heaven. And in the end that accursed heaven will no longer exist!

### Notes

1. This was recently shown by F.W. Fetter in "Lenin, Keynes and Inflation," *Economica*, vol. 44, no. 175, February 1977, pp. 77–80.

2. TN: Destabilization of the regime, as Negri defines it here, involves direct and even violent confrontation with the state, and is associated with the vanguard actions of specialized groups. Destructuring of the system, on the other hand, involves mass activity of insubordination aimed at subverting the discipline of wage labor and the extortion of exchange value. In *Domination and Sabotage* Negri is attempting to overcome the divergence or opposition between these positions.

3. The reference is specifically to Lapo Berti's studies in *Primo Maggio* and to Christian Marazzi and John Merrington's presentation to the British Conference of Socialist Economists in 1977.

4. For example, John Holloway and Sol Picciotto, "Capital, Crisis and the State,"

in *Capital & Class*, no. 2, summer 1977, pp. 76–101.

5. In *La forma-stato*, Milan: Feltrinelli, 1977, pp. 297–342. [TN: This is a reference to the text published in this volume under the title *Toward a Critique of the Material Constitution*.]

6. *L'infamia originaria: Facciamola finita col cuore e la politica*, Milan: L'Erba Voglio, 1977. [TN: Lea Melandri (b.1941) has been a prominent Italian feminist and psychoanalytic critic from the sixties onward.]

7. "Per un dibattito su militanza e organizzazione proletaria" in Furio di Paola et al, *Bisogni, crisi della militanza, organizzazione proletaria, Quaderni di Ombre Rosse* 1, Rome: Savelli. [TN: Furio di Paola is a researcher in philosophy of mind and epistemology at the University of Naples.]

8. TN: Raniero Panzieri (1921–1964) was a Marxist theorist whose work paved the way for the workerist movement in Italy; originally a member of the Italian Socialist Party (PSI), he moved further to the left during the Fifties and ultimately became involved with the radicals Negri, Mario Tronti and Romano Alquati in the founding of *Quaderni Rossi*, the major journal from which workerism emerged, in 1961. Here Negri is probably referring to unrecorded conversations he had with Panzieri, but a similar idea is expressed in Panzieri's brief text "Intervento sul Congresso del PSI," published in the posthumous anthology *La ripresa del marxismo-leninismo in Italia*, Milan: Sapere Edizioni, 1972, pp. 305–06. See also two of Panzieri's influential essays that have been translated into English: "Surplus Value and Planning: Notes on the Reading of *Capital*," translated by Julian Bees, in *The Labour Process and Class Strategies*, London: Stage 1/Conference of Socialist Economists, 1976, pp. 4–25, and "The Capitalist Use of Machinery: Marx versus the Objectivists" in P. Slater, ed., *Outlines of a Critique of Technology*, London: Ink Links, 1980. Steve Wright's discussion of Panzieri in *Storming Heaven*, London: Pluto Press, 2002, chapters 1 and 2, is also helpful.

9. In his book *Konstitution und Klassenkampf*, Frankfurt: Verlag Neue Kritik, 1971, Italian translation *Costituzione e lotta di classe*, Milan: Jaca Book, 1973, by S. de Waal—a book which, with the passing of the years, is becoming increasingly important.

10. *Die andere Arbeiterbewegung: Die Entstehung der kapitalistischen Repression von 1880 bis heute*, Munich: Trikont Verlag, 1975. [TN: Karl-Heinz Roth (b.1942) practiced medicine in Germany during the sixties and seventies, while at the same time becoming deeply involved with the extraparliamentary left; like Negri, he was accused (and acquitted) of involvement in terrorism, and his 1975 historical analysis of the "other workers' movement" parallels the work of Negri and other workerist theorists.]

11. "L'altro movimento operaio negli Stati Uniti: L'operaio-massa e gli Industrial Workers of the World," in *La Formazione dell'Operaio-Massa negli USA*, Milan: Feltrinelli, 1976. Original German edition: *Die 'andere' Arbeiterbewegung in den USA, 1905–1922: Die Industrial Workers of the World*, Munich: Trikont Verlag, 1976. [TN:

Gisela Bock (b.1942) is professor of modern history at the Free University of Berlin; her 1976 study of the IWW was widely influential on Workers' Autonomy.]

12.  TN: This is an ironic allusion to Hegel's dismissive description of Schelling's notion of the Absolute: "[Schelling's philosophy] is a monochromatic formalism ... we see all value ascribed to the universal Idea in this non-actual form, and the undoing of all distinct, determinate entities ... Dealing with something from the perspective of the Absolute consists merely in declaring that, although one has been speaking of it just now as something definite, yet in the Absolute, the A = A, there is nothing of the kind, for there all is one. To pit this single insight, that in the Absolute everything is the same, against the full body of articulated cognition, ... to palm off its Absolute as the night in which, as the saying goes, all cows are black— this is cognition naively reduced to vacuity" (Hegel, *Phenomenology of Spirit*, translated by A.V. Miller, Oxford: Oxford University Press, 1977, paragraph 16, p. 9).

13.  And in particular his methodical treatment in *The History of Sexuality*, vol. 1, New York: Vintage, 1978, translated by Robert Hurley.

14.  Regarding Cacciari's *Krisis*, Milan: Feltrinelli, 1977, see my review in nos 155–156 of *Aut Aut*.

15.  TN: The New Philosophers [*Nouveaux Philosophes*] were a group of young French philosophers who attacked both the ideology of the established left parties and the theories of the (post)structuralist left (especially Althusser, Derrida and Deleuze and Guattari); the most prominent were André Glucksmann and Bernard-Henri Lévy.

16.  TN: Negri is referring to Tronti's book *Sull'autonomia del politico*, Milan: Feltrinelli, 1977.

17.  Marx, *Theories of Surplus Value*, vol. 1, Moscow: Progress Publishers, 1963, p. 388.

18.  See the articles published in *Operai e Stato,* Milan: Feltrinelli, 1972. [TN: English translations of these articles are included in Negri, *Revolution Retrieved*, London: Red Notes, 1988.]

19.  TN: In English in the original.

20.  TN: In English in the original.

21.  TN: In English in the original.

22.  TN: In English in the original.

23.  Michal Kalecki, in "Trend and Business Cycles Reconsidered," in *The Economic Journal*, June 1968, pp. 263 and following.

24.  Cf. Joan Robinson in *New York Review of Books*, 4 March 1976, and in particular George R. Feiwel, *The Intellectual Capital of Michal Kalecki*, Knoxville: University of Tennessee Press, 1975. [TN: Michal Kalecki (1899–1970) was a Polish socialist economist who specialized in the analysis of business cycles in capitalist economies and planning for balanced growth in socialist economies; he was sometimes regarded as a left-wing Keynesian.]

25.  Kalecki, "Class Struggle and the Distribution of National Income," in *Kyklos*, XXIV, 1971, pp. 1ff.

26. TN: In English in the original.

27. TN: In English in the original.

28. Although Geoffrey Kay draws attention to the problem in his *Development and Underdevelopment,* London: Macmillan, 1975.

29. A propos of this, see the fine essay by A. Graziani, "Commento," introducing R. Convenevole's book *Processo inflationistico e redistribuzione del reddito: La dinamica del salario relativo,* Turin: Einaudi, 1977; republished in *Quaderni Piacentini,* no. 64, pp. 113ff.

30. Note that certain theoretical positions that exist within the Official Labor Movement, and which have nothing to do with Marxism—such as the famous theory of the "autonomy of the political"—ape these bourgeois assertions.

31. See the articles by Robert Zevin and by Roger A. Alcaly and Helen Bodian in Roger E. Alcaly and David Mermelstein, editors, *The Fiscal Crisis of American Cities,* New York: Vintage, 1977.

32. TN: Eurocommunism is the general term used to describe the development in Europe during the sixties and seventies of national communist party programs that were largely independent of Soviet control and designed to work through alliances with other parties within the institutions of parliamentary democracy; the Italian Communist Party's program of "Historic Compromise" with the center-right Christian Democratic party was the first major project of Eurocommunism.

33. TN: In English in the original.

34. Christian Marazzi, "Intervento al seminario sulla spesa pubblica," École normale supérieure, Paris, April 1977, mimeo, p. 9.

35. In addition to the work of Romano Alquati, see the article by G. Bossi, "Note su bisogni operai e 'autonomia del politico'" in *Aut Aut,* 159–160, maggio–agosto 1977, pp. 73–87.

36. See Sergio Bologna, "The Tribe of Moles," originally in *Primo Maggio* no. 8, spring 1977; English translation in *Working Class Autonomy and the Crisis,* London: Red Notes/CSE, 1978.

37. See Glen G. Cain, "The Challenge of Segmented Labour Market Theories to Orthodox Theory: A Survey," in *Journal of Economic Literature,* December 1976.

38. A propos of this, see the useful notes by Michel Aglietta: "Panorama et nouveaux developpements sur les théories de l'emploi," mimeo, INSEE 14/1/1977 MA/SP, 320/3564.

39. See N. Branson and M. Heinemann's fine *Britain in the Nineteen Thirties,* London: Panther, 1973.

40. TN: In addition to its literal meaning, the word "salami" bears the idiomatic connotation of "idiot" in colloquial Italian.

41. TN: The phrase "putting salt on its tail [*mettendogli il sale sulla coda*]" alludes to an Italian proverb that jokingly offers this as a method for capturing something that cannot be captured.

42. TN: This refers to Negri's former student and comrade Massimo Cacciari

and others who, like Cacciari, had abandoned the extraparliamentary left in order to join the PCI at the end of the sixties.

43.  TN: Roughly, "The historical lesson of Germany is once again demonstrated."

44.  See W. Nordhaus, "The Falling Share of Profits," in *Brookings Papers on Economic Activity,* no. 1, 1974.

45.  TN: The Italian title of this chapter is "Non abbiamo più nulla a che fare …". The concluding phrase, "che fare," is the Italian translation of Lenin's title *What Is to Be Done?*, but we have not found a way to reproduce this allusion in English.

46.  TN: The following three paragraphs, which have often been cited to "prove" Negri's complicity with and/or participation in terrorism, were omitted from Ed Emery's original translation and replaced by this note: "In translating, we found the first two pages of this section almost incomprehensible. Consultation with comrades in Italy produced a suggestion that, since they add little to the argument, we should omit them. Furthermore, Toni Negri himself, in a clandestine 'Interview from Prison' … has stated that in this section, in emerging from the confines of political concepts, he hit on difficulties of self-expression and 'dubious literary quality.' Therefore we have omitted most of pages 42–43 of the original…" (*Working Class Autonomy and the Crisis,* p. 116). However, Negri chose to include this passage in the Italian re-issue edition that forms the basis for this translation, so we include it here as well.

47.  TN: Negri is referring ironically to an exchange of political prisoners that took place in December 1976: Soviet premier Leonid Brezhnev freed Russian dissident Vladimir Bukofsky in exchange for Chilean dictator Augusto Pinochet's freeing of Chilean communist leader Luis Corvalan. The exchange, a public-relations coup for the Pinochet dictatorship, proved to be a serious embarrassment to the Soviets because of the overt equation it established between their regime and Pinochet's right-wing dictatorship.

48.  Epicurus, "Vatican Sayings," in *The Essential Epicurus,* Buffalo: Prometheus Books, 1993, no. 41, p. 81, translation by Eugene O'Connor slightly revised.

49.  TN: Georges Sorel (1847–1922) was one of the most important theorists of anarcho-syndicalism; in his major work *Reflections on Violence* (1906), he interpreted fundamental tenets of Marxism as "myths," images that would inspire the working class to violently overthrow the capitalist system. Chief among these "myths" was the general strike.

50.  TN: Ernst Bloch (1885–1977) was a messianic German Marxist who sought to recuperate the practice of utopian thinking by identifying the elements of revolutionary potentiality in everyday life; his major works are *The Spirit of Utopia* (1918) and *The Principle of Hope* (1959).

51.  Sergio Leone, *Spartito di un nuovo film.* [TN: This work has not been identified.]

52.  This is stressed—and is one of the most important and misunderstood

points—in Alfred Sohn-Rethel's work in *Intellectual and Manual Labour*, Atlantic Highlands: Humanities Press, 1978.

53. TN: See section two above.

54. Shakespeare, *Cymbeline*, Act II, scene 5.

55. However, for an internal analysis of the general mechanisms of "big-business criminality" and the "mass illegality of capital," see Antonio Bevere's article in *Critica del Diritto*, no. 9.

56. TN: A term drawn from medival Scholastic philosophy meaning a destructive step that should then lead to a constructive step or *pars construens*. See Michael Hardt, *Gilles Deleuze: An Apprenticeship in Philosophy*, Minneapolis: University of Minnesota Press, 1993, pp. xii–xiv, 28–30, 115–17.

57. See Glucksmann, Lévy, Legendre, Holder or many others.

58. Interview in *Les Revoltes Logiques*, no. 4; English translation: "Power and Strategies," in *Power/Knowledge: Selected Interviews and Other Writings 1972–1977*, New York: Pantheon, 1980, p. 138, translated by Colin Gordon et al.

59. I am paraphrasing Michel Foucault's *Discipline and Punish*, New York: Vintage, 1979, pp. 3–31, translated by Alan Sheridan.

60. See the splendid examples of academic imbecility in *Towards Balanced Growth*, edited by the National Goals Research Staff, Washington DC: US Government Printing Office, 1970; G. Becker, "A Theory of the Allocation of Time," in *The Economic Journal*, no. 75, September 1965; J. Schmooker, *Invention and Economic Growth*, Cambridge, MA: Harvard University Press, 1966.

61. Allen Ginsberg, "Sunflower Sutra" in *Howl and Other Poems*, San Francisco: City Lights, 1956, 1959, p. 37–38.

62. And added that it was "unfree" and "unsocial"—Marx, "Über F. Lists Buch," in *Archiv-Drucke* 1, Berlin: VSA, 1972, p. 25. English translation: "Draft of an Article on Friedrich List's Book: *Das Nationale System der Politischen Oekonomie*" in Marx and Engels, *Collected Works*, vol. 4, New York: International Publishers, 1975, p. 279.

63. TN: Arthur Rimbaud, "L'Orgie parisienne, ou Paris se repeuple" in *Œuvres complètes*, Paris: Bibliothèque de la Pléiade, 1954, p. 82. Instead of using a standard translation, we have translated this poem so as to make Negri's allusions in the following paragraph more noticeable.

64. TN: Cf. Marx, letter to Ludwig Kugelmann, 12 April, 1871: "… the present rising in Paris—even if it be crushed by the wolves, swine, and vile curs of the old society—is the most glorious deed of our Party since the June insurrection in Paris. Compare these Parisians, storming heaven, with the slaves to heaven of the German-Prussian Holy Roman Empire, with its posthumous masquerades reeking of the barracks, the Church, the clod-hopping junkers and above all, of the philistine" (Marx & Engels, *Selected Correspondence*, Moscow: Progress Publishers, 1975, p. 247), translated by I. Lasker.

# Index